Red Rivers
in a
Yellow Field

Red Rivers
in a
Yellow Field

MEMOIRS OF THE
VIETNAM ERA

To David & Nancy

EDITED BY

Robert M. Craig

Red Rivers in a Yellow Field
Memoirs of the Vietnam Era

Published by Hellgate Press
(An imprint of L&R Publishing, LLC)
PO Box 3531
Ashland, OR 97520
email: sales@hellgatepress.com

Editor: Robert M. Craig
Book design: Michael Campbell
Cover design: Robert M. Craig and L. Redding
Cover photo: "Three Servicemen," Frederick Hart, 1984, Vietnam Memorial, Washington, DC. Photo by Robert M. Craig
Back cover photo: "Brothers." Photo by Robert M. Craig

Cataloging In Publication Data is available
from the publisher upon request.
ISBN: 978-1-55571-915-9

CONTENTS

INTRODUCTION

THE GENESIS of this volume of recollections of military service during the Vietnam years was a brief email correspondence in 2011 between two classmates of a small high school in St. Louis, both of whom were in the class of 1962. They had served briefly as Navy officers after their college graduation, and then returned to the pursuit of different careers in civilian life. The two had not seen each other for almost half a century, and in 2011 they were about to attend their 50th high school reunion, held jointly with the high school class of 1961. "Why don't we meet with others of our school mates who were in uniform during the 1960s, and share sea stories?" Steve Wells suggested.

Usually 50th high school reunions are times to recall our youth and innocence, share with past friends our lives and careers after school, and simply catch up at a time many of us are nearing retirement. Neither of the two high school friends, who planned the impromptu gathering of former sailors and soldiers, had been "career military," and yet, fifty years later, it was the military experiences of fellow classmates about which they were intent on learning. Steve Wells, son of a Navy captain, had served during the Vietnam era as a demolitions disposal expert, defusing unexploded ordinance. I had been responsible for approximately ten thousand meals per day serving as food service officer on an aircraft carrier, population over 3,000. My ship, USS *Intrepid* (CVS-11), had been sent on three deployments to Yankee Station off Vietnam (I was aboard only at the end of the third deployment), but even then, as I headed for the Tonkin Gulf in December 1968, I was aware that another high school friend and St. Louis neighbor, Peter Van Vleck, was a pilot whose squadron was assigned to *Intrepid* and who, now on the other side of the world, would be there to welcome me aboard the ship, in between his flying sorties over Vietnam.

Looking back, Steve Wells and I realized that crossing paths in this manner was not unusual for our classmates. In the 1960s and early '70s, just months after graduation, friends from Principia[1] (both high school and college) found themselves in Southeast Asian jungles, rice fields, or river deltas rescuing other friends from Principia who were under attack on Swift Boats, or patrolling an Army base near the DMZ, or flying reconnaissance over Laos. Fifty years later, as Steve and I thought about friends from our years at Principia's "upper school" and college, buddies who had donned the uniform to serve their country during the Vietnam era, our conversations ran something like this:

"Did you ever talk to Franke, or Karen Van Vleck's older brother, or Johnnie A. about their time in the military? I'll bet they'll be at the upper school reunion. Franke piloted Swift Boats, of all things — now he returns regularly to Vietnam on business; Peter flew jets — later headed up Adventures Unlimited in Colorado; John was a submariner (like his dad, I think), and then he became a speech writer for Nixon," and on and on the conversation went. And then, thinking beyond the high school reunion, we remembered Principia College friends who had not previously attended the high school but were equally comrades in arms:

"Dick Upshaw flew 'coptors near the DMZ, I heard, and Jim Chamberlin was in 'Nam and then had a career in the state department."

"Remember Roy Kussman and Rick Halladay?" Steve would respond, "They were in the training class behind me, and I later ran into them in the Mekong Delta."

Then Steve and I surmised, "… come to think of it, there seems to have been a lot of us in the late 1960s who kept bumping into each other in Vietnam, or aboard carriers, or on military bases world-wide. Small world, eh?"

---

1 Principia Upper School (high school) and Principia College (a liberal arts four-year college) are units of The Principia, a private educational institution for Christian Scientists with units from pre-school/kindergarten through college. The graduation years of authors in this book are indicated by US62 and C66 (meaning upper school/high school class of 1962 and college class of 1966, to give two examples). Authors in this anthology attended either the high school or college, or both, and/or had some other affiliation to the school.

Well, it wasn't such a small world, but it appeared to us that Principia Upper School and Principia College, with as small a population as each campus had in the 1960s (graduating classes of less than 150), produced a notable number of Vietnam era vets. We were a brotherhood of short-term military enlistees and junior officers, who answered our nation's call to duty in the 1960s, before pursuing our intended careers in banking, insurance, education, business, or politics. Steve and I already knew that a significant number of our high school friends (some of whom had gone on to attend Principia College) had joined the Navy, or Marines, or Air Force, or Army soon after graduation. Moreover, we were aware that our classmates' military duties took them all over the world, and repeatedly fellow graduates of the 1960s and early '70s encountered one another in uniform at these distant outposts — in Saigon, or at supply depots and ports in South Vietnam, on Swift Boats in the Mekong Delta, or at homeports or dry docks world-wide. And that was just the Navy, the branch Steve and I had joined! As we contemplated the wider circle, Steve and I concluded that the military record at "Prin," a school with no ROTC program, was not half bad. "Mert was career Air Force; Kiss was career Navy; Brian (our swim coach) joined the Marines and then came back to the college; and Rob Ostenberg enlisted in the Army as a private and rose to the rank of major general, while his brother Chip was a command sergeant major, the highest enlisted rank in the Army." Who knows who may show up at the 2011 high school reunion, we remarked, and who knows what we might learn about guys we knew as teenagers, if we schedule a gathering of vets "to share their stories"?

Our informal email conversations in 2011 encouraged Steve and me to learn more about Principians' role in the military throughout the long Vietnam Era. Many of the boys we personally knew best were in high school as the decade of the 1960s opened and then joined the Principia College classes of 1964, '65, '66, '67, or '68. The latter class of 1968 (two years behind our own) would graduate on the eve of the Tet Offensive and the USS *Pueblo* incident. It was by all accounts a tumultuous time. By 1968 some of us were already in the military, and we later learned that one of our classmates (academically number one in our class), was in a submerged submarine, the closest Navy ship to the *Pueblo* when the latter ship was captured by the North Koreans. It turned out that the executive officer of the *Pueblo*, Edward R. Murphy, who spent eleven months in captivity in North Korean prisons, was also a Principian.

Among our fellow students, even the most unengaged in contemporary affairs could not avoid an increasing awareness that our school years were becoming a period of personal uncertainty. We were living in a historic period that witnessed the cold war, the space race, civil rights struggles here at home, and an increasingly active war in Southeast Asia. Safe in school, we held our breath during the Cuban missile crisis under President Kennedy, and then we learned (when an art appreciation class was interrupted for the announcement during our sophomore year in college), that John Kennedy had been assassinated. Soon, that very distant country, Vietnam, began to shape our lives personally: as young men, we matured during the presidencies of Lyndon Johnson, who waged the war in Vietnam, and of Richard Nixon, who brought it to an end. High school and college friends, with whom we competed in sports, or acted in plays, or engaged in academic debate, by the later 1960s became grunts and platoon leaders, military intelligence officers, pilots of F-4 Phantoms or Hueys, supply officers, Army artists, line officers on destroyers, admiral's assistants, Swift Boat captains, and chaplains. Barely out of school, our classmates were being sent to Westpac fleets, to Army bases in Germany "to listen to the Russians," to rivers and villages and military outposts in "'Nam," and to military bases and training facilities state-side. Some had to check the atlas to recall where Cambodia or Laos or "Phu Bai near Hue" were located, but soon, for some, the Cà Mau Peninsula became as familiar and horrible as Corregidor or Guadalcanal had been for our fathers.

Of course, there were soldiers and sailors from other Principia classes (earlier and later than Steve's and my high school class of 1962 or college class of 1966), as well as marines and air force personnel and national guardsmen who wore the uniform and served in Europe or elsewhere during these years. Not everyone saw combat, but what we all had in common extended beyond our Principia education as history or art majors, as star athletes, or as leaders of student government. Life was no longer academic and isolated. From diploma to enlistment was a reality check big time, and our classmates, indeed our generation, embraced the full range of experiences in the military services, wherever duty took us, and whatever we were asked to do for Uncle Sam. It was now a half century later and class reunion time, but on that evening in 2011, the Principia alums were not talking about their 40-year careers since school as businessmen or educators, nor recalling former high school sweethearts, nor sharing current hopes for anticipated cruises or other pleasure travel now that most of us were close to retirement or already retired. That night at our high school reunion, in addition to being alumni, we were vets.

I majored in history in college—Steve in biology—and our real careers ultimately followed those interests. But we were about to find out about episodes that disrupted our lives during the late 1960s, about whether or not our brief military experiences were much different from others among our high school buddies or college friends of a half century ago. The first question was, "Where had the military sent us?" I had seen those posters about "Join the Navy and See the World," and I have to admit I already had a head start as a world traveler, thanks to Principia. After graduation from college I joined a "Principia Abroad" history and art study tour to Athens and Rome, Florence and Milan, Paris and London. Later, after the Navy, and not too many years into my career as a university professor, I went to China, I spent seven months living in France, and I married a lady from England where I return periodically to visit my new English relatives and to look at architecture. But at that high school reunion in 2011, I found myself talking very little about any of that, but, instead, about Cubi Point and Subic Bay in the Philippines, where I first arrived in Southeast Asia in December 1968. I learned that others gathered that night had never been to China or France— even England "where they spoke the language"— but that *many* of us knew about Subic Bay. And when one of us started to tell a tale about Olongapo City, another vet would interrupt and say, "Ah yes, Olongapo City, I remember the night we crossed the bridge just outside the base..." and off we'd go recounting another "sea story."

Steve was right; we had had experiences in common. Indeed, as an historian, I could conclude that the collective experiences of the graduates of our small liberal arts high school and college in the Midwest was a microcosm making up a small slice of the larger cultural experience of all of America, during what has been called the Vietnam era. We were the children of the "greatest generation," and as we looked back to our military years in the 1960s and early '70s, we discovered a common and sobering theme regarding our individual responses to our country's call to duty. Principians (our fellow alums) appear to have answered that call to service in large numbers. Moreover, no matter what individual path we Principians took in the military, we all sought to ensure, as John McCain has written in his family memoir entitled *Faith Of My Fathers*, that our actions would meet with the approval of our fathers. We were the sons and grandsons, nephews and cousins of the generation that had been victorious in World War II, and we could do no less.

On the other hand, there were conflicting views, during the Vietnam era, about what constitutes patriotism, duty, loyalty, and honor. For some vets, who returned to the states to less than warm reception from crowds of protestors and anti-war activists, there was added conflict at home and returning Vietnam vets met with domestic disapproval, condemned for even being in the military in the 1960s, as though service itself was a disservice. To be sure, even before they signed up, some young men faced dilemmas of conscience, and this may have been especially acute in a high school and college community guided by a firm moral compass. Sara Barnacle's essay about her husband Tom Gallant, entitled "War-Averse Sailor," touches on a universal theme of our generation, indeed, any generation asked to go to war.

In the 1960s, news casts described that some of our age-group were looking for ways to avoid the draft, and a familiar phrase entered anew into the lexicon of the times: conscientious objection. Anti-war activists suggested to our generation, "Just burn your draft card and disappear — move to Canada — no one will know." Thus, as our student careers at Principia drew to a close, the issue of military service in this, the age of Vietnam, became highly personal. Very few of our generation realized that at the very moment we were weighing our personal decisions about enlisting, a Navy pilot was in a Hanoi prison facing daily decisions about honor and loyalty under far more trying circumstances. "Sign a confession," his captors encouraged in between episodes of torture; "Put your name below a statement criticizing the war and disavow the dishonorable cause that you Americans have been asked to serve," demanded the captors who would beat him again and again when he refused. "No one will know," the Viet Cong interrogators repeated, pressuring the captured pilot to sign. That pilot, now Senator John McCain, has written "… the men I had the honor of serving with always had the same response: *I will know, I will know.*"[2]

Before such heroism was even known in the West, but nonetheless sustained by a parallel commitment to honor and character inherited from the greatest generation, the children of that generation, including Principians, did not run to Canada but enlisted; they volunteered for hazardous duty, entered combat zones, and lived the standard of service and good character that their alma mater considered to be central to its educational mission. John McCain, although he had no association with Principia, understood such ideals and principles, and later wrote that "character is destiny." "No one will know," his Hanoi tormentors had promised. "I will know, I will know," McCain repeated, as he experienced daily challenges in his fight to retain the faith of his fathers. Inspired by each other's moral strength, fellow downed pilots, individually and by the dozens, faced sometimes even more severe beatings and torture than McCain in order to persuade them to sign confessions because "no one will know," but they responded likewise: "I will know; I will know." McCain reminds us that this inner thought "is good character." Thirty-five years later, at the end of his book, *Character is Destiny*, the elder statesman McCain

2 John McCain with Mark Salter, *Faith of My Fathers: A Family Memoir* (New York: Random House, 1999), p. 255.

addressed his younger readers of today's generation saying, "I hope it is your destiny, your choice, your achievement, to hear the voice in your own heart, when you face hard decisions in your life, to hear it said to you, again and again, until it drowns out every other thought: *I will know, I will know, I will know.*"[3]

Steve Wells and I understood that the Principians who served in uniform, no matter where or under what circumstances, had shared that sense of duty and good character embodied in the phase, "I will know." As Principians, whose education focused on character, we all knew about the "still small voice." The simple decision, to serve or not, pales in the face of what we now know about imprisoned pilots like McCain or about the capture, incarceration, and sufferings of the officers and crew of the USS *Pueblo.* But for some young men, uncertain of the potential consequences of being in the military, the very enlistment and commitment to an unknown fate was itself an act of courage. In each case, the decision was a highly personal one, and this volume records individual experiences that resulted, without commenting on the rightness or unpopularity of the war itself or the way it was conducted by military or civilian leaders.

What does emerge, for even the general reader unfamiliar with the school that happened to educate this group of military servicemen, is that the collective experiences of Principians in the military, if not entirely typical, is in a large part a reflection of the American experience. Vietnam era vets are part of a national brotherhood and embrace an *esprit de corps* perhaps impossible to convey in words, although Peter Stone and others offer us insight within these pages.

So, Steve Wells's reunion gathering in 2011 opened the door to a wider collection of memoirs and recollections contained herein. Before we left our high school reunion, Steve and I committed to each other that we would try to document and publish, in book form, a representative sample of the personal recollections of Principians in uniform, covering roughly the years from 1960 to the Fall of Saigon

---

3 John McCain with Mark Salter, *Character is Destiny: Inspiring Stories Every Young Person Should Know and Every Adult Should Remember* (New York: Random House, 2005), p. 300.

in 1975. I would serve as editor, and Steve (whose idea to share "sea stories" it was in the first place) would join a small editorial advisory committee. We would put out a limited call through our alumni network and ask fellow vets to respond. We had no idea what we'd get, but we hoped to have a book in hand by the date of the 50th *college* reunion of some of our authors. This publication finally appears fifty years after the Tet Offensive.

The heading for Part I, "Children of the Greatest Generation," brings focus to our generation's inspiration from our fathers, men who journalist Tom Brokaw called the "greatest generation," a now commonly accepted reference to the military of the World War II era. Based on interviews and information that he collected from this "greatest generation," Brokaw authored a series of essays about World War II vets both well known and unknown. Our compilation differs: Steve and I asked the military personnel of the next generation to write their own stories, to recount events as "first hand" recollections of the experiences they lived. The children of the greatest generation are those individuals who served their country throughout the Vietnam Era. We sought, in this small sample, to include the experiences not just of those who served in combat or even only those men who went to Vietnam, but to sample the whole generation who wore the uniform, serving in any military duty assignment anywhere during the period. What notably characterizes the sample, is that each author attended the same school.

What follows below are the stories of over thirty authors, presented as essays, poems, short stories, and short memoirs. My opening essay, "The Wall," offers a dedication to our high school (1962) and college (1966) classmate John Sweet, who died in Vietnam following the crash of his helicopter, and to others who lost their lives as a result of their military service. The memoirs in the main body of the book are organized in seven parts, the first inspired by the theme of our fathers passing the baton to our generation. The relationship to the military experience of World War II is implicit in my poem about D-Day entitled "When I was New and Only Eight Days Old," a poem written on June 6, 1994, the 50th anniversary of the Normandy invasion. The connection to our generation's fathers is made explicit in Dave Nysewander's essay, "Full Circle," and Barrie L. Cooper's reminiscence. In the "In country Vietnam" section of this volume, it is perhaps Allen Orcutt who best captures the spirit and sense of duty embraced by many of this second generation, in his quoting of the inscription, *Nulla Quiat Alibi*, "No Rest Elsewhere." "There would be no rest elsewhere for me," Orcutt writes, "but in doing my duty…" The several authors contributing to Part I of this volume, in their individual ways, speak to the pride and sense of duty implicit in their service in the military and in their continuation of the spirit of "the greatest generation," finding honor in walking in the footsteps of their fathers.

Members of Rackham Court West, Principia College, singing house song, "Um Yah." Left to right: Jim Johnson, Bill Franke (USN), Nelson Smelker (National Guard), Mike Workman, Bill Franks, Steve Metcalf (Air Force), Jay Anderson, Bill Bollinger, Marv Harris (career Air Force). Photo: *Principia Sheaf,* 1964, courtesy The Principia

Another classmate, Bill Franke, graduating a month behind me at the Navy's Officer Candidate School [OCS] in Newport, told me at my commissioning that he intended to volunteer to serve as a Swift Boat officer in the rivers of Vietnam. "Are you crazy?" was not an unexpected response. "That's about as dangerous as it gets," I reminded him, but Franke was determined to serve. Almost thirty years later, his alma mater's alumni magazine, *Principia Purpose*, published an account of a rescue effort involving Franke's Swift Boat and two escort boats under attack in the Mekong Delta, a story reprinted here. The account became one of the inspirations for this book, telling the first of many stories of Principians in the military, many with different jobs to do, unexpectedly encountering other Principians in uniform. Franke's rescue may have been one of the most dramatic, but collectively, as Rod Carlson and Mike Kneeland suggest, the young men of this second generation comprise a brotherhood of a kind that most of us could not have imagined a few years earlier when we were studying in the more isolated world of a bucolic Principia College campus at Elsah, Illinois, overlooking the Mississippi River, or singing rousing fraternity house songs on a late weekend night.

Parts II and III recount experiences in "officers' boot camp" [OCS], assignments in Europe or state-side, and activities at non-combatant posts. "In Country Cambodia" and "In Country Vietnam" announce the themes of Part IV and V, with journalist Elizabeth Pond's news articles recounting her capture by the Khmer Rouge and Steve Heubeck's essay "Beetle Bailey Isn't Funny Anymore" providing another reminder that Principia's vets' active duty comprised more than just an inconvenient, three-year disruption in our lives. "In country" essays are from Army, Navy, Marine Corps, and National Guard authors, both enlisted and officers, and cover episodes and military assignments both ordinary and hazardous. Some of our authors returned home with Purple Hearts, various commendation medals, and, in the case of Dick Upshaw, as many as thirty-seven air medals with combat V following thirteen months in combat in Vietnam. Part VI "At Sea" continues with accounts of service on ships written by carrier officers, carrier squadron pilots, submariners, and others. The concluding Part VII draws the memoirs to a close, suggesting that memory is "still on patrol," and referencing something of the afterlife of the Vietnam era.

My own ship, USS *Intrepid* CVS-11, as does USS *Ranger* CVA-61, appears more than once in these pages; Principians were aboard these carriers each in different capacities over the years. Dubbed "the oldest and the best," *Intrepid* is an *Essex*-class carrier whose history during World War II included surviving several strikes by *kamikaze* planes; *Intrepid*'s role as a recovery ship included retrieving returning space capsules during the space race, and its final deployment to Vietnam, the third of three, is recorded in these pages. *Intrepid* was decommissioned in the 1970s, but the ship was soon resurrected from moth balls and today provides a venue of military history in New York as the *Intrepid* Sea, Air, and Space Museum. It is now a place for us to revisit the storied history of the carrier, including exhibits about the sailor's life aboard *Intrepid* during the 1960s, the latter based in part on a scrap book I kept and shared with curators allowing the ship museum to reconstruct some of the mess decks I had remodeled in the late 1960s when I was aboard as food service officer. My wife notes that she had to go to the New York museum, push the button on a kiosk showing my BUPERS mugshot in uniform from 1968, in order to find out what her husband did in the Navy. She can now read in these pages about my role as "interior decorator for a warship." This "sea story," as well as other more light-hearted accounts narrated in these pages, seeks to depict the other side of military service in the Vietnam era.

A few classmates with whom I corresponded about this book declined to participate. They served during the Vietnam era, but however raw their memories remain, however sensitive or classified their work was, and for whatever personal reasons, they declined, and we respect their wishes and are reminded by them that the era was fraught with issues of war that were both universal and personal. Those absent from these pages remind us of the full picture, and in prefacing the collection of essays with this editorial foreword, I am encouraged to paint with a wider brush and put these essays in a larger context.

As noted above, the 1960s and early '70s was a controversial time, with anti-war demonstrations, civil rights controversies, and domestic unrest often at odds with patriotic attitudes of loyalty, duty, and service held by those in uniform. During the 1960s, while still in high school or college, some of us were folk singers, and as we listened to popular tunes that we liked melodically, and as we admired guitar work and harmonies behind the lyrics, it was sometimes less apparent to us that Pete Seeger and Peter Paul and Mary were actually singing protest songs. We might recall that the anti-war anthem, "Blowin' in the Wind," was written by Bob Dylan in 1962 and made even more famous by Peter Paul and Mary in 1963, the years that Franke, Orcutt, Nysewander, and many other authors of this volume entered college. At the time these men graduated and joined the military, a counter culture was widespread, and domestic turmoil was marked by repeated crises. Martin Luther King was assassinated while Franke and I were at our first Navy assignment at Officers Candidate School in Newport, and two months later, while I mustered for morning reports at the Supply Corps School in Georgia, it was announced that Robert Kennedy had been killed in Los Angeles. As we were then wearing the uniform of our country, many of us wondered whether we would have an immediate change of duty, assigned to respond to domestic unrest and violence, not to action in a foreign war. The following year, in 1969, while Principians and others were in the Mekong Delta, or on a fire base near the DMZ, or stationed near the border of Laos, John Lennon of the Beetles recorded a hit single, "Give Peace a Chance." And from August 15th to 18th of that year, ten days after our Principia classmate, First Lieutenant John Sweet, was killed in Khanh Hoa province, an event took place in a muddy field in upstate New York: "An Aquarian Exposition: Three Days of Peace and Music," a venue known ever since as simply "Woodstock."

Such contrasts describe two worlds in the late 1960s, and those who respectively encountered each, clearly held differing views about Vietnam. Rod Carlson, Mike Kneeland, and Steve Wells describe one of those worlds as a remarkable coincidence of Principians unexpectedly meeting in foreign places, classmates who answered the nation's call and who, in so doing, formed a special brotherhood lasting to this day. However, few if any of us heard then a phrase that we overhear more frequently today, whenever we encounter active military personnel in airports or near Army or Navy bases: that unsolicited remark from a stranger, "Thank you for your service." This salutation

Red Rivers in a Yellow Field

did not characterize many soldiers' and sailors' and pilots' receptions home as Vietnam veterans. For those mates not found within these pages, as well as to the authors here represented, we say now, if we failed to say then, and in all sincerity, "Thank you for your service."

Robert M. Craig, May 2015
Ocean City, Maryland

Dedication: the Wall

ROBERT M. CRAIG

THE DAY WAS WARM, but not hot, certainly not one of those sweltering humid summer days for which Washington is famous. I was doing what I loved to do, touring old buildings, photographing every angle and picturesque view of the city's architecture, famous and not, thinking that some day, for some class or academic conference paper, this new photograph will be indispensable to my job as a teacher of architectural history. The cloudless blue sky and sharp shadow lines cast against white marble were especially striking that day. Washington is a city of monuments and columns, classical in the tradition of ancient Greece and Rome. Today's sky and clarity of bright white architectural forms appeared almost to reach the levels of Mikonos or Santorini; it was a splendid Kodachrome day.

I was near the west end of the reflecting pool and intent on seeing the Vietnam Memorial — The Wall, it was called, and a controversial monument because it was black in a city of white. Maya Ying Lin had been an architecture student at Yale, and rumor had it that she got a "B" for the project that developed into the Vietnam Memorial. I had never been to The Wall before, and I thought, dismissively, "there's probably not much to it — not up to the standards of Robert Mills or Henry Bacon,[4] but what memorial designs these days were as noble as theirs? Admirers of classicism and traditionalist writers had called The Wall, with a critical grumble, regrettably modernist and abstract, fabricated of polished black granite from Bangalore, India, when half of Washington shone with Georgia white marble or Indiana lime-stone. How inappropriate the black wall was, the critics had argued, a misguided memorial to a misguided war. After a quick visit, I could check it off my list, and maybe still have time for another viewing of

---

4 Robert Mills was the architect of the Washington Monument, and Henry Bacon designed the Lincoln Memorial.

Daniel Chester French's seated Lincoln nearby. Now *that's* a monument!—the famed president, who presided during a different war, memorialized inside a glorious temple on the hill. But first, the Wall.

I had walked a fair distance from the central mall and across an open lawn, when I glimpsed for the first time the dark slab slicing across the landscape, low at one end, and from my vantage point, hidden by trees at the other. I wondered if a knife or bayonet metaphor was intended. But it was starting to get hot, so, before visiting The Wall, I wandered off to seek some shade in a copse of trees. Within minutes, I happened upon a realistic bronze casting of three, over-life-sized soldiers,[5] their bodies profuse with sweat from the jungle heat, one bearing an M-60 machine gun across his shoulders, canteen on his hip, belts of ammunition, and a broad-brimmed hat; the second figure, an African-American; and the middle infantryman, a Marine with holstered pistol on his hip, wearing body-armor vest and poised with his body weight shifted to his left leg in a distinctly male stance that I had seen so often before. Each man was alert—no, rather, tense—hesitating at mid-stride with strong arms whose pronounced veins seemed to pop out in ridges as rugged as the wrinkles on the uniforms. Energy flowed over biceps and forearms down to monumental hands, embodying in these youth the potential power that Michelangelo had brought to his figures centuries ago. There was a toughness and humanity expressed in each soldier. They appeared to have just returned from a mission, bodies were slightly turned, and a frown on the forehead of the middle soldier seemed to draw you into his eyes. What was he looking at? What had they all three momentarily paused to observe, as they emerged from the jungle?

And then I saw The Wall. The soldiers, in fact, were looking at The Wall, and their momentary pause was to lend respect to their fallen comrades. The eyes of the central figure, the Marine, were instructing me to look to the northwest, to move to The Wall, much

---

[5] "Three Servicemen," sometimes known as "Three Fighting Men" or "Three Infantrymen" is a larger than life-size sculptural group by Washington sculptor Frederick Hart, unveiled in November, 1984. The piece was cast by Joel Meisner and Company Foundry.

as the Marine might, in silence, and only with his eyes, instruct his platoon to head out.

At first The Wall appeared ordinary—dark, and from this distance somewhat bland. Sunlight was highlighting certain sections, and the spotlighting almost immediately displaced the infantrymen as the object of my attention. Had the abstraction of The Wall won over the unmitigated realism of the infantrymen? Which one of these was the real Vietnam monument? The infantrymen were so tangible, I could almost smell the jungle odors. The GI tropical trousers, the GI towel across the shoulders of the African American soldier, the tropical "Boonie" hat—all these were familiar to in-country Marines and combat troops, and conveyed that guerilla warfare, like these soldiers, was raw, virile, and male. But the soldiers themselves had paused with a certain solemnity to look across the opening to their brothers in arms—sailors, pilots, Marines, and Army infantrymen—who had come home, at least in name, to this place.

I found myself drawn to The Wall, walking slowly to its west end. It was a magnet like no other monument I had experienced, pulling me forward on a personal journey along its length. Thousands of inscriptions came into view, one of which, for every visitor here, had respectively drawn thousands of others like me, in search of a familiar name. The Wall was abstract, and yet each name recorded fully articulated narratives, like the one in which I was about to play a part, just as I had played a small part in the Vietnam war. This memorial was not about the black granite, or the surface sheen, or the formal relationship of architecture or sculpture to the landscape, the latter so prominent in Maya Lin's intentions. It was all about the names.

I felt totally unworthy even to be here. Yet, I *was* a Vietnam veteran, and only then did I begin to understand, in part, what that designation means, at least what it means to me. It was an appellation I had rarely considered relevant to me, because such an honor belonged to the heroes. But here I was, with scores of other Washington tourists, visiting one of the city's many monuments, but like some of them, I had come here as a Vietnam veteran. As a consequence, I was very much a part of this place, more so than I knew.

When I got to the west end of The Wall, I became aware of others around me, and I almost laughed out loud, realizing that neither I, nor they, appeared properly dressed for this honorific place. Some wore army-navy surplus camouflage, and I wondered if any of them were ex-military at all. Others sported baggy shorts and tee shirts, baseball caps and sleeveless undershirts——the summer "dress uniform of the day" of "the ugly American" as sculptor George Segal has so humorously depicted "sartorially challenged" American tourists. What *was* the preferred dress code for Everyman? It seemed not to matter. Everything about this crowd, and this place, was different from what I expected. It was a public park, but no one was slouching, brazen, rude, or loud. There was no boom box or skate board, pan handling or fowl language, no flirting teenager or oblivious lout bumping into strangers. It was wholly a place of respect.

And then I noticed the hush, the total silence. Even the city street traffic seemed distant. Except for the rustle of leaves as limb brushed against limb in the near-by wood, all was silent. The three infantrymen were frozen in time. The path to The Wall beckoned as though inviting one to join a funereal march, and if anyone spoke, it was in a whisper, as though we were in some ancient *temenos*. The Wall itself was a landmark, marking the land as a sanctuary and holy ground.

John Sweet is here somewhere, I remembered. He was a high school classmate from Louisville, Kentucky, and later a Buck House brother studying at the college during the mid 1960s when I was in Rackham West.[6] Because Principia College was so small—a little over 500 students when John and I attended—everyone there knew everyone else. So I knew John, although not very well. He signed his contemplative picture in my high school yearbook, and his college yearbook picture shows him with a broad smile on his face, looking out the window of a convertible automobile, eyes embracing you as a friend, and happy as a clam. He died in Khanh Hoa province in coastal south-central Vietnam on August 5, 1969, three years after he graduated from Principia College. I wanted to find his name here on The Wall.

---

6 Lillian Brewer Buck House and Rackham Court West were two men's residence halls at Principia College, in many ways comparable to college fraternities.

At first I chastised myself, wondering if this was mere curiosity, but I began to think of nothing else, here in this place, and no one else but John Sweet, and the life he might have had. I had no flowers or tokens to leave here, but John was here, and I guess I just wanted to say good bye.

I looked him up in the directory of names to determine on which panel his name was inscribed, and I started walking along The Wall. The unexpected length of the polished black granite invoked a spirit and solemn gait akin to a religious pilgrimage. Many had come great distances to this sacred destination, a site that was their personal Santiago de Compostela.[7] For all these Vietnam era pilgrims, the sacred journey ended not at the realistic sculpture of three infantrymen, but at the black granite wall. Like hundreds before them, many that day had brought letters, personal keepsakes, and tokens of remembrance, and these oblations lined the base of the wall. There was no graffiti nor any evidence of tampering with the personal items that family members of servicemen had left here. In all, there was a level of respect that not even Maya Lin could have anticipated. And the silence was palpable. Only the shuffling of feet, occasional whispers, and muffled sobs could be heard as fellow veterans, brothers, fathers, and sons were remembered.[8]

I had come here alone, and I approached John's panel with a macho attitude that the quiet weeping I could hear further along the path, and other emotional reactions were somehow "them," and I was different, in control, and besides, I hardly knew the guy. I checked my scrap of paper again for the panel number, which was still several panels away, and I started paying more attention to the roses, and letters, and flags, and teddy bears—an endless row of offerings, extending along the base of the granite, each momento

---

7 The reference is to the shrine of St. James in Santiago de Compostela, Spain, the goal of medieval pilgrimage routes extending from Paris, Vézelay, and other French Romanesque sites, southward and across the Pyrénées, then westward across northern Spain to Santiago.

8 There are eight women on the wall, seven Army nurses and one Air Force nurse. 7,484 American women served in the Vietnam War, according to the memorial's website.

leaning against the wall below a soldier's or sailor's, or airmen's, or marine's name. There were so many names.[9] The panels were taller in the center of The Wall, which meant even more names displayed, and each was somebody's son or father or boy friend or husband. I continued my slow gait, looking at the endless rows of names, but still not finding his. John was, indeed, a casualty of the war, but, because of The Wall, he would not be anonymous. I suddenly realized that I didn't even know how John was killed. What does it matter *how* he died, I told myself, he was here among heroes, killed I learned later when the helicopter he was piloting crashed. Some here were still MIA, some (God forbid) had been killed by friendly fire, some died in accidents, but the inscriptions seemed endless. There were so many names, recording that so many had died. Some names have rightfully been added to The Wall many years after the end of the war, recorded here too, because their death occurred after the war but was attributed to war injuries or effects of Agent Orange or other war causes. I still couldn't find John's name.

And then, there it was: panel 20 west, row 99: John H. Sweet. I stared at the name carved in gray against the black polished surround, and all the other names disappeared. I was suddenly overcome with grief. My arms felt a chill, I wanted to take a deep breath but could not, my shoulders and legs tensed, and I felt tears welling up in my eyes, uncontrollably. I sobbed, and then I cried openly, as I reached out to touch the name. And I just stood there alone, not caring who was around me, or who heard me, or who thought this wasn't manly, and the incised letters of John's name started to blur through tears I could not control. *I hardly knew the guy*, I heard myself thinking, as though my rational side was asking my emotional side what was going on. But it made no difference. I felt a loss that seemed to embody the losses recorded on the entire wall. John was a fellow Principian; he had gone to Vietnam; and he had not come home. I felt my shoulders

---

9 As of Memorial Day, 2017, there are 58,318 names listed on the Memorial, including approximately 1,200 missing in action (MIAs), prisoners of war (POWs), and others.

pulsating as I wept. Someone handed me a tissue, and then disappeared, leaving me, again, alone.

I don't know how long I stood there in front of John's name. But I started to remember what I had read about The Wall before coming here—the magazine articles and the critiques in architectural journals that spoke of the black memorial, and the black war, and the black cause, and I thought, almost out loud, *They just don't get it, do they?*

Vietnam Memorial "The Wall," John H. Sweet inscription.
Photo by Robert M. Craig

When I finally regained my composure, a lady was standing next to me, and ever so slowly turned to me and said, "Which one did you know?"

"John Sweet," I said, pointing. "We were in high school and college together."

"I'm sorry," she said.

John Sweet was my connection to a realization that this might have happened to me, and I started to hate myself for wondering whether that is why I had cried. But John's name on The Wall was not only about sacrifice, about duty, and ultimately about loss. As the focus of my pilgrimage, John had given me part of himself. John's gift to me that day was a bond sealed by a moment of remembrance—remembering a yearbook picture and a broad smile, a shared moment between two college kids whose lives crossed at one of life's happiest times, and then crossed again here, at one of its saddest moments. Since those halcyon days at college, John and I, and so many others, had graduated into a world that called us all into war. What I learned at The Wall was that even though I didn't know him well, that kid in the Austin Healey 3000 and I are both Vietnam vets, part of a brotherhood that brought challenges to us when we were far too young to contemplate the possibilities. Oh, yes, we were innocent, and the Vietnam War carried some of our fellow vets "to hell and back,"[10] as Audie Murphy described his World War II experience. But for John, and so many others here, there was no return.

At The Wall, I stared at the inscribed "John H. Sweet" now standing out again in focus against the black granite background. I then stepped back to see the full panel, and then looked right and left to see the long range of other panels and the countless names. These thousands of names, in quiet dignity, proclaim a national sacrifice at a scale not easy to comprehend; the seemingly endless wall both approximated and personalized our national loss. All our comrades who died, or who are still missing in action, are listed here, and First Lieutenant John Sweet is here. I suddenly thought how relatively inconsequential my own military role had been during those same years, how short in duration my time off the Vietnam coast had been, where I had been a supply officer aboard *Intrepid*, the aircraft carrier which, ever since, I have considered "my ship." However dangerous work aboard an aircraft carrier really was, my war experience paled by comparison to what in-country infantrymen had gone through, or what skippers of river patrol boats experienced, or what pilots engaged in night sorties lived through, or what ordinance disposal teams endured. Some of these men recount their experiences in this volume.

---

10 "To Hell and Back" was the title of a 1955 Cinemascope [Universal-International] film, starring Medal of Honor recipient Audie Murphy who played himself, depicting Murphy's war experiences in World War II, as detailed in Murphy's autobiography, also entitled *To Hell and Back*. (New York: Henry Holt and Company, 1949).

John Sweet was in the Air Force, as were some others from his and my college class. I joined the Navy. By joining the military, we all knew that our civilian lives were being put on hold for two, three, or more years. Throughout the country, soldiers, sailors, air men, and marines did the same thing by the hundreds of thousands, but from a small school in Elsah, Illinois, a remarkably high percentage of college men had volunteered, and each did their fair share. No one in my acquaintance had given more to his country than John Sweet, and his name on the Vietnam Memorial Wall conveyed to me that day as powerful and personal a message of heroism, as any monument in this city of monuments. That I share John's status as a military man who served in Vietnam is an honor, and for what John and these other heroic souls on The Wall did, in the mere act of serving, I am very proud.

John Sweet, college yearbook picture, *The Sheaf* 1966. Photo courtesy The Principia

I found a scrap of paper and a pencil, and I slowly raised them to the level of his inscription. I carefully started to rub, and the name John H. Sweet appeared outlined in charcoal gray. John made the wall personal. I stuffed the rubbing into my pocket and stepped back. Then, forgetting that I was not in uniform, I stood at attention, raised my arm, and I saluted John Sweet.

As I started to leave the Wall, I saw a woman with two young children in hand, a little boy and his slightly older sister, walking toward a nearby panel.

"Where's Daddy?" the little boy asked in a tone both serious and childlike.

"He's just down here," his mother said, and her voice appeared to break just slightly.

"No, I mean, where's Daddy really."

The woman stopped as both children looked up at her awaiting their mother's response. She put her arm around her daughter's shoulder, almost needing the child's support as she faltered, and then turned to face her innocent son. She slowly placed her other hand over her heart, and the woman said, "He's here, my darling. He's right here with us, because we remember."

ROBERT M. CRAIG is what is sometimes called a lifer—not in the Navy but at Principia. He began school in Principia's kindergarten and continued his education at Principia through the Lower, Middle, and Upper Schools and on to Principia College where he graduated in 1966 with a double-major degree in History and Education. His father taught Latin and mathematics at Principia's Upper School (high school) and was Captain of the Ocean City [Maryland] Beach Patrol throughout his career. The younger Craig earned a master's degree at University of Illinois, Champaign-Urbana, in 1967, breaking away from graduate school in the fall of 1967 to attend Principia Abroad in Europe. He taught history briefly at Meramec Junior College in St. Louis in the fall of 1967 before beginning officer's training at the Navy's Officer Candidate School, Newport, Rhode Island, in January, 1968. In preparation for his work as a supply officer, Craig attended the Navy's Supply Corps School in Athens, Georgia, and upon graduation was assigned to USS *Intrepid* (CVS-11), then operating off the coast of Vietnam. After discharge from the Navy Craig earned a PhD (1973) in the history of architecture and urban development from Cornell University, the first doctorate awarded an architectural historian in this new field of study. Hired immediately by Georgia Tech, Craig remained at the Atlanta university for thirty-eight years, retiring in 2011, although he continues to advise doctoral students as Professor Emeritus.

Craig is the author of three books and co-author of three others. Considered a founder of SESAH (the Southeastern Chapter, Society of Architectural Historians), Craig also served on the board of directors of the parent national society (SAH) for fourteen years, ten years as secretary of the society. Active throughout his career in the Southeastern College Art Conference, Craig edited the society's scholarly art journal [*SECAC Review*] for five years during the 1980s. He has also served as President and later Treasurer of SESAH, President and later Treasurer of the interdisciplinary Nineteenth Century Studies Association (NCSA), and President of the Southeastern Society for Eighteenth Century

Studies where he was instrumental in founding the academic journal, *New Perspectives on the Eighteenth Century.* Considered a specialist more on the early twentieth century, Craig is best known for his books on architects Bernard Maybeck, John Portman, and Atlanta architect Francis Palmer Smith, as well as his book on Art Deco Atlanta. He has presented more than 160 academic papers throughout the country, lectured at venues from China, Australia, Canada, France, and throughout the United States, and recently served as architecture editor for Oxford University Press's five-volume *Dictionary of American Art.* Craig has recently completed work on the Georgia entries for *Archipedia,* an online encyclopedia of American architecture, and is working on *The Buildings of Atlanta* and *The Buildings Georgia,* all three projects for SAH. He is editor of the current collection, *Red Rivers in a Yellow Field: Memoirs of the Vietnam Era.*

Like many of the authors represented in this collection, Craig's military career involved a six-year commitment during the Vietnam era including three years active duty. *Intrepid* was just completing its third deployment to Vietnam when Craig reported aboard to serve as disbursing officer, one of several supply corps positions aboard the carrier. Six months later, Craig was transferred to become Food Service Officer, and among his accomplishments in this area was his remodeling of the ship's mess decks and lounge spaces for enlisted crew; some of these features of the ship's interior, have been reinstated by curators of the *Intrepid* Sea, Air, and Space Museum (founded 1982) in New York, who are preserving the carrier and have consulted with Craig in their effort to document "the sailor's life" aboard ship in the 1960s. While Craig was Food Service Officer, *Intrepid* was recognized in the Ney Award competition as the best food service operation among all Navy large ships afloat, world-wide, and *Intrepid* took third place in the awards program among all Navy food operations (large and small ships afloat, as well as Navy shore facilities). Craig's wife, Carole, a Brit, remains "gobsmacked" declaring "he can hardly boil an egg."

After Vietnam, *Intrepid* spent time in the Philadelphia dry docks, engaged in exercises in the Caribbean, trained pilots in the Gulf to execute carrier launches and landings, and even sailed up the Mississippi River delta to New Orleans for Mardi Gras. Soon after Craig's discharge in 1970, *Intrepid* was decommissioned and temporarily put in moth balls, but the "Mighty I" was resurrected and moved to New York where visitors today can go to Pier 86 W 46th St. and 12th Ave. to tour the *Essex*-class aircraft carrier, as well as to see Craig's remodeled and now partially reinstated mess decks.

"Three Servicemen," Frederick Hart, 1984, Vietnam
Memorial, Washington, DC. Photo by Robert M. Craig

PART I:
Children of the Greatest Generation

◆

Help in the Line of Duty

WILLIAM E. FRANKE & STEVE SANDBERG

This article was first published in the Principia Purpose *(Fall/ Winter, 2006, 13) and is republished here with permission.*

On September 5, 1969, Lt. (jg.) Bill Franke (US'62, C'66) was thinking about his college days, and his friendships at Principia as he was about to take his Swift Boat out to sea and up the coast of Vietnam to a U.S. Navy repair facility in Cam Ranh Bay for overhaul.

Between the battering sea and enemy fire, Bill's boat was beat up, and he wondered if it could last the three-day trip.

Since he was in an area controlled by North Vietnamese and Viet Cong military forces, he would need two boats to accompany him as escorts for safe passage from the river to the ocean.

As his boat approached the mouth of the river, Bill and his crew entered an ambush. One of the two escort boats became disabled and had to be pulled out of the ambush. Six crew members suffered wounds that were life threatening.

Being on open water, Bill requested Sea Wolf helicopter assistance to lift those most in need to safety and care. To permit the helicopters to carry the additional load, Bill hand-signaled the gunner's mates in the helicopter to jettison their munitions and everything else of any weight into the river.

"Loading these men into a helicopter over the water was difficult," remembers Bill, "not only because of our exposed position, but because the blades of the copter barely cleared our radar and only cleared our whip antennas when the antennas were held back.

"There was no more than a 12-inch clearance—not very much with a bouncing boat and a helicopter being buffered by the wind and updrafts caused by the blades. It took tremendous skill on the part of the pilot," he recalled as if it were yesterday.

Standing on the munitions bunker after lifting the last of the men into one of the helicopters, Bill looked at the pilot to signal for him to get going. The pilot was intensely engaged in keeping the helicopter close to Bill without being swept into the boat or crew.

"The skids of his copter occasionally brushed my legs," Bill added. It was an incredibly skilled and heroic effort on his part. He had to do it perfectly."

Bill Franke college yearbook picture, The Sheaf, 1966.
Photo courtesy The Principia

As Bill focused on the pilot's face, he had a strong feeling that he knew him. "My recollections of his concentration," he says, "his selfless act of patriotism and his concern for these sailors remains to this day very emotional for me. There were so many dramatic images of that series of events. The one that remains crystal clear in my mind, though, was the pilot's calming influence upon me."

"The noise of his engines was deafening. The up-blast off the water was overpowering. The anguish of the wounded and stress of the circumstances were huge. But that pilot at that moment provided me with the resolve and the strength to complete what had to be done. I will never forget it."

On that same day in September, 1969, Lt. Steve Sandberg (US'61, C'65) received an order to head up the river for a medevac of crewmen from a Swift Boat that had been ambushed.

En route he was figuring out "how to hover over the back end of the board in order to get the wounded crewmen into the helo."

When he first saw the boat, "It was not a pretty picture," he says. "I thought, 'Is that a Swift Boat or just scrap metal floating on the surface?!'

Steve Sandberg college yearbook picture, *The Sheaf,* 1965.
Photo courtesy The Principia

"On board the Swift Boat, those still able to stand were getting ready to lift the first badly shot-up crewman. I was, at the same time, trying to get close enough and low enough to place the helo's landing skid on the aft end of the boat without whacking it with my rotorblade or [hitting] the boat's pilothouse, radar box, and antennas, as this floating scrap heap bobbed up and down, up and down.

"As I looked down from my airborne perch, I sighted a familiar face. And although it was heavily disguised with a full growth, it rested atop that six-foot four-inch body I had not seen since '65 but had known growing up at Principia Upper School in the late '50s and the College in the '60s.

"Bill, with help from another, was able to body press the crewmen above shoulder height in a maneuver necessary to get the wounded up and into our helo's cargo door opening—up, over, around the helo's rocket pod, M-60 machine guns, and canister of ammo.

"I heard later that the wounded crewmen lived to tell their stories!"

Postscript

While many Principia alumni served valiantly in Vietnam under the United States Air Force, Army, Coast Guard, Marine Corps, and Navy, this story was about two Principians meeting under difficult circumstances in the line of duty. The story would not be complete, however, without the mention of two other Principians, referred to by Bill and Steve. Lt. Doug Dixon (C'62) was the executive officer on the LST (landing ship tank) that helicopter pilot Steve Sandberg was assigned to. And Lt. (jg.) Rick Alt (US'64, C'68), a diving officer with the Navy's Harbor Clear unit, helped raise one of the Swift Boats that sank due to the heavy damage in the ambush referred to above.[11]

---

11 Rick Alt was the brother of CNN correspondent Candy [Alt] Crowley, a journalist who was the second female to moderate a televised presidential debate [Obama/Romney, October, 2012)] and was anchor for the CNN interview program, "State of the Union" that aired on Sunday mornings. An alumna of Principia (kindergarten through high school (US66), Crowley retired from CNN in late 2014, after 27 years with the network.

"When I was new and only eight days old"

ROBERT M. CRAIG

written on the occasion of the 50th anniversary of D-Day
June 6, 1994
printed here in tribute to the "Greatest Generation" [our fathers]

When I was new and only eight days old,
Below the darkened clouds, on misty sea,
Where fate was poised along the destined shore
On sandy thresholds of eternity,
The gods of virtue stopped, to hold their breath,
Among great battleships of lifeless gray.
From each, surveying eyes searched distant points—
Each soul, his separate imprint on this day.

When I was new and only eight days old,
A thousand leadened vessels offshore lay,
Nine hundred thousand brothers wait aboard,
And thousands more above in peppered gray.
Each soldier, sailor, fly-boy innocent,
With tear-filled eyes of youthful memory,
Now faced events that storied heroes make,
Each nameless face to rewrite history.

When I was new and only eight days old,
On sandy Utah beach and Omaha,
Where salt-foam-reddened stains at high tide line
Marked waves of onslaught nature never saw,
The landing craft of time's immortal force
Slapped steel-hinged gates against the shallow shore,

Disgorging men whose shoulders bore the hope
And war machines and armament and more.

When I was new and only eight days old,
The cliffs grew tall, no longer viewed from sea,
Each Joe looked up against the spitting fire
To find a courage never known to me.
With rope and spike beyond the hallowed beach,
They clawed their way up rocks in swarming mass,
To rest forever on these liquid hills,
Now marked in rows of white in sea of grass.

Now, I am fifty years and eight days old;
In hardened eyes of men to shore returned
I see the memory undimmed by time
And hearts in which each story has been burned;
They lift their weary arms in last salute
Above the crosses, stars, goodbyes longed craved;
And through these tear-filled eyes I learn the truth:
When I was eight days old, the world was saved.

D-Day, Normandy Invasion. Photo: National Archives,
Franklin D. Roosevelt Collection

Full Circle

DAVID R. NYSEWANDER

In some ways, my Vietnam war experience comes full circle in my mind back to my father's service in World War II. He spent three years overseas as a military chaplain: a year in Australia, a year in New Guinea, and a year in the Philippines during World War II. In fact, the first time he ever met me was when I was three years old when he returned briefly just before the end of the war. I am told that I cried when this strange man came in and hugged my mother when he returned. Before then, "Daddy" was a photo on the fireplace mantle. I do remember seeing glimpses of him later in Indiana when I was a kid. After the grownups bundled the children off to bed, Dad would entertain folks and church members with his stories and photos of his experiences overseas, memories and narratives mixed in with other socializing and card games of Canasta. It all seemed sort of exotic and mysterious to me. My father passed away when I was sixteen years old, and so I did not have a very long time with him. But as you may see, in many ways his influence persisted after his passing, and he still affects me to this day in many little ways.

When I finished my college days at Principia College and gradu-ated in 1965, my draft board in Indiana was "pursuing" me, so I began to ponder how I should meet this required service for our country. Military service seemed like a big detour from the type of work I loved, working with wildlife, as I was a biology major at Principia. Just after graduation, I was working at the college during the Principia summer sessions where people would occasionally come up to me, recognize my last name, and comment on how my dad had helped them during their time in World War II. I began to wonder if being a chaplain was a better way to fulfill my service requirement than just being a foot soldier. I was not a conscientious objector and did not want to shirk from what I perceived to be my duty. I decided to become a military chaplain.

Although I went through the chaplaincy training, attended related graduate school, and eventually became a chaplain—a non-combatant status to be sure—I chose the service (U.S. Army) and training (air-borne qualified) that I thought would put me right where the majority of other troops were, whether front lines or otherwise. Possibly because of my youth, conditioning, and the airborne qualifica-

tions, I was sent to Vietnam; indeed, there was some consideration of assigning me to Green Beret units when I first arrived in South Vietnam. Eventually the decision was made for me to be stationed at a large logistical center, Cam Ranh Bay, from which the U.S. supplied all of its troops scattered between the South China sea and the Laos/Cambodia border in what the U.S. military called II Corps; this includes the coastlines, mountains that came closer to the coast there, and the upland forests and grasslands that existed between central Vietnam and the Saigon area. As it turned out, this was fortu-

Dave Nysewander,
college yearbook
picture, *The Sheaf,*
1965. Photo courtesy
The Principia

itous in that I was freer and more likely to be able to serve both the Protestant aspects of my chaplaincy as well as Christian Scientists who might be stationed at a number of different Army units and who would pass through or be associated with this area.

I served as a Protestant chaplain primarily for several logistical supply units (fuel, ammunition, and the like) based out of Cam Ranh Bay from February 1970 to April 1971. My experiences were neither heroic nor battle-filled but may parallel those of the large number of support personnel who stood behind, supplied, and cared for the combat soldiers in Vietnam. It has been said that some nine to ten support personnel like me, whether supply officers, repair and maintenance personnel, administrative staff, or chaplains, served for every one combat soldier or front-line fighter, a ratio higher than the 4:1 ratio of World War II or the 7:1 ratio in Afghanistan. In this light, it would seem that my experiences likely reflected what many soldiers in Vietnam encountered during their Vietnam service experiences, a day-to-day life most would not characterize as heroic.

My routine as a chaplain and our challenges in this support, were more related to boredom, drug overdose, accidents, keeping morale up, and finishing our thirteen-month tour. We lived in a very beautiful exotic setting, a large protected bay set in the tropics with a mix of palm trees, villages, occasional larger cities, green rice fields, blue mountains, sand dunes, and sandy beaches, with jungles and pine forests up 5,000 feet in altitude only fifty miles to the west. However, the nature of guerrilla warfare meant that it was hard to recognize and distinguish the good guys from the bad guys, so to speak. And so the American troops would have their own bases and were often kept mostly segregated during their off hours from the general Vietnamese public. I had more leeway in this respect, and would use my greater contact with some of the Vietnamese locals in my job both to benefit my troops as well as to broaden my own experience there.

I was part of the administrative staff of officers in charge of base troops, and we were involved with keeping up morale and alertness. We organized a wide range of activities including volleyball contests and snorkeling along the tropical sea coasts. We were available for counseling and arranged for troops to work with the local Vietnamese civilians through orphanages and other such outreaches. We did not have to worry much about attack on our main base for a number of reasons that ranged from having trained dolphins patrolling our docks, to the extensive activity on and around our main base. Located on a remote outer peninsula in a spectacularly beautiful bay, the bases appealed to and were used by German, French, Japanese, and other navies over the years. The bases were beyond the range of the type of rockets that the communists were able to carry down from North Vietnam via the Ho Chi Minh trail. As a result, there were only ten deaths in my three battalions over the year I was there (three accidents, two drownings, two drug overdoses, and three losses of life from explosions, the latter associated with the convoys we would run inland up 5,000 feet into the mountains of Vietnam from the coast). There was sort of a "wild-west" feeling associated with our supply convoys—wagon trains going through some mountain passes to the interior. These were the most likely occasions when some improvised explosive might be used to harass the convoys and perhaps injure someone. I would sometimes go on these convoys or travel by helicopter or plane to supply bases scattered inland and along the coast, but more often I would find myself occupied on the main base: counseling, giving training sessions, conducting religious services, attempting to help resolve personal issues among the troops, or simply going out to visit and help keep awake duty guards at night, stationed at the fuel tanks in case this was the one night when a "sapper" might try to sneak in and blow up a fuel tank in order to score some propaganda points before an upcoming election.

Dave Nysewander in Vietnam, 1970.
Photo courtesy Dave Nysewander

In some ways, I liked the informality in dress, ceremony, and schedule of the Army in Vietnam, so much so that I thought of extending and finishing out my service time there, but the military was not letting officers extend at that time. I remember meeting Jim Brown, a Principian, in Saigon; Jim was working in Vietnam as a civilian, and I wondered if I might return and do similar work since I had some growing affection for the country and its peoples. At any rate, I returned to Fort Lewis, Washington, and finished out my active service requirement there. When other things beckoned, I did not go back.

In the end, my Vietnam experience was more than just a series of vignettes in the life of an American soldier just doing his job and fulfilling the duties that his country requested of him. My time at Cam Ranh Bay became a window into another culture for me, perhaps in a *Lord Jim* Conrad-esque way, but also in a way that allowed me to see my own culture differently for a while. I remember when I first returned from Vietnam after thirteen months away and was whisked away from the airport, how fast freeway traffic seemed after having never gone more than twenty-five to thirty miles an hour for the last year. I wondered at the greater solidity of the buildings, how colors seemed darker and different, how even the American people, especially women and older folks looked differently to my eye,

Dave Nysewander
at Cam Ranh Bay,
Vietnam, 1970.
Photo courtesy, Dave
Nysewander

having been around mostly younger American men and the Vietnamese people for such an extended period of time. This feeling lasted for only a week or two before everything seemed normal again, but this was probably the only time I had been outside my own culture long enough actually to see my own culture and country, however briefly, as outsiders' eyes might.

One hears of lots of different reactions by Americans to the Vietnamese people, some positive and others not so much, depending upon the experiences of the troops, or the wartime stress they may have faced. The Vietnamese people I knew while in Vietnam opened my mind and heart to their uniqueness, beauty, history, and culture, so much so that a number of years later when my first marriage dissolved, I eventually remarried, this time to a Vietnamese lady I met in the United States. Now, after thirty-two years of marriage with her, through all the ups and downs that any relationship seems to face, I am grateful that we made this journey together, and I wonder in my mind whether it might ever have occurred, if I had not spent time in Vietnam. I do remember kindly the warm mild nights, the blue mountains and green fields, the eyes on the small wooden Vietnamese fishing boats, the small child-like appearance of the Vietnamese women, the sandy beaches and sparkling seas, the old French Colonial style roof-tiled buildings, the ancient Cham temple ruins scattered here and there, the water buffaloes in the fields, the statues of Buddha in Nha Trang, and all the other exotic images that float in the back of my memories.

Sixty-five years after World War II and thirty-five years after the Fall of Saigon, I viewed the many episodes on HBO cable television of a 2010 series on WWII in the Pacific. I watched, in part wondering if I would gain any new insight into my father's experiences. Partway through the series, the episodes cover troops recovering between battles at some bases in New Guinea, just back from the front lines, and the images captured the ambiance of that place and time. It struck me that there were a number of strong similarities between those scenes in New Guinea and what I experienced at Cam Ranh Bay in Vietnam. I sensed that in some ways I was truly a child of the "greatest generation," as Tom Brokaw characterized the WWII troops, that my dad's experience had come full circle in my Vietnam experience. I do not know if I fulfilled the promise when my time came. I only know I tried and that I am the person I am now, the offspring of my father, in part because of it.

DAVID NYSEWANDER'S father was a military chaplain during World War II, and David followed in his footsteps, serving in the Army from 1969-72 including a tour in Vietnam. Nysewander attended Army Chaplain School in Fort Hamilton, New York, as well as airborne training at Fort Benning, before taking on his own responsibilities as a protestant military chaplain at Forts Benning and Lewis, and at Cam Ranh Bay, Vietnam. He was awarded a Bronze Star for Service, and the Vietnam Service Medal for his tour in 'Nam.

Born in 1943 in Indianapolis, and raised there, Nysewander attended Principia College graduating in 1965 with majors in biology and geology. His sister Bobbi would follow as a graduate of the college class of 1969. He was a member of Phi Alpha Eta, the scholastic honorary society, served as substitute reader one quarter in the college chapel for services sponsored by the Christian Science College Organization, played intramural sports, and spent much of his free time in "assorted wildlife related activities." A member of Brooks House South, he was a housemate of Steven Heubeck who graduated the year after Nysewander and also joined the Army, Heubeck as a member of the Eight Special Forces Group Airborne.

Nysewander went on to earn a Bachelor of Sacred Theology degree from Boston University before his military service and an MS in wildlife science from the University of Washington after his departure from the military in 1972. He married for the second time Lanh T. Nguyen in 1981, a Vietnamese woman he met while visiting friends in the state of Washington in 1980, and has one step son, George Dixon, and three grandchildren through this relationship. Nysewander has lived either in Alaska or in the state of Washington since 1972, active as a U.S. Fish and Wildlife Biologist and Supervisor 1975-92 in Alaska and a Washington state wildlife biologist and project leader 1992-2010 specializing in marine mammals, birds, and waterfowl work during all of these years in both regions. He is currently retired, living in Olympia although his list of activities and interests would hardly suggest so: marine wildlife, boating, gardening/farming, rescue of large working dogs, bicycling, and outdoor survival.

The War College

ROD CARLSON

I expected to be in a war. My grandfather had been in the Army in the First World War, and I'd grown up hearing about my father's Navy experiences in the Pacific in World War II. With major wars coming like clockwork every twenty years, more often if you count Korea, a war for me was no surprise.

What was a surprise, however, was war itself. I'd seen John Wayne, Randolph Scott, and Robert Mitchum whipping the Axis, so, like other movie-going civilians, I knew all about war. I knew it was loud and dirty, and people got killed, mostly the enemy, and it was as awful as it could be. The movies taught America that war had redeeming aspects that made our victories well worth the effort.

Principia cadets, 1924. Photo courtesy The Principia

But, to my surprise, off the silver screen, war wasn't at all like that. Whatever was good about it in the movies was missing in real life. There was no drama, certainly no theme music to foreshadow or announce excitement or tension or sadness, and there was nothing historic or noble or romantic, nothing like Humphrey Bogart telling

Ingrid Bergman that the war was bigger than the problems of two little people, as if that revelation makes being obliterated no worse than having a bad day. In my war, there was no dramatic tension of John Wayne motivating his Marines to keep slogging through *The Sands of Iwo Jima*, no romantic tension of James Garner's philosophical arguments with Julie Andrews in *The Americanization of Emily*, and no Errol Flynn and David Niven cavorting around the countryside and drinking French champagne in *Dawn Patrol*.

To me the war in Vietnam was sprawling, amorphous, and as impossible to define or label as the middle of the ocean. I couldn't imagine anything that even Hemingway would have found interesting enough or appealing enough to write about. Any novel that I might have written would have been as short as *The war was getting up in the dark, hitting the rack in the dark, flying endless hours oozing rivers of sticky, greasy sweat, and misery offset only by the extreme joy of reading mail from home.* That best-of-times-worst-of-times sentence could have been punctuated with: *but, I wasn't alone.* I really wasn't, and, frankly, that was a surprise.

Within the hour of joining my Marine squadron, a fellow Principian Dick Upshaw taxied up to the ready room in a helicopter with a string of fresh bullet holes only inches from his leg. Worse, he was completely nonplussed, as confident as ever and gave me a huge welcoming smile as though almost getting killed didn't warrant a flinch and was all in a day's work.

Upshaw was just the beginning. During my thirteen months in Vietnam, I was always running into Principians. A while later, Steve Tupper exposed himself to hostile fire and gave me a cheery wave as we barely escaped a mortar attack at his Special Forces camp, little more than a bunker surrounded by barbed wire at a place called Thuong Duc.

When I was flying search and rescue at Chu Lai, Peter Sappenfield gave me shelter and his bunk. His nights were being spent flying bombing missions far into North Vietnam. A month later, Dick Hammer also gave me a place to stay at his Navy Explosive Ordinance Disposal Team's base, threw a couple of M-16s in the back of a jeep, and drove us up a treacherous jungle road to the top of

Monkey Mountain where we checked out an old French colonial lighthouse perched high above the South China Sea. And it seemed like I was always running into Peter Stone, either on his aircraft carrier, in the officers' club at Marble Mountain Air Facility, or somewhere in between. In Vietnam, there were Principians everywhere. Sometimes it seemed like an extension of the men's quad.

Why so many of us in that war? Sure, there was the draft, but they could easily and legally have beaten it, thousands of guys beat the draft, but the Prin guys I kept running into had volunteered for Vietnam, and most had worked hard and made longer commitments to serve as officers. In other words, they chose to get jobs that would put them in harm's way, not occasionally, but in many cases every day for the entire year or longer that they were there.

Principia cadets, 1924. Photo courtesy The Principia

What was it that made these Principians serve on land and sea and in the air and survive and succeed at their chosen fields of military endeavor? The answer is Principia itself. Its founder Mary Kimball Morgan held the firm conviction that the purpose of education is to develop self-discipline, character, and the ability to think vigorously, fearlessly, and accurately. The school instilled those qualities along with other traits and capabilities required for success. Expecting Principians to play many roles in society, Mrs. Morgan knew that education must empower them to respond to any leadership challenge thrown at them. It had to free them from flaws and weaknesses; it must make them whole men embued with fully-developed spiritual, moral, intellectual, social, and physical dimensions of good character. Mrs. Morgan's Principia turned out young leaders with courage, and ability, and above all, good character — leaders capable of winning in the real world where she knew the game was played for keeps.

But for military service, Principia added an ace in the hole, an extra ingredient stirred into its education, something unknown to West Point or Annapolis. With its dedication to Christian Science, Principia gave its graduates an understanding that would enable them to accomplish whatever was their duty to do, without being harmed or fatigued, and to stay healthy under all conditions. What could be more valuable to warriors going to war than this kind of confidence?

While I wasn't surprised to find myself in a war, I was eventually surprised when it dawned on me that in spite of calling itself a liberal arts school, all of us who'd gone to war had been educated at a first rate military academy.[12] We were all in Vietnam together, in our right place, doing exactly what Mrs. Morgan had in mind.

ROD CARLSON was a captain in the Marine Corps and served in Vietnam in 1968-69 as a pilot. From Marble Mountain Air Facility adjacent to Danang and Phu Bai farther north near Hue City, he flew a variety of medevac, resupply, and other combat missions with two helicopter squadrons: HMM-361 (in post-Korean War Sikorsky UH34Ds) and HMM-265 (newer, tandem rotor Boeing Vertol CH46As). Two of his thirteen months overseas were spent flying off the amphibious assault carrier, the USS *Tripoli* (LPH 10) on station in the South China Sea. Carlson accumulated enough mission credits for 25 air medals and was also awarded: Vietnam Service Medal, Vietnam Campaign Medal, Meritorious Unit Citation, the Vietnam Cross of Gallantry, and an honorable discharge. After Vietnam, while at New River Air Station in

---

12 Principia was a uniformed military academy during the earliest years of the institution, from 1905 to 1936 (including the junior college level from 1910 to 1927).

North Carolina, his squadron steamed aboard the USS *Guam* to South America and flew earthquake relief missions in the Andes.

Rod's father served as an officer in the Navy and fought in the Southwestern Pacific, serving aboard a tank landing ship LST 751 which saw service in Leyte [landings, November, 1944] and Luzon [Lingayen Gulf landing, January, 1945].

Born in 1943 in Duluth, Minnesota, Rod was raised in Duluth coming to Principia College in 1961 where he studied history and graduated in 1965. A member of Rackham Court West, Carlson played intramural sports, served on the fire crew, and spent considerable time hunting and boating on the Mississippi River with his adopted family of local "river rats." He married classmate Barbara Burton, and their children Nancy and Mark both attended the College. After the Marines, Rod earned an MBA from the University of Virginia and worked in New York City, Minneapolis, and Miami in advertising and marketing. He is now retired and is a charter member of the Veterans Writing Workshop, a nationally acclaimed program that provides writing opportunities for veterans of all wars.

Small World (Schoolmates in Every Port)

MIKE KNEELAND

I was amazed at the number of Principians going through training for and serving in Vietnam. It was common to see Prin friends in flight training in Pensacola and at other Navy training bases. I also ran into them overseas.

While on USS *Ranger* (CVA-61), I read the lesson[13] on Sundays with Bill Hanzlik. I think once, while flying tanker, I aerial refueled classmate Dave Jones in his F4. In port we always seemed to run into other Principians.

Many of those night combat missions gave me ample opportunity to think back to what I'd learned in those four short college years. Orion was my favorite constellation in Dr. Hooper's astronomy class. Returning from night missions over Laos, I could see Orion in the bombsight as I flew back to the carrier. Those experiences carried me back to Elsah.

In April of 1971 I flew exchange duty with the Air Force Forward Air Controllers (FACs) over Laos. In exchange, they visited the carrier and experienced carrier landings with us. The FACs flew out of Nakhon Phanom (NKP). While in NKP for our three-day stay we visited the control center that we worked with while doing our all-weather bombing missions. During the day we flew with the FACs who were spotting targets for the A6s, flying visual day-bombing missions. Because I was rather junior, I was "bumped" for the return trip to the ship and spent an extra three days in NKP.

---

13 Christian Science weekly readings from the Bible and *Science and Health With Key to the Scriptures* by Mary Baker Eddy (the Christian Science textbook), studied daily by Christian Scientists, and comprising the sermon in Sunday services in Christian Science churches world-wide.

As I was getting ready to leave the last day, my BOQ (bachelor officer quarters) roommate came in. He told me that he had just met another pilot from my squadron and that they had attended the same high school and even dated the same girl. He then said that he'd had an even more amazing experience while on R&R (rest and relaxation) in Bangkok. He was swimming in the hotel pool and met an American stewardess who was there. He told me that after meeting her he found that she had attended "a small school about forty miles from St. Louis." I asked him her name, and I think he said Ginny Brown. I told my roommate that I had graduated with Ginny. My roommate then stated, "Then you must know my cousin, Pete Van Vleck." I told him that Pete and I had flown from USS *Coral Sea* when Pete flew photo F-8s and I flew A-6s. Had we played the "who do you know" game earlier, we could have visited more about our Prin experiences.

One of my roommates on USS *Ranger* was Bill Cadieux, a Marine Corps bombardier/navigator. Bill and I kept in touch after the service. One day, about twenty-five years after serving together, Bill and his wife, Joyce, were visiting us in Minnesota. Joyce casually mentioned Bill's roommate in Japan, Pete Sappenfield. Pete had flown A-6s in the Marines with Bill. When I mentioned that I had gone to college with Pete, Joyce told me that she and Bill had been good friends with Pete and his wife Jan. I served with Bill for almost two years and kept in touch with him for another twenty-five, and I never knew that he, and Principians Pete and Jan Sappenfield, were good friends.

About ten or fifteen years ago, John (Cap) Andrews was visiting my father, his cousin, in our hometown of Deerwood, Minnesota. John served on a submarine in the Pacific Theater during WWII. John related many tales about his demonstrations[14] and experiences while in the U.S. Navy. John said that he was once up on the bridge with the submarine's captain as they sailed into one of the Pacific ports. John recognized another Principian on the pier. Apparently this had happened many times. The ship's captain asked John how many students attended this college called Principia. When John told him

14 The term "demonstration," in this context, references a healing or demonstration of God's presence and protection.

about five hundred the ship's captain exclaimed, "They must all be over here in the Pacific!" That was also my "small world" experience in the military. I am grateful for the lessons I learned at Prin. They gave me a solid foundation to weather my Vietnam experience and afterwards return to civilian status. As Principians we have joined an amazing fraternity. The lessons learned at Prin have continued to benefit me throughout the years.

MIKE KNEELAND wore several hats during the six years of his military service in the Navy. A Navy pilot flying sorties from the carrier USS *Ranger* (CVA-61), Kneeland was assigned to squadron VA145, an attack squadron established in 1951 and nicknamed "the Roadrunners" but known since about 1954 as "the Swordsmen." Kneeland flew A-6A and A-6C Intruders as part of Air Wing 2 during the *Ranger*'s 1970-71 deployment to Yankee Station. *Ranger*'s planes, together with those from the carriers *Kitty Hawk* (CV-63) and *Hancock* (CV-19), hit a wide variety of targets, including Vietnamese and Laotian infrastructure (ferries, bridges, truck parks, and rail facilities) as well as military installations, airfields, antiaircraft guns, and SAM sites, the coordinated effort disrupting and destroying entry corridors leading into South Vietnam from Laos. For Kneeland's service, he received seven air medals, the Navy Commendation Medal with combat V, Meritorious Unit Commendation, and Vietnam Service Medal plus the other medals awarded to all who served in Vietnam. Kneeland also served as electrical branch officer, later as a flight instructor/avionics division officer, and a public affairs officer before his active Navy service ended in 1972. Kneeland remained in the reserves drilling for two years and serving in the inactive reserves for twelve years. He continues to serve as a civilian flight instructor. Mike was chosen as the FAA 2001 Flight Instructor of the Year for the Great Lakes Region.

Kneeland's first association with Principia was when he was age 3, attending pre-school from 1946 to 1947 when his family lived in St. Louis. In 1948 the family moved to Deerwood, Minnesota. Mike returned to Principia in 1962 when he resided in Rackham Court East (serving as house manager), majored in mathematics, played football during his first two college years, and graduated in 1966. During his college years he volunteered and served on the campus fire crew all four years, and spent three years on the stage crew assisting the drama department and stage management needs of the concert and lecture program

at the college. He was also on the projection crew for three years and Chapel
Custodian for three years. A third generation Principian, Kneeland notes that
both his father and grandfather were Principia college graduates, and both had
served in the military in the two previous World Wars. The Kneeland family
tradition continued when Kneeland's younger brother Todd (C69) followed
Mike's example both in graduating from Principia College and serving in the
Army in Vietnam.

Kneeland married Lorri Mullenmaster in 2010. Mike has a daughter, Dr.
Jessie Kneeland who works as a Senior Environmental Chemist at Gradient,
an environmental consulting firm, and a son David who served five years in
the Marine Corps and is now attending college with the intention of obtaining
his law degree. Kneeland returned to live in Minnesota after the military
and pursued a career there of over thirty-seven years as a low income public
housing director. In addition, for forty-one years Kneeland served as a school
bus driver, and for most of the period continued to give flying lessons. An
elected public servant for twenty years, he was elected mayor of Deerwood,
Minnesota, as well as school board chairman. Now semi-retired, Kneeland
lives in Brainerd, Minnesota.

United States Navy Officer Candidate School emblem

PART II:

OCS and Flight Training School

Conduct Unbecoming

ROBERT M. CRAIG

I was late to boot camp. I couldn't help it, and it was not an auspicious beginning to my military career, but I was late. Although I never considered the military *was* my career, it was clear that the training officer at the Officer Candidate School, who was now nose to nose "in my face," believed sincerely that he now owned me for a time.

"Nice of you to join us, candidate Craig," he said, and added, "that *is* your name, eh?… because I certainly don't want to forget the only person in living memory who had the gall to be late to OCS!"

I need not add that the tone of his voice was indicating an increased enthusiasm for relaying to me "up front and personal" his welcoming message.

"Oh, yes, I most definitely want to remember correctly the name Craig. You see, Mister Craig, we have been waiting for three hours for the pleasure of your company."

Somehow this last did not sound like an intentional expression of politesse.

"But you WILL NOT, Mister Craig—I repeat, you WILL NOT soon forget the necessity for punctuality. Hit the deck and give me twenty push-ups!"

The reason for my being late seemed of no interest whatever. I was reminded that I had known for four months that I was to report to the Navy Officer Candidate School (OCS) in Newport at the appointed hour, and no later, on that cold day in January. My less than cordial reception at 3pm (instead of at high noon as "expected") was now referenced in terms intended to impress me further. In military jargon I was informed that I had been AWOL for three hours.

Good God, is he going to call out the firing squad at dawn?

Eighteen… nineteen… twenty—I made it, that's twenty push-ups, and as I started to get off the ground, I heard my nemesis bark,

"That twenty was for the first twenty minutes AWOL, now give me twenty more."

I had arrived at the parade grounds behind the wheel of my rather sporty burgundy Firebird convertible, (a conveyance which did little to mitigate the present circumstance, since in the eyes of my reception committee, I was now perceived as some upper middle class twit). But I was exhausted from the road trip. I had driven almost straight through to Newport from St. Louis, targeting an arrival at the appointed hour, but, alas, I had missed my ETA.

"I'm sorry," I whined pathetically.

"Not yet you're not — twenty more!"

And then to add insult to injury (given the fact that I had a master's degree in history), he added, "Craig, you probably would have been late to D-Day — twenty more!"

The rest of the class of officer candidates just stood around and smirked, shaking their heads with amusement since it was increasingly clear that this "example" of discipline at my expense was intended to impress everyone, regarding the potential consequences of any infraction that might bring displeasure to our commandant. One poor sod from Alabama told me later, "Better you than me, suh." That first day was not the last during which I was reminded that I had "volunteered" to join the Navy, and so whatever treatment I got, I had actually asked for it. Arriving late to officers' boot camp was not a good start.

I had, in fact, picked the Navy, among several options to keep me occupied during what turned out to be the three years (1967-70) between my master's degree and PhD The circumstance of my "volunteering," I had to admit, had been a bit harrowing — no doubt much like the experiences and angst of many of my contemporaries regarding entering the military in the Vietnam era.

The Vietnam "conflict" — it seemed never to be called a "war" in official circles — was never far from the minds of male high school and college students in the mid 1960s, aware of the increasing national commitment to the "conflict." It was clear to most young men in their twenties, that as troop calls were increased, the odds of being drafted and sent to Vietnam were appreciably higher than the likelihood of seeing the name of the Homecoming Queen on your dance card. In my (admittedly imaginative) mind's eye, any image of yours truly, toting a rifle along a jungle path in southeast Asia, seemed simply too uncharacteristic. What I did not know at the time was that throughout the summer of 1967, while I was weighing my life options under the shadow of the high likelihood of being drafted, virtual hero John Wayne was at Fort Benning, Georgia, filming the movie *The Green Berets*.[15] I resisted any notion that Col. Mike Kirby was to be my role model: I was more of an Ensign Pulver[16] type, so my thoughts regarding the military soon shifted to the nautical.

Growing up summers on the ocean, coupled with my athletic experiences in college as a four-year letterman in swimming, I soon concluded that my path in the military pointed to the Navy or Coast Guard, not the Army. On the other hand, as I struggled that day in January to complete my sixtieth push-up, imposed as penance for three hours AWOL, I wondered if it was too late to declare myself a conscientious objector.

The previous academic year (1966-67), I had been happily enrolled in a masters program in history at the University of Illinois, a course of eight credits that began during the summer of '66 immediately after my graduation from Principia College. Graduate school was interrupted in the fall term by my joining a "Principia Abroad" four-month study tour in Europe. To "join the Navy and see the world" was not yet on my radar, but I was seeing a part of the world I really relished. "Prin Abroad" was a grand tour in the tradition of eighteenth-century grand tours: study visits to art, architecture, and archaeological sites in Greece, Italy, France, and England, an itinerary essentially designed by Principia art historian Frank Parker and now conducted by Professors Jim and Barbara Becker. (That memorable fall-term trip abroad

---

15 *The Green Berets* (1968), distributed by Warner Brothers-Seven Arts.

16 Jack Lemmon played Ensign Pulver in the popular 1955 movie *Mister Roberts*, distributed by Warner Brothers. The film starred Henry Fonda, James Cagney, William Powell, and Jack Lemmon, and was based on the play *Mister Roberts* (by Thomas Heggen and Josh Logan) which in turn was based on Heggen's novel, *Mister Roberts*.

was highlighted by our group's being present in Florence, Italy, to witness the famous November 1966 Florence flood, when the Arno overflowed its banks, severely damaging Cimabue's crucifix, marring Donatello's *Mary Magdalene*, and dislodging from the baptistry doors five of the ten renowned panels sculpted by Ghiberti, part of what Michelangelo called "the Gates of Paradise.") I loved going on tours abroad, but "tours" increasingly meant something else to most of us in the late 1960s — a friend was assigned a "tour" in Vietnam, a brother was heading back for his second "tour," someone else was said to have miraculously survived three "tours."

In January 1967 I returned from Europe and Principia Abroad to the University of Illinois to finish my master's degree, taking "one day at a time" while my draft board in April reclassified me 1-A — "available" — promising me that my dreaded "Greetings" draft notice would be tucked into my Master of Arts diploma, with both documents scheduled to be "awarded" in August. Without doubt, Vietnam beckoned.

So, in 1967, I applied for both Navy and Coast Guard officer training programs, specifying for the Navy that I wanted to be in the Supply Corps (the "business school" of the Navy). It seemed to me that the idea of my learning a little accounting or gaining some business experience offered greater potential for translation to civilian life than marksmanship and hand-to-hand combat in a jungle. On the other hand, I was ill prepared for such a specialized school because as an undergraduate I had elected almost no college course work in business, economics, or accounting, and so I wondered whether the Navy would even consider me for the Supply Corps under such circumstances.

Then a letter arrived from the Coast Guard offering me a place in their officer's training program, but with a short two-week deadline for my accepting or not. The dilemma was real: if I said, "No" to the Coast Guard, and the Navy then said, "No" to me, then the Army would extend a hearty, "Yes," and flashing before my mind's eye was that WWII finger-pointing image of "Uncle Sam Wants You." I said a prayer, gulped, wondered if I were a fool, and declined the Coast Guard.

I then waited for the Navy. And I waited. When the letter finally arrived, accepting me into the Navy's officer candidate school, it included an assignment after OCS to report to the Supply Corp School in Athens, Georgia, and so, everything was set in place on the trajectory that led me to these eighty push ups on a wet Rhode Island field in bitter-cold January, 1968. My orders were to report to Newport and Navy OCS *at noon—sharp*.

My initial career plans had not envisioned the Navy. I planned to teach high school history, and Eric Bole, headmaster at Principia Upper School, had offered me a contract to teach "American Backgrounds" and other high school course work, but I could not accept the appointment due to the draft. But then, with my September acceptance letter from the Navy in hand, I had four months (September-January) with nothing to do. A family friend who headed the English Department at a St. Louis area junior college mentioned to my dad that a popular history professor there had unexpectedly died, and the college needed someone to teach his classes, including, ironically, his already outlined course work on the history of Vietnam and SE Asia. With my master's degree in history, Meramec Junior College was prepared to hire me immediately, if I could take over his course work the day after tomorrow! I did, and the experience redirected my teaching interests toward the university level, rather than high school, but four months later it was this junior college post that made me late to OCS. At the end of term, with final exams to read, with grades to calculate and turn in to the registrar, and with a more than one-thousand-mile drive to Newport, it was my destiny to arrive one exhausted and pathetic soul, and (did I mention?) I was three hours late.

So now we're caught up in my story. I had always wanted to see Newport (although I had the Breakers and Chateau-sur-Mer in mind), but here I was, on a brisk January afternoon, fully engaged in the ritual of "welcome to officers' boot camp,"— fifty-seven... fifty-eight... pant... fifty-nine... sixty.. pant pant!—demonstrating to one and all how *not* to do a push-up properly. "Seventy-eight, seventy-nine, eighty!" *This too, shall pass*, I told myself, wondering what time was "lights out."

At OCS throughout the next four months, our class went through the standard fare: harassing 2am awakenings to assemble and march about on the parade grounds, now in February snow, dressed only in our Skivvies, and barefooted, unless you took the time to put on shoes and be twenty seconds late.

"Craig, hit the deck and give me twenty—ten for each shoe. Oh, and hand over your shoes, you're out of uniform."

"But, it's snowing…"

"*Craig*…"

"Yes, sir… one, two, three, pant pant, four…"

We were warned about, and experienced, the USS *Buttercup*, a make-shift ship's hold, perforated with multiple holes to train officers in damage control and leadership. Five or six of us were put into the compartment, water started flowing from every conceivable crack, hole, and burst pipe, as the instructor closed the hatch overhead shouting, "Don't start patching until the water reaches your waist" (which it already rapidly had done). "If you find and plug every hole, before the water rises to the overhead, you won't drown."

"Nice!" I said, and then saw a classmate begin to panic, and I quickly said, "Oh, he's full of hot air; do you really think they'd let us drown?" by which time the water was chest high, and we heard the hatch above us slam shut, and toggles creak "locked," so I suggested we'd best get started. All kinds of damage control plugs, rubber tubing, rags and bands were available to stuff here and there, wrap around pipes, and slow, then stop, the leaks. We floated as the water rose, tread water in order to stop ceiling ["overhead"] leaks, dove underwater to find more leaks, and finally the bubbles and the rising water stopped. We had completed the exercise and passed.

"What grade do you get if we had failed?" someone asked.

"*Requiescat in pace*," I said. I couldn't resist; my father taught Latin.

Our OCS class had to wait six weeks before any liberty was allowed, and on that first weekend off base, even that was "arranged": our first Saturday night of freedom we were to attend, in uniform, a dance organized by the girls of Salve Regina University. The school was housed at Ochre Court, which was an added bonus for anyone like me interested in architecture, although my interest in French Renaissance chateau architecture, with Louis Seize "rococo" ornamented interiors, did little to impress either the Navy or the females who viewed the resplendent surroundings of their daily school activities with an attitude frightfully blazé.

Back "home" in the barracks, life went on: leadership training was inexplicably linked to polishing boots, polishing linoleum floors, and polishing brass. I spit polished the corridor several times before I was adequately trained. My military decorum, when it came to presenting myself in uniform, was hopeless. What appeared to me to be excessive concern by my superiors became, as a consequence, a subject for repeated demerits: everyone's day was ruined if my brass belt buckle was not precisely aligned with my shirt buttons, and as for any discovery of lint during morning quarters: heaven forgive my superior should discover a stray atmospheric settling of residue on my shoulder or person! To find such sartorial infraction, during an inspection, invoked a level of displeasure that I'd be more inclined to reserve for a felony violation. Was the entire institution of the U.S. Navy so impeccably faultless?

My high school classmate Greg Arthur [US62], who became company commander of November Company at OCS, recalls a "Prin[cipia] encounter of the close kind" involving Mark Youngberg [C68], two years behind me at Principia College. Arthur crossed paths with Youngberg at Navy OCS: "he was in his first two days, and I was in my last days." Arthur describes the incident: "...Remember that 'mock' period," Arthur muses, "when you got red gigs for just about anything you did whenever you went anywhere at any time... when everything you did was wrong, and you were sure that you were living what you later found to be the first half of *The Shawshank Redemption?* I watched that sweaty and rumpled collection of candidates [Youngberg's rookie class] trying to form into a section for hours as they scrambled, scrubbed, scrabbled along the p-ways [passageways]... and all along [collecting demerits as they went] they were being warned that they were looking pretty sorry, and that they would never be presentable for the looming inspection by the company commander.

Late that night," company commander Arthur continues, "just before they were going to be told that they were going to start over again with a clean slate, my inspection took place, and I sternly strutted down the line and gave red gigs for just about everything until I got to Mark. And I made him the Golden Boy: all blue gigs for everything about him. 'All you other guys should take special note of this candidate who obviously had his shit together,'" Arthur announced to the knees-shaking assemblage. Mark's eyes were bulging straight ahead, sweat pouring down his face, uniform soaked. I spun on my heel," Arthur recalled, "walked out, graduated, left for Norfolk, [and I] never saw him again. I often wonder what he thought had happened. Did he even know that it was me?"

As for candidate Craig, at a similar stage just a few days before OCS graduation, my target for a last hurrah was not just [my] Mike company but the entire school. Like Greg Arthur, just prior to leaving Newport, I could hardly contain myself. It was time for Ensign Pulver's revenge. A few weeks prior to commissioning day, it appeared that half the school was "down" with food poisoning from something that had been served at Ney Hall, the school's central dining facility. The top brass swore it was a stomach virus, but most officer candidates thought it was a salmonella outbreak. Eager for some little gesture of retaliation, I schemed with the only co-conspirators that I thought could get away with expressing our views on the matter: my fellow singers in the Navy OCS glee club. I had been given the charge to devise the musical part of the program for our class's commissioning ceremony, and I took the liberty of adding a specially re-written lyric to the closing number. Some thought my gesture boarded on "conduct unbecoming an officer," but I reminded one of my Principia classmates (who was in the class behind me at OCS), that I was a Rackham Westie,[17] and "rowdy was good," indeed, marginal conduct was adequately normal. Nonetheless, for this august occasion at Newport, I was warned, that the front row would be filled with admirals, rear and otherwise.

---

17 Member of the Rackham Court West [fraternity] residence hall at Principia College

"I'll be conducting the glee club," I said, "so I won't be distracted by the reaction of the top brass. My back will be to them, and maybe they won't recognize me. And what can they do? throw me out of the Navy?"

And so at full voice, with officer candidate Craig conducting, we immortalized the outbreak of food poisoning at Ney Hall. To the tune of the Broadway title song "Mame," we sang with noticeable enthusiasm:

> *You coax the blues right out of the horn, Ney Hall;*
> *You charm the husk right off of the corn, Ney Hall;*
> *You got our stomachs churning and fluids flow enough to*
> *beat the band;*
> *Now OCS is hummin' since salmonella's back to plague*
> *the land.*
>
> *You make your sailors whoosy and weak, Ney Hall;*
> *You make the strong among us quite meek, Ney Hall;*
> *You cause our constitutions to*
> *Whither at the mention of your name;*
> *Your special fascination'll*
> *Prove less than constipational—*
> *Try to be less sensational,*
> *Ney Hall... Ney Hall... Ney Hall!*

I lowered my conducting arms, but I dared not turn around to face the audience.

"The Admirals are getting up," whispered a tenor in the front row.

"Are they coming after me?" I asked.

"No, I think it's a standing ovation."

So despite it all, I got my commission, and I left Newport as Ensign Craig.

My Principia College classmate and fellow Westie, Bill Franke, an officer candidate in the OCS class behind me, scurried to be the first to salute me, since the tradition is that whoever offers you your first salute as a new officer is supposed to be paid a dollar. The commissioning ceremony was barely over when Franke rushed to the front of the hall and hastily saluted, with his other hand extended, palm up. I paid up, and Franke became so wealthy that he later used my dollar (and a few others) to buy the *St. Louis Globe Democrat* newspaper. I would be the last to suggest that Franke owes all his financial success to me, and to that dollar he collected in May, 1968, and clearly invested. I wonder how much my dollar is worth today, amortized annually with compounded interest... Of course, Franke has always claimed he had to pay it to somebody else, when he was commissioned the next month, but I wonder.

Oh Dad, What Have You Done?

STEVE WELLS

This remembrance is my account of the impact of my dad on my time in the Navy. It's another one of those "who'd a thunk it" tales.

My dad retired from the Navy after twenty-eight years, and in retirement he supported his wife who was Dean of Women at Principia College. Dad liked to joke that he was the Unofficial Assistant to the Dean. Among his many "duties" was to ensure there always was properly brewed coffee available in their apartment, and several men made regular morning visits to the apartment in Howard House to have coffee with "The Captain" and to hear sea stories. I've heard their testimonies about the influence my dad had on them, and several joined the Navy at least in part because of these visits. But I doubt any of them had their Navy lives so impacted by having known dad as were my own three years.

It began at Officer Candidate School (OCS) in Newport, Rhode Island. I reported for duty in July following graduation from college. I was assigned to Golf Company in class 701. My company officer, who governed every moment of my life, was Lt. Emil Novotny. The lieutenant didn't like me from the start, and I began getting demerits immediately. I got demerits for having a *Science and Health* in my locker, because it was "unauthorized." I got demerits because the inside of the receptacle in my desk lamp was dirty. It was dazzling. I couldn't do anything right, and I was confined to the base every weekend. By marching for several hours on Saturday, I could work off my demerits. But when I worked off one demerit for marching, everyone else in the same marching detail would be credited with three. I fast approached the limit of accumulated demerits and was close to being "washed out" to the fleet to be a sailor instead of an officer. They allowed me to call home and explain my predicament.

I called my dad. He heard my story and told me to relax. First, he explained that he'd spent much of his four years at the Naval Academy aboard their prison ship, so I was just maintaining family tradition. But then he asked me to repeat the name of my company officer. I told him it was "Lt. Novotny." His response was to explain that he had dropped Lt. Novotny from the flight training program at Pensacola when Dad was executive officer at Whiting Field. The lieutenant was clearly getting even. I was a gift to him that dropped into his lap. What are the odds of this happening?

Dad then said, "I know what your problem is, and I know what your solution is. Hang on and let me make a phone call." It turns out that the admiral in command of the entire Newport Naval Base had wrestled with Dad at the Academy. Dad called the admiral, and my life immediately got better. I was commissioned and allowed to begin training to join the EOD Teams.

EOD training takes about a full year. I completed that training and got my orders to report to the EOD Group in Hawaii where I would join the teams and from there be given deployment orders. Eager to get to work, I showed up in the commanding officer's office at the appointed hour. I gave him my orders, which he read very carefully. He then looked up at me and said, "Are you the son of Harold Wells?" My heart raced. After all this, I wondered what my dad had done to my new commanding officer. Was all that hard work getting to this point for naught? All I could do was say. "Yes Sir." He paused, then smiled at me, and said, "I wouldn't have graduated from Stanford if it weren't for the support I got from your father." Dad had been assigned to the Navy ROTC Unit at Stanford when my CO was a struggling undergraduate. Then the CO added, "I owe you big time."

My first deployment was with a team that spent three months diving in Micronesia. Every day a new coral reef on a beautiful atoll. Some of the best diving in the entire world. It was an adventure that these days civilian divers spend thousands of dollars to enjoy, and I got to do it because my dad had influenced yet another young college man.

Thanks, Dad.

STEVE WELLS traveled to Vietnam for two tours of duty, serving in the U.S. Navy as a bomb disposal expert. Assigned to EOD Group Pacific, Wells saw duty in Hawaii, Micronesia, Yankee Station (in the Gulf of Tonkin, Vietnam), and the Mekong Delta. He was officer in charge EOD shipboard and mobile units, earning a Bronze Star with V [the "V" designation to denote combat heroism or to recognize individuals who are "exposed to personal hazard during direct participation in combat operations"]. He also was recognized with a Combat Action ribbon and Meritorious Unit Commendation. Wells's father was also a Navy man, serving from 1935 to 1962 (the year of Steve's high school graduation), so Steve grew up in a military family.

Those who knew Steve Wells in college also recall that his mother was Dean of Women at Principia College, and indeed, there continued Principia connections throughout his family: his mother, uncle, sister, and two children are alumni of the college, and three grandchildren currently attend Principia Middle and Upper Schools. Steve graduated from both the Upper School (US62) and College (C66). Wells was a swimmer at college and also captain of the school's soccer team. A member of Rackham Court West, Wells distinguished himself in academics; majoring in biology, he was elected to Phi Alpha Eta, the school's honorary scholastic society. He also served on the campus fire crew, a volunteer fire company that helped protect the isolated rural campus from fire. Following his military service, Wells pursued graduate studies earning a M.F.S. [Master of Forest Science] degree at Yale University and "abd" (all but dissertation) doctoral-level studies at University of Washington. Married to Janice Oldenberg, Wells has two daughters, Kimberly and Karin. A resident of Tacoma, Washington, Wells is owner of Maas Boat Company, a manufacturer of rowing shells) and describes his current activities as "homemaker, teacher, bureaucrat, and sales[man]."

U.S. Navy recruiting poster, Vietnam Era.
Photo: U.S. Navy

To Fly My Own Jet With My Name On It

H. TUCKER LAKE JR.

I was introduced to the U.S. Navy at my birth at North Island Naval Air Station, Coronado, California. My father was career Navy, joining before World War II in 1937. He was one of the youngest chiefs in the Navy at the time and received his commission during the war. The first ship I remember being on was the USS *Boxer* (CV-21), an *Essex*-class aircraft carrier. At the tender age of three years of age, I got to climb on airplanes, and seven years later a friend of ours who was a Navy fighter pilot took me out to see his plane, a jet called a Cutlass. I was hooked on naval aviation, and being a naval officer was all I wanted to be.

Flash forward to my freshman year at Principia College in 1965-66. A team of recruiters from NAS Olathe, Olathe, Kansas, visited the small Illinois college campus. Needless to say I was intrigued. The Vietnam War and the military draft were becoming of vital interest to young men. For me, it was all about becoming a U.S. *naval officer* and being able to "fly my own jet with my name on it." Imagine that picture. I bought that line from the recruiting lieutenant who told me about the Aviation Reserve Officer Candidate Program (AVROC). I took the tests, flew out to Olathe, Kansas, had the flight physical, and then waited and waited and waited. A trend of "hurry up and wait" was starting to develop. Finally, in September of 1966, I heard that I was accepted into the program, and I was sworn into the Naval Reserves later that month. My only job now for the Navy was to graduate and to attend two summers of OCS down in Pensacola, Florida. Up until then, I had never flown in any military planes, or small aircraft of any kind for that matter.

So that first summer I boarded a commercial flight to Pensacola with stops in Atlanta, Georgia, and Jacksonville, Florida. The weather in the late afternoon down South can be quite turbulent, and the flight was horrible: we bounced all over the air. I was not in the greatest shape when we got into Pensacola about 10 p.m. The first thing I did when we got on the ground was to find a place to heave. I then entered the world of indoctrination battalions and Marine drill instructors: an eye-opening time and military reality check. I had been advised not to check in early as indoctrination starts no matter what time you arrive. I should have gotten in earlier. Trying to keep up with all they had us do, I did not get into bed until 3 a.m. First lesson: don't listen to others; just do what you are told. Anyway, it was an eventful time. The most memorable thing was lining up getting our heads shaved and not being able to recognize the guys we had lined up next to. I survived the two weeks of INDOC and then moved with my class to join the battalion and regiment. Principia College fraternity brother John Kistler was there and just graduating from OCS, on his way to a career in the Navy. He and his wife Karen would take me to church on Sunday mornings, a nice escape from the program for a few hours. I managed to accumulate thirty-five demerits that summer. Forty, and you are out, so I survived the first summer.

The second summer was another testing time. We had classes covering navigation, military history, geography, and, best of all, a speed reading course. That helped all through college. We also had a course in leadership. To me, this was a waste of time since the answer to every problem that could arise appeared to be a "breakdown in the chain of command." So the class was boring but only effected my evaluations slightly: I graduated first in my class and number one in academics, although I was seventh militarily because of that leadership class and those thirty-five first-summer demerits. Despite receiving no demerits the second summer, I missed being an honor graduate which would have allowed me to augment into the regular Navy. Anyway, at graduation, because of those two number ones, the admiral asked where I went to school. I told him Principia College. He said we need more from there, and I thought that was nice. I was on my way back to Principia to complete by undergraduate schooling.

The selective service draft was starting to become more of a big thing, and the antiwar movement was really gaining momentum. I noticed two things while on campus. The students were more aware of what was going on. Whenever President Lyndon Johnson talked about calling up the reserves I had numerous people come up and ask if I had heard the news and how did that affect me. Was I going to get called up? I would assure them my job in the Navy was to graduate, and I was not at risk. I also got questioned a lot about the war and my personal feelings about it. My answer was pretty much this: I am going to be a naval officer and a pilot, and if the war is where I was sent then that is where I would go. Naïve? — probably yes, but I

Tucker Lake college graduation, 1969. Photo courtesy H. Tucker Lake Jr.

believed in the United States, and I was ready to serve. Up to that time, other than the graduation from OCS, the greatest moment for me was to graduate from Principia College in full dress white uniform. I felt like I was making my personal statement in support of my country. I got my baccalaureate diploma and was sworn in as an ensign. Later that day Admiral Alan Shepard, famed astronaut and father of my Principia classmate Laura Shepard, came over and introduced himself to me and said, "It is a great adventure you have started on." That was really cool, and he was right.

I received my orders to report to Pensacola that September of 1969. When I headed down to the naval air station, my dad's departing words were, "Remember there is nothing in your contract that says that the Navy has to be fair." Off I went. When I arrived in Pensacola too many trainees had been ordered to come down to flight school, and the pipeline for pilots was full. One night four of us were talking in our room at the Bachelor Officers Quarters, and we felt we needed a name for this pool of waiting would-be pilots. That night we formed a squadron named VT-0 The Pool of 1969. We designed a squadron logo for a patch. We got it approved by the admiral, and we were able to wear it on our flight jackets. All the while, however, we were still going to have to sit and wait and wait and wait. Recurring theme.

VT-0 The Pool of 1969 patch.
Photo courtesy H. Tucker Lake Jr

The Navy finally came up with jobs around the country for us to do. I was sent to NAS Memphis to work at the naval reserve unit there. Of all things, I was now the recruiting officer telling young college guys to "imagine your own jet with your name on it." The line still worked. Our office recruited both college kids for programs as well as sailors getting off active duty for the reserve program. The office staff included a large group of sailors and two female civilian clerk typists. I took the place of the yeoman as he went off to attend a twelve week class, so I had the sailors and two civilians working for me. The circumstance provided my first challenge and opportunity to activate the skills I had learned from that boring leadership class. The two civilians were allowed forty-five minutes for lunch, during which they would play Scrabble, and it appeared that each day the game took longer, and so did the lunch break. One day, one of my sailors came to me and asked, "Mr. Lake, when do *we* get our Scrabble game?" I realized this could become a big problem. I did not want to screw up the program, and I certainly wasn't going to bother the skipper with something I should be able to handle thanks to my fantastic leadership classes. Moreover, I needed those ladies to be happy, as they could type out contracts four times faster than I could. So I figured I had to do something quickly and quietly. That first night after the ladies left for the day, I took all the "I's" out of the Scrabble box. The next day's game was not quite as long. The following day I removed the "E's." That got the game back to short time and the lunch back to forty-five minutes, and harmony re-ensued throughout the unit. About a week later, my sailors brought me a gift: a desk name plate saying Yeoman Chief ENS Lake. They gave it to me with a wink and a smile.

Tucker Lake at Saufley Field VT1 after first solo in a T-34 Jan 1970. Photo courtesy H. Tucker Lake Jr.

The lottery for the draft took place while I was in the reserve unit in Memphis. We were swamped with calls from mothers trying to get their boys into the reserves. The college kids could try to get into the different OCS programs, but there was nothing we, as recruiters for reserve programs, could do for them. All we could do was to recommend they go see the regular Navy recruiters. During this time we also visited college campuses, but we were not the most popular people on campus. A Chrysler convertible was vandalized, so we would hide our cars. We experienced people throwing rocks and spitting at us. Others would come up and ask how we could kill babies and innocents. I was an ensign fresh out of college: I had done nothing. A Marine gunnery sergeant accompanying us would come over and bail me out offering answers that made most protesters just walk away. He had already been to Vietnam twice and was sent home having been wounded numerous times.

Finally, it was back to Pensacola and flight school, and the beginning of that adventure about which Alan Shepard had spoken. My first four flights of straight and level flying wound up being very interesting. I was the first student my instructor ever had, and I was a challenge. I got airsick numerous times. I would fly, then say, "You got it, sir," heave, and then take back control. Throughout our first flight together, this repeated occurrence bothered him. He took over the controls as we came in for a landing and brought us back to earth. It was the worst landing I ever saw. We bounced down the runway like a real rookie. I smiled and told the instructor not to worry: "They will think I was flying." He did not chuckle. After the fourth flight like this, I saw the flight surgeon who gave me some pills, and all was good. I could fly, and land, and eventually even soloed. By then we all realized that only a few pilots got jets, and many, like me, decided that jets might not be the greatest thing to fly anyway. They had glide ratios lower than rocks. That is when I decided that I would like to fly helicopters.

Tucker Lake on wing of a T-28, prior to a solo flight at
Whiting Field, VT-3, circa May, 1970.
Photo courtesy H. Tucker Lake Jr.

Before going on to the next phase of training called Basic Flight, I went home for a week, and it was again like being in the recruiting office. I was flying home in uniform, and as I walked thought the airport I was called all sorts of names and spit at. To this day it bothers me that Americans could treat service personnel so vilely. I can only think how hard such treatment was on the guys who really faced the enemy. It hurts me, so I can only imagine how they feel.

So I was next off to Whiting Field and the T-28 — a fun plane to fly. I made it through basic and soloed. It was a great life for a young guy: flying planes and living at the beach. Life was grand. But then it hit. The government was running out of money for pilots, and the shortfall was reflected in the latest federal budget. There I was, enrolled in instrument training, and we had a stand down. People's flight grades were suffering and the rumor of cuts was bothering all of us. A Navy captain came down from Washington, DC, to assure us that there was no truth to rumors of cutbacks, but two weeks later we were marched into the gymnasium in alphabetical order and told that on a chair was a letter for each of us. The letter informed us whether we were going to remain in the program or were being released with the ability either to switch branches of the service and fly, to go to flight officer school, or to leave the service altogether having fulfilled our military commitment.

I went to my detailer who suggested I become a flight officer. I was not about to let someone else fly me around. I am a terrible backseat driver. He offered the Marines where I would have been a first lieutenant and could go on with my training. It was not a good choice as I had not been to Marine OCS nor to basic school. I asked about riverboats, as word was they were looking for junior officers. He asked where I went to OCS, and when I told him Pensacola, he said, "Can't do, as I did not go to 'boat school.'" I pointed out that the Navy felt I could fly in a multi plane environment. But he said. "No Go." Then he offered underwater ordinance. I said, "Swim?" "Planes and boats, Yes, but swim? No." So I left the service.

At the start of the next budget year, I went down to Pensacola and met with the admiral. We talked for half an hour. It was the same admiral that had given me my graduation certificate. He said, "Send in your letter, and we will get you right back down here." Again, a case of "hurry up and wait." So, I waited and waited. Because I needed to pay bills, I got a job on Wall Street and was happy. Seven months later I finally got orders to report to flight school. It was too late. I had waited and waited and waited, and it just took them too long. Again my father's words came to mind: "There is nothing that says they have to be fair." The same thing could happen again. The Navy's mission was slowly winding down, and I could envision continuing major cutbacks by the time I would have my wings of gold. So I wrote a letter returning the orders. There would be no drills with the reserve, but I did get promoted to a full lieutenant, and in 1976 I got my final military discharge. 10 years as a reservist, and I never left the sunny shores of Pensacola. Thus ended my military career and the dreams of that three-year-old climbing into airplanes.

Tucker Lake at age 3. Photo courtesy H. Tucker Lake Jr.

 **TUCKER LAKE** wanted to follow his father's footsteps and be a career Navy man. The elder Lake had served twenty-one years, retiring as a lieutenant commander. Tucker rose to the rank of lieutenant in the Navy, spent most of his career at Pensacola where the Navy flight school remained more than a temptation, but as his story just told indicates, his dream of becoming a Navy pilot was not to be.

Born in Coronado, California, Lake was raised in Andover, Massachusetts, before coming to Principia College to join the class of 1969 and to study history. A four-year letterman in track, Lake also lettered three years in football. He was a member of Rackham Court West, serving his house as freshman head, volunteering for the campus fire crew, and serving as vice president of his senior class. He married Principia alumna Sharon Brittenham (C67), and they have three children: Christopher, Joshua, and Jessica, the latter two also Principia graduates. Lake's older sister Pam, a member of the college class of 1965, was the first in the family to graduate from Principia. After Lake's discharge from the Navy, he pursued a career as a securities trader. Today he lives with his wife in Washington, New Jersey.

USS *Intrepid* CVS-11. Photo courtesy *Intrepid* Sea, Air,
and Space Museum

PART III:
Service Domestic and Abroad

The Real Glory

DONALD L. HUBER

I joined the military shortly after college graduation—it was 1967, Vietnam was gaining traction, and military duty was not only required, but expected. It never occurred to me that I wouldn't serve or couldn't kill an enemy if necessary. It was simply a duty to protect our country and defend democracy, and I think most of my classmates felt the same way. This may be a far cry from what most college grads think today, but joining the military was one of the best things I ever did.

I can't say that, like some of my classmates, I was a skilled fighter pilot, an elite Ranger, or a Navy Seal. On the other hand, my entry career field *was* a bit sexy and highly classified—a nuclear ICBM launch officer. However, true to form for the military, that assignment was abruptly changed during Officer Candidate School (OCS) in order to meet Air Force needs. I was to become, instead, a mundane logistics supply officer, and little did I know how that would later evolve.

Even prior to signing-up, divine doors were opening. My draft board guaranteed that if I didn't go to graduate school, I would be quickly drafted. While I applied for graduate school, acceptance didn't beat the draft board who assured me that the military was my best option. So, my next applications were to OCS. The Army test took only minutes, was passable by any eighth-grader, and offered only two career choices—tank driver and infantry rifleman. I could already drive and knew how to shoot, so I declined. The Navy test was a little harder, and the Navy was my first choice, but apparently I flunked, or so I was told. The Air Force test was quite long and the most challenging, but I passed with a high mark, and so I signed-up. Soon thereafter I was notified by the Navy that there had been a mistake in my test scoring and that they would be happy to have me. Too late—Providence had already taken care of which branch of the military I would serve.

My first military experiences were quite comical at times. The entry physical was done by an Army doctor who walked along a row of us standing in our skivvies and looked over each of us for about ten seconds. Little chance I'd flunk this exam! However, he did ask the guy standing next to me, who had flatter feet than a duck, to step out and answer a question: "Son, do you ever have trouble with your feet?"

"No, sir," he replied. "Only when I walk!"

Scratch one happy recruit, soon to be home again. And Providence stepped in for me again when the test for a potentially disqualifying problem I encountered never showed up on my physical exams. Both of us were blessed.

About two weeks before graduating from OCS at Lackland AFB in San Antonio, Texas, classmates were getting their assignments, usually to large bases or training schools. My orders read, "Assigned from Lackland AFB to Lackland AFB." Clearly a mistake I told the personnel office. Not so, they replied, and paid me all of 35 cents for travel expenses across the base! I had a great father-like commanding officer, who quickly followed initiation tradition for new second lieutenants and assigned me to be a munitions officer in an area which, in his words, had some really "big" stuff—small arms ammo, obstacle course explosives, USAF Olympic Team special munitions, and hundreds of mostly empty bomb bunkers. The bunkers were large, as were the snakes that inhabited them. But again, Providence was already at work paving the way even in this small, isolated ammo dump.

I had been in this assignment only ten days when my operations sergeant arrived straight from two years of twenty-four-hour shifts in Vietnam managing the full range of the real stuff—aircraft bombs, missiles, canon rounds, and gunnery munitions. He was 6' 4" tall, weighed about 250 pounds, and sported seven stripes and more ribbons than a battle banner. Plus, he came with fifteen other seasoned airmen of all sorts and colors as his crew.

It only took another week for S.M. Sgt. (Senior Master Sergeant) Bowman to pull me out of my first jam. The office and lounge area only had one bathroom, and one day, while I was seated comfortably, a six-foot rattlesnake about the size of my calf crawled under the tin siding and was starting to curl around the ceramic facility. I quickly jumped on top of the seat and banged on the wall loudly "explaining" what was happening. In just a few seconds S.M. Sgt. Bowman appeared with shovel in hand, duly executed the snake, and extended a hand so I could navigate around the still convulsing corpse. Talk about being embarrassed and caught with your pants down! I can still hear their laughter.

In another instance, my commander asked me to write an analytical report requested from higher up. I duly researched it, wrote it, signed it, and handed it in. He responded that it looked great, except for one thing—he would sign it, not me. That was my first, but not last, lesson in how the military chain of command worked.

Shortly after the slithering snake episode, our first annual inspection was scheduled, and this is where I got one of my most important military lessons. S.M. Sgt. Bowman quietly asked for a chat to get us ready. It was lighthearted and went like this—"Lieutenant, you're a likeable, bright guy, but let me tell you how it works here. I take care of you, and you take care of me. I run the shop, you learn the ropes, and we both get an afternoon off one day a week to play golf." "Sounds like a plan," I replied, trying to balance by initial surprise with being prudent. As an officer, in the military hierarchy, I outranked him, but his was no *suggestion* that I should abdicate my authority. He was a dedicated coach, an expert in a dangerous profession, and we worked together to build a team—the best team on the tarmac—but his team. Thus, I learned early that it was the sergeants that made the military work.

Bowman also told me our warehouse locks were outdated, and we'd get gigged at inspection, but when he mentioned it in passing to the colonel, the colonel said they were okay and too expensive to change. "What do you think?" Bowman asked me. "Change them," I replied. "Good," he said. We passed inspection with an outstanding rating. But, I did get duly "reminded" by the colonel that not following his wishes is how second lieutenants don't make first lieutenant. Fortunately, however, I put a lot of effort into the job, and in the next two years I got outstanding ratings, received a top USAF Supply Officer award, earned a regular commission, and did make first lieutenant. (Admittedly, at that time, only officers who had committed a crime didn't make first lieutenant!) Senior M. Sgt. Bowman became Chief M. Sgt. Bowman and retired with one more well-earned stripe.

Lackland AFB was, indeed, a bit of a country club, but duty there was important preparation for my military journey, where the next stop was to be Udorn AFB, Thailand—a major air base for gruesome Vietnam bombing runs and jet-jockey fighter support.

In stepped Providence again. My commander urged me to apply for an MBA in Computer Science, compliments of the USAF, and I was accepted. Cancel Thailand; start graduate school in Washington, DC. It seems that graduate school was in the plan all along. The Air Force had a highly sophisticated, worldwide, computer-managed logistics supply system, and working with that, plus a computer MBA, would serve me well later.

Fast forward a few years to MBA graduation, and another cancellation of my career field shifted me to become a special agent in the Office of Special Investigations. (The OSI is the Air Force version of television's famous Navy CIS.) This assignment was to entail everything from counter-intelligence tracking of foreign military attachés and suspected Air Force spies to investigating base murders/suicides and fraud, as well as to designing a military-wide, computerized background investigation system. Each of these skills was instrumental in my being hired by future employers. After OSI training in Washington, DC, I could have been assigned anywhere in the world—to a U.S. or overseas field office, to an embassy, or to an industry assignment, etc., but in another twist, I was asked to remain at the Washington headquarters, a somewhat unusual duty for a new agent. The assignment was to be for three years, and I loved Washington, but little did I know I would be there for another thirty-five years.

All of this experience came with the price of a five-year service obligation. But, I was a career officer with a regular commission, the training was great, officer colleagues were superb, benefits and the future were good, and the military was challenging and well-run. Also, various new friendships, many that remain today, were forming in

Washington. Fellow or future Principians such as Marv Harris (career Air Force and an officer at the Pentagon) became a good buddy, David Bradley (future owner and publisher of *The Atlantic* magazine) and his family emerged as longtime good friends, and George Moffett (later international journalist and president of Principia College) became my future best man, to mention a few. While these three were particularly special friendships, numerous other Principians and church friends all around Washington greatly enriched my assignment in the nation's capital. True to the unseen plan, in a few years to come there would be an especially good Washington relationship that would be life-changing. So, serving a longer military obligation in DC, which had many attractions, a large Principia contingent, and active Christian Science churches, was fine with me.

Then Vietnam ended. Officers were in oversupply, and I got an offer I couldn't refuse: a free pass out. There would be no active duty obligation; instead, only a two-year reserve assignment at the Pentagon in — you guessed it — munitions logistics. Obviously that first munitions assignment in 1967 was no fluke: the resulting experience in my record qualified me for the Pentagon slot. Also, unknown to me at the time, trading my regular commission for a reserve one allowed me to add all of my active duty military years to my future federal service years for retirement. My military experience also landed me a job with an international consulting and educational firm in the Watergate Office Building, where I worked for six years (yes, I was there the night the Plumbers broke in!), as well as my first government position in the International Trade Administration directing background investigations on foreign companies. It even helped one of my sons attend the Air Force Academy. But, maybe the best result of all was that this timely exit from the military lead to my meeting my lovely wife of thirty-five years during a very short two-week overlap period when we were both working in the Watergate. This was clearly both divinely guided and life-changing.

I spent eighteen more years in the reserves becoming proficient in the "big stuff," and it was indeed big! It included active duty tours in the president's east coast version of NORAD's Cheyenne

Mountain;[18] working in a highly classified weapons vault in the Pentagon developing a close relationship with the Air Force's conventional and nuclear arsenal; getting working exposure to the Pentagon's underground war room munitions control station; assisting with the preparation of SALT[19] background materials and nuclear weapons destruction guidelines; standing in awe under rows of alert-ready aircraft with multiple nuclear warheads; and being restricted for overseas travel because of what I knew. I ultimately retired early as a lieutenant colonel to accept a very rewarding position directing a presidential trade program that provided many special trips (often with my wife) to United States embassies and related embassy events, to overseas trade shows such as the Paris and Farnborough Air Shows, and to major defense and industry shows.

So, it ended up being an exciting adventure after all, for as Mary Baker Eddy has written in *Miscellany*, "We live in an age of Love's divine adventure to be All-in-all."[20] I learned that the glory in the adventure was God's, just as Job wrote: "For he performeth the thing that is appointed for me: and many such things are with him."[21] My experiences demonstrated God's perpetual care, guidance, and protection—protection not from bombs or in combat, but from leaning just on my own understanding. I recognized, with great gratitude, His well-laid plan—which was certainly formed long before I knew about it.

---

18 NORAD: North American Air (now Aerospace) Defense Command, founded in 1957 in Colorado Springs, Colorado. A bi-national organization (U.S. and Canada) whose mission is to detect, validate, and warn of attack against North America whether by aircraft, missiles, or space vehicles and to ensure air sovereignty and air defense of U.S. and Canadian airspace (including after a 2006 expanded agreement), maritime warning.

19 SALT: Strategic Arms Limitation Talks under President Richard Nixon and Soviet General Secretary Leonid Brezhnev, these two rounds of bilateral conferences and international treaties [notably the Anti-Ballistic Missile Treaty of May 26, 1972] initiated old War agreements to limit the number of nuclear missiles in American and Russian arsenals.

20 *The First Church of Christ, Scientist, and Miscellany* by Mary Baker Eddy: 158:9-10. Used courtesy of The Mary Baker Eddy Collection.

21 Job 23:14.

LIEUTENANT COLONEL DON HUBER served in the Air Force from 1967 to 1972 assigned to the Pentagon as a special agent in the Office of Special Investigations, a U.S. federal law enforcement agency that reports directly to the Office of the Secretary of the Air Force. His specialty was munitions logistics/supply including logistics-nuclear. Among the several medals recognizing Huber's military service are the Vietnam Service Medal and an outstanding unit medal with four bronze clusters.

Born in Chicago, Huber grew up in Kansas City traveling to St. Louis to complete his high school education at Principia's Upper School (US61) and then briefly attended Principia College (C65). He was a member of Rackham Court East before transferring to the University of Kansas, where he joined Tau Kappa Epsilon and majored in sociology and business. Following his graduation from KU, he entered the Air Force [his brother served in the Navy] and headed to San Antonio, Texas, for Officer Training School (OTS). Several years after graduation from OTS he was assigned to Washington, DC, to obtain his MBA at George Washington University in conjunction with his new regular commission as a career officer.

Huber's post-military career included six years with the International Management and Development Institute and thirty years with the federal government's International Trade Administration. Married to Elizabeth "Nimmie" Addison, Huber has a daughter and two sons (one of whom attended the Air Force Academy). His son Andrew attended Principia Upper School.

Carrier Flight Deck. Photo by Robert M. Craig

War-averse Sailor

SARA MITCHELL (GALLANT) BARNACLE

Thomas Martin Gallant became a Principian in 1985, when he brought his family from Maine to St. Louis to put daughter Leah in Upper School and daughter Rachel in Lower School. He plunged whole-heartedly into his role as a Prin dad, staff spouse, and volunteer in many activities, such as driving vans on school trips, leading a Prin-based Girl Scout troop, joining and serving in the Dads' Club, running a Sunday-afternoon recreational program for boarders, painting theater sets, and curating the first and perhaps only Principia staff and alumni art show. He started a small contracting business, through which he improved the homes of many in the Principia community. Word of mouth opened up one job after another.

As a high-schooler, Tom had followed his father's footsteps into the U.S. Navy. Clifford H. Gallant, Sr., had served as a chief engineer during World War II and stayed in the reserves through the Korean War and on until retirement. Proud of his father's service, it was natural for a young son to follow suit. Tom had weekend duty and a three-week training cruise every summer. A highlight was the day, serving as quartermaster, that he navigated his ship into Portland, Maine, harbor — his home city.

Then came the Vietnam War. By then, Tom was in college at the University of Maine. Exposure to the array of political ideologies on campus in those days expanded his worldview. His youthful pride in military service was challenged. Some young men he knew fled to Canada. Others squeezed out every avenue for exemption. Others served grudgingly. Others served willingly. Some never returned, some returned seemingly unscathed, while others returned sadly changed. While still loyal to his country and his obligation to complete the active duty segment of his reserve enlistment, Tom agonized over the prospect of being sent to kill fellow beings who he perceived to be no real threat to America or to true American interests. At some point, this view caused him to opt out of officers' training and accept the reduced pay of a lower grade, balanced by an earlier end to his military service.

During this time, Tom exercised his legal right for deferment of active duty in order to attend college. In 1969, he met and married fellow art student Sara Mitchell. Sara had just returned from a college term studying art in France and Italy, and Tom's earnest wish was to see for himself the works of the great masters in art and architecture before he might die in Vietnam. The new couple took the fall semester off to take an extended honeymoon hitch-hiking from cathedral to museum to palace to historic town around Europe.

Back in Maine, they returned to college, and before long they started their family while attending college part-time. Months before the first baby's birth, Tom learned that his deferment had expired, and it was now time to serve the Navy with honor, or serve time in prison. He chose the honorable route, and prayed most earnestly to be led into the best use of his talents when called to active duty.

He had become interested in Christian Science through observing the life of a college friend, before he met Sara, who had grown up in Christian Science Sunday schools. In typical fashion, Tom plunged into this new way of life with all his heart and energy. His first demonstration was the healing of dyslexia. The trouble which had so hampered his high school studies melted quickly away, and he became an A student.

Tom served his active duty, based out of the former Naval Air Station at Quonset Point, Rhode Island. After a few weeks of hauling trash, he was assigned to be a yeoman in a legal office. The healing of dyslexia made this paralegal duty possible, and his natural bent toward helping others was expressed in the care he took with cases that came before his boss. Among his most satisfying achievements was helping arrange the best discharges possible for young men who could not safely serve after their homosexuality had become common knowledge among the sailors.

Another word about the trash-hauling duty. Periodically, Navy ships are required to off-load the total inventory of perishables, such as mattresses, efficiently replacing them all at once. It may have been illegal, but Tom rescued a number of still-good items that had been designated "trash" under this all-or-nothing policy. Once he returned home for the weekend with several cot-sized mattresses still in good condition strapped to the roof of his Saab. One mattress, freshly upholstered, went on top of a large wooden box in his in-laws' back hall breezeway, making a guest bed out of a blanket chest. The other mattresses found new homes elsewhere. No wonder his mother-in-law came to call him laughingly, "St. Tom the Provider."

Tom's ship was one of the *Essex*-class aircraft carriers based at Quonset Point, USS *Intrepid* (CVS-11). His final assignment was to serve as a photographer on that ship from April of 1971 to November of 1971. Daughter Rachel recalls her dad explaining how he had earned this posting. He stood up for a fellow sailor, a male ballet dancer from New York City who was being bullied, and as a reward was offered any open position in his grade. He leaped at the chance to further his artistic and technical education in the photo lab.

Tom and Sara's baby, Leah, was born just two months before *Intrepid* left Rhode Island. The ship had just returned from active participation in the Vietnam War. Tom was in the large contingent that came on board to replace half of the war-weary crew. The ship and the remaining half of its crew were being sent on a diplomatic (R & R) cruise up and down the coast of Europe. To be included in this adventure was a coup for this loyal American but war-averse sailor. Tom hardly dared attribute his "luck" to his living Christian Science. But there he was — assigned to be an official government tourist/diplomat as his wartime service.

Sara and Tom exchanged letters almost daily, which have been preserved.

Life on ship was not easy for Tom. He loved to work and work hard, but creativity and spontaneity were his style, not protocol and endless rules. One photo sent home shows him among a row of full-dress sailors under review by their captain. Tom's caption: "Why is Gallant making a fist?" Finding quiet space for religious study was always a project. His bunk was very close to some big, noisy machinery. However, Tom became adept at finding some of the quieter nooks onboard.

Tom ran a clandestine barber shop, seating his clients on an overturned, empty trash can. Reason? The black sailors who usually wore their hair in the full-bodied afro of that day, had to learn how to keep it appearing short and neat to pass inspection. In sympathy, Tom figured out how to cut their curls so their hair could fit neatly under the uniform cap, but fluff out more fully for going ashore. The ship's barber would have buzz-cut the afros.

Tom was always on the look-out for ways to earn extra money to send back home, but he turned down the opportunity for the pay raise that would have gone with assignment as the photographer who hid in a small pit on the flight deck to take the mandatory pictures of each plane as it landed. This was exciting but dangerous duty, to be under landing fighter planes and near the cable that caught and stretched like a giant bowstring to arrest their speed. Some photographers had been hurt in that line of duty. Tom feared he might not be around to return to that growing wonder child and her mom.

He did, however, climb into jet engines to record cracks or other problems needing repair. The photos were mailed back to the States for advice on repairs. Every activity on board, it seems, was recorded photographically—formal dinners, the arrival of foreign dignitaries in various ports, and common events all over the ship. The photo lab provided excellent schooling in the techniques needed for both black and white and color work. When on leave, the photographers were encouraged to take their cameras and capture the flavor of the ports for the ship's cruise book, as well as for American official publicity. Tom took full advantage of this, coming home with slide shows of Herculaneum, Pompeii, the Swiss and French Alps, the German cities and countryside around Lubek, and the northern beauties of Scotland and Norway. He also was allowed to develop film sent from home, so Sara provided him with a constant record of Leah's growth.

Although never in real danger, *Intrepid* was under regular surveillance by Russian planes and ships, especially as they cruised north of the Arctic Circle.

Tom's most satisfying shipboard moment occurred during a major storm at sea, while on an earlier cruise across the ill-famed  "Bermuda Triangle." The normally stabilized aircraft carrier began to pitch and heave. So high were the waves that they broke over the flight deck, many stories above the usual waterline. Tom had been in the enlisted mess decks and was helping put away the dining tables, which were on wheels when folded. Before they could be properly secured against the rolling of the ship, the tables broke loose and began to race back and forth across the mess deck crashing forcefully into each other. Tom reached up and grabbed an overhead pipe to lift himself above the lethal army of advancing and retreating tables. Then he saw his work partner, a small man, standing nearby — petrified and potentially going to be crushed, maimed, or worse. Hanging from the pipe with one arm, Tom reached down and with the other arm drew the man up out of the way of the tables, holding both of them safe until help arrived.

Tom Gallant. Photo courtesy Sara Barnacle

In relating this story at home later, Tom told it in such a self-deprecating way, illustrated by hooking one arm up in the air and the other pulling up an imaginary person, that his experience became a fun family story. But in fact, it had been a serious situation, and a great saving of limb and maybe of life. The sailor he rescued was ever grateful.

Christian Scientists have been protected while fulfilling many different military roles, from being assigned to serving behind the lines (in the days when battle involved "lines"), to emerging safely from combat or imprisonment. Some have found alternative service. As with all those earnest seekers, Tom was put in the place he could do the most good, learn the most for his future, and serve his country honorably and well.

Tom passed on in November of 2008. Most of the copies of his Navy photo-work were donated to the new naval museum aboard *Intrepid*, now permanently docked in New York. His wife and daughters remember visiting that museum during an earlier visit to New York City. Tom had been tremendously excited to be stepping back aboard, and was generally pleased with the changes made to accommodate displays and the public. The high point for him would have been to take his family to the photo lab, the scene of such an important era of his life. Imagine his consternation to find the lab converted into a chapel, somber by comparison to the lively scenes in the seventies.

That naval tour of duty augmented and confirmed the direction of the rest of Tom's life. The specific techniques learned in the photo lab parleyed afterwards into several jobs, a lifelong pursuit of photography as an art form, and even his major hobby of collecting old cameras. The mundane duties on board gave him valuable background when dealing with people, notably his public service as a school board member in Waldoboro, Maine, and when designing the new public library there. After leaving the Navy and graduating from college, Tom studied architecture at Boston Architectural Center and worked for many years as an architectural designer; but the masterpieces he had studied so eagerly in Europe fired his lifelong avocation as an art historian and artist.

TOM GALLANT had several jobs during his active military career, notably in 1971 serving as an enlisted photographer's mate aboard USS *Intrepid*. *Intrepid* is an *Essex*-class aircraft carrier, commissioned in World War II, with distinguished service on three tours to Vietnam, and whose homeport during Gallant's service was at Quonset Point, Rhode Island. The carrier is now the *Intrepid* Sea, Air, and Space Museum in New York City, and many of Gallant's photographs are now part of the museum's collection. Gallant's father, Clifford H. Gallant, had served in the Navy during World War

II rising to the rank of chief petty officer, but (as Gallant's wife recounts in the previous essay), Tom's decision to join the military was not an easy one. He was an artist, had certain qualms of conscience regarding the war, and had married during his college years and had a baby on the way. Nonetheless, honor, for him, dictated enlistment, and in 1965 he joined the Navy. Following boot camp at Great Lakes, Gallant's early duties included various assignments including service as a yeoman in a military legal office, and, in 1971, Gallant had an opportunity to begin work as a ship's photographer aboard *Intrepid*.

The ship had recently returned from three tours to Yankee Station Vietnam, but was now home ported in Rhode Island so cruises during Gallant's time aboard the ship were Atlantic, not Pacific tours. Tom's cruise in 1971 took him to Europe, including to Scandinavia and the Mediterranean. As an artist who may well have envisioned the final months of his military tour as an eighteenth-century "grand tour," Gallant was eager to spend hours during liberty visiting such ancient sites as Roman Pompeii, touring Italian and German cities, or recording photographic images of the natural beauties of the Alps and Scandinavian coastlines. Even when not on cruise, Gallant no doubt found the New England home port of *Intrepid* suited him just fine, as he was born in Chelsea, Massachusetts, had been raised in North Yarmouth, Maine, and earned his Bachelor of Arts degree in art at University of Maine at Orono.

Gallant's artistic interests shaped his work as ship's photographer, although much of his work was documentary, including recording liberty sites for the ship's cruise book. His civilian career would be similarly that of a man of artistic bent. A studio art major in college, Gallant also attended the famed Boston Architectural Center, and although he did not graduate, his post-military career was as an architectural designer. A second civilian career soon emerged for Tom as a Principia dad and active volunteer at the school, after he brought his family to St. Louis to enroll his two daughters in The Principia School (then known as the Lower School (elementary) and Upper School (high). Tom was proud to be closely associated with Principia. His two daughters would both graduate from Principia Upper School, Leah Gallant McFall in 1989, and Rachael Gallant Feeney in 1993. Rachael would attend Bryn Mawr College. Leah, who graduated from Principia College in 1993, would go on to earn a Masters of Science in Education from Southern Illinois University Edwardsville in 2006; she returned to Principia College in 1999 where she is currently working as Costume Director/Designer in the college's theatre and dance department. Tom's wife Sara Mitchell (Gallant) Barnacle worked in the publications office of the school from 1986 to 1997, eventually becoming Associate Director of Publications. They were married for thirty nine years, until Tom's passing, and Sara is the author of this account.

News from Somali Wally: "Now You Know the Rest of the Story"

WALLY WETHE

In 1989 I was assigned to an obligatory one-year unaccompanied tour to the remote country of Somalia. When the orders came through, I asked my assignments officer where Somalia was. He said, "Well, it's not the end of the world, but you can *see* the end of the world from there!" I was the deputy commander of the Office of Military Cooperation (OMC), and managed two military foreign aid programs there. I also was one of four pilots assigned to the U.S. Embassy in the capital city of Mogadishu. We flew a small but beautiful six-passenger Beechcraft Super King Air turboprop airplane, and we navigated the country by means of what is called "dead reckoning" because there wasn't a single operational radio aid to navigation in the entire country. This tour took place years before GPS satellite navigation became readily available to one and all, as it is today. Looking like the number seven, located at the northeast corner of Africa, the narrow little country of Somalia truly did feel like the end of the world. But it was a world of adventure!

What follows is a true story. Do you think the best stories are fictional and have to be thought up from scratch? Many are. But I think the most interesting, the most inspirational, the most fun stories are not contrived or invented, but simply assembled from experience, from events that are going on right in front of us. They may appear to be unrelated pieces in a cosmic puzzle, daily occurrences that pass by us unnoticed. Whether these fragments are recognized or not, depends on how alert we are. Reassembled in this volume, our stories are recorded as memoirs of true experiences. They often tell us more than we initially heard on the evening news. The people and the events in this account of Somalia are real although I used a little artistic license here and there for fun. As the legendary news broadcaster, Paul Harvey,[22] would say, "Hello Americans! You know what the news is. Now you're going to hear the rest of the story."

October brings cooler fall weather to most northern climes, but not in the endless summer heat of equatorial Somalia. The sun rises and sets at nearly the same time every day of the year. This particular morning, Colonel Abdulahi Sheik Omar, chief of engineering and construction for the Somali ministry of defense, awoke to what he knew would be another hot and dusty day in Somalia's capital city, Mogadishu. As he prayed the first of five daily Moslem prayers to Allah, he gave thanks that fate had not seen him assigned to the war-torn North, near Berbera or Hargeisa, where it was even hotter and filled with the incredible instabilities and sorrows of civil war. He had problems enough of his own to handle right here in Mogadishu!

He and his friend, the chief of logistics, Colonel Mohammed Abdi Hashi, were trying to manage with Western management techniques, their part of a fledgling governmental system barely twenty years old, but rife with centuries-old nomadic traditions of graft, family favoritism, and corruption. The president's appointed ministers, all family members, were getting rich by dipping generously into the country's limited, imported wealth, intended by its donors to benefit the nation, and frustrating the two colonels' efforts to keep track of millions of dollars worth of equipment, supply stocks, spare parts, and now fuel.

The failure of Mogadishu's main electric power generating plant near Gezira Beach, just south of the city, had taken an entire month to repair. During that time, Colonel Omar's men at the Gezira generating station had been ordered by minister after minister to provide truckloads of diesel fuel from the tank farm to power the private

---

22 Paul Harvey (1918-2009) was a radio broadcaster and syndicated news commentator, one of the most listened to radio personalities of his generation. Although he had worked in radio since he was fourteen, Harvey's most famous broadcasts were "The Rest of the Story" episodes, mixtures of news, history, mystery, and feature stories, which he broadcast from 1976 until his death in 2009.

backup generators of privileged family members. Colonel Omar had to comply. It wasn't wise to deny a member of the president's family.

But he hadn't recognized the magnitude of this drain on his fuel stocks. As it came time to fire up the huge diesel-guzzling city power generators, a terrified Colonel Hashi came running down from the tank farm to his fellow officer and friend, Colonel Omar, with horrible news. "Abdulahi, Abdulahi!" he gasped, "The diesel fuel is almost finished! We will not get more from Mombasa for two weeks!! The lights in Mogadishu will go out, businesses will not be able to do business, and the president's family will be after our heads!"

"My friend, Mohammed, calm yourself!" said Colonel Omar, summoning his own reserves of leadership and experience, combined with faith you might expect from praying five times a day. "Do not panic and run so wild-eyed like the little dik-dik![23] Allah will provide, Allah will provide. We must pray!"

Moslems prefer to pray together. Exactly what Colonel Omar and his friend prayed for as they bowed themselves toward Mecca, I could not tell you. But I would say from the talks I have had with my Moslem friends, that it was less a prayer of petition, and more a simple acknowledgment of God's greatness, and a willingness to become receptive to the idea that Allah might be willing to help them, wanting to help them, waiting to help them! If only they could become conscious of the solution He was trying to give them. I can tell you surely that the solution was there all the time. But to find out what it was, you have to know "the rest of the story!"

First, I want to tell you that the country's annual celebration of its 1969 military coup d'état, called the "21 October Revolution Day," came and went without another revolution—for which we were thankful! On the anniversary day, there arrived in Mogadishu, a seemingly endless parade of tribes from all over the country dressed in their special colors and featuring the people's most popular article of footwear, the flip-flop!

---

23 Named for the alarm calls of the females, dik diks are small antelopes (genus Madoqua] indigenous to the bush in eastern and southern Africa.

That night at our OMC compound, nicknamed the Villa Somalia, our retinue of military officers, the U.S. ambassador, and his embassy officials and their ladies (the ones who had them), stood in the reception line and met all of Somalia's leaders, including President Siad Barre, who was looking fit as a fiddle for all of his eighty years. It was a stellar event, fireworks and all.

Wally Wethe in front of the C-12 [Beechcraft Super King Air] six-passenger airplane, Mogadishu, Somalia, circa August, 1989. Photo courtesy Wally Wethe

We also had a three day visit from the deputy director of security assistance of our command headquarters, Central Command, or CENTCOM, located in Tampa, (MacDill Air Force Base), Florida. We gave them a complete orientation, had lengthy consultations with the ambassador and senior officials from the Somali ministry of defense, and threw another "wingding" of a party for 200 in their honor on the beautiful and quite large patio of the OMC chief's residence.

But the bottom line from CENTCOM was that although they "love us like brothers," we're on our own out here in Somalia when it comes to determining the future of our mission. Washington is too involved in other matters, and the political situation is too fluid on the Horn of Africa, not only in Somalia, but in Ethiopia, Sudan, and elsewhere for quick policy decisions to be forthcoming. The relative importance of the entire continent of Africa was once laconically referred to by 1970s Secretary of State Henry Kissinger, as "a dagger pointed at the heart of Antarctica!" This situation was actually quite instructive, and we were simply carrying on like a commander does on the field of battle. A field commander remembers his loyalties and presses on as he has been trained to do to accomplish his mission as he understands it without having his plays called in from the side-lines. This is what my friends Colonel Omar and Colonel Hashi were doing as best they could. And we discussed their dilemma at the CENTCOM party along with others of Somalia's many dilemmas.

At the party, the two colonels told me that they would not be at the ministry of defense headquarters in Mogadishu for a few days. They were going to investigate a situation south of the city. A huge derelict ship had washed onto the shore in a little fishing village called Baraawe, pronounced Brava. The wreck actually happened late in September, but it hadn't created much interest. Authorities made attempts to find out where she had come from. She was big enough that no one in Baraawe could board her. It turned out later that the ship had been sailing southeast across the Arabian Sea, bound for Singapore and Jakarta, when she caught fire. The crew, afraid that an explosion was imminent and after initial attempts to fight the fire failed, had jumped overboard, only to watch helplessly from their raft as the fire burned itself out, and the ship drifted away from them. The ship's owners were attempting to get into Somalia to get their freighter back, but according to international rules, the unauthorized entry of a vessel into sovereign waters is grounds for confiscation. In any case, the action to be taken finally fell into the lap of our friend Colonel Omar, the chief of engineering and construction. He was ordered to go to Baraawe and meet with the townspeople who wanted only to get rid of this huge, ugly eyesore still stuck on the beach.

Omar and his friend, Colonel Hashi, took off from the military ramp in Somalia's only military helicopter, a UH-1A, and headed south past the Gezira Beach generating station which was rapidly burning up its last hours of fuel. Colonel Omar really had more important matters on his mind, but he was taking time out to placate the good people of Baraawe. After a short meeting with the local town commissioner, they decided that the deck of this ship was listing only slightly and that a small search party would accompany them in the helicopter and land on the foredeck to conduct a search.

The initial reports were accurate. There was no one on board the stranded behemoth of a ship, and there was clear evidence of a fire that had since burned itself out. Colonel Omar went toward the bow and ordered his men to open the first cargo hatch. He peered into the dark hole and sniffed a familiar smell. He looked at Colonel Hashi who, in spite of his friend's advice, was beginning to jump up and down again like a little dik-dik! They ran over to the next hatch, and it smelled the same. Colonel Omar fell down onto his knees and called on his men to do the same, because Allah indeed had provided, and had done so weeks before anyone had even become aware of the need. The ship, which had been abandoned in the Arabian Sea, had been loaded in the Persian Gulf and had drifted over two thousand nautical miles, coming to rest at the very backdoor of the Gezira Beach generating station.

Colonel Abdulahi Sheik Omar, the chief of engineering and construction and the man who knew that Allah would provide, was on his knees on top of 800 metric tons (over 2,000,000 pounds) of fresh, clean, grade A, number one diesel fuel. It was enough to keep the lights on in Mogadishu for the two weeks it would take for their scheduled shipment of fuel to arrive from Mombasa. And that's exactly what it did!

And now you know the rest of the story.

This is Somali Wally writing you from the U.S. Embassy in Mogadishu, Somalia, on the Horn of Africa. Good day!

WALLY WETHE'S father was a Marine Corps pilot, so it was no surprise when the younger Wethe embarked in 1970 on a career in the military serving in the Air Force for twenty-six years. He retired in 1997 at the rank of lieutenant colonel. He too was a pilot, commanding various aircraft, assigned to posts worldwide, and serving as chief of air operations for the Defense Intelligence Agency (DIA).

Wethe was born in 1946 in Minneapolis, Minnesota , and lived in Laguna Beach, California, at the time he decided to travel back to the Midwest to attend Principia College as a member of the class of '68. He majored in music and business administration, lettered in track and field, and served as freshman head of his residence hall, Rackham Court West. During his senior year, Wethe organized and conducted a ninety-piece orchestra to perform at Parents' Weekend at the college. His other major, business, would be advanced in graduate school where he earned an MBA at National University. Married in the Principia College chapel to classmate Nancy Milliken after her graduation in 1970, Wethe has two children, a son Jordan, who graduated from the college in 1993, and a daughter Kimberly. Wethe's uncle may have been the family member first associated with the school: Alan Wethe attended the college briefly after World War II. In the few months before beginning his Air Force pilot career, Wally Wethe worked for the dean of men at Principia as a house pop at Rackham Court residence hall in the fall of 1970. After the military, Wethe was a commercial airline pilot and worked for two years at FAA Headquarters in the Flight Technologies and Procedures Division in Washington, DC The Wethes now live in Burke, Virginia, where Wethe serves as clerk of his local church.

USS *Manley* (DD-940), USS *Vogelgesang* (DD-862), and
USS *Edson* (DD-946). Photo: Department of Defense

Vogie Vignettes

DAVID POTTER

I was descended from warriors. My dad was a supply officer in the Navy in the South Pacific during World War II. My granddad was in the Army during the Spanish American War. My great-grandfather was a captain in the First Iowa Cavalry during the Civil War. And, if we take it back five or six more generations, I had soldiers on both sides of the Revolution.

ROTC

My military experience started when I was nineteen. It was the summer before my junior year at Principia. My dad was a retired captain in the Navy Supply Corps and knew an active duty captain at Great Lakes Naval Training Center, someone who could help me get into an ROTC program while I was in college. My dad and I went down to see him. We had coffee in his office, and he explained the program. I asked a few questions and found out that I would have to spend the next two summers in "boot camp" somewhere to get commissioned as an ensign when I graduated from college. I thanked him for his time and told my dad on the way home in the car that I'd take my chances of getting into the officer candidate program after I graduated. My father was not amused. Apparently he had worked pretty hard to get me in front of the captain and thought I was making a big mistake. He was probably right, but I got lucky.

OCS

The summer before my senior year at Principia, I went down to Chicago (we lived thirty miles north in Gurnee, Illinois) and took the test to get into the officer candidate program. They put me into a room with about twenty other guys. The test was difficult. It seemed to be mostly math and science, and I was a political science major. I couldn't go fast enough and never did finish all the questions. I figured I was destined to hearing from my draft board soon and heading for Vietnam with an M-16 in my hand. An officer came into the room and directed everyone somewhere else except me. Now I was really worried. He then told me that I had passed the test and that the Navy would get in touch with me about actually going to Officer Candidate School after graduation from Principia. I was pretty happy about the outcome, and I think my dad was too. He had kind of gotten over the ROTC offer.

I headed back to school in August for my senior year at Principia. I thought I wanted to go to law school, so I applied to three or four of them. Sometime in November I got a call from the Navy. I had been accepted into the officer candidate program and had two weeks to say yes or no. I contacted all the law schools that I had applied to, but they all said they couldn't give me an answer until the following April. I was getting a little tired of school by then, so I called the Navy back and told them "yes." I had to report to Officer Candidate School the July after I graduated from Principia.

Bruce McRoy and Mark Youngberg (both College '68) ended up going to Officer Candidate School with me. Bruce lived in Connecticut, and Mark lived right down the road in Waukegan, Illinois. Mark and I got out to Connecticut and met Bruce at his house. The three of us drove together to Newport, Rhode Island, to the Navy's Officer Candidate School. I don't remember exactly, but I think we got hung up on a bridge or something, but we were thirty minutes late to our first assignment. The upper classmen in charge of greeting us weren't happy about us showing up late. I was wearing a pair of shoes with a hole in the sole, 'cause I figured I wouldn't need them once I got to OCS. Turns out I got to wear them for about a week since the first thing we missed was "shoe issue." That little hole got bigger as the week went on.

Officer Candidate School was eighteen weeks long. And, up until about two weeks before graduation, most of us were convinced we were going to flunk out any minute. Getting "rolled back" four weeks for academic failure was a fate worse than death. That could also happen if you got really sick, and missed a lot of classes. One of the guys in Juliett Company (my company), got hepatitis about half way through the training. They were going to quarantine all of us but only ended up "rolling back" this poor kid from Rutgers. He said it had something to do with a girl he'd met one weekend.

We marched everywhere (to class, to meals, back to the dorm), and we were encouraged to make up marching cadences. One of our seamanship instructors was a master chief bos'nmate [boatswain's mate] named Schneider. It appeared to us that Master Chief Schneider had a slight drinking problem, so we made up the following cadence: "If Schneider were the new CO, the scuttlebutts would pump VO." (For you landlubbers, CO is commanding officer, scuttlebutts are drinking fountains, and VO is a brand of whiskey.) As we marched by Master Chief Schneider's classroom, he would usually bring his cup of coffee out on the porch and smile at us. I think he liked the attention.

We put our civilian clothes in a little box the day we arrived and spent the next eighteen weeks in our Navy uniforms. My fiancée (married to her nearly forty-nine years now) came out to visit after I'd been there several weeks. We decided to go to the Newport Jazz Festival. So, I got to go in my whites with my new white hat. This was 1968 and not 2017. I did not have anyone come up to me and thank me for my service or thump on their heart to let me know how they felt about the military. This was the era when you could count on someone shouting "baby killer." But, nobody punched me out, and we enjoyed the music.

My dad and mom showed up for graduation, all the way from Illinois. My dad could still get into his uniform. During World War II he had served as a supply officer for a construction battalion (Seabees) in Fiji, New Caledonia, and Funafuti. He was very proud of me in spite of the fact that I didn't always take his advice. He did tell me that I should go into the Supply Corps because it was the business end of the Navy, and that I might actually learn something that might do me some good later on. I think he was right that time.

The Wall

After Officer Candidate School, several of the new graduates went to the Navy Supply Corp School in Athens, Georgia. Bob Browne, another new ensign, shared an apartment with me in Callaway Gardens Apartments. Supply school lasted about eight months. Toward the end, we got to fill out a form with our top twenty duty choices after graduation. I really wasn't very interested in going to Vietnam, so all my choices were east coast. Bob's twentieth choice was Saigon, and that's where he went. Bob grew up in Corpus Christi, Texas. His goal in life was to do his tour in Saigon, transfer to San Juan, Puerto Rico, save his money, buy a charter boat, and live in the Caribbean. He got killed when the helicopter he was flying in to go on liberty hit a mountain. I wrote to his mother when I heard he died but never heard back from her. Years later, when I was working in Billings, Montana, they brought the "mini wall" to town. It was a scaled down version of the Vietnam veterans wall in Washington, DC. I knew Bob's name would be on there as well as Denny Gonzales who went to high school with me. We played on the football team together. I had a hard time finding Bob's name because I forgot that he had an "e" on the end of his last name, but once I found it, I noticed that he and Denny got killed about three months apart. I didn't think "The Wall" would be a very emotional experience after all those years, but it choked me up. I found it odd that Denny and Bob would get killed three months apart in a place so far away — probably didn't even know each other.

Boston

After Supply Corps School, I was assigned to the USS *Vogelgesang* (DD-862), a destroyer in the Boston Naval Shipyards. I was newly married by now and sent Carol apartment hunting in Boston. I told her how much of a housing allowance I got as an ensign, and I think it was $180 a month. We were staying with friends of my parents west of Boston. When I got home that night Carol was in tears describing the places she could find for that kind of money. We expanded our search to Quincy and ended up there for a few months before she left for Norfolk (my homeport) for a teaching job. The landlord wanted $190/month, but was willing to knock off ten dollars per month if we'd paint the place. We were official "Southies" and didn't even know it. (Southies were residents of South Boston, typically of Irish descent.) We also discovered that it isn't "Quin See" but "Quin Zee." Before Carol started teaching, we were so broke we used to window shop in the penny candy store. Once she started working, and I got promoted to Lt. (jg.), we seemed always to have money we didn't know what to do with.

Vogie (my ship) was in the shipyards when I arrived. As disbursing officer (one of my duties as supply officer on *Vogie*), I was the one that got to pay the crew—in cash. I made a trip down the pier every two weeks to the Shawmut National Bank with my leather bag and my .45 caliber pistol. The Navy issued the pistol to me but never really showed me how to shoot it. Of all the times that I had to tote cash around, the Boston Naval Shipyard was the only place I actually got the gun out of the holster, chambered a round and put it back in the holster with the flap off. I thought those shipyard workers would have killed me for my lunch money.

Uniform Code of Military Justice

As *Vogie*'s supply officer, I was also the supply division officer. If any of my men got in trouble, it was my job to accompany them to captain's mast and stick up for them. I supervised the cooks, store-keepers, ships servicemen, disbursing clerks, and stewards. Two of my cooks got into a fight on shore with two Marines. They proceeded to take off their uniform belts, wrap them around their hand and beat the two Marines bloody. The shore patrol arrested all four of them, and I had to bring them before our captain, Commander George W. Mau. The captain asked for our version of the story, and I told him. He asked who won the fight. I told him that our sailors won. He dismissed all charges against my cooks.

I also had a young storekeeper named Murray. Murray had a hard time with the Navy. He had been a couple of semester hours short of graduation from college when he joined up. He was a real smart kid and actually got to be a third class petty officer. But, he had trouble with things like getting out of bed in the morning and following orders. His senior petty officers started a program of trying to show him the benefits of doing what he was told. It involved getting beaten regularly when he didn't do what he was supposed to do. The laundry had a lock on the outside, and Murray spent more than one session in the laundry with one of the senior petty officers discussing his behavior.

Eventually his supervisor, a first class storekeeper, came to me and told me he was tired of beating Murray and that we should just write him up and take him to captain's mast. I agreed, and we took him to see the captain. At captain's mast, Murray had a pretty good shiner under one eye. The captain asked Murray how he got the shiner, and he replied, "Fell down a ladder, sir." The captain asked if we had attempted to work with Murray within our department to solve his behavior problems, and I responded that we had been diligent, but it didn't seem to be working. Murray got busted down to E-3 from E-4, lost some pay and got a couple of weeks of extra duty. Forty-three years later, Seaman Murray is probably chairman of Intel or a college professor somewhere.

The Night Baker

Once the *Vogelgesang* got out of the shipyard, we cruised down to Norfolk, Virginia, our home port. GITMO (Guantanamo Bay, Cuba) was our next port of call. They called this refresher training. The cruise was a chance to test out all the new equipment and train the crew since a lot of them were new to this ship. I had a cook named Stowe who was just an average cook, but a tremendous baker. Stowe drank a little. It impacted his performance in port, but once we got out to sea for a few days, he sobered up and became the night baker. Stowe baked pies, cakes, cookies, and bread. The crew loved it. Most all of the officers on the ship knew that Stowe baked at night and were good about sending the messenger of the watch down to the galley to alert

Stowe of any planned movement of the ship. One night, one of the junior officers forgot to tell Stowe and made a fairly sudden maneuver that caused all the cherry pies he was baking to hit the deck and hit Stowe. He gathered up what was left of two of the pies and climbed up the two ladders to the bridge to report to the officer of the deck: if anyone had any complaints about no pie on the menu they could talk to the junior officer who had ordered the starboard turn.

Soul Food

In 1969 we were all trying to be more aware of diversity and "black" issues, and so we were encouraged to put "soul food" on the menu. My senior commissaryman,[24] CS1 Smith, was black. I didn't know much about cooking, but I was supposed to help Smith prepare the menus for the week. When I encouraged him to put "soul food" on the menu, he told me "Boss, soul food is just poor food. These young black sailors have a little money and can afford to eat better. They'd take a burger ahead of collard greens any day." I accepted his advice and signed off on his menu choices for the week.

Benjie's Balloons

Vogie had a "Ship's Store," operated by Ships Serviceman Third Class Benjamin. Known as the "gedunk" store, it was located in the after passageway near the stern of the ship. As the store operator, you could stand in the store and touch all four walls. But, it carried some very essential products. Prior to entering a foreign port, senior petty officers coached the younger sailors about avoiding STDs. (I think they mostly called it "the clap" back then.) We accommodated their coaching with sales of "Benjies Balloons." Benjie posted signs on the store windows encouraging their use.

---

24 The Navy terms have evolved from cook, to commissaryman, to mess management specialist, to culinary specialist.

Gitmo

Guantanamo Bay was not the Gitmo that makes headlines today, the prison that holds Middle Eastern enemy combatants. I think the base was only twelve square miles on the tip of Cuba. There were two hundred Cuban nationals that worked on the base and walked through the gate every day. They got paid by the Navy to do their job, but they made a lot of extra money selling the pocketful of Cuban cigars they carried in with them every morning. The worst thing I recall that happened in Guantanamo Bay was when Castro shut off the water to the base forcing the military to bring water into the base on a ship. When our ship was steaming around Cuba, we were told to keep an eye out for refugees in little boats trying to escape. I think we only saw one. Several of us got promoted to lieutenant junior grade [Lt. (jg.)] while in Cuba. Drinks at the officer's club were a dime, and you could really get a snoot full for $1.20. I went to Cuba twice while I was on active duty. I didn't know it at the time, but we went through the Bermuda Triangle both times, going and coming back. I didn't disappear mysteriously, and I am still here to tell about it.

Cassette Tapes

In today's world of cell phones, texting, tablets, wifi, and computers, it's funny to remember that Carol and I didn't speak to each other for six months when I deployed to the Mediterranean. Making a long distance phone call from Europe back to the states was something like $15 for a few minutes. We agreed to exchange cassette tapes and mail them back and forth. When I left for Europe Carol was two weeks pregnant. So, when I returned from the deployment she was about 7 ½ months pregnant. My shipmates found a picture of a very pregnant former Miss America in her bikini, so I would know what to expect when I got home. Carol came running down the pier, when we came back home, so I figured she was still in pretty good shape.

Snoopy Ship

When we got to Europe we became a "snoopy ship." They brought what looked like a trailer aboard and placed it on the main deck. Several communications technicians and one officer worked in that trailer and not one of us, including the captain, was allowed to go in. We trailed the Bulgarian and Russian Navy and apparently listened to their electronics. One time, to get them to communicate, we shut everything down and went completely silent. The other guys got curious and turned their equipment on to see what we were doing. Their crew used to line up along the main deck before meals with little metal pails. We would watch them through binoculars. They saw us watching and proceeded to give us the international friendship symbol. (Yes, it really is international.)

Getting Cash Overseas

The ship put into San Remo, Italy, a port in Northern Italy near the French Riviera. As paymaster, I had to get $10,000 worth of Italian lire to pay the crew. I rented a little Fiat Cinqacenta and drove down the coast to Genoa. I got the money at a bank in Genoa, stuck it in my little leather bag and drove back to San Remo with the $10,000 in cash. Since we were overseas, I couldn't have brought my .45 even if I did know how to shoot it. When we deployed for six months, I was directed to get enough cash to pay the crew for six months. No checks. So, when we left the states, I had $250,000 in cash stuffed in my little safe. Each country we stopped in had its own currency (no euros). So, by the time we got back to the states, I had eight or nine kinds of currency in the ship's safe. Before the crew headed ashore, we used to set up a card table in the helicopter hanger and exchange foreign currency for U.S. dollars. In Alanya, Turkey, I took my disbursing clerk (Chuck Pace), two blank government checks, and a piece of carbon paper to the local agricultural bank to get $10,000 in Turkish lira. I was twenty-two years old in my Navy khakis and with my black leather bag, asking these guys to cash my check. It took about three hours, and we had to drink a lot of tea, but we got it done.

Haze Gray

The ship put into Naples, Italy. We planned to sail to Tunisia next, and the captain wanted the ship painted so we'd look sharp. I headed over to the Navy Supply Center in Naples to arrange for some haze gray paint and discovered they didn't have any because someone stole it all. I had to buy most of the food and supplies in port so I asked around about anyone that might know who stole the paint. One of the vendors told me he had an idea and would have that person contact me. A man came to see me that had a lot of haze gray paint. Not only that, he agreed to have his crew paint the ship as well. I couldn't give him cash, but he accepted a large quantity of hawser (big rope), brass damage control fittings, and a wrist watch out of the ship's store. We got the ship painted. When we lifted anchor for Tunisia, the captain asked me how it got done. I told him it was best not to ask about everything and that he should hope that we didn't have a big fire on board any time soon, because our damage control supplies needed replenishment.

Planter's Cocktail Peanuts

The commanding officer of the *Vogelgesang*, Commander George W. Mau, had an affinity for Planter's cocktail peanuts. He bought them from my ship's store. Unfortunately for me and for the store operator, Ships Serviceman Third Class Benjamin (of Benji's Balloons fame), we ran out of them out at sea in the middle of the Mediterranean. I figured that peanuts were peanuts. We carried at least six different kinds of peanuts, so three of us brought samples of each of them up to the captain's sea cabin so he could tell us which one he would like. He told us, in no uncertain terms, that he wanted cocktail peanuts and nothing else. We began plan B. We could not get replenished at sea for several weeks but there was a chance that we would come across another Navy ship.

Sure enough, the next day we came along side another ship for underway replenishment. The weapons department (we called them deck apes) had to transport something from ship to ship so they flung the monkey's fist (a lead ball covered in rope) to the other ship and set up a line between the two moving ships. I went up to the signal bridge and asked the signalmen to send a semaphore message to the other supply officer about Planter's peanuts. Outgoing message traffic was supposed to be released by the commanding officer, but the signalmen accommodated me on this one. Besides, the captain was pretty busy keeping *Vogie* from running into the other ship. Their supply officer had the peanuts, but needed a box of nickel cigars for his commanding officer. We had them, so shortly there was a little canvas bag coming across on the line with peanuts. The cigars made the return trip. I'm sure the commanding officers knew what we were doing, but no one ever said anything about it. It's why they called supply officers dog robbers.

Underway Replenishment

Out at sea, on deployment, we were replenished by helicopter from a supply ship. It was an all-hands event. We lined the crew up on the starboard side of the ship and as the stores were dropped on the fantail in a big net, crew members advanced to the stern of the ship, grabbed a box and headed forward to stow them down below. Canned hams were popular. With a loaf of bread from the night baker, they made great sandwiches. I knew that a few of them would disappear during underway replenishment, so I would just send my chief storekeeper to talk to the engineers and arrange for them to get three or four hams if they would make sure it didn't turn into more than that. As a young (twenty-three years old) Lt. (jg.), I mistakenly thought I had to be in the middle of the underway replenishment. I hung out on the fantail, right in the middle of the helicopter and two hundred men. On a trip up the port side I caught a wave chest high that nearly swept me overboard. After that I took my chief storekeeper's advice and spent my time on the bridge drinking coffee with the captain.

Coffee with the Admiral

Sometimes we practiced shooting. The ship had two gun mounts. One forward and one aft. The guns were called 5″ 38's. The shell was five inches in diameter and looked like a great, big piece of ammunition like you'd put in a rifle. My job when we shot guns was to act as a "checksight observer." I had to sit in the forward gun mount and look through a telescope at what we were shooting. If I saw that we were shooting the wrong thing, I was supposed to shout "Cease Fire" into my microphone. On one occasion, we were shooting at a sled being towed by another ship, a ship that happened to be the admiral's flagship. When the weapons people on the *Vogelgesang* put the guns on automatic, the guns started to track on the cable pulling the sled, instead of the sled itself. Target sighting started moving up the cable toward the ship and soon proceeded to drop shrapnel on the fantail of the admiral's flagship. When I noticed what was happening, I started shouting "Cease Fire" into my microphone. It took the gunners mates a moment or two to shut down the guns, but it wasn't soon enough to keep us from peppering the admiral's ship. The next day our captain was invited to have coffee with the admiral. I don't think the coffee was very good.

Cash on the Line

Since I had to pay the crew every two weeks, in cash, I had to keep a fair amount of money in my safe on the ship. And, I had to count it and verify that it was all there every week. On one of our trips to Guantanamo Bay, Cuba, I decided to count the cash one evening. I locked the office door, dragged all the cash out on the desk and proceeded to count it. We were in rough seas and the ship was rocking. I had two port holes in the office, one located next to where I was counting the money. As the ship rocked, a wave hit the port side of the ship, and the water poured in the port hole. The water hit the deck where I had set the cash and soaked some of it. I gathered up the money but had to figure out a way to dry it out. I ended up stringing something like clotheslines across the office and hanging the bills to dry. I didn't get any sleep that night because I couldn't walk away from the cash. The next morning I put the cash back in the safe. It was pretty dry, but for the next few paydays some of the crew got some damp cash.

Clear the Mess Decks

Payday out at sea took place on the mess decks (the cafeteria). The procedure was normally pretty routine. My disbursing clerk, Second Class Petty Officer Chuck Pace, and I brought a leather bag full of money, a big flashlight called a battle lantern, and my .45 pistol to the mess decks. The crew lined up to get paid. On one occasion, soon after we got set up and had paid some of the crew, we heard the engines slow down and stop. We had lost the load, and the lights went out. The mess decks were below the main deck and got really dark; I took my .45 out of the holster, racked the slide to chamber a round, and shouted, "Master-At-Arms, clear the mess decks." The crew must have known what a lousy shot I was. They all vacated the mess decks, with exemplary military dispatch, and didn't come back until the lights came back on.

Laundry "Chits"

Vogie had a ship's laundry, for which the supply division was responsible. We washed uniforms for all personnel and ironed uniforms for the officers, chiefs, and first class petty officers. The only requirement was that each crew member fill out a little form called a laundry "chit." One of the officers, Lt. (jg.) Steve Harrison, refused to fill out his laundry "chit." The ships servicemen who ran the laundry were always having to run him down to make sure they had the right number of uniform items. I even talked to him on a couple of occasions. It didn't seem to help. He continued just to toss his bag of laundry through the door of the laundry without a "chit."

Lt. (jg.) Harrison got transferred. Just before he left, he dropped off all his khaki uniforms at the laundry. No "chit." The man running the laundry that day asked me what he should do. We were out at sea steaming around in the Atlantic. I told him to throw the bag over the side. He asked me to say it again, and I did. Over the side the bag of uniforms went. About a week went by, and Steve inquired about his khakis. I asked him what khakis he was talking about. He told me he dropped them off at the laundry. I asked him where his laundry "chit" was. He told me he didn't fill one out. Never did. Never will. Not his job. I told him "Then I guess we don't have your khakis." It was a good lesson for everyone about not screwing with the supply officer.

Oil on the Water

In the summer of 1970 we were steaming in the Mediterranean, somewhere off the coast of the French Riviera. Our commanding officer, Commander Ron Campbell, had been relieved by Commander George Mau, and we were having the "change of command" at sea. Everyone was dressed in their whites and lined up on the fantail to listen to the two commanders read their orders. My roommate, Lt. (jg.) Ned Young, was standing next to me. We were both at parade rest and enjoying a sunny day at sea. Ned was one of the junior officers in the engineering department. I looked over my left shoulder at the water and noticed something black pouring out a discharge pipe on the starboard side of the ship. I elbowed Ned and gestured to the black stuff with my chin. Ned looked that way and said, "#@%." He ran for an open hatch and disappeared below decks, and the black fluid stopped shortly thereafter. A few minutes later Ned was back in formation standing next to me and muttered something about an open valve that wasn't supposed to be open. I don't think anyone noticed, and fortunately we didn't make headlines for polluting the French Riviera beaches.

In Norfolk, Virginia, we often went to sea on Monday and came back to port on Friday. On one of those trips, we sailed with the aircraft carrier *John F. Kennedy* (CVA-67). The exercise was supposed to include refueling *Vogelgesang* while the carrier launched aircraft. We came alongside *Kennedy* and sent lines across so they could send us fuel lines. They got everything hooked up and started to pump fuel into *Vogelgesang*'s tanks. *Kennedy* continued launching aircraft but didn't have as much wind as they wanted. I don't know much about launching airplanes off a carrier, but I think the pilots like to have as much wind in the face as possible. When the *Kennedy* officer of the deck realized that they didn't have as much wind as they wanted, he started to come to port to get more wind. The trouble was, he forgot to tell us. As *Kennedy* started turning to port, we saw what was happening and followed them to port. Then they realized that they hadn't told us about their maneuver and began to come back to starboard. Now you had two ships bearing down on each other with fuel lines hooked up in between them. To avoid a collision, *Vogelgesang* turned sharply to starboard just as *Kennedy* pulled away from us to port. These maneuvers resulted in pulling the fuel lines out of our tanks and blowing diesel fuel all over the Atlantic. The good news was that *Kennedy* didn't run over *Vogelgesang*, and *Vogelgesang* didn't hit *Kennedy*. But, we left a little fuel floating around in the ocean. It turns out that the officer of the deck on *Kennedy* was my neighbor downstairs in the apartment complex in Norfolk. Needless to say, he and I had some discussion about paying attention to what's going on while you're launching aircraft.

NATO

At one time *Vogie* sailed as part of a NATO task force. There was a Canadian ship, a British ship, and a few others. The Brits threw a party one afternoon on their ship and all the officers on *Vogelgesang* put on their dress whites and went to the party with our spouses. I recall chatting with one of the British naval officers and noticed all the ribbons on his uniform. I didn't recognize any of them and asked him what one of them was for. He told me he got that one "for dancing on the rooftops of Haifa." I didn't ask for any further explanation. It was good enough for me.

I left active duty in October, 1971. I joined up at twenty-one and left at twenty-four. Just a kid! If someone would have told me that when I graduated from Principia I would get a job supervising forty men, mostly older than me, a little rough around the edges, and be the expert on supply, logistics, and payroll, run a retail store, a laundry, and a barbershop, I would have thought you were nuts. I stayed in the reserves for twelve years. I got promoted to lieutenant, lieutenant commander, and commander. I was commanding officer of Advance Supply Base 213, officer in charge of a cargo handling detachment, and logistics officer for a construction regiment of 1000 engineers, sailors, and marines. I got rid of most of my uniforms when I left the reserves thirty years ago, but still have a set of blues hanging in the closet with my sword and hat with the "scrambled eggs" on the brim. I don't know what to do with them. I'll never wear them again. The gold on the sleeves is pretty "salty," but I can't throw them away. I have mostly fond memories of my Vietnam era service, and I would do it all over again if I had the chance.

DAVID POTTER was born in 1946 in LaGrange, Illinois, and lived in Gurnee, Illinois, when he was accepted as a student at Principia College in 1964. Majoring in political science, Potter also lettered in football and wrestling, and served on his house board of governance as a member of Rackham Court East. Potter also hosted a weekly radio show on WTPC, the campus radio station, playing such jazz artists as Thelonius Monk and the Dave Brubeck Quartet. In the days before electronic media, "I learned how to 'queue up' a record," Potter recalls. "That's when we broadcast through the water pipes in the houses…I estimated my listening audience at four people."

In 1968 Potter graduated and would later earn an MBA at the University of Montana. But in the meantime, the military beckoned, and Potter was off to the Navy's Officer Candidate School at Newport. His father was a retired reserve captain in the Navy Supply Corps, serving in World War II in a CB battalion [later "Seabees"] in the South Pacific. The senior Potter was part of the construction battalion that developed the major allied base of Nouméa [formerly Port-de-France] on the archipelago of New Caledonia and built an airstrip on the atoll at Funafuti (Tuvalu [formerly Ellice Islands]). The base at Nouméa was established with 50,000 American troops and served as the headquarters of the Army and Navy in the South Pacific housing the fleet that turned back the Japanese fleet in the Battle of Coral Seas (May 1942). As was the case with many authors of this collection, Potter followed his father's example in becoming a Navy Supply Officer. After graduating from the Navy Supply Corps School in Athens, Georgia, the junior Potter served as Supply Officer aboard the destroyer USS *Vogelgesang* (DD-862), home-ported in Norfolk, Virginia.

Vogelgesang operated as part of the Navy's Atlantic fleet and during the period of Potter's service engaged in naval exercises at Guantanamo (twice) and cruised to the Mediterranean. For this latter ship assignment, the crew was recognized for "meritorious service" in connection with the "Black September Coup," an involvement of the Navy's 6th fleet, positioned off the coast of Israel near Jordon during the Jordanian Civil War (September 1970-July 1971). The conflict pitted native Jordanians (Jordanian armed forces under King Hussein) against the Palestine Liberation Organization (PLO) headed by Yasser Arafat. During "black September" of 1970, President Nixon ordered an additional carrier task force and a Marine assault ship to the region to protect American interests and to respond to the capture by Palestinian forces of some fifty American (and German and British) citizens in Jordon. The conflict ended with the expulsion of the PLO leadership and Palestinian fighters to Lebanon. Potter was discharged about the same time, returning to civilian life and a career in banking, again following in the footsteps of his father, a banker by trade.

Married to Carol Maki for forty-nine years, David Potter has a son Thomas, daughter Bethany, and three grandchildren. He is now retired and lives in Riverton, Wyoming, where he serves on the board of the Wind River Development Fund, a native community development financial institution in Ft. Washakie, Wyoming.

Join the Navy and See the World: From Athens to Vietnam

ROBERT M. CRAIG

Athens

After Officer Candidate School, I quickly learned that a six months tour to the Supply Corps school in Athens, did not mean Greece. To be sure, Athens was in a foreign country, but the Athens of my next duty assignment was Athens, Georgia, and the foreign land: The South.

My grandfather always loved the word, copacetic, and he used to say life is not always copacetic. As a youngster, I had no idea what the word meant, but during those few months in Georgia in the late 1960s, he might well have said that my living in the South in 1968 was less than copacetic. Martin Luther King Jr. had been assassinated in April, while I was at the officer's candidate school in Newport, and it was only two months later that I and my fellow officers at the Navy school in Georgia found ourselves at 8:00 a.m. morning muster hearing the announcement of yet another assassination: this time, Robert Kennedy. What was the world coming to? More to the point, what might we in the military face, in terms of domestic duty assignments, in this atmosphere of racial conflict, irrespective of Vietnam? Lester Maddox was governor of Georgia, and although Alabama was enjoying a brief respite between the several gubernatorial terms of George Wallace (he had just left office in January 1967 but would return in 1971), to me, the South seemed to be a foreign country, with wacko state governors.

The South was full of characters which writers love to stereotype, because they are so true to *Suth-un'* life (or myth), ranging from members of the Daughters of the Confederacy to red necks, rural tenant farmers, and poor Uncle Remus blacks. Stereotypical Southerners included poor white trailer trash, old family patriarchs who wore white suits, local "hicks" who were about as couth as gum-chewing Rod Steiger in *In the Heat of the Night,* and aging, but surviving [and/or wilting], "southern belles." The latter were a cross between Scarlett O'Hara and Blanche DuBois, to say nothing of the supporting cast of small-town beauty-parlor socialites of the kind later depicted in *Steel Magnolias* or frustrated country and western singers named Savannah Sue or Dollie Lou who will sing some day at the Grand Ole Opry. Georgia, Alabama, and Mississippi, seemed the heart of this foreign land called the New Old South (somehow different from Virginia or even the Carolinas).

Since Atlanta-born Jeff Foxworthy was only nine years old when I first arrived in Georgia in 1968, red neck jokes were not yet funny, although it appeared to me, the state was full of candidates for such lampooning from top to bottom. In an almost symbolic choice of habitation, my roommate Ensign Ed Fox and I were residing in Athens in a rented trailer, a step we elected to take in order to save money, since living anywhere other than the BOQ [bachelor officers quarters] on the Supply Corps School campus qualified us for an additional housing allowance. With a musty upholstered sofa in the trailer's side yard and an old tire swinging from a magnolia tree, all Ed and I needed was a torn, sweat-stained, and sleeveless undershirt and a twenty-year-old car with its hood propped up and parked in the dirt yard atop well-established pools of oil drippings in order to qualify for a Foxworthy one-liner. Ensign Fox was reading a biography of Lester Maddox, and he roared with laughter every night: "This would be horrifying if it weren't so laughable," he'd say. We went to Atlanta to attend a performance of a play entitled "Red, White, and Maddox," a satire on Lester Maddox, who was high on the list of Georgia's state curiosities. Lester Garfield Maddox Sr. was the axe-handle-wielding proprietor of the Pickrick Restaurant in Atlanta who closed his eatery permanently rather than serve blacks, and who was subsequently elected governor of Georgia due to a consequential upsurge of his popularity among whites.

We became aware that the South had its own Vietnam era conflict. In June 1963, as I completed my freshman year at Principia College, a civil rights activist named Medgar Evers was shot in the carport of his Jackson, Mississippi, home, where he lived with his wife and three children. He was a World War II veteran of the Battle of Normandy, honorably discharged, and had been working in Mississippi toward the elimination of Jim Crow laws and to improve voting rights for African Americans. Earlier that day, President John Kennedy had been giving a speech in support of civil rights. Five months later Kennedy was assassinated; it was in November of my sophomore year at Principia College. In the meantime, the 16th Street Baptist Church in Birmingham had been bombed (September 1963), and the following June three young men working in Mississippi to increase African American voter registration, were murdered in Nashoba County, a year almost to the day following the assassination of Medgar Evers for his similar efforts The following month, in July 1964, President Lyndon B. Johnson signed the Civil Rights Act, followed by the Voting Rights Law in 1965. Race riots broke out in 1964 in Harlem, in 1965 in Watts (Los Angeles), and in 1966 and 1967 in Atlanta, San Francisco, Oakland, Baltimore, Newark, Detroit, and elsewhere across the country. A five-day march from Selma to the Alabama capitol in Montgomery took place in 1965 and nearly cost the life of John Lewis, now a U.S. congressman from Georgia. At the Edmund Pettus Bridge in Selma, just as the march had started, state troopers and local police, some mounted on horseback, attacked the peaceful demonstrators, using bull whips, billy clubs, rubber tubes wrapped in barbed wire, and tear gas. John Lewis was knocked unconscious and seriously injured.

These events were in the recent memory of anyone living in the South in 1968. They had all occurred during the four short years while I was an undergraduate student at Principia College. Now, in 1968, newly arrived in Georgia and an admittedly naive kid just out of school, I wanted to travel to a long list of Southern towns and across any rural Southern landscape to see interesting pieces of antebellum architecture. For me, the South was *Gone With The Wind,* not the Lorraine Motel in Memphis. But when I encouraged a fellow supply officer candidate (and native of Atlanta) to join me for one of my weekend architectural jaunts, indicating that the itinerary included Birmingham and Selma, Alabama, he said "Are you nuts?" Maybe New Orleans instead? That was enticing, but you had to drive through Mississippi to get there.

I must admit I had already lost my friend's confidence on a previous trip. The previous week, he and I had gone on a double date weekend to New York, which included, upon my recommendation, a tour of the Dutch Colonial Dyckman Farmhouse on Broadway at 204th Street, a local landmark. On the way to north Manhattan, we stopped at 125th Street to see an old theater, and when my Atlanta friend found himself at the Apollo, in the heart of Harlem, I thought he was going to turn apoplectic.

"Do you know where we are?" he suddenly exclaimed with eyes bulging.

"Of course," I said, beginning my history lesson. "Harlem was originally a Dutch village founded in 1658 and named for the city of Haarlem in the Netherlands…"

"No! more recently!" he said, turning pale, and frantically looking over his shoulders. "Harlem? Are you out of your $%^^&#% mind? You and I are lily white, and we're standing here in the heart of Harlem?

"I noticed that," I retorted, but this building is a musical landmark: Ella performed right over there," I explained. "You know: 'a-tisket, a-tasket, I lost my yellow basket…'"

"She may have lost her basket, but you've lost your marbles; let's get outta here!" And that was the end of our afternoon touring meccas of jazz and the Harlem Renaissance, or even pre-Revolutionary Dutch colonial sites.

But I *did* go to Birmingham and Selma and to New Orleans, Charleston, and Savannah, visiting historic houses, small southern towns, and places of architectural interest along the way. I simply liked old buildings. Weekends were truly "liberty." It was only during the week that supply corps duties consumed every moment as I wrote up countless exercises in double-entry accounting, became familiar with Navy requisition forms, and studied the Manual of Naval Procurement as though it were a military Bible, which more than one instructor said it was.

I had entered the Navy Supply Corps School thinking that with a master's degree already under my belt, how hard could this be? I found out from day one. It was very hard. The standard practice was that any officer who did not succeed in passing a Thursday weekly quiz on that week's material, would have to stay over for remedial work on Friday, rather than being allowed to leave for early weekend liberty. This was especially motivating for me, as my every weekend was booked with a scheduled road trip somewhere in the South to look at architecture, and the last thing I wanted to do was spend Friday at what we called "dummy school." Alas, one week I found myself early Friday morning marching across the supply school compound to dummy school with two other officers who had likewise failed the Thursday quiz.

"Out of curiosity," I asked them both, "What is your background?" And then I admitted to myself that maybe I should have been an undergraduate business major in order to survive this ordeal.

"Don't worry," one of my fellow dummy school enrollees remarked, "He's a graduate of the Wharton School at Penn, and I have a degree from the Harvard Business School. You're in good company."

We later discovered that J. Sterling Livingson, founder of the Sterling Institute, had taught supply officers during World War II, returned to Harvard for his PhD, and was a professor there for more than twenty years. Rumor was that Harvard had helped set the curriculum at the Navy Supply Corps School and that Livingston was the man in charge of writing the Manual of Naval Procurement. By the time I finished the Supply Corps program, I thought I deserved a Harvard degree.

My reward was something else. A few weeks before we were to graduate and to receive our post-school duty assignments, the Navy presented us a "duty request form" by which we could "select" our preferred duty assignment. The qualified promise to us was that we would likely get either a "ship type" or one of the "home ports" we selected. Of course, we had to fill in ten of each, so the odds were high the Navy could claim everyone's pick (one of the twenty) was honored. I looked over the form and saw two columns numbered one thru ten to suggest priority. Column A was ship type and column B was home port. Clever me, I had researched what ship types were home ported where, and so I started listing ship types that I knew nothing about except that they were home ported in exotic places. I acted like I was looking at cruise brochures. I listed Holy Loch, Scotland (never mind that it was the U.S. Polaris nuclear submarine base — it was Scotland!), or Rota, Spain (a base that supports Mediterranean Amphibious Readiness Group, whatever that was), or perhaps Naval Air Station duty on Malta or in Sigonella, Sicily, — yes, the Mediterranean *would* be nice. Recalling a miserable episode of sea sickness in my youth, I started with the largest ships I could think of: cruisers, battleships, or an aircraft carrier, and what the %#&^ was a submarine tender? In the end, I got choice #6 in both columns, the carrier USS *Intrepid* CVS-11, homeported in Norfolk, Virginia.

"Could be worse," I noted recognizing that Norfolk was as close to my summer home of Ocean City, Maryland, as any Navy base, and I concluded that a carrier on the Atlantic coast would be touring the Mediterranean for sure, not the Pacific and SE Asia. So I started envisioning my weekend liberties in Naples and Rome, side trips to Florence and Venice, sailing to the Greek Isles, and maybe some north African sites with ancient Roman ruins, and then there's Casablanca! Ah, Casablanca! That would be romantic: Bogart and Bergman. "Play it again, Sam." I was planning my architectural tours off *Intrepid* already.

We all compared duty assignments, and I learned that fellow supply officers were being sent all over the world. Unlike supply officers on smaller ships who were responsible for all of the supply divisions, I would join a supply team of five or six supply officers on an aircraft carrier, and there would be others, not me, responsible for requisitions of repair parts, for ordering provisions, and for management of food service operations. I was to be *Intrepid's* new disbursing officer, a popular fellow I presumed, as I would pay everyone. And, I told my roommate, "It looks like I won't be going to Vietnam."

But then, I was encouraged to read my orders more carefully, which I did, eager to know the date when I should report to Norfolk. I found myself asking "Hey, Lieutenant, Where is Yankee Station?"

"Oh, I forgot to mention, Ensign Craig: *Intrepid* is indeed home-ported in Norfolk, but that's not where it is now; your ship is on its third deployment to Vietnam. We'll fly you out there and land you aboard asap, because there is an officer aboard due to be released in a couple of weeks, and he's anxious for his replacement to arrive."

"But Norfolk is east coast, not west," I insisted, seeing the Mediterranean dissipate in the fog of my neutralized dream of weekends in Capri.

"Ah, yes, that's the rub. *Intrepid* is the only Atlantic fleet carrier serving in Vietnam."

"How did it get there?"

"The same way Magellan did."

And then another officer piped in, "Come on, Craig, you should be proud. *Intrepid* is an *Essex*-class carrier, commissioned in 1943 during World War II — a great ship with a fine record of service."

"Oh," I said.

"And the "Fighting I" has been reconfigured. When they added steam catapults and the angle flight deck, the 1943 carrier doubled its speed of launches, and *Intrepid* is currently a major player in Vietnam."

"Oh," I said, again.

Vietnam

My new duty assignment was the subject of water-cooler conversation back home in St. Louis, and I soon found myself the recipient of a request from a neighborhood Mom who had just learned that my path, and that of her Navy pilot son, would soon cross. My mother was chatting with Teenie Van Vleck when Mother informed her friend that "Robert has just been assigned for duty on *Intrepid*, and he'll be heading to the Tonkin Gulf off Vietnam next week."

"Oh, Peter's flying off *Intrepid*," Mrs. Van Vleck exclaimed with delight, "Robert can take him some of my chocolate chip cookies."

"Of course," my mother said, "He'd be happy to," acknowledging that this imminent meeting of the two sons on the other side of the globe was a serendipitous coincidence that any mother could not pass by, and so I dutifully accepted the tin of goodies for Lieutenant Peter Van Vleck.

Peter Van Vleck yearbook picture, *The Sheaf*, 1965.
Photo courtesy The Principia

"Peter normally flies off the carrier *Hornet*," she said, as though my mother was familiar with the entire fleet, and Peter's Mom was referencing some frequent flyer program.[25] But Peter's squadron had been temporarily reassigned to *Intrepid* while *Hornet* was undergoing repairs. "So isn't it grand that Peter will be on board to welcome Robert to Vietnam?"

---

25 Historically, of course, this was unlikely since United Airlines would not introduce such a concept for another four years.

So off I went to San Francisco, cookie tin under arm, to board a commandeered Pan Am plane and to island-hop across the Pacific. We had brief stops in Honolulu (I always wanted to see Hawaii, but thirty minutes in the airport was hardly worth mentioning), and another hour to refuel in Guam, until finally we landed in the middle of the night at Clark Air Force Base in the Philippines. From there, with a few other half-asleep sailors, we headed to various Navy ships, but were first bussed to Subic Bay [Cubi Point Naval Air Station], where a BOQ bunk bed awaited. *Intrepid* was at sea, so reporting aboard the ship itself would have to wait.

Naval Air Station, Cubi Point, Bataan, Philippines.
Photo by Robert M. Craig

My orders awaited me at Subic Bay: "Report to [a designated hangar] at 0600 (6:00 a.m.) tomorrow morning, and if there is room on the daily prop COD, we'll fly you out."

"What's the daily prop COD?" I asked.

"Carrier Onboard Delivery — it's a propeller-driven junk plane they use to deliver mail and any repair parts ordered by the ship's S-1 division from requisitions processed the day before, and if there's room, they stuff you in the tail section with the spare parts and delivery you as well."

So daily, at 0400, reveille sounded in the form of a civilian alarm clock, and I dragged myself to the air field to learn there were too many spare parts and not enough room for a passenger seat to be stowed in the tail, so: "report back again at 0600 tomorrow." It was not my custom to get out of bed at 4:00 a.m., but the Navy was forming new habits. This went on for days:

"COD overloaded, come back tomorrow morning."

"Isn't there an afternoon flight?" I ask rubbing sleep from my eyes.

"What the %^#% do you think this is, a vacation spa? 0600 tomorrow. Be here!"

Olongapo City, Philippines. Photo by Robert M. Craig

I spent the rest of the several days, in between abortive 6:00 a.m. visits to the hangar, checking out camera and stereo equipment at the Navy exchange on the base, following my dad's recommendation that Nikon cameras and Sony stereo equipment might be bought to good advantage "if I ever got to Japan," and this exchange in the Philippines seemed as close as I'd likely get. I bumped into another supply officer who had been on leave and was returning to duty, and, like me, he was also waiting for transportation to a ship in the Tonkin Gulf. We were both bored with the limited entertainment at Subic Bay, and he seemed anxious to share with me his wider knowledge and experience regarding local sites, namely the local bars and other pleasures of Olongapo City. Olongapo was a real sin city at the other end of the bridge just beyond the gate to the naval base. "I'll pass on the various 'indulgences,'" I told him, "but I'll go with you, just to see the town." My new friend was, according to local sailor patois, "feeling horny," so I thought it might appear prudish of me to suggest any interest in Olongapo City's vernacular architecture.

"You'll get propositioned at least ten times in as many minutes," he warned, and then repeated several times "wear your watch high on your arm to forestall pick-pocket artists who will strip you of your Bulova." It sounded more likely that sailors got stripped of their virginity, and a lost watch or two was only part of the price to pay for an evening in Olongapo City, but I slid my Omega up past my elbow, and off we went.

My buddy could not believe I didn't drink beer, so he drank enough for both of us, as we took in the various sights of abject poverty and sleeze. "You come here often, sailor boy?' was heard from petite and not unattractive, but hard driven, Filipino girls, whose main job at the bar was imbedded in the next question, "You buy me a drink? Maybe we have good time?" About the fifth such encounter, I started replying in French, out of self defense, but soon the whole ritual got tiresome, and when we returned to the base, my officer friend discovering he was sans Bulova.

Jitney on the road to Manila. Photo by Robert M. Craig

"Maybe tomorrow, if the prop COD is full of parts and equipment, and we get bumped again, we should hire a jitney and driver and go to Manila."

"Now you're talking," I said, and we found two other junior officers interested in the trip, and a driver. We encountered some unexpected historic sites along the way. We noticed several roadside markers that indicated our route was crossing that of the famous Bataan death march, during which in April of 1942, Japanese troops murdered countless Filipino and American prisoners of war during a forced march in Bataan province. "That could have been our fathers," we noted as markers landmarked the death march.

Road to Manila, Philippines. Photo by Robert M. Craig

We spent the afternoon and evening in Manila, and were back on base in time to drag ourselves, one last time, to the 0600 hangar muster and finally board the prop plane. It seemed almost Biblical that "on the seventh day," the parts order was adequately small to cram two passenger seats in amongst cogs, airplane parts, equipment repair paraphernalia, and miscellaneous metal bits and pieces. My fellow passenger for the flight to *Intrepid* was an enlisted mail clerk whose gathered sacks of mail picked up on shore gave him priority seating. He seemed barely out of high school but took great glee in serving as the experienced traveler to Yankee Station, eager to give me "all the information I would need about a COD flight." He explained what was important for me to know, not "if" we ditched, but "when" we ditched. His confidence level in the COD, which he called an aeronautical bucket of nails, was nil. It seemed to me that the flying contraption did shake an inordinate amount, and with only one tiny side port hole disclosing only a cloudy blue haze, we could only sense that we were in the air, but exactly where remained an unknown.

"How will we know when we get there?" I yelled above the loud clatter of shaking metal and whirling props. I thought the question sounded like a toddler asking his parents the same question during some family vacation trip.

"You'll know you're there when the rubber band catches you," the postal clerk said with a smirk.

"What do you mean when the rubber band catches you?"

"Well, we'll be traveling at about 80 knots and then, three seconds later, we'll be dead stopped on the flight deck. The hook——it must be attached to the outside bottom of the plane just below your chair there somewhere—the hook on the plane will be grabbed by the cable on the carrier deck, and we'll be stopped faster than if you'd hit a brick wall at a drag race." And then he stroked his chin, adding, "Well, on one condition, that is…"

"What's that?

"If the pilot comes in too high, he'll get waived off and try again."

"And if he comes in too low?

"Cur-r-r-r-tains!" he said with a teasing melodic lilt.

"Oh, swell"

About this time, I could feel the plane banking and the tiny window revealed the horizon, where a light blue sky met the darker blue water. The postal clerk stretched toward me to peer through the window.

"There she is," he said.

"Where?"

"There"

"No, you don't mean that match box! We can't land on that!"

"Sure, piece of cake. It'll get bigger as we get closer," and then the ship disappeared behind the edge of the porthole, and we saw nothing but blue again.

Before long, we sensed a few coughs of the engine, as the pilot slowed the plane for landing, and a couple of sudden drops to correct our approach, and then "WHAM, the wheels hit the deck, the cable engaged, our chests slammed against the restraining seat belts criss-crossed against our upper bodies, and the plane was still.

Navy band. "Welcome to Vietnam."
Photo from *Intrepid 1968 Cruisebook*

"Whoa" I said, and my "cabin mate" let out a whoop that reminded me of some rodeo cowboy just after the gate has released him and his bronco started bucking.

"Welcome to Vietnam" the postal clerk said.

As the prop taxied to one side of the carrier's flight deck, the under belly of the tail of the plane started lowering, our feet descending with it, and I looked out into bright daylight to see Lieutenant Peter Van Vleck, standing in front of a small Navy band, the latter playing military music; I was too distracted to determine which Sousa march. Peter's hand was extended—I thought with the purpose of shaking my hand in welcome.

"You got my cookies?" he said, and then grinned, knowing that was not a proper greeting. He outranked me, and I don't remember if I even saluted him, but he said quickly, "Just kidding, Ensign Craig. Welcome aboard. What do you think of the welcoming committee I arranged for you?" Pete said, looking over his shoulders at the oom pah pah tuba, and the other gleaming brass instruments, played by energetic sailors.

"Do you arrange that reception for everyone reporting aboard?" I asked him.

"Nope, just for Principians" he joked. "How'd ya like your first carrier landing?"

"I don't know, my head is somewhere off the port bow; I don't think it stopped with the rest of me."

"Well, there's no snow here, but Merry Christmas," Peter said, reminding me that the date was Dec 24th. You'd best report to the supply officer and check in."

So off Peter went, returning to his squadron, and as the band played on, I headed off to find my new boss. Commander Q. B. Morrison greeted me cordially and said, "Lt. (jg.) Rost, the current disbursing officer, is moving to S-2 division, so that Grude, the S-2 supply officer can be discharged and go home. Craig, you'll be in charge of S-4 (disbursing), and that needs to happen tomorrow, if possible, so if you want to count the money you're about to sign for, Lieutenant Parrott can show you the safe; you'd best start counting right away."

It did seem prudent, because as of tomorrow I would be responsible for whatever money was on board, and I'd better know that it was all there to the last dime. Talk about balancing your checkbook! Whenever I, in turn, would leave the S-4 division, a closing

net balance would be checked; my disbursements and receipts, calculated against this starting balance, would create a closing balance,
an amount I would then sign over to someone else, so the balances
and the arithmetic had better come out right, both now and then. I
guessed (without any basis) that the safe probably held a couple of
grand, but that was no chump change.

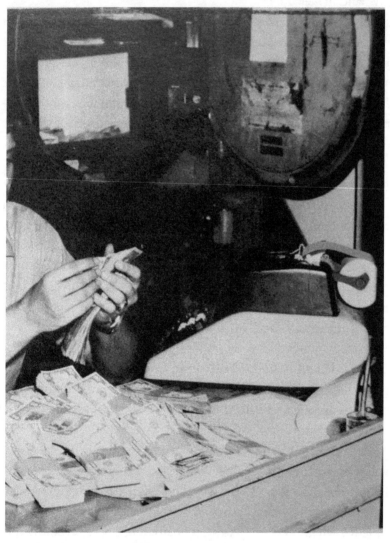

Disbursing Officer duty: verifying the cash on hand.
Photo from *Intrepid 1968 Cruisebook*

"That shouldn't take long," I responded.

"Ah, yes it will," my new boss warned. "There's a million three in the safe, plus you'll have to check all the postal stamps on board. Oh, did I mention: as disbursing officer you'll also be responsible for the ship's post office? By the way, Ensign Craig, if you finish counting by tomorrow, you might hang around the enlisted mess and hanger deck; we've got a special guest coming aboard for Christmas dinner."

Just what I need! I thought to myself, Santa Claus is coming to Yankee Station off Vietnam. I dismissed such a possible visit from the North Pole as less important to me than making sure that "the million three" was present and accounted for, so I started confirming Lt. (jg.) Rost's totals by counting endless bound stacks of dollar bills, and fives, tens, twenties etc. I was still counting throughout most of Christmas Day, and I missed the special event. I wondered if Commander Morrison was the one who would be dressed up as Santa Claus.

Forty years later, my dad gave me a copy of Bill White and Robert Gandt's history of *Intrepid*,[26] with a foreword, by the way, written by Senator John McCain. I found an interesting coincidence that soon after McCain had finished flight school (about eight years before I reported aboard) his A-1 Skyraider Squadron had been assigned to *Intrepid*. In 1967, the year before I arrived aboard *Intrepid*, McCain's plane (flying off another carrier) had been shot down, and he was captured and imprisoned. That Christmas eve, 1968,[27] while I was playing Scrooge counting bagfuls of money, McCain was in a POW camp. On Christmas Day itself, McCain's captors at the "Hanoi Hilton" POW camp, organized a propaganda event intended to deceive the West by staging a church service for the POWs, and filming POWs in an effort to demonstrate they were being treated well. POWs were instructed to

---

26 Bill White and Robert Gandt, *Intrepid: The Epic Story of America's Most Legendary Warship* (New York: Random House (Broadway Books, 2008).

27 Interestingly (and also unknown to me at the time), the promise of Principia dad Alan Shepherd's historic first American space flight was being extended at that same moment by Apollo 8 [Bill Anders, Frank Borman, and James Lovell] that first orbited the moon on Christmas Eve, 1968, just six years and three months after President Kennedy's 1962 challenge to reach the moon before the end of the 1960s.

be quiet throughout the filming. The future Arizona Senator McCain, however, wounded and in pain from mistreatment and torture, defied his captors and shouted, "F-%^# you, you sonofabitch!" and McCain began to communicate on camera the ill treatment he was receiving.

Admiral John S. McCain Jr. and Captain V. F. Kelly aboard
Intrepid, Christmas, 1968. Photo from *Intrepid 1968 Cruisebook*

The POW's father was Commander, United States Pacific Command, and *Intrepid* (along with all other U.S. Navy ships in the Pacific fleet) was under McCain's command. For propaganda reasons, when the North Vietnamese learned who their prisoner's father was, they offered the younger John McCain an early release from prison, preferential treatment due to his father's prominence. But McCain refused any out-of-sequence release from prison camp, insisting POWs be released in order of their capture and that all the POWs be released, or he would not be; McCain remained a POW for five and a half years, until March, 1973.

What neither John McCain nor I knew at the time was that McCain's father, Admiral John S. McCain Jr. was spending Christmas 1968 on *Intrepid* while his son's defiance was being filmed by the Vietnamese who had hoped to soft pedal the physical condition of the POWs. In his introduction to White and Gandt's history of *Intrepid*, the senator did not describe the display of defiance that the television public saw on film at the time, but McCain did mention that his father was aboard *Intrepid* that Christmas Day. So when Commander Morrison, my boss, spoke to me of a special guest for Christmas dinner, it was not Santa Claus but Admiral John McCain, the future Senator McCain's father, who was sharing Christmas dinner on the third deck with the enlisted sailors now serving on his son's former ship. In 1968, the name McCain would have meant nothing to me. Fragments of this story, including the younger McCain's POW experience, got pieced together later.

But forty years later, as I read McCain's book foreword, it dawned on me that the welcoming patriotic music of Peter Van Vleck's military band on the flight deck, was not for me at all. "Well, I'll be!" I muttered aloud. "Peter Van Vleck, you so-in-so! *That's* what that Navy band was for, when I arrived in Vietnam COD. The band wasn't welcoming me; they were rehearsing for Admiral John McCain!"

Lieutenant Van Vleck never told me, and when I saw him at our 50th high school reunion in St. Louis nearly half a century later, I told him I had finally figured it out. Peter just smiled, and thanked me again for the cookies.

Lattitude 00° 0' Longitude 140° 42': Crossing the Equator

My sojourn to the waters off Vietnam was short lived, because in December 1968, the ship was preparing to end its third deployment and head home to Norfolk. A recreational stop was planned for Sydney, Australia, where I traded extra duty at sea for a second day of liberty in Sydney. I wanted to bodysurf at Bondi Beach, and visit the already famous Sydney Opera House, then under construction. I toured parks and a few other sites, including the famed Sydney zoo, while 90% of my shipmates went to local bars. Bondi Beach interested me because it was then noted for its lifeguard competitions, and due to my dad's summer career as Captain of the Ocean City Beach Patrol, and my five years lifeguarding at the Maryland ocean beach, I thought Bondi might offer some great waves for bodysurfing. It didn't. But what *was* memorable was my initial arrival into Sydney harbor by ship, seeing from that vantage point the "sailboat sails" of the Opera House, and the harbor's sublime Art Deco suspension bridge.

Sailing past *Intrepid* in Sydney Harbor, 1969.
Photo by Robert M. Craig

On our return from 'Nam, we would stop another day at Wellington, New Zealand, and then, because the ship's angle flight deck meant that *Intrepid* could no longer fit through the Panama Canal (it could just squeeze through in its 1943 configuration), the ship headed all the way around Cape Horn. I was nearly blown off the flight deck by a gust of wind while watching an underway replenishment [refueling] off Chili. There are, thankfully, nets to catch any such foolish personnel in flight so I wouldn't have blown far, but it did give me a fright. I thought it much fun that we were following part of Magellan's 1519-22 route (when his ship circumnavigated the globe, although Magellan sailed east to west). *Intrepid* rounded Cape Horn through the straits named for Magellan, and headed north up the east coast of South America. We stopped again for two days liberty in Rio before reaching, finally, the ship's home port of Norfolk, Virginia.

Sailors on liberty in Rio. Photo by Robert M. Craig

When we first left Vietnam waters, I thought this anticipated itinerary to be splendid news: two days liberty, each, in Sydney, Wellington, and Rio. But then someone mentioned crossing the equator before we even got to Sydney.

"So we're crossing the equator! So what?" I said.

"Don't you know about the Navy tradition regarding crossing the equator?" I was asked.

I gave a shrug to indicate I didn't know what the guy was talking about.

"Ah, well you better prepare yourself, 'cause you're a pollywog."

"I'm a what?"

Crossing the equator: shellbacks awaiting polliwogs.
Photo from *Intrepid 1968 Cruisebook*

"A pollywog—a sailor who has never cross the equator on a Navy ship. Get ready 'cause all the shellbacks on board will give 'ya hell in a hazing ceremony that makes fraternity initiations seem like a ladies tea party. Oh, and by the way, Craig, since you just reported aboard last month," my friend continued, "and because most of the crew has already been on three separate deployments to 'Nam, which means that most of the ship's crew has crossed the equator many times, I'd estimate that you pollywogs are outnumbered about 3000 to 50 at best. I sure wouldn't want to be a pollywog on *this* trip home!"

"It can't be that bad," I assured him with a naivety for which I was becoming renown.

On the day in question, my friend suggested that under my trousers I wrap my knees in heavy socks, but "Don't let any shellback know you've done so, whatever you do." I soon found out why.

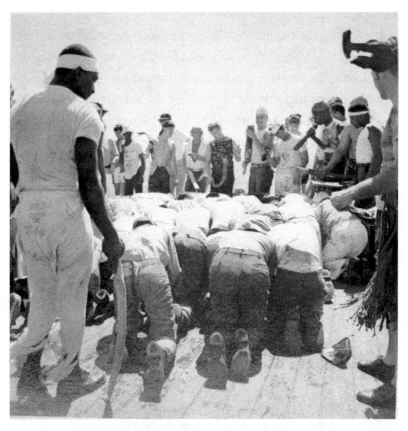

Crossing the equator: gauntlet.
Photo from *Intrepid 1968 Cruisebook*

On the morning of the designated crossing day, pollywogs were gathered like cattle on the hangar deck level, required to make their way on hands and knees to the forward elevator [a huge platform that lifts jets and equipment to the flight deck], passing through a gauntlet of whooping shellbacks armed with three foot lengths of canvas fire hoses which they swung heartily to "spank" the pollywogs as they tried to crawl, with some dispatch, down the long line. The surface of the hangar deck was rough, but nothing like the tight jagged surface that awaited on the flight deck. The flight deck had a heavily textured coating intended to provide traction for acceleration of planes during take off, as well as surface friction for slowing planes upon landing. For pollywogs, it was like crawling on broken glass, and while I suspected everyone knew pollywogs had been warned about wrapping their knees, the message was always accompanied by the suggestion that if you got caught doing so, there would be hell to pay. I took the chance, and it helped a little, although I suspected my sore behind and back made it difficult to feel pain on my knees. The flight deck surface was so hot, I found myself pulling my shirt sleeves down over my hands, and wishing uniform shirts were made of asbestos.

Crossing the equator: flight deck welcoming committee. Photo from *Intrepid 1968 Cruisebook*

Temperature-wise, as the forward elevator leveled itself to the topmost level under the equatorial sun, and we crawled out onto the flight deck, we had symbolically crossed the River Styx into Hades.

Our eyes squinted in reaction to the harsh sunlight of high noon at zero latitude, and you could taste the thick heat. The flight deck had been converted to a festival of Davey Jones imagery, pirate paraphenalia, skull and cross bones, swarthy sailors in make-shift costumes, and various secular "stations of the cross" that each pollywog must visit. One sailor, the fattest on board, sat enthroned with his fat belly covered with axle grease, and pollywogs were required to pay homage by having their faces smudged into the slimy, sweaty stomach, and rubbed around a bit. Pine coffins were lined to one side of the flight deck, and any infraction (such as perspiring) was cause enough for a pollywog to serve time in the coffin. The coffins were filled with carefully selected samples of the ship's garbage, and I found myself laid out, face down, head resting on a half grapefruit for a pillow, while the coffin lid was renailed in place. It was dark, odiferous to say the least, and warm to the point of becoming stifling. We were on the equator after all.

Crossing the equator: belly rub.
Photo from *Intrepid 1968 Cruisebook*

"Are you ready to meet Davey Jones?" a shellback yelled, and assuming this did not mean burial at sea, I answered, "whatever's next on the program."

"Ah, a smart aleck? Five more minutes in the coffin."

Crossing the equator: coffin filled with garbage.
Photo from *Intrepid 1968 Cruisebook*

Eventually the lid came off the coffin, and I was released for more fun and games. What seemed to be an endless period of creative harassment included an obligatory drinking of pollywog blood which turned out to be pomegranate juice à la tobasco sauce, followed by a ceremonial blind folding after which I was given pollywog eyeballs to bite and then swallow (grapes), and finally a visit to one old salt who was referred to as the ship's dentist, leaving you to wonder quite what he intended to do with his instruments of torture. In the end, all pollywogs were told they would receive their shellback certificates at the end of the day.

Visitation hours at sick bay were declared to be open all afternoon, because for each equator crossing there are always some shellbacks who get carried away; it was announced that we might well find a fellow pollywog with skinned knees and "medium rare" flanks recovering under the care of Blackbeard's personal physician. As well, let it also be known, the ship's PA system also announced, that the mess hall was open for a special "crossing the equator" meal, and that sounded like good news.

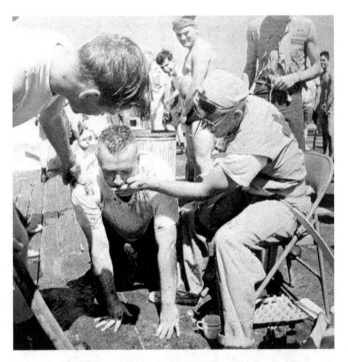

Crossing the equator: ship's dentist scourging mouth.
Photo from *Intrepid 1968 Cruisebook*

When I arrived at the mess deck, however, I found a pollywog menu quite different from the soup, salad bar, rib steak, franconia potatoes, mushroom gravy, corn, and chocolate layer cake that the shellbacks were being offered. To be clear, the day's menu was printed in two columns. Having not yet received our certificates, we pollywogs

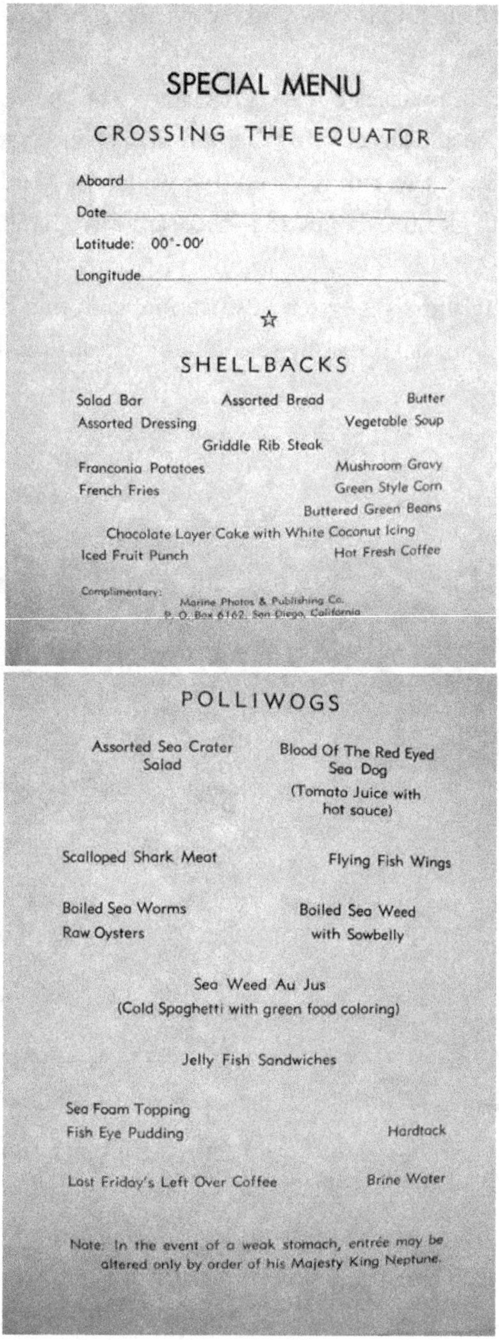

SPECIAL MENU
CROSSING THE EQUATOR

Aboard_____

Date_____

Latitude: 00°-00'

Longitude_____

☆

SHELLBACKS

Salad Bar	Assorted Bread	Butter
Assorted Dressing		Vegetable Soup
	Griddle Rib Steak	
Franconia Potatoes		Mushroom Gravy
French Fries		Green Style Corn
		Buttered Green Beans
	Chocolate Layer Cake with White Coconut Icing	
Iced Fruit Punch		Hot Fresh Coffee

Complimentary: Marine Photos & Publishing Co.
P. O. Box 6162, San Diego, California

POLLIWOGS

Assorted Sea Crater
Salad

Blood Of The Red Eyed
Sea Dog
(Tomato Juice with
hot sauce)

Scalloped Shark Meat

Flying Fish Wings

Boiled Sea Worms
Raw Oysters

Boiled Sea Weed
with Sowbelly

Sea Weed Au Jus
(Cold Spaghetti with green food coloring)

Jelly Fish Sandwiches

Sea Foam Topping
Fish Eye Pudding

Hardtack

Last Friday's Left Over Coffee

Brine Water

Note: In the event of a weak stomach, entrée may be
altered only by order of his Majesty King Neptune.

Crossing the equator: menus Shellbacks vs Pollywogs.
Photos from *Intrepid 1968 Cruisebook*

must select from the right hand column: "assorted sea crater salad, blood of the red-eyed sea dog (tomato juice with hot sauce), scalloped shark meat, flying fish wings, boiled sea worms, boiled seaweed with sowbelly, raw oysters, seaweed *au jus* (cold spaghetti with green food coloring), jelly fish sandwiches, sea foam topping, fish eye pudding,

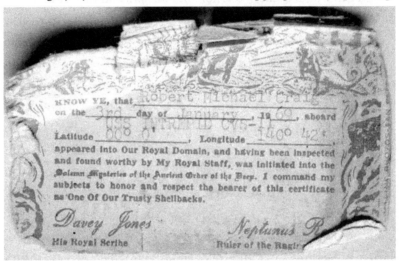

The certificate a Navy man never loses.
Photo by Robert M. Craig

hardtack, last Friday's left over coffee, and brine water." The menu's disclaimer read, "In the event of a weak stomach, entreé may be altered only by order of his Majesty King Neptune." His Majesty was a particularly unseemly character we had already met on the flight deck. So it is no surprise that fifty years later, I still have (and keep guarded) my shellback certificate, as do all Navy men who carry proof they've already crossed the equator and are disinclined to repeat their "crossing the equator" pollywog-to-shellback initiation. In the event we find ourselves on another cruise crossing zero degrees latitude, we want it known that we are now trusty shellbacks.

Running Aground

When the ship finally returned to Norfolk, the crew learned, to its distinct displeasure, that rather than dock at Norfolk where families were waiting to see returning sailors, the ship's new captain announced that *Intrepid* would anchor off shore with very limited or no liberty. This infuriated the crew, because the crew had not been home for over six months. Rumor was that the captain thought the entire crew would get drunk, if allowed ashore in Norfolk, and he would not be able to get underway on time to an awaiting Philadelphia dry dock.

In any case, *Intrepid* continued its cruise north to Philadelphia where it spent the next six months undergoing repairs and rehabilitation in dry dock at the Navy Yard of the City of Brotherly Love. Before this work was completed, scuttlebutt spread through the ship that the home port had been changed from Norfolk to Quonset Point, Rhode Island, and that the perceived political pull of our post-Vietnam new captain, Horace Moore, was likely to blame. In September 1969 *Intrepid* headed north to its new home port, entering Narragansett Bay on September 8th. The ship's arrival was on a dull day with low clouds trying hard to form a dense fog, and, as is customary, a pilot boat met the ship. A maritime pilot familiar with the bay came aboard to confer with the captain and guide the ship in, although the captain, of course, remained responsible for his ship. Before the fog set in at its most dense, it appeared that every sailboat, fishing boat, and private nautical vessel in Newport had filled the bay with onlookers gathered to welcome the carrier to its new home port. A fire boat sprayed jets of water skyward, and *Intrepid*'s flight deck was lined with sailors in white uniforms manning the rail; the whole waterfront was in full regalia. Then the fog set in like pea soup.

One of my disbursing clerks had a friend in the ship's OA division (operations department) working in CIC (combat information center, or ship's operations room); his team was below decks, manning radar and sonar, and radioing soundings and suggested instructions to the captain on the bridge. Repeatedly, as the ship approached the edge of Jamestown Island, it appeared that the bridge was ignoring the information being communicated from the radar room. When the last coordinates were conveyed to the bridge, the radar operator said, "If they ignore this one, we're running aground," and soon thereafter, following an extended sensation that the ship's hull was scraping crunchy sand, braking slowly, and finally coming to a complete halt, *Intrepid* was "dead in the water."

Two black balls, *Intrepid* aground.
Photo by Robert M. Craig

Local newspapers reported that observers on nearby pleasure craft heard distinct expressions of amusement from the sailors manning the rail. Within minutes a signal was heard piercing through the fog: one long and two short blasts, signifying "I am not under command"

and the bridge displayed two black balls hung vertically, barely visible in the fog, to declare the ship was stuck in muddy sand. Having dragged up huge amounts of fine aggregate, sand, and grit into its Westinghouse geared steam turbine engines, the ship was not going anywhere. Navy tugs, helped by a high tide two hours later, got the ship off the sand and pulled and pushed her to the dock, where the chief engineer spent countless hours and days up to his elbow in grease and oil, cleaning and repairing the engines. As a supply officer, periodically on duty as officer of the day during the following days, I had to handle the chief engineer's requests for hundreds of O-rings, gaskets, rods, and the like which had to be found and then requisitioned from shipyards from Charleston to Boston, wherever I could find them. Those extra Friday classes at "dummy school" in Athens paid off. Eventually the engines were repaired, and *Intrepid* was operational again. *Intrepid* retained Quonset Point Naval Air Station as its home port until the ship was decommissioned in 1974, and the base itself was deactivated the same year. But the reputation of the grounding of *Intrepid* continued for years as local bars in Newport served drinks called "*Intrepid* on the rocks." I would guess that the whole affair was very likely career-changing for the captain, as well.

Flight deck nap, *Intrepid* returning from Vietnam, 1969.
Photo by Robert M. Craig

Cambodian captives, released June 1970: Richard
Dudman(l), Elizabeth Pond (ctr), Michael Morrow
(rt). Photo courtesy United Press International.

PART IV:
In Country Cambodia

Out from Cambodian Captivity: "Don't Shoot, We are International Journalists"

ELIZABETH POND

Series by Elizabeth Pond. Reprinted with permission from the June 22-26, 1970 issues of *The Christian Science Monitor*. ©1970 The Christian Science Monitor)

Dateline Saigon, June 22, 1970

PART I

Probably the basic fact to report is that the three of us never quite accepted the premise of an adversary relationship, even at the moments when we were most frightened. It seemed to me and to my companions — Richard Dudman of the *St. Louis Post-Dispatch* and Michael Morrow of Dispatch News Service International — that the most practical hypothesis to base our responses on was that we would be treated civilly by whoever had arrested us, as journalists seeking insights rather than as enemies either to be destroyed or to be converted.

Mike is a young idealist who has refused induction into the American Army to fight in Vietnam. His wife of a few months is Vietnamese and Mike speaks considerable Vietnamese and understands well the Asian forms of politeness. Dick is a newspaper professional through and through, one long identified personally and editorially in his newspaper with an antiwar position. I am a woman whose reporting in Vietnam has tended to be dispassionate rather than committed to a point of view. Personally, I had been deeply dismayed by the American decision to send troops into Cambodia.

When the two men with rifles, one Vietnamese, one Cambodian, stepped from behind a tree and motioned our automobile to stop, we stopped.[28] As we got out of the car, Mike said in Vietnamese, "Don't shoot. We are international journalists, not military people. We are Canadians, not Americans." (This was true in his case for his mother is Canadian.)

We were ordered to drop our things on the ground, to empty our pockets, and to walk westward on the road away from the Cambodian provincial capital of Soai Rieng. We complied, our hands in the air.

Mike initiated bits of conversation in Vietnamese to keep communications open between us.

Then the order came to run, apparently because of approaching planes. I soon lagged behind Mike and Dick despite the importunings of the soldiers. So when a bicycle overtook us on the road, I nodded toward it to ask if I might ride. The Cambodian on the back of the bicycle relinquished his seat to me until I caught up with the others.

Several kilometers from where we had stopped we were brought to rest under a tree. Mike and Dick were asked to remove clothing to reveal any possible hidden weapons. They had none, of course, and this search revealed only Dick's American passport which he had kept in his pocket up to that point. We were given tea to drink and asked if we knew how to ride bicycles. We then rode bicycles down a side road to a house where perhaps ten people were gathered. I was taken upstairs and searched unsympathetically by a woman. The several women at the house offered me no gentleness.

---

28 In a later article, "Sanctuary in Captivity," published by Elizabeth Pond in *The Christian Science Journal* (April 2011) Vol 129, no 4, pp 48-51, she wrote, "A mixed group of Viet Cong and Khmer Rouge stepped from behind trees, trained their rifles on us, and ordered us to get out of the van with our hands up. We were on the fringes of the "Parrot's Beak" area that was quickly becoming the arena of fierce fighting. At this stage the Khmer Rouge were new, unknown guerrillas; only later, after they had murdered more than a quarter of their fellow ethnic Cambodian population, did they get their "Killing Fields" reputation. Also, at this early stage of the Cambodian war there was as yet no established pattern of dealing with captured Western journalists." [48]

There was turmoil about us, with hard eyes and closed faces on some, with more tentative eyes elsewhere. One of the moderate faces — that of a young Cambodian — had a clear look that was to be a prototype of many we would see during our stay in Cambodia. Repeatedly we stressed our position as journalists, Mike in Vietnamese and I in French.

PAC [Public Affairs Conference] Student Admin.
Committee (standing, l to r: Bob Priddy, Arend Lijphart;
sitting l to r: "Beb" Pond, George Happ, Barbara Lewis).
Photo: *The Sheaf* (1958) courtesy The Principia

Eventually the Cambodian village chairman arrived who was of the hard persuasion, and a distance prevailed between us. Conversation by us was greeted with derision. We were prevented from stepping outside to get water. Dick's watch was taken — 'borrowed" the man said who took it. Dick responded by offering it as a gift. After some vacillation by the soldiers the watch, too, was put on a pile of our belongings that was being inventoried, and it, too, was wrapped up and added to the inventory list. One soldier saw the broken lens cap on Mike's camera and asked if they had broken it. Mike explained that he himself had broken it—as he had in dropping it to the ground initially.

We were taken on the back of motorbikes and bicycles to a nearby village and stood inside the porch. The atmosphere was such that a kind of kangaroo court could have flared up at any moment.

Plans changed again, however, and almost immediately we were taken to a waiting truck which was camouflaged on top with fresh branches. We mounted a plank and were seated toward the front on the floor of the truck and instructed not to look out of the windows. Space was left between us and the guards at the back of the truck. We traveled through several hamlets brushing the entry arches in each. In the hamlets we slowed down and were announced as American captives, primarily by a young student from Phnom Penh who was a weather vane of the first day. At the original house he had begun by being open and talkative, and we had conversed in French. Then he had been told abruptly by the village chairman not to talk to me, and he had moved away from me, with a conscious air of establishing his reliability in the command structure.

Caught Up in Emotions

Now in the truck he went beyond this to become caught up in the emotion and act as one of our main announcers.

Hatred flared up in the villagers' voices and was fanned by mob excitement, clearly comprehensible even in an unfamiliar language. Villagers thumped the truck, springing up on it to look at us. Now and then a less inflamed person did appear. As I looked at the people I tried to convey to them that I bore them no ill will, that I loathe war and the passions of war, destruction, and hatred and enmity between men—and that if any of them had lost loved ones my heart went out to them.

Toward the end of the ride two guards trained rifles or machine guns at us. One instruction was given to Mike in Vietnamese, which he misunderstood to mean he should lie on the floor. That he did so angered the person giving the order, and the student explained to me in French that we should just sit normally.

Then we were blindfolded — tightly — and led off the truck, stooping to descend the plank. I was kicked once on the way, but for the most part the villagers did not touch us.

My sense was that we might be close to being killed in this period. We were walked — holding hands — through a gauntlet of villagers, who shouted at us but again did not touch us very much. Then Mike, holding my right hand, heard in Vietnamese what sounded like talk of killing us and told me to speak to the student, who was on my left. I asked the student a question, which he answered, but it was difficult to tell if it broke any of the tension or not.

The ground became rougher. Suddenly Mike's hand was wrenched from mine and a stranger took Mike's place. He did not hold my hand, but gripped me by the wrist in a clear assertion of force.

"This is a school"

The student shifted from holding my left hand to imitate this. Mike and Dick disappeared ahead of me in the midst of shouting. The student told me they were being questioned. I was taken to a building and seated on a chair. "This is a school," the student told me in a neutral tone, "A school of the Cambodian people." I acknowledged the school, then asked if I could have a drink of water. "This is a school," the student repeated in the same tone. "There is no water here." I must have been saying something to him about the truth of our being journalists, for his parting words, still in the slightly mocking tone, were, "Truth is very important."

A period passed — the duration of which I could not judge — in which waves of people, Cambodians I believe, came in and stared at me and then receded. I was glad for the blindfold. No one touched me except for one man with an angry voice who snatched off my sandals and threw them against a wall. There were pockets of quiet, and during one of these I sat on the dusty floor out of tiredness. A little later as I sat, I thought I could ask again for some water. A cup was brought to me in quietness. I drank it and asked for another. It also was brought.

A little later I felt I could slip the blindfold from my eyes. It was just about dusk. I indeed was in a school room, and there was one guard at the door. After another interval the guard tried to attack me and took my rings. I said aloud that this was not necessary, that he was my brother, and I was his sister. Nothing happened for a few minutes, and then he replaced the rings on my fingers.

Officer Intervened

Another interval, and a new soldier appeared to indicate that I could rest on one of the tables if I wanted to sleep. I learned later that he had been sent by a higher official to ensure that I was not mistreated. This higher official had just found out about our arrests, it appeared, and had swiftly intervened to restore correct treatment to us.

Shortly thereafter a solder came to conduct me to another building. He retrieved my sandals and directed me across the yard. As I walked through the door of this new building, I saw Dick and Mike sitting on a bench. We expressed our mutual joy at seeing each other, and Dick explained that we would be fed and would be allowed to wash.

Dick said that he and Mike had been run behind a motorbike for a kilometer or so, then had been hit in the head and thought they might be tortured. They had been rescued by the same officer who had sent someone to look after me. Now we were to be fed — the first meal that day for any of the three of us.

Phrasing Unclear

The civil treatment that was to be accorded us for the rest of our time was established that evening. It was explained to us that if we were journalist rather than spies we had nothing to worry about. This was somewhat muddied by an alternate phraseology that if we were "good people," we had nothing to worry about. We accepted the clean interpretation of this and anticipated that we would be allowed to work as journalists. We accepted as well the apology of a ranking officer for the rough handling we had received that afternoon before the intervention of higher authority.

Letters not Received

We said we understood the feelings of people at war and suspicion in war that we were spies, and we welcomed an inquiry that would establish our bonafides as international correspondents. We asked to write letters to our families notifying them that we were alive and were told that we would be allowed to do so. Unfortunately, these letters have never been received, and our families did not know until our final release that we were alive.

PART II:
TYPICAL DAY IN CAPTIVITY

A kind of typical day was established only after we passed an initial probe of about a week's duration. We had accepted an investigation into our claim to being journalists, and we proceeded on this basis. Things grew more relaxed as time went on, but even from the beginning the soldiers with us never mounted formal guard. They did, of course, carry weapons, as did all the soldiers in the villages.

At the first house and always thereafter, however, we were introduced as friends, and nothing in the bearing of the soldiers toward us contradicted this. An escape attempt was the last thing that any of the three of us would have tried, and this appeared to be understood. As time went on, weapons were freely left in our presence, even in the absence of soldiers.

Conversations

There were, however, three unpleasant interrogations in the first week in which it was suggested but not actually charged that we were spies. We feared at the time that the authorities were considering the possibility of framing us. This period passed, however, and we came to be spoken to more and more in the vein of journalists. Conversations with the two soldiers who discussed ideology became more frequent. The conversations began at their initiative, which we welcomed, and we expanded their range to topics and questions of our own.

By the second week or so, then, we had settled into something of a routine. The best part of a typical day, in my eyes, came after nightfall. Then, when the local villagers had finished their turns, the three of us could go out to the well and wash. The primary joy came in getting outdoors after being cooped up all day in a house. The moon might be full and shimmering over a rice paddy. The stars might be brilliant, with the Southern Cross hanging in the south and flares shining in the east. Or it might have rained, and all the frogs in the ponds might have been stroked into song.

The second joy, of course, was simply to achieve at least relative cleanliness.

Not the Custom

We were given sarongs at the beginning as a change of clothes, and by pooling our personal discoveries about techniques, we three quickly became expert at washing under sarongs in order to maintain the propriety of the villagers. We learned this early, for in one of the few indiscretions, Dick bathed in the raw the first night, and a soldier politely informed Mike that this was not the custom of the villagers.

I always lingered to prolong the time outdoors. But at last the moment would come to return to the house, wash the mud from our feet with a coconut shell dipper, and climb the ladder to the house. We would hang up our washed clothes, then sit up for a bit and talk.

One of the soldiers might readjust his pack—this was an unending process for the heavy compact satchels. The host of the house—or one of the soldiers—might build a kitchen fire anew and make tea, and two or three little glasses would be placed on the slat floor and shared among us. A glow would be cast on faces by small homemade kerosene lamps.

On special occasions one of the soldiers might pull out of his pack a plastic bag of sugar and make sweet tea. Afterwards we would simply shift our positions on the floor from sitting to lying, and retire for the night. Later, if we were to travel at night, one of the soldiers would wake us, tell us to get ready to go, and we would leave. The added instruction to roll up our pant legs meant we would be walking across wet paddies. Mike and Dick would throw our meager things into their overnight case and Pan Am flight bag (which had been returned to us the first night), and we would set out. "It's nice to have some belongings," Mike noted once, and it was.

For the most part, there was less walking at night than we would have liked. Our moves were generally made by vehicle, and tended to be rather cramped, what with the three of us, the basic five soldiers assigned to us, and sometimes one or two women and small children who were fleeing the area of fighting, all together in the vehicle. When we did move, we would arrive at our destination before daybreak. We would settle in, often at some inconvenience to the host family, as we would invariably be given the most honored place in the house.

The first of our two daily meals would be prepared—all the rice we could eat, meat, and often the greens that were the Viet Minh staple when they were fighting the French for independence.

Prerogatives of Age

The houses usually had teak beams, thatch roofs, and coconut palm sidings. Woven fish traps, mattacks, parts of yokes, and other tools often hung around the room on wall supports. Several places had hand-embroidered pillows, flower-painted mirrors, a clutter of little bottles saved from time unknown, perhaps a woven cradle.

Communications between us and the host families varied. One 70-odd-year-old man bronzed and content in his children and grandchildren, was one of the first to spend time with us. It came in the first week of our detention, when the soldiers assigned to us still did not want families to talk to us. The old man asserted the prerogatives of age, however, and just waved the soldiers pleasantly aside to approach us.

Chess Games

We spoke no mutual language, but it did not matter. The grand-father admired Mike's size and strength, then got his son's school diploma out of a chest in the corner and showed it to us. Mike asked for some Cambodian words, and the man turned out to be a natural teacher, drilling Mike repetitively and severely until he could repeat the basic vocabulary swiftly.

After breakfast the three of us were apt to talk among ourselves. The soldiers would be busy elsewhere, discussing where they might buy a chicken or who was going to go into the market for soap. Con-versations of our mixed group were more likely to take place in the afternoon, over tea, perhaps, or after supper.

The last few weeks we had one new diversion: a chess set. We had been taken out to some woods to spend the daylight hours — pri-marily, we discovered later, to be allowed to relieve ourselves more than the original twice nightly schedule permitted. Dick, who had always wanted to whittle a chess set, found some sticks and got to work with his little penknife, and Mike and I helped. The owner of the house we were then staying in invented a board by chalking the slats on the floor, and Mike, Dick, and I took our turns at the game. The strategy and tactics involved appealed greatly, as was only natural, to our guerrilla veterans, and it was not long before two of them could be drawn away from the game only by the most critical overflight of planes or helicopters. Once that took place, the standard ending to the day, in the last light of dusk, became the last possible chess game before the kerosene lamps had to be lit.

PART III:
PROFILE OF JOURNALISTS CAPTORS

There were five soldiers who stayed with us for almost the entire 5 ½ weeks of our detention — Hai, Ba, Tu, Ban Tun, and Wang.

Hai (a code name meaning "two") was the oldest, in his mid-40s. The prime ideological spokesman, he had a gray brush cut, a pug nose, and apple cheeks. He wore loose black peasant trousers and

customarily kept his undershirt rolled up around his chest for cool-
ness. Some of his language and pronunciation was southern; much
was North Vietnamese. He did not speak Cambodian.

Ba ("three") was in charge of security. Although he was only in his
mid-30s, he was a longtime professional soldier and appeared to be a
reasonably high-ranking officer. He had little patience and amenities.
Even in casual conversation Ba gave the appearance of being always
watchful, always preoccupied with the next move and all emergency
possibilities. He would be the first to spot a plane on the horizon,
the first — on one occasion — to run to another part of the woods
and shoot his rifle in order to draw the attention of maneuvering
helicopters away from us.

An Interest in Soccer

He had been a good soccer player, he said, had once played three
consecutive games without break, had once written a book on soccer.
He was the one who kept the major supply of sugar in his pack. He
was southern Vietnamese but must have been in Cambodia for some
time, as he spoke good Cambodian.

Tu ("four") in his early 30s, was more or less Hai's understudy. He
would talk to us about ideology, too, and he was the person who at
the beginning handled the mechanics of caring for us. He would tell
us when to wash, when to eat, when to get ready to move. Tu turned
out to be the one in the group with barbering skills also, cutting everyone's hair to his specifications, stropping the double-edged razor blade
on the palm of his hand. He moved with the economy and grace of
a cat. He, too, was southern Vietnamese and spoke no Cambodian.

These three were all battle veterans and had been wounded several
times each. They were officers, as they carried pistols in their belts. In
common with the practice of the National Liberation Front (South
Vietnam) and now of the Cambodian National United Front (as the
Communist-led forces now call themselves), the men did not wear
uniforms or insignia. The command relationship among them was
handled completely informally.

Ban Tun was the only Cambodian of the five. In his mid-30s, he looked much younger. He had a handsome square-cut head that could have been the model for sculpture. He was strong, and he exalted in his strength. In the mornings he would spring from prone sleep to standing wakefulness in one bound, then glance around to see if anyone was watching him.

Exuberance Exhibited

Where the Vietnamese were careful, Ban Tun was exuberant. On night marches, when we would come to rest in a villager's yard, the Vietnamese would stand quietly and vigilantly in shadow, Ban Tun would fling himself down on the ground with a loud sigh, imitate the sounds of battle in the air, and improvise his own vocal jazz out of them. He would Indian-wrestle the Vietnamese, somewhere to their embarrassment, and always win; or he would prod them into imitating some Cambodian dancing around the room. On one occasion he went into a parody of a Buddhist chant, which all the soldiers laughed at—and which he himself grew more and more absorbed in, until it became the real thing. As an amulet against getting shot, he wore a rope necklace with two Buddha figures wrapped in it. Ben Tun apparently became an officer in the course of our time in Cambodia, for in our last few days there he too was wearing a pistol.

Background Mixed

Wang was part Vietnamese ethnically and said he had grown up in Phnom Penh which seemed likely from the naturalness of his Cambodian. One of the other soldiers told us that Wang's family was well-to-do, and this also seemed likely. In his late 20s, Wang was not yet married and sometimes had to parry offers of old woman to introduce him to eligible young girls in the villages. In our party cooking and shopping usually devolved on Wang, though others occasionally pitched in, too.

In addition to the basic five, there were others who joined us only briefly: the nurse and cook who was with us for perhaps a week; the boy who looked about fifteen, said he was seventeen, and resented any implications that he was still a boy; the interrogators (North Vietnamese, and considerably less personable than the men assigned to us).

Goals Suggested

The self-identity of all of our basic five soldiers — and especially of veterans Hai, Ba, and Tu — seemed to reside completely in fighting for the revolution. Their psychology appeared to be less that of the natural warrior than of the single-minded revolutionary, with a vast capacity to sacrifice for the cause. This cause, as developed in the course of many conversations, embraced primarily nationalism and social justice. As presented to us, these meant broad concepts rather than doctrinaire niceties. Nationalism in one conversation would mean Vietnam for the Vietnamese, in another Indo-China for the Indo-Chinese. Whichever it was, the essential objective was to get the Americans out of Indo-China. (Formally, the Cambodian front was always referred to as an independent Cambodian entity, but there was much less stress on this than on broad nationalism and social justice).

Family Life Foregone

For all of the soldiers with us, personal identification with the cause meant foregoing normal family life. Hai, Ba, and Tu had not seen wives or children for periods ranging up to ten or eleven years. As for friendships, they could be warm and valued, as we saw in the relationships among the five, but they were always to be subordinate to the cause. A kind of Confucian humanism of doing unto others as one would have done to him was preached and practiced with friends (and, so far as we would observe, with villagers).

Friends, however, are carefully defined. An enemy, if he is just ignorant or mistaken, can be reeducated to goodness (a familiar Confucian as well as Maoist concept). The meaning, in this context, is that he can be reeducated to support the revolution. But there is no room for an alternate truth or perception of truth. An enemy who refuses the revolutionary truth can be killed without compunction. The religion of revolution shows no mercy for heretics.

Nor is there any feminine softening of this definition of oneself and one's friends. The nurse might carry a pink and white polka-dot purse in her pack, but that was the only touch. Every other phrase in her conversation was: "according to the revolution."

PART IV:
LAST DAYS OF CAPTIVITY AND A FAREWELL DINNER

The word that we would be released came to us on June 9 in a rather casual way. To our pleasure we had been taken out to the woods before dawn that day. That meant we would get some sun, walk around a bit, and enjoy the trees and the birds. There was a tiny hatch hut we would sit in that housed several sacks of rice.

In the afternoon we heard helicopters approaching and quickly pulled into the hut the wet clothes that were spread out so as not to draw attention to our position. The tea kettle was black and therefore posed no problem. The white dishes had already been put under a bush and covered with an additional branch or two. The hut itself had foliage put over it at one time. But these branches had long since browned and withered, leaving a rectangle of thatch that might easily become visible from the air if rotors were close enough to agitate the branches of the tall trees above us.

This time it was no overflight to somewhere else. There were four helicopters, and they were working over our immediate area, descending and rising in a pattern as they searched the woods. They were not shooting—yet—but the hut was a likely target if they saw it. In one breathing space the three of us had scrambled under the raised floor of the hut—under the rice sacks—but this would have been no protection if the helicopters had fired their rockets.

Diversion Tactic Tried

One of our guards, Ba, feared the worst as two of the helicopters, which were maneuvering at a distance of about eighty meters from the hut and at an altitude of only forty meters, were indeed sweeping the high foliage in a way that might reveal the hut. He therefore ran through the woods on the far side of the helicopters, shot his M-16 into the air, and ran in the other direction to divert the pilots away from the hut.

Hai and Tu, who had been in the village, rather than in the woods, with us when the helicopters approached, independently ran to the same area that Ba did, also to draw the aircraft away. Ba next circled back to us and moved us, with great urgency, to a camouflaged glade in another section of the woods. Then he disappeared to reconnoiter further. Ban Tun stayed with us, giving us fresh branches to cover ourselves in case the helicopters should return—and also giving us some wild oranges he had discovered en route. When Ba came back to the glade once more, he explained that we would now have to leave the area that night, unexpectedly. The safest way to leave was to walk, and he made sure that we were all in good health and that none of us had any foot trouble. We assured him that we were felling very well and that we could walk a long distance with no difficulty.

Instructions Repeated

"No matter what happens, don't run," Ba said, repeating an instruction he had given us at the height of the crisis. (It was a superfluous command. We feared the helicopters as much as everyone else did.) Now Ba added what he had not said before: "I have a pistol here, and in a dangerous situation I could shoot you....I am letting you know, no matter what happens, I would not do that. But if you brought the American helicopters here, it would make much difficulty for the friends that live here."

We told him that we would never run, and he nodded, adding that he did not say much, but he saw a great deal, and he knew this was the case. "I want you to live," he said, "I want to see you safely back with your families...I just want them to see you face to face again... Sooner or later you will be released."

Photograph Taken

That evening, we were visited by a high commander in the region who informed us officially that we would be released soon. No more than half an hour later we said goodbye to the Cambodian family we had been staying with and began our long last night walk. Some niceties remained. There was our formal and polemical interview with a Cambodian introduced as the regional commander. There was one photograph of us with packs and hats standing with Ban Tun, who had just been promoted to officer. (We asked to have copies mailed to us.)

There was one brief recording session in which Dick read the joint statement we had been asked to write about our treatment and impressions. Mike read an article he had written about high morale among the pro-Communist and pro-Sihanouk front troops—as a dog yowled inconsolably in the background. (I was recorded in French at the interview when I thanked the commander for the interview and for the hospitality and good treatment we had received in Cambodia.)

There was a gala good-bye dinner at which just about every front official we had met in our 5 ½ weeks showed up.

Chess Set Accepted

And there was one session which Mike, Dick, and I initiated in which we gave modest presents from our own belongings to our five escorts. They would not accept anything we had brought to Cambodia with us, but they did accept the chess set. In doing so, they said they would always remember our whittling it.

We were scheduled to be released on June 14 and on that afternoon set out across the fields to meet a vehicle. To our surprise the vehicle turned out to be a full-fledged taxibus. To our further surprise, we took a main road full of people, an unprecedented event. To our final surprise, we turned into a village school yard where a celebration was beginning. There was a gathering of about 1,000 villagers; there was an honor guard of Cambodian irregulars; and there were new banners that were translated for us thanking American people who oppose aggression by the Nixon administration in Cambodia. We were shown places at a small table in front of the podium.

Names Mentioned

There was a speech given in Cambodian over the loudspeaker system that was not translated for us. At one point our names were announced, although we did not seem to constitute the focus of the speech. At the end, I was asked to thank the assemblage in French. I said—sincerely—that we appreciated greatly the hospitality of the homes we had stayed in. Then the heavens unloosed a monsoon torrent, and the crowds fled.

The rain made travel difficult on mud roads, so we changed our plans and returned to our last house, rousing the family, which had already retired for the night. Wang (the guard who had done most of the cooking) had bought some pastry in the village. We dried out over tea and pastry, and we wondered what Hai, Tu, and Ban Tun, who had quit our party that day, might be doing.

The next afternoon and night we traveled by jeep and a relay of motorbikes to a part of Highway 1 controlled at night by the front. We had white flags of sorts and money that the soldiers had given us to make sure we could get back to Saigon. The following morning we hitched a ride with an empty South Vietnamese convoy that was returning from Phnom Penh to Saigon.

Our Cambodian sojourn was at an end.

PART V:
FREED JOURNALIST'S
QUESTION: "WHY US?"

The continuing absence of some twenty newspaper correspondents in Cambodia, presumably detained by pro-Sihanouk forces, poses serious moral issues for a journalist who has been released. Why us? Are we precedent or exception? And if precedent, what kind of precedent? These questions have haunted me since our release. So have others—questions about the nature of friendship and the trust of friendship, of freedom, of moral responsibility and moral ambiguity.

The three of us never said anything we did not believe, either in conversation or in the few statements that we were asked to write. Nor, I believe, would we have. In that sense we were honest. Yet honest views offered voluntarily and honest views offered under implicit sanction are two different things. Perhaps I should specify here exactly what we did and did not do during our detention.

Requests Limited

It could be argued that we were asked for relatively little. We were not asked to sign statements written by others, nor were we asked to change statements we had written. We were not asked to make any statements about Vietnam.

At the beginning we were asked to list our newspapers, samples of our articles, and names of journalists, especially "progressive" journalists who could vouch for us. The inquiry was described as seeking to establish clearly that we were bona fide journalists, not spies. But verbal criticism of our first of two listings included political diatribes against some of the references we had listed and a stern demand why I had not written more against the war. The joint statement that the three of us were asked to write after we had been told we would be released concerned our treatment and our impressions about such things as the morale of the pro-Communist and pro-Sihanouk front troops and the behavior of South Vietnamese troops in Cambodia.

Statement Sketched

In this statement we said that we had been very well cared for after the first day. That the morale of the five soldiers we were with was excellent, and that, prior to our arrest, we had seen South Vietnamese troops stealing civilian rice reserves and household goods in the town of Prasaut. We did not generalize from these observations (which were all accurate), and we were not requested to elaborate.

As for our many informal conversations, we freely expressed in them our views about the war. These were favorable to the front in that the three of us deeply regretted the entry of American and South Vietnamese troops into Cambodia—and that we hoped, as journalists, to be able in some way to alter American policy.

We could have made a different choice. We could have been silent about our views. We could have refused communication because a policy of our government—even though we differed from it—defined those who had arrested us as enemies. Or we could have challenged frontally the assumption that there can be no independent observers, only those who are for or against a cause. We could have drawn a line, perhaps, at writing anything while under detention, or at being recorded. There is no ethical code for journalists in situations of this sort, and I am not sure that any could be established. In practice, in the shock of danger and the heat of sudden events, one makes instant decisions, then lives with them.

Conclusions Reached

As it turned out, we made a choice that was not one of confrontation. We expected to be treated as journalist once it was ascertained that we were not spies, and we acted this way. We proposed interviews and trips whenever we could. We posed questions. We took—in the latter period—copious notes, which were not censored. We lived, to come extent, the "other side" of this bitter war with an immediacy that we had never imagined possible.

In addition, in the close daily contacts of 5 ½ weeks, we came to know something of our escorts as men rather than as political automatons—and they too came to know something of us.

Each of the three of us has his own political as well as personal conclusions from our experience. My conclusions do not favor the American action in Cambodia.

I look forward to the release of the other journalists soon. Prince Norodom Sihanouk, chairman of the Cambodian National United Front, who arranged for our release, has assured us that he will do everything he can to arrange a similar unconditional release of other correspondents who may now be detained by his military forces.

This is the precedent I hope we have established.

ELIZABETH POND: When this volume of essays was first announced and a call went out soliciting submissions from potential authors, we described both the intended character of the planned book and indicated we sought authors who had attended Principia (high school or college) and then served in uniform during the Vietnam Era. The book would not be limited to combat zone experiences in Vietnam, although we knew we would hear from some Principia alumni who had served in dangerous regions "in country" or on carriers at Yankee Station from which pilots flew sorties over Vietnam. It was possible that such combat memoirs would constitute the bulk of the book, but not the whole. We intended a broader look at military experiences during the era no matter where a soldier or sailor or military intelligence officer might have been stationed (or what may have been his job).

The common theme for subjects and authors would be a shared membership in three communities: 1) the generation born during, or soon after, World War II, 2) alumni of Principia high school or college, typically from the classes graduating at the height of the Vietnam conflict, and 3) individuals who wore the uniform of their country as members of the armed forces of any branch, serving (it appeared likely for most authors) relatively brief commitments in the Navy, Marines, Air Force, or Army during some of the years of the active Vietnam conflict, roughly between 1960 and the Fall of Saigon in 1975.

The first response received was from Elizabeth Pond (college class of 1958). "I'm not sure how broadly or narrowly you are casting your net for [the projected book]," she began, "but in 1970 I was captured in Cambodia by the Khmer Rouge and held for five and a half weeks," she reported matter-of-factly. Further emails disclosed that she was an international journalist and had been detained at gun point, and that she and two other journalists were suspected of being spies, kept under guard, interrogated, and shuttled from village to village until they were ultimately released in June, 1970. "So you might like to include my story," she offered. We shared ideas about the projected character and scope of the book, and the project was underway. *If this is the first inquiry I received about our collection of essays, what might be coming next?* I pondered (no pun intended).

Indeed, Elizabeth Pond is listed by the Defense Prisoner of War/Missing Personnel Office as a Vietnam War POW, captured May 7, 1970, in Cambodia at "loss coordinates" 111000 North, 1054000 East, and released June 15th. For two decades, from 1967-1988, she was a foreign correspondent for The *Christian Science Monitor*, an international newspaper that first published her account of Cambodian captivity only a week after her release (as reprinted here with permission). Assigned to Saigon, from where she reported on the war, Pond was in Japan when Nixon made his historic trip to China, covered the Brezhnev era from the Soviet Union, and reported from Germany when the Berlin wall came down ending the cold war and reuniting the two Germanies. Today, she lives and writes in Berlin. Her work has appeared in *Foreign Affairs, the Wall Street Journal, the Washington Quarterly, World Policy, and other newspapers and magazines.* From 2000-2005, she was the first editor of the English edition of *Internationale Politik.* Pond has authored ten books, mostly on foreign policy and international affairs of Europe and the Balkans.

"Beb" Pond, who hailed from Allentown, Pennsylvania, gave evidence of these interests from the start at Principia. She was a government major and served on the administrative committee of the 20th annual Public Affairs Conference [PAC] in 1958, the student-run intercollegiate conference that brought Dr. Henry Kissinger and William Elliott of Harvard University to campus to serve as experts as college students from across the country discussed "the cold war," the PAC topic for 1958. Dr. Kissinger would go on be Secretary of State and win the Nobel Peace Prize for ending the Vietnam War Pond had been a member of the international relations club on campus, served on the staff and editorial board of the campus newspaper, and was a member of the debate club and the scholastic honors society, Phi Alpha Eta. Even with all this interest in world affairs, Cambodia was not on Beb Pond's radar in 1958. A dozen years later it would be.

Huey helicoptor insertion and pick up in Vietnam.
Photo courtesy Rob Ostenberg

PART V:
In Country Vietnam

Beetle Bailey Isn't Funny Anymore

STEVEN HEUBECK

It was the 14th day of October, 1966, a Friday. I was sworn in at a military reception station at Fort Holabird, Maryland. I met a major with a 1st Cav shoulder patch on his right sleeve indicating combat tours with the 1st Cavalry in both Korea and Vietnam. He had a handlebar mustache. I enlisted for a three-year tour of duty. I was promised an assignment in a classified military occupation specialty (MOS) with military intelligence (MI). It had begun.

I departed Baltimore that evening via Greyhound bus for Fort Bragg, North Carolina. Fellow inductees were from the Maryland and Virginia area. We didn't talk much. I ate a box lunch and spent the rest of the ride memorizing my military service number RA (for Regular Army) as opposed to a draftee whose number began as US11568387. That little bit of memorization would save me push-ups once we got off of the bus at the reception center at Bragg.

Fort Bragg is the home of the XVIII Airborne Corps, the 82nd Airborne Division, and the U.S. Army Special Forces known as the "Green Berets." Both the 82nd and the Special Forces would come to play a role in my life, although at the time I didn't know it.

Fort Bragg was also the home of a basic training brigade (2nd Brigade) that used old World War II wooden barracks to house the trainees. The 2nd Brigade trained draftees and volunteers from Maryland and south. Because I enlisted at Fort Holabird, I went to Bragg along with my other bus mates.

It was about "Zero Dark Thirty" (sometime between midnight and 6:00 a.m.) when we got off of the bus into the waiting arms of cadre screaming at us to "double-time" and get into formation. We were taken to a large classroom and filled out paperwork. I saved myself from push-ups by being able to recite my service number from memory.

I saw fellow recruits turn in "Skin magazines," switchblade knives, and handguns during the reception process! Interesting world. Finally, I was given a bed in a WW II barracks. All too soon, I was awakened in the morning to a crashing of trashcans, bright lights, and a screaming sergeant who in his own special way got us out of bed and herded us to the mess hall for breakfast.

One of the recruits got a hold of the Sunday paper and was reading the "funnies" when he looked up at me and said, "You know something? Beatle Bailey isn't funny anymore."

Push-ups were the preferred method of ensuring compliance with directions and orders in basic training and other Army training programs. One morning during formation the company first sergeant called me out of formation and told me to "drop for ten," meaning ten push-ups. I did twenty and stood at attention not knowing what particular problem I was causing the sergeant. He said that I filled out my religious preference card not by marking Protestant, Catholic, or Jewish but by indicating that I was a Christian Scientist. So he dropped me for another ten, and I gave him another twenty.

When I returned to attention, I told him that I would do push-ups for him all day, but it was not going to change my religion. He then looked at me with what can only be described as understanding (a *big* leap for a basic training first sergeant), and he said, "Son, we only have these three religions in the U.S. Army, and that is all that you can chose from." I said that it would be considered Protestant, made the change, and moved on.

The curriculum, lessons, and teaching methods were memorable. I did the usual live ammo crawl under machine gun fire; threw the hand grenade; practiced rifle marksmanship, bayonet skills, and marching; and learned that when you smell whiskey and onions, your sergeant is up close and personal and is giving you "one on one" instruction!

I also learned that "Men-ses" was the drill instructor's plural for "Men"; that, and sentences that began with "people" meant that collectively we'd done something wrong and were going to pay.

We learned that there were scams to avoid. One was a gilded, leather bound Bible with a picture of the recruit in uniform (we all looked alike in those pictures); another was the American flag that could be sent to our mothers for about $100. We made $93 a month as recruits. There was a payment plan, or a loan shark, and we could pick our poison.

We were told that there were some 82nd Airborne Division paratroopers from Detroit who were robbing basic trainees in the barracks at night at gunpoint. They got caught while I was there.

I also learned that there were young women who sought out and married basic training recruits who were going to be infantry soldiers. The women would get $10,000 in death benefits from the government, and this became a business enterprise. One guy returned home from his combat tour in Vietnam to learn that his loving wife of a year or so had married another infantry soldier while he was overseas. It was always a problem for the girls when the guy survived the tour.

On graduation day, as we were leaving our basic training company "Echo 6, 2 All the Way Sergeant!" [Echo Company, 6th Battalion, Second Brigade], a fellow basic trainee from North Carolina came up to me and asked to speak to me in private. He told me that I was assigned to E, 6, 2 so that he could watch me on behalf of Military Intelligence (MI). Later that day another recruit called me off to the side and told me the same thing. It was interesting. Both gave me high marks, so I was pretty sure that I was not doomed to a three year stint as a potato peeler and pots and pans washer.

I got on another Greyhound in my uniform and rode from Fort Bragg to Baltimore, then on to Boston, where my parents met me and took me home. The basic training experience and bus home trip were interesting, and I got a good look at the South: the way of life of the families who sent their sons to serve our country as they could not go to college, and they chose not to go to Canada! These people are the "salt of the earth."

On a cold, rainy January night in 1967, my aunt and uncle who lived in Baltimore dropped me off under a dismal excuse for a streetlight at another reception center at Fort Holabird (we called it 'The

Bird') in Baltimore, where I was held in "casual status," meaning that my training was not ready to begin. My aunt cried, and my uncle shook my hand.

There I met a fellow student named Ray Mushal, a Connecticut Yankee whose father was a groundskeeper at Yale University. Ray got to go to Yale for free. We became fast friends. Ray served two tours of duty as an MI officer in 4 Corp, Vietnam, and used his savings to put himself through Penn Law School. He married Barbara, a wonderful lady from South Carolina, whom he met in DC. They had two children and lived in Bethesda, Maryland. Ray became an environmental attorney with the Department of Justice and recently died from cancer brought on by a thirty-year smoking habit. At "The Bird," as we called it, he would smoke his morning cigarette, and I would hide in the hallway and read the lesson![29]

The MI training was classified, but I can say that we learned the tradecraft that is so eloquently detailed in John Le Carré's, *Smiley's People*. We had wonderful instructors with fascinating careers. One was Major Hishoro (not his real name), a Japanese American from Hawaii who during the Korean War would infiltrate into North Korea to conduct intelligence operations. During one mission he had to hide in a rice paddy, his body completely submerged under water in the paddy, and to breathe through a reed until the Korean Patrol searching for him left. He then made his way back to the submarine. Rice paddies are fertilized with human waste, and he developed a high fever when he returned to the submarine.

He was in sickbay when there was another mission that was critical to the success of an Allied mission. He volunteered for it, went back into enemy territory, returning after the mission was completed. All with the high fever! He knew that what he did in the mission would lead to saving American lives, and the mission was more important than his well-being. He taught us great lessons about character, devotion to duty, and the importance of the true mission of intelligence work.

---

29 The weekly Christian Science study of the *Bible* and *Science and Health, With Key to the Scriptures* by Mary Baker Eddy.

I learned where Ulan Bator[30] was, and about operations into East Germany and Russia. During one segment of instruction about crossing borders into "denied areas" our instructor told about the guards, electric fencing, and land mines. We were told how we could overcome each of these obstacles.

Then he told us about the dogs! He said that when the dog attacks, he goes for your groin, so, to defend yourself, you bend over and give the dog your arm to bite. Then you pull the dog up to your chest and break his back. The class was silent for a few minutes thinking about that one, but as we "sort of kind of" thought about it, most of us felt that if it came to that, we could do it. Then the instructor said with a twinkle in his eye, "Oh, yes, and men, the dogs attack in pairs!" Most of us decided that if the dogs were there we would look for another way into where we wanted to go.

Later when I was traveling in the former East Germany, on a train ride through the country I noticed the watch towers that the Soviets placed every few hundred yards along the fields and roadways. Interesting to see in the real world what I was trained to deal with so many years ago.

A second language was something that would make us better operators in our jobs, and so our class took the Army Language Aptitude Test. I selected Russian, German, and Vietnamese, thinking that I could land an assignment in Germany, ride around in a Porsche, chat up gorgeous German women, and save the world from Communism.

I didn't make the cut for those languages, but I was selected for Spanish language training at the Army language school in Monterey, California, known as the Defense Language Institute West Coast (DLIWC). Ray Mushal got French, and we were off to California.

During this period the intelligence branch had a critical need for officers in my MOS. The training for officers and enlisted personnel was the same, and as I had a college degree I applied for a direct commission in my specialty and the MI branch. Ray and another student

---

30 Ulan Bator was a fictitious country devised for training purposes in military intelligence training exercises.

in my class also applied. During my training at the language school, Ray and I were interviewed by a panel of officers for the commission.

The lieutenant colonel who headed up the panel opened the inquiry by noting that I failed Economics 101 while in college. I responded that I also withdrew from an earlier class and struggled through a third try at Econ 101 finally passing with what I called a "gentlemen's 'C'." The interview was all downhill after that, although Ray and I eventually became officers.

Photo taken at the Gatun Locks Drop Zone, Canal Zone, Panama, parachute qualification course run by the 8th Special Forces Group: Following a unit jump [left to right: Sgt. Bob Ritter, unidentified Lt., Warrant Officer Ted Gullege, 1st Lt. Steve Heubeck]. Photo courtesy Steve Heubeck

The language training was highly focused and very rewarding. Classes were small. Two of my classmates were Lt. Col. Richard V. Atkinson and his wife Dee. They were going to Panama where he was to be the second in command of the 8th Special Forces Group in Panama. He had several tours in Vietnam, and at one time Atkinson headed the program where special forces troopers from the 5th Special Forces Group trained and led the Vietnamese mountain tribesmen known as "Montagnards" to fight the Viet Cong. After I received my commission, I was transferred to the 610th MI Detachment, 8th Special Forces Group and was under Atkinson's command.

I made the cut in language school and was assigned to the 470 MI Group in Panama. We were located in Fort Amador, Canal Zone, Panama. There was one other building on the post with no windows, and that belonged to our 'rivals," the CIA, whom one MI boss more or less affectionately called "the three-toed sloths" after the furry, South American jungle dweller.

Steve Heubeck (l) with Captain Ray Orr.
Photo courtesy Steve Heubeck

About a year into my tour I was commissioned as a second lieu-tenant and made "an officer and a gentleman" by an act of Congress. It was then that I was sent to the 8th Special Forces Group.

I went through basic airborne (parachute) training in Panama along with about twenty other officers and enlisted personnel who were not airborne qualified but who had been assigned to the 8th which was an airborne unit. It was intense. The training cadre looked as if they were taken straight from Hollywood's "central casting" to play the role! They were great, and, despite the intensity of the training, they had a sense of humor. Humor, that is, by Army paratrooper standards.

There was Sergeant Serois who was from Lawrence, Massachusetts, and who had me do push-ups because I lived in Haverhill, Massachusetts, where his high school football team lost to my high school football team on Thanksgiving Day, 1962! All in fun.

There was another cadre member named Sergeant First Class (SFC) Max Armillo. Max was to be assigned to my unit after the parachute training was over. Max won a Silver Star and Purple Heart in Vietnam during a Special Forces operation that won Second Lieutenant Roger Donlon the Congressional Medal of Honor. Max was wounded by a bomb dropped by U.S. aircraft during the desperate fight for survival, and Max had to have one of his shoulders repaired as a result of his wounds.

The sergeant in charge of the airborne training cadre took me aside and asked if there were going to be any problems between Max and me because Max had me do push-ups and hollered at me during the training. "Absolutely not," I told the sergeant, "Max was a hero in my eyes," and I would take care of him and see that his transition into our unit was smooth and harmonious. And it was.

During the first week of airborne school, we officers left formations early at lunchtime to be served at a private dining area of the mess hall. The airborne trainees had to file in behind the garrison troops, and many of them did not have enough time to finish their lunch. So, I spoke to Sergeant Armillo about the situation and asked if he could talk to the mess sergeant to let our guys get lunch before the garrison troops. We worked it out, and from that time on I would get in line behind the last of the enlisted trainees and made sure that they had food before I did. Sorry to say that none of my fellow officers followed my lead.

I did my five parachute jumps to qualify for my parachute wings. Max gave me his parachute wings when I graduated! And I went on to do night equipment jumps as practice for infiltrating enemy territory. I can still smell the kerosene from the turbo jet engines of the C-130s in moist air that envelops you when the door opens and you are about to make your jump, wearing, by the way, a piece of equipment made for the U.S. government by the lowest bidder! I made thirty-three jumps before I left the service.

One day in Panama I gave a ride to another lieutenant and during our conversation he mentioned that he graduated from the University of Wyoming. I said that the only person I knew who went to that school was Dick Schneider, a friend of Bob Craig and my roommate at the Belote house in Elsah.[31] He did a double take telling me that Schneider was best friends with him! So the small world thing was beginning to make sense.

On another occasion I was in the Canal Zone airport, getting ready to take a flight to the States, when I looked up and saw a fellow "Southie"[32] named John Snyder. John was a newly minted second lieutenant and was in Panama to go through the Jungle Warfare School before being deployed to Vietnam. We spoke briefly, and he asked me if I had any advice for him as he was going through the course. Since I worked in the POW[33] side of the training, I told him not to get captured!

I lived outside of the Canal Zone. I was married at the time and had a nice apartment behind the Panama Hilton Hotel. When I was commissioned, I kept living there but went to work in a uniform instead of plain clothes.

The communists were active and violent in Panama at that time, and they took two shots at me that happily failed. On one occasion someone removed four of the five lug nuts on my car's wheel, and the wheel almost came off during my return home from the Christian Science Society meeting one Sunday. I never found out who did that one. The second effort at sabotage was a little better and almost worked. I had my vehicle serviced at a Canal Zone facility. Apparently

---

31 Residence [in Elsah, Illinois] of James Belote, Professor of History at Principia College. Heubeck and Schneider roomed at the Belote home; Craig roomed at another professor's house across the street. James H. Belote and his twin brother William M. Belote wrote three major military histories of WWII, on Corregidor, on Okinawa, and on the development and operation of aircraft carrier task forces during WWII.

32 Member of Brooks South residence hall at Principia College.

33 Prisoner of war.

someone cut the brake line or damaged it to the point where it would fail when I applied the brakes. I was crossing the Isthmus from Fort Gulick (the 8th Special Forces Group location) to Fort Amador, and when I hit the brakes….nothing! There was a military two-and-a-half ton truck ahead of me, so I swerved onto the narrow shoulder of the road, pulled on the emergency brake, and was able to stop in time and not go over the embankment. I never found out who did that one either.

While serving in the 8th I knew that I was surrounded by men who fought in three wars. Their bravery and commitment to the fellow soldiers were symbolic of the warrior heritage that was handed down to me. One sergeant major (the senior enlisted rank) was a bear of a man: at age eighteen he was an enlisted glider pilot who took part in the Normandy invasion, landing his glider with paratroopers in a field in France.

Our command sergeant major was featured on the television program "What's My Line," where he was identified as a U.S. guerilla fighter with missions in Korea. There was another master sergeant who was recruited by Army Intelligence in Berlin during the end of WWII; he became a Yugoslov border guard and crossed over to the Allied side with the first AK 47 rifle to fall to the U.S. Army's hands.

The Canal Zone General R. O. Johnson was a Bataan Death March survivor and would talk about his experience as a POW at our officers' formal dinners called "Dining Ins."

Finally, there was Sergeant Joseph De Long. Joe worked in the operations and training unit at the 8th Group's headquarters. I would talk to him on a daily basis as I scheduled training in South America for our Group.

The 8th sent a mobile training team to Bolivia, the team that trained the 2nd Bolivian Ranger Battalion that chased and captured the infamous "Che" Gueverra from Cuba. Che was Castro's right hand man, and was in Bolivia to foment a revolution, but was caught and killed before he could achieve any measurable success. We had his fountain pen and a knife in our display case at the 8th Group headquarters.

Joe went on his third or fourth tour of duty in Vietnam. He was a radio communications specialist by skill set. The 5th Special Forces Group was sending teams of American and Vietnamese military into North Vietnam on operational and intelligence missions. If a team was not heard from after the parachute infiltration, the protocol was to send in two radio operators and radio equipment under the assumption that something had happened to the first team's radio operators and or the equipment. Joe, and another radio operator, and that "A" Team were never heard from again.

Parachute training, 1969, Gatun Locks Drop Zone, Ft. Sherman, Panama Canal Zone [Captain Ray Orr, 610th Military Intelligence Detachment, 8th Special Forces Group (Airborne)]. Photo courtesy Steve Heubeck

Later, in 1975, I was in Puerto Rico working as an FBI Agent and was reading the "Army Times." I was looking over the names of military personnel who had died in Vietnam prison camps in 1974, and I saw Joe's name. Joe and the "A" Team had been compromised by a U.S. Navy Spy group (The Walkers) who forwarded the infiltration information to the North Vietnamese who were waiting for them when they landed in North Vietnam. The FBI worked the Walkers spy investigation, and ended up arresting several family members who were part of the spy ring.

One day my unit commander, Lt. Col. Mervin Brock, told me a story about something that happened during his tour in Vietnam. The Viet Cong (VC) captured two Army Intelligence officers, one CIA field officer and two Christian Science nurses. The VC released the two nurses making them promise as a condition of their release that they not tell anyone which direction they were going. When a military rescue unit found the nurses, they stayed true to their promise and did not cooperate with the rescue team. This, Lt. Col. Brock claimed, doomed those three men to torture and certain death. He, of course, asked why, and I told him that it was their personal choice not to help, but that the religion did not have anything to do with it.

After I left the Army I took up skydiving. I met a fellow jumper named Carl Beck, a WWII veteran. Carl had been on a full football scholarship to Syracuse when the war broke out, and he enlisted in the Army, volunteered for parachute training, and was ultimately assigned to the 82nd Airborne Division. He parachuted into France (I think it was Ste. Mère Église) during the invasion and was horribly wounded in the face.

Carl lost hearing in one ear and lost one eye. He told me that he had over fourteen operations on his face after the war. The ear and eye problem meant that he could not free-fall straight down. He was always listing to one side and slid away from us as we maneuvered in the air to make what are known in the sport as "stars" groups (of eight or more jumpers in a circular formation holding onto the other jumper's jump suit sleeves). So we would have to "fly" down to Carl, grab him, make adjustments to his body position, and then build the "star" around him. We were finally able to get him his coveted eight man star patch. It was the least that we could do for someone who gave so much of himself for America. Carl Beck would make several commemorative jumps in France during the anniversary of the D Day Invasion, usually ending up with a malfunction of some sort. He was a link, to me, to "the greatest generation."

The military taught me many things about people, myself, duty, honor, mission — lessons I have embraced and used for my adult life. It was an honor to serve my country, even though it was during a dirty and horrible war in a contentious time. From where I was coming, it was my time to serve, and I did. I later continued my service to my fellow countrymen, and to this nation, by joining the FBI, a goal of mine since I was twelve years old.

STEVEN HEUBECK was sent to Fort Holabird for further training in intelligence work after basic training at Fort Bragg, North Carolina, where he attended the Defense Language Institute West Coast (Spanish) School. Assigned to the 470 MI Group, Ft. Amador, Panama Canal Zone, Heubeck was subsequently advanced by direct commission to the rank of second lieutenant. Transferred to the 610 MI Detachment, 8th Special Forces Group Airborne [SFG(A)], Heubeck spent part of his Canal Zone duty at Fort Gulick, Panama, a post on the Atlantic side of the Panama Canal on Gatun Lake from which the 8th Special Forces Group operated in Central and South America. [Famously, it was the 8th SFG(A), just prior to Heubeck's arrival, that had participated in the training of a Bolivian Ranger unit which pursued Ernesto "Che" Guevara and his guerillas. Che was the Marxist leader of the earlier Cuban Revolution who in the mid-1960s promoted similar socialist revolutions in the Congo and then in Bolivia. In late 1966 and 1967, Che led a well-equipped guerrilla force of about fifty men operating as the National Liberation Army of Bolivia and mounted successful skirmishes in the mountainous Camiri region [Cordillera Province] of Bolivia. By late summer 1967 the Bolivian army began to turn the tide against the guerillas, and with the aid of a CIA special-divisions operative, Bolivian special forces were able to locate and execute Che in October 1967.] Soon after, Heubeck spent time in Bolivia as part of a Mobile Training Team conducting training for the Bolivian army at the request of the U.S.

Military Group at the U.S. embassy. Recipient of a good conduct ribbon, National Defense Ribbon, and Army Commendation Medal, Heubeck was also parachute qualified and awarded parachute wings.

After completing his military career in 1970, Heubeck spent twenty-eight years in the FBI assigned to the investigation of violent crimes, including bank robberies, kidnappings and extortions, and drugs. While in the FBI Heubeck was Bureau Firearms and Defensive Tactics Instructor, in charge of FBI SWAT Teams in New York and New Haven, Connecticut. He was also police training coordinator of the New York office, coordinating FBI instructors in the training of local, state, and federal law enforcement officers, for which he received the FBI's master police instructor award. He has taught at the Rockland and Westchester Police Academies. As Director of the City University of New York (CUNY) Public Safety Training Academy in New York City, Heubeck was responsible for the training and re-certification of 500 peace officers.

Born in Baltimore, Maryland, in 1944, Heubeck was raised in Andover, Massachusetts, and began his studies at Principia College in 1962. A resident of Brooks House South, Heubeck joined the varsity track team and was a member of the soccer club, Prisoc, which developed into a recognized varsity campus sport by the time of his senior year. He also served on the campus fire crew. Majoring in political science and international relations, Heubeck received his BA degree in 1966, entering the military later that same year. Heubeck married Nancy Neil, a college co-ed from the class of 1967; they have a son Daniel Alan Heubeck. Still active as a police training coordinator, Heubeck is currently working to become a certified Adaptive Alpine Ski Instructor so he can teach Wounded Warriors to ski.

"The Lieutenant was Shot at, and They Missed": Infantry Missions from Chu Lai to Marble Mountain

ROBERT (ROB) B. OSTENBERG

In 1965, I graduated from high school in St. Louis, Missouri, (Principia) and went to Miami, Florida, where I would begin my college career. It was inevitable, and I was resigned to the idea, that there was an uncertain date in the not too distant future when I would be called into military duty. During the summer between my freshman and sophomore years, I was working full time on the night shift as the foreman and lead melter in a lost wax metal foundry in West Palm Beach. I continued taking courses during the summer since it had become a routine, and I would have extra college credit hours.

In February, 1967, my father passed away, and my mother relocated to St. Louis to be a house mother in the girls' dormitory at the high school I had attended. At the same time my older brother got his draft notice, and months later, he was in the Army. My brother served three consecutive tours in Vietnam.[34] This validated my apprehension about my certain future. After my sophomore year, I transferred to a college in Elsah, Illinois (Principia College). Following a review of my transcript, I lost credit for courses such as humanities, engineering, data processing, journalism, and more. I was back to being a third-quarter freshman. Losing my II-S Selective Service student deferment classification was a real possibility. To graduate on time, I had to take a foreign language for five of my six remaining college quarters, and recoup over a year's worth of credit hours. Short story is, I was able

---

34 See William H. Ostenberg IV, "Answering the Call," in this volume.

to graduate with my class in June, 1969, by taking extra courses each quarter and courses in the summer. I also participated and lettered in football, wrestling, and track each season.

During this time, I was seeing news coverage of protests, some peaceful and many not so. America was deeply divided by reactions to counter culture agendas and to the war itself. Vietnam was not a popular war, and those who served in the military were not held in high regard. However, many of my classmates volunteered for military service following graduation in 1969.

I, on the other hand, feeling lucky, packed my car and went to Martha's Vineyard for the summer. I planned to return to St. Louis later in the fall and enlist in the Army. I lived in Vineyard Haven and worked near Edgartown. Life and people there were fantastic. After the Edward Kennedy / Mary Jo Kopechne incident on Chappaquiddick Island, visitors inundated the island, and I escaped by finding a job as a first mate for a family sailing up the coast to Maine. The next month was wonderful and the family very gracious as we sailed into ports to spend several days before moving on. Once a week, I would · find a pay phone and call to check in with a friend in Vineyard Haven. We were returning and in Booth Bay, Maine, when I called and was told that I had a registered letter from the Selective Service. I told my employer my situation, caught the next bus back to Falmouth, Massachusetts, and then caught the ferry to the island. I packed my car, and drove to St. Louis, having heard that if you enter the service there, you would be sent to Fort Ord, California, for basic training.

After enlisting, I went to the St. Louis Induction Center (MEPS), took some tests, and had a physical exam. Found fit for duty, California here I come! I entered the Army on October 23, 1969. While hundreds of the recruits got orders for Fort Ord, a small group of us were sent to Fort Dix, New Jersey. In hindsight, this had something to do with our test scores, as we all were selected later to go to Officer Candidate School (OCS).

My company of basic trainees, had incredibly gifted young men, including a sub-four-minute miler from Notre Dame. We ran a mile in combat boots for physical training, and he set the post record, at four minutes and fourteen seconds I recall, which likely still stands today. Another was a Citadel graduate who declined the commission to second lieutenant (2nd Lt.), and another had a PhD: both enlisted "to get the experience." We were all competitive and always tried to get the maximum scores in every aspect of training.

After basic training, we went to Fort Leonard Wood, Missouri, for combat engineer Advanced Individual Training (AIT). They called Leonard Wood "little Korea," and it lived up to the reputation in January and February. It was great training, and, by the end, Infantry OCS was a lock for the group from St. Louis and for several other soldiers.

Encampment, Vietnam.
Photo courtesy Rob Ostenberg

In early March, 1970, I was at Fort Benning, Georgia, where for the next six months, the 220 candidates would try to survive the training to become infantry officers and earn the rank of second lieutenant. Some of my college classmates were there eight weeks ahead of me, and I would see them at church. At the end of OCS, only forty-nine in my class graduated, and I decided to change my branch to armor. I was sent to Fort Knox, Kentucky, where I had a great experience and worked with dedicated soldiers. I might add that my company commander was a captain and a Medal of Honor recipient. It was due to his influence that I volunteered for duty in Vietnam in March of 1971.

After a three week jungle operations training course in Panama, I flew to Cam Ranh Bay, Vietnam, about 180 miles northeast of Saigon. Looking out the window during the decent, I saw an expansive field of bomb craters in the ground below, and my first thought was, "What have I gotten myself in to?" From Cam Ranh Bay I flew north to Chu Lai which was in First Corps (I Corps). My assignment was as an infantry platoon leader in A Company, 1st Battalion, 6th Infantry, 198th Infantry Brigade, 23d Infantry Division (Americal).

Huey helicoptor insertion and pick up in Vietnam.
Photo courtesy Rob Ostenberg

My platoon, while never at one hundred percent strength, was very effective, and they were good soldiers. I have been asked about drugs in Vietnam. We were subject to unannounced testing, and I never had anyone in my unit test positive. It probably had a lot to do with our operational tempo. Generally, we were inserted by "Huey" helicopters into a natural clearing or landing zone (LZ) in the mountainous jungle west of Chu Lai where we would operate against the North Vietnamese Army (NVA) who were moving supplies south or building up caches in preparation for attacks on our bases. We would then spend on average fifteen to twenty days looking for contact. Rules of engagement were simple. It was a "free fire" zone with only enemy forces in the area. So if it moved, eliminate it. We kept moving every day, stopped at night to rest, and continued on the next day. We did not wear "flack vests," or helmets, and everything we needed was in our backpacks (rucksacks), which weighed around eighty-plus pounds. At the end of a mission, when the six or seven helicopters were coming to pick us up, we carried lots of "C4" explosives to blow the trees and vegetation down to make a large clearing for the extraction. One helicopter at a time, with six men on each one. I was first in and the last out. We would be in the rear for three days and would run night ambushes the first two nights. Then, on the third day, we'd refit, and then back out into the bush.

On day three of my very first mission, we were cutting across a trail when a sniper fired on us. The bullet went right by my neck, grazed my shoulder, and went right through my ruck sack frame. The threat was taken care of, and a comment followed: "the lieutenant was shot at, and they missed, so that's done; it will be a smooth mission from here on out." It is worth mentioning that I carried my religious books and tried to get inspiration and thoughts of protection from them, and it proved most helpful. In addition, some of the girls at the college in Illinois, were typing out the weekly Bible lesson, and sending it to several of us, and Christian Science was an absolutely vital part of helping me keep my head in the game, focused and alert, and maintain our high moral standards.

Several missions later, in the morning of the fifth day, I received a called from my company commander. He told me there were signs of activity in the area that he and another platoon were searching, and he told me to come as soon as possible (ASAP). I looked at my map, plotted their location, and figured that, with the terrain, it would take several hours. We moved out, and I was really disappointed because the route passed through an area recently searched by another platoon. If this were discovered by the enemy, they would be very alert and possibly waiting to ambush any of our troops. It also meant that there weren't any stashes of food or enemy equipment to find. About halfway there, I sensed a mildew or odd rotting cloth smell that was out of place. I had a thought, or an inner voice, that directed me to

do something that defied common sense and contradicted the movement order I had received earlier. I told my point man to move ninety
degrees to the left, and about thirty meters in, and I directed my men
to set up a perimeter. I am sure they were all thinking I was nuts, but
I was being directed to search. With the perimeter secure, I selected a
few of my men to begin a search. Within minutes, we found a cache
of mortars, rifles, ammunition, food (including several large woven
bamboo containers holding an estimated three tons of rice), and plans
for an attack on one of our own fire bases. It was the largest find by
any unit in the area, and with its capture, we eliminated the ability
of the North Vietnamese to carry out the planned attack against us.

Cache of weapons. Photo courtesy Rob Ostenberg

I requested helicopter support to extract the weapons, and we were
able to get most of them out, but we would have to remain in the area
overnight and resume the next morning. That night, from below our
defensive position, we could hear the clucking of chickens and what
sounded like a goat. The next morning the extraction continued, and
we loaded the last of the mortar shells. My commander radioed to
make sure all the rice was sent back too. The only way we could have
gotten it out was to carry it, one hat full at a time, up to the landing
zone that we cut for the helicopters, and I do not know how loose
rice could be flown out; so I apologized to the captain and told him
we had already blown up the containers and the rice was scattered
over the steep mountain side. He approved and told me to come to

his new location, and he gave me the grid coordinates. As we moved out, I blew up the bins of rice.

I decided to walk point (the lead person in the formation). When we were a safe distance away from the cache site, I called in a tactical air bomb strike at that location. It was approved and executed, eliminating whatever might be in the tunnels below. Normally, I did not like to walk on the trails due to booby traps and enemy ambushes. However in this particular case, we were in steep and rough terrain, so we used a trail. At one point, rocks began to fall from above. Without hesitation, two of my men took aim on the location above us as I scrambled up the steep slope. There was nothing there, and we assumed it was an animal.

Rocket fire, Vietnam.
Photo courtesy Rob Ostenberg

About one hundred meters away from the other platoon, there was a direct route straight to their location that would take us about five minutes to join the others. However, it was across open ground, and I was not comfortable with the exposure. We stopped for a moment, and I listened for guidance. I elected to follow the tree line and circle to the opposite side, then climb up a steep cliff to enter their perimeter, a route that would take about thirty minutes. When I was about ten feet from the top of the cliff, I could hear a soldier hitting a tree with a machete, some talking off to our left, and movement at the top but off to our right. I radioed the platoon and told them that we were close and to let their perimeter guards know. The reply was that they didn't have perimeter guards, and we would have that task when we arrived. I told the other platoon that we heard movement coming toward them. I quickly got to the top of the cliff where there was some concealment and saw the North Vietnamese Army soldiers with rifles and grenades moving toward the sound of our sister platoon. I was able to get my radio man and two others with me, and we engaged the NVA, eliminating an attack that probably would have ended with thirty to forty of our soldiers killed.

1st Cavalry Regiment, 196 infantry brigade.
Photo courtesy Rob Ostenberg

In October, the division left Vietnam, and several of my men and I were reassigned to A Troop, First Regiment, First Cavalry, located at Marble Mountain, near Da Nang to the north. I was a platoon leader and had three M551 Sheridan tanks, six M114 armored personnel carriers (APCs), and one mortar track, providing lots of fire power. Missions were in the low lands, and we were very effective. I had a Kit Carson Scout (a North Vietnamese soldier we captured who agreed to work with our army); he was very good, and I trusted and had absolute faith in him. He never let me down.

In mid-April, 1972, American combat forces were down to 96,000, and our unit left Vietnam. I out processed at the Oakland Army Base, California, where I received my steak dinner and watched the movie *Bambi*. I had heard about the poor treatment received by those military, and specifically soldiers, returning from Vietnam, and it bothered me. However, when I left the base, I went un-noticed and faded into the fabric of those who, other than my short hair, looked pretty much like me.

Months later, I was pondering my service and realized that I had some character building experiences and learned some life lessons that one could only have as a member of our military. Not for any one reason, but perhaps for not having regrets in the future, I joined an Army Reserve unit nearby, and, over the more than thirty-nine years of my total military service, I served in every leadership position from platoon leader to commanding general of a division of 14,000 men and women. From 2001 to 2005, when I was reassigned, over 9,500 of my soldiers deployed to Afghanistan and Iraq and seven other countries. My time with them there made me proud of all who selflessly serve in the military. My final assignment was as a Director, North American Aerospace Defense Command (NORAD) and

"Kit Carson scout," A Company, 1st Squadron, 1st Cavalry Regiment (196th Brigade). Photo courtesy Rob Ostenberg

United States Northern Command (USNORTHCOM) in Colorado Springs, Colorado, where I retired at the end of 2008.

At my retirement ceremony, an ambassador and good friend gave me a gift of an old military compass in a display box which I cherish. The inscription reads: To Major General Robert B. Ostenberg 'His Compass is True.' My parents, my family, my religion, my educators, and my military experiences that tested my metal, all contributed to the perception of who I am. I have no regrets, and I am grateful that I gave the military another go after Vietnam. I am proud that the public opinion, in many polls since 2001, ranks the military in the top three most respected professions. And today, as Americans celebrate the 50th anniversary of the Vietnam War, they too are expressing gratitude toward those who served there.

ROBERT B. OSTENBERG began his military career as an enlisted soldier. After boot camp at Fort Dix, New Jersey, he attended the Infantry Officers Candidate School at Fort Benning, Georgia, and was commissioned a second lieutenant in September 1970. Active duty assignments took him to Fort Davis, Panama, Chu Lai, and Black Hawk Hill/Marble Mountain, Vietnam. His service in Vietnam from 1971 to 1972 was as a platoon leader with the 1st Battalion, 6th Infantry and with the 1st Regiment, 1st Cavalry of the 23d Infantry Division. Following active duty, Ostenberg continued in the Army Reserve and was assigned to the 91st Division (Training), in San Jose, California. He remained in the reserves for another thirty-six years (1972-2008), rising to the rank of major general. He has held every military leadership position from platoon leader to commanding general of a division of 14,000 active duty troops, reservists, and civilians. Between 2001 and 2008 military duty has sent Ostenberg three times to Kuwait, twice (each) to Afghanistan, Uzbekistan, and Guantanamo, Cuba, and to Qatar and Iraq.

Ostenberg came from a military family. His father, Captain William H. Ostenberg III, served in Africa and Burma in the U.S. Army Air Corps during World War II. His father-in-law Captain Jack Troster served in the Marines in the Pacific during World War II. (*His* father, Army Colonel Oliver Troster had chased Poncho Vila with his cavalry unit in 1916 and subsequently served in both World War I and World War II.) Ostenberg's great great-grandfather Colonel George L. Godfrey served in the Civil War. More recently, Major General Ostenberg's brother, Chief Sergeant Major William H. Ostenberg IV, served three tours in Vietnam, and two cousins, First Lieutenant Steve Ostenberg Spaulding (Army, Vietnam) and Staff Sergeant Clark Spaulding (U.S. Air Force, Okinawa, Japan, supporting Vietnam), were also military veterans; cousin Steve and brother William (Chip) are also authors in this anthology.

Born in 1947 in Scotts Bluff, Nebraska, Robert Ostenberg's hometown at the time he went to college was Palm Beach, Florida, although he whimsically lists the "girls' dormitory, Principia Upper School" as hometown, since his mother had moved to the boarding school to serve as housemother after the death of Rob's father, so the housemother's apartment was "home." Many in his family would have Principia connections: his father had attended Principia College for a year prior to transferring to the University of Colorado. His brother Chip graduated from both the Upper School (1964) and College (1973) and another brother Thomas graduated from the college in 1971. His sister Helen (Elswit), following her Upper School graduation in 1969, earned her college degree at

Principia in 1974. Another sister Susan (Henn) worked in the admissions office at the college in the 1970s. If Ostenberg's rise from enlisted platoon leader to Army major general was a case of "from rags to riches," his Principia career was not dissimilar. As a student he worked as a waiter, dishwasher, and clean-up worker in food service, a staff worker in the "Pub," and a grounds keeper. At the same time he lettered in varsity football, wrestling, and track. After graduation [C69] he would become Prin Club president, a member of the alumni board, and a member of the trustees council.

Among Principia's alumni, Major General Ostenberg has had one of the most distinguished military careers in the school's history. His military education includes Airborne School, Jungle Operations, Armor Officer Basic and Advanced Courses, the U.S. Army Command and General Staff College, and the U.S. Army War College. In 2005 the commander of the Joint Chiefs of Staff named Ostenberg Director, Reserve Forces, with additional duty as one of five Domestic Attack Assessors (DAA) which included Attack Assessment and Engagement Authority (EA) at North American Aerospace Defense Command (NORAD) and United States Northern Command (USNORTHCOM), Peterson Air Force Base, Colorado. In recognition of his service, Ostenberg has received the Distinguished Service Medal, the Defense Superior Service Medal , the Legion of Merit (with Oak Leaf Cluster), the Bronze Star with "V" device (with

Oak Leaf Cluster), the Purple Heart, the Meritorious Service Medal (with Silver and Bronze Oak Leaf Clusters), the Air Medal (with numeral 2), the Army Commendation Medal, the Army Achievement Medal, the National Defense Service Medal (with two bronze service stars), the Combat Infantry Badge, and the Parachutist Badge. In civilian life, Major General Ostenberg is an Advanced Field Underwriting Consultant for Financial and Estate Planning, Metropolitan Life, San Jose, California. In late 2013, Ostenberg returned to Vietnam on a Principia Adult Continuing Education [PACE] tour. Married to Gretchen Troster Ostenberg (US 67 and C71), Ostenberg has one daughter, Daisy (US99, C03, married to Rick Holland (C01), and two grandchildren. Major General Ostenberg is retired and lives in Woodside, California.

Artillery raid 175mm. Photo courtesy Jim Chamberlin

Shelling the Ho Chi Minh Trail: Travels with Mobes

JAMES W. CHAMBERLIN

After I graduated from Prin in 1967, it was pretty clear that I would be drafted if I did not maintain my student deferment. I decided that law school would be easier than graduate school in mathematics, and I managed to get into the University of Georgia Law School. After I finished my first year, however, my draft board said no more student deferment. When I went for my draft physical, one of the doctors encouraged me to apply for an officer candidate program that would only mean a two year commitment, like the draft, if I did not get commissioned. As a result I sort of volunteered for the draft with the option of going to officer candidate school. My military career was a bipartisan effort; I was essentially drafted by Lyndon Johnson in 1968 and sent to Vietnam by Richard Nixon in 1969.

I went through basic training at Fort Leonard Wood in Missouri during the winter of 1968-69. The majority of trainees in my basic training class were not going to Vietnam; they were in either the National Guard or the Army Reserve and were going back home after their training. We had an African American drill sergeant, and I still had a pretty strong southern accent justifying my Prin nickname of "Mobes" for saying my hometown of Mobile, Alabama, with such a drawl that nobody at Prin could understand it. Because I had been to college and was going on to OCS (Officer Candidate School), the drill sergeant made me a squad leader. As the training went on, it turned out that most of the other trainees who were going on into the regular Army and then to Vietnam were African American. The drill sergeant ended up putting all the African Americans in my squad, presumably to make us all learn to live with each other. One man in my squad was from the old Pruitt-Igoe slum housing development in St. Louis. He periodically threatened to kill me by having an accident at the firing range. The drill sergeant had us fight each other with pugil sticks, giving him the chance to beat the tar out of me. But he remained in my squad, and we continued to make it through basic training. At the end of our training, we made identical scores on our physical training test, and he congratulated me. I was amazed. It seemed as if we had developed some kind of a bond, thanks largely to our African American drill sergeant who was good at his job, and we moved on to the next stage of our Army careers.

Jim Chamberlin. Photo courtesy Jim Chamberlin

I remember flying home to Mobile on leave, probably for Christmas, on the same plane with an old high school classmate who was also in training at Fort Leonard Wood. He had also finished one year of law school, but was in the National Guard, going back home after training, not to Vietnam. He went on to become attorney general of Alabama.

From Fort Leonard Wood, I went to Fort Sill, Oklahoma, for advanced individual training [AIT] in artillery. Compared to basic training, AIT was relatively uneventful. The main thing I remember is that one of the men in our unit was a professional, minor league baseball pitcher, whose main job seemed to be to pitch for the company baseball team and who seemed destined to stay in AIT forever.

From AIT, I moved to artillery officer candidate school at Fort Sill. I was serious, but I was influenced by the general anti-war feeling in the country, so that I was not inclined to put up with a lot of foolishness, and it seemed like there was a lot of foolishness at OCS. I was pretty constantly in trouble, and the main penalty for being in trouble was being forced to run something they called the JARK.[35] It consisted of running 4.2 miles up what they said was the highest mountain in Oklahoma (a medium sized hill) with a full pack, combat boots, etc. However, I did it so often that I could pretty much do it with my eyes closed, and it probably meant that I was in the best physical shape of my life. In addition, I could knock off twenty-five or fifty fairly decent pushups several times a day.

About half way through OCS, there was a big celebration of the first Air Force "Ace" who had shot down the requisite number of enemy planes. It turned out that he had a mustache, which until then had been banned by the military. Because the publicity said that mustaches would now be allowed, I started growing one. It took a few days for anybody to notice, but when they did, all hell broke loose. I did enough pushups and jarks that I could no longer be blasé, and my muscles began to notice, not to mention my response to cleaning latrines and doing any other terrible things that the OCS instructors could think of. But I was still in the program.

That ended, however, when a few weeks before graduation our whole company was restricted to the barracks during a three-day weekend on some general principle that we weren't good enough to deserve any free time. I decided to take food orders and get everybody

---

35 An unofficial history of the artillery OCS notes that the first commandant (1941-42) of the artillery OCS at Fort Sill was Captain Carl H. Jark, who went on to be a general. Describing the 4.2-mile "Jark" run, the history records, "The term 'Jark,' was coined by the OCS Cadre to describe a fast-paced disciplinary tour from Robinson Barracks to the top of Medicine Bluff 4 (MB4) and back at port arms, a physically onerous task. The 'Jarks' were held every Saturday and Sunday afternoon for those candidates who had accumulated an excessive number of demerits or other violations...The step was thirty inches and the pace was 130 steps per minute. The prescribed uniform varied throughout the school's history, but in most cases it was the fatigue uniform, baseball cap, pistol belt with full canteen, poncho with first-aid kit, combat boots, and rifle." "Artillery Officer Candidate School, 1943-1973, OCS Historic Overview Fort Sill and Field Artillery School History" (Revised 9/17/13). *http://www.faocsalumni.org/documents/faocshistorybook.pdf*

burgers and fries from a hamburger stand on base. I thought that if I did not leave the base, I would get in trouble, but not get thrown out of OCS. I was wrong. I got thrown out, along with about ten of my colleagues. One ended up being one of my best friends. His offense was to go outside the barracks to speak to his wife in the company parking lot while she sat in the car. When we started OCS, there were several candidates from Ivy League schools, one from Cal Tech, and my friend who had finished one year of law school, as I had. I don't think anyone who had gone to an elite school or who was working on an advanced degree finished OCS. I think this was at least partly due to the fact that the war was starting to wind down. When we had signed up for OCS about a year earlier, it had looked like the U.S. would need more officers than it did as graduation approached. So, the class took a big hit about a week before graduation. For most of us it was not entirely bad, because we reverted to a two-year service obligation.

Getting kicked out of OCS was a guaranteed ticket to Vietnam. My law school colleague and I ended up with basically the same orders, sending us to Dong Ha, Vietnam, near the DMZ (demili-tarized zone). We ended up as "chief computers" for two different batteries in the same heavy artillery battalion. Chief computers were specialist-5 section chiefs who ran the fire direction centers of the artillery units. The fire direction center talked to the troops in the field and figured up the data to send to the guns to shoot the fire missions requested by the troops in the field, or more often from some intelligence officer back in the rear. Since artillery usually cannot see what it is shooting at, the fire direction center figures a direction and elevation that the guns apply from a fixed reference point to hit the target. It is basically an exercise in trigonometry that could be done easily and instantaneously by a calculator or computer today, but was more difficult back then. We did have computers to figure the data, although we always had to double check them by figuring the data by hand. The FADAC computers were about the size of a footlocker, ran on several car batteries that had to be charged continually, and displayed their results in old nixie tubes that contained light bulb filaments shaped like numbers.

We arrived from the United States at Cam Ranh Bay, where we waited for a plane to Dong Ha. I remember looking at a map there, where the dot for Dong Ha would not fit entirely in South Vietnam, but jutted across the DMZ into North Vietnam. This was what the Army called northern I Corps. From Cam Ranh Bay we flew to Da Nang, where I was amazed at the busiest airport I had ever seen, with fighter jets and transports tailgating each other down the runway. In the terminal, however, things looked pretty normal. Everybody was pretty clean and relaxed looking. One soldier, though, looked like someone out of the old Willie and Joe cartoons from World War II. He was dirty, his uniform was ragged, and he had a glazed, far-away look in his eye, the only one like that of the hundreds in the airport. My friend asked him where he was from. It turned out that he was from the DMZ. When my friend told him we were going to Dong Ha, he said something like, "I just came from there. I heard the A-2 base was overrun the night before last. I suppose you are going to replace some of the men who were killed there." We were not pleased to be going to where the one man in the airport who looked like he had been in a war had just left.

I remember flying into Dong Ha on a C-123 transport plane. I don't know whether the pilot was putting us on or not, but he said that they had had a lot of planes blown up on the ground in Dong Ha, so they were not going to stop. They would land, slow down, lower the back cargo door, and we should grab our stuff and run away from the plane as fast as we could. We did, and the plane accelerated and took off without turning around. There we were in the bright sunshine, in the middle of a quiet, green grassy landing strip that could have been a park in any American city.

That night we joined twenty or so other men in a tent waiting for assignment. There was a lot of drinking and poker playing going on despite some shooting heard outside, until someone came running in to say that we were under mortar attack and Vietcong were using the lights in our tent as their target. The next day I was assigned to A battery of the 2/94th Artillery, a heavy artillery battery with eight-inch howitzers and 175 mm guns, which was stationed with one brigade of the 101st Division at LZ Sally, near the town of Quang Tri.

Replacing a gun tube. Photo courtesy Jim Chamberlin

It felt pretty good to be stationed with 101st Airborne. The LZ Sally base camp was on a ridge looking north, and we could often watch the firefights in the valley below. From our safe distance the tracers were like a fireworks show. There was different fireworks show every night when another artillery battery would adjust fire for defensive targets on our perimeter using white phosphorous rounds which lit up the sky so that you could see them easily.

During one firefight, the battleship USS *New Jersey* [BB-62] was off shore, and she joined us in providing support to the troops in the field. When we talked to her on the radio, it was like listening to a commercial FM station back in the states, compared to the weak hissing and cackling communications we had with individual forward observers with the infantry. When it shoots close support for troops, an artillery battery tells them, "Shot" when the guns fire and "Splash" about five seconds before the rounds hit, so that they know to duck to avoid shrapnel from the friendly fire. When *New Jersey* told the troops, "Splash," everyone in our battery who could, ran outside to try to see the 2,000 pound rounds go off, but we never saw or heard them.

There were some Cobra helicopters stationed on the LZ which would periodically go out and shoot at stuff on our perimeter. Watching the Cobra miniguns fire a solid stream of tracers was pretty impressive. Even more impressive was watching the occasional visit of "Spooky" to shoot around the perimeter. An even bigger column of tracers streamed out of the side of the converted cargo plane. During these operations there were usually loud speakers broadcasting the "Chieu Hoi" invitation to the enemy to surrender.

After a few months, we parted ways with the 101st and went off on our own to an old Marine fire base called LZ Sharon. The Vietnamization of the war was starting, so instead of American infantry protecting us we had Vietnamese troops and American air defense artillery. At LZ Sharon, the Vietnamese troops were draft dodgers who had been caught, but the Vietnamese Army would not give them guns; so they had clubs and knives. Our air defense artillery was a quad-50 machine gun, four 50-caliber machine guns mounted together on the back of a five-ton truck. Because it was closer, when it fired the tracers made almost as good a fireworks show as the platoons of infantry back at LZ Sally. For some reason, probably because as chief computer I was pretty good at calculating how to aim artillery, I had my own 81 mm mortar. However, I only had illumination rounds to support the quad-50; I did not have any high explosive rounds. Most of our battery's shooting was done at night. Usually around 4:00 in the morning everything would quiet down, and the guys on the quad-50 and I would be about the only people awake. I would shoot some illumination rounds along our perimeter, and the quad-50 guys would look for any movement. If they saw any movement, we would have to clear a whole map "grid square," a square kilometer, with higher authorities before the quad-50 was allowed to shoot. It was not exactly rapid response, but perhaps it let the bad guys know, if there were any out there, that somebody was awake.

We were at LZ Sharon during monsoon season, and the moisture meant that the powder in the eight-inch howitzers burned more slowly. As a result there was usually a huge flash as the projectile left the barrel and the unburned powder hit the air. In our fire direction center, the explosion would make the dust on the desks and the floor rise up about an inch and then settle back down. One night, after a particularly loud shot, the plywood walls of the "hooch" where we were working fell off, and we were left standing in the two-by-four framing in the middle of the night.

Bob Hope Christmas Show, Phu Bai, December 1969.
Photo courtesy Jim Chamberlin

I think it was while we were at LZ Sharon that I saw Bob Hope's Christmas show in December, 1969. It was at the Phu Bai combat base near Hue, which was a long drive for us. I don't remember much except telling my mother to look for me on TV, sitting about ten rows behind the guy with a monkey on his shoulder. She always claimed that she saw me, although it was unlikely in that sea of uniforms. Still, it was very patriotic of Bob Hope to come, and it was encouraging when there was so much opposition to the war to feel that there was someone publicly supporting us.

From LZ Sharon, we moved to Firebase Barbara on a mountaintop west of Quang Tri, close enough to Laos that we could shell the Ho Chi Minh trail that ran along the border. At Barbara we had two eight-inch howitzers and two 175-mm guns. The eight-inchers could fire about ten miles, and the 175s about twenty miles, but less accurately. They gave us pretty long coverage up and down the Ho Chi Minh trail. We also did more close support of American troops than we had done since we had parted from the 101st division. I never knew who we were shooting for, but they sounded like Special Forces, if only because they were so calm in combat. We would be adjusting fire for them, walking the rounds in closer, and they would very calmly say something like, "They are in the wire, too close for you to shoot at now; you'll have to wait awhile." I only learned from a *Time* magazine subscription I had that an American Special Forces base at Mai Loc had been overrun. I recognized the name because it was marked on our charts as a no-fire zone. I wondered why we had not been asked to shoot support for them, but I realized that they were east of us and our battery was designed to shoot west, terraced down the western side of the mountain. If we had tried to shoot east, we would probably have blown off the top of the mountain. Somebody on the internet says that former Secretary of Veterans Affairs General Eric Shinseki (then Captain Shinseki) was sent to relieve Mai Loc, but obviously didn't make it in time.

Road to Firebase Barbara. Photo courtesy Jim Chamberlin

One night we received a warning from our battalion headquarters back in Dong Ha that intelligence (probably infra-red sensors) showed a large group of enemy soldiers assembling at the bottom of our mountain. At Barbara, we had swapped our old anti-aircraft quad-50 weapon at Sharon for a pair of "dusters," old anti-aircraft tracked vehicles that fired twin 40mm cannons, again a steady stream of tracers. Because these anti-aircraft artillery units were almost always stationed in the "boonies" in somewhat dangerous locations, they had a reputation as "space cadets" who didn't pay much attention to doing stuff by the book.

Duster. Photo courtesy Jim Chamberlin

They were our main defense, although in theory we also had Vietnamese infantry to defend us. After the attack warning, our battalion supply officer in Dong Ha came on the radio to tell us not to give any gasoline to the dusters. We had gasoline to run our fire direction center generators. He said it was too difficult to resupply us, and the dusters were notorious for not maintaining their supplies. However, we decided that if the dusters were our main line of defense, we were going to give them all the gas they needed. The dusters blew away a grid square (a square kilometer) or more where the intelligence said the enemy was forming, and no attack occurred. We never knew whether we had averted an attack or the intelligence had just picked up a herd of deer grazing at the bottom of the mountain. I think Barbara is the only place I remember seeing an air strike by Phantom jets. They bombed one of the mountains nearby, but we never knew why.

On April 29, 1970, while we were firing at something on the Ho Chi Minh trail, the breech blew out of one of the 175-mm guns, killing two of the crew and wounding several others. The names of those who died, Paul Kosanke and Willie Austin, are inscribed on the wall of the Vietnam memorial.

Charlie I entry to base. Photo courtesy Jim Chamberlin

A more pleasant memory was when a helicopter flew out a huge bladder of water, which it tried to drop on the mess hall, a bunker. He dropped it from too high up. It bounced off the roof of the mess hall and rolled down the mountain. Later, a flatbed truck made it all the way to the base along the dangerous, often-mined road back to the coast, carrying a new "tube" (barrel) for one of the 175-mm guns. He was almost at the top of the steep, winding road up the mountain, when the tube began to slip off the back of the truck, and it too rolled down the mountain. Since it weighed several tons, it's probably still there.

From Firebase Barbara we went back near Dong Ha, to Charlie-1, one of the bases along the DMZ. It was in theory the safest of these bases because it was the southern-most and eastern-most of this line. Those closest to the DMZ were labeled A, as in A-1, A-2, etc. B Bases were the next line, and C bases were the third and last line. The numbering started from the east, near the coast with 1, and went up as you went west. Presumably Khe Sanh would have been the western anchor of this line of bases.

Carpet bombing near DMZ. Photo courtesy Jim Chamberlin

At Charlie-1 we did more shooting during the daytime. Often an Air Force forward air controller would fly up and down the DMZ in a small plane like a Cessna. If he found something big, he would call in an air strike, but if he found something small he would call us. Often he would call a fire mission on "footprints in the sand." We would start shooting where he said the footprints disappeared, and usually someone would emerge running back toward North Vietnam because they knew that we were forbidden to shoot into North Vietnam. We would try to get him before he could get back to the river dividing the north from the south.

At least once, maybe more times, the Air Force would fly what we called an Arc Light mission. A fleet of B-52s would fly over the DMZ and carpet bomb it. The rumble and shaking was like an earthquake. We could see many vapor trails in the sky, but I don't remember their being challenged by the North Vietnamese.

As I neared the end of my two year hitch, the Army offered a deal to let people out a few weeks early to go to school. I needed to leave a few weeks early to make it to the first day of law school. I wrote to both the University of Georgia, where I had finished my first year, and the University of Alabama, where I was a state resident. For some reason, Alabama replied quickly and said that they would accept me. I used the Alabama paperwork to get my early release approved. Just before I left Vietnam, Georgia finally replied that I could return, but by then the paperwork for Alabama was done. It turned out that my friend from OCS had done the same thing, and we left together for law school in Alabama.

When I had first arrived in Vietnam, the officer in charge of the fire direction center had persuaded me to sign for all of the equipment in the section. His argument was that if anything went missing, he as an officer would be personally responsible, while I as an enlisted man would not be. He had been a forward observer at Khe Sanh and had a Silver Star; so I agreed. The equipment included our generators, computers, radios, an M-60 machine gun, but also an M-577 mobile command post (an armored personnel carrier with a high roof) and a trailer to carry the generators. On an artillery raid, the trailer axle broke, and I gave it to the motor pool sergeant to repair. He either buried it or sold it on the black market. After I had been in law school in Tuscaloosa for a few months, I got a "report of survey" from the Army billing me about $1,000 for the missing trailer. I went to see an Army lawyer at nearby Ft. McClellan. He gave me some forms to fill out, and I never had to pay, but the Army had followed me to law school.

JIM CHAMBERLIN followed a family tradition of Army service. His great-grandfather served in the Confederate Army, his grandfather (buried in Arlington Cemetery) served in the Spanish American War and World War I, and his father served in World War II and Korea. Jim joined up in 1968 at the height of military action during the Vietnam War, and his Army assignments in Vietnam with a heavy artillery battery in I Corps took him to the demilitarized zone (DMZ) supporting the 5th Mechanized Division, to Quang Tri province (north central coastal region of Vietnam) supporting the 101st Division, and to the Laotian border firing on the Ho Chi Minh Trail. His battalion headquarters were at the Dong Ha combat base, the northern-most U.S. base in South Vietnam and a strategically significant facility supporting Marines and Army troops along the border of the DMZ. Chamberlin was a specialist-5 with the 2/94th Artillery, whose service is recognized by the Vietnam Service Medal and Army Commendation Medal.

Born in Miami, Florida, in 1945, Chamberlin was raised in Mobile, Alabama, and took on the nickname in college of "Mobes." He studied mathematics at Principia College, graduating in 1967. A member of Rackham Court West, Chamberlin served as house treasurer, participated on the debate team, and was as "rowdy" as the rest of his brother Westies, known for their house spirit. Married to Anderson Eastie Cheryl Racicot, Chamberlin has one step-son David Marshall. Following graduate school at the University of Alabama where he earned a JD degree, Chamberlin became a Department of State Foreign Service officer with overseas assignments in Sao Paulo, Bangkok, Brasilia, Warsaw, and Rome, as well as many assignments in Washington. At State he worked on nuclear proliferation and other science-related issues, participating in the creation of the Missile Technology Control Regime (MTCR) and the ending of the nuclear rivalry between Brazil and Argentina. During a Washington assignment working on environmental issues, he was State's representative to meetings of the World Heritage Convention. An oral history of his Foreign Service career is located in the Library of Congress at www.loc.gov/item/mfdipbib000192. He now lives in Lakewood, Colorado.

Answering the Call

WILLIAM H. "CHIP" OSTENBERG IV

When I completed basic and advanced individual training and got my orders for Vietnam, I went to Vietnam not knowing what it was all about except that our country ordered me to go, and it was my duty to go. I lived in Florida and traveled across America, so I had been in high temperatures and humidity. I arrived in 'Nam in February, 1968; Tet had just begun, and my education began at the reception station.

We got our orders telling us what unit and location we were assigned. During the course of talking about our orders, a master sergeant back for his third tour asked us where we were headed. I told him the 1097th Medium Boat Company located at Dong Tam. He shook his head, and I asked him why. He just said, "Ten minutes." I asked what that meant, and he said that ten minutes was the expected life span at Dong Tam.

The unit transformed to "Mobile" by converting some of the boats to various purposes: an orderly room, where the administrative work and commander's office were; the maintenance platoon, where the machine shop and mechanics worked; and the mess hall, where, of course, the food was prepared and soldiers fed. I was disappointed that we went mobile on the day we did, because the Bob Hope show was held that night. I did see Joey Heatherton. I learned that the boat I was assigned needed maintenance, so I went to our now land-based "rear area," although, that didn't mean behind the lines, as I learned later in my first tour.

I spent a couple of weeks doing work around the orderly room, including filing, and then I was sent to the 159 Transportation Battalion, our higher command, to do some electrical work. The assignment resulted in my promotion and designation as a classified messenger. I flew, or was transported by one of the boats, to the several companies in the battalion as well as to the 4th Transportation

Command, the battalion's higher headquarters in Saigon. I performed this duty for about two months when I was then promoted to sergeant (E5) and assigned as the non-commissioned officer in charge of the intelligence and operations sections. Normally, the position is manned by a master sergeant (E8), but none was available, so the battalion leadership chose me. I held the position until February, 1970, after my third tour. Our mission was moving equipment and personnel throughout the Delta, and occasionally we pushed artillery barges into position for their fire missions. Our compound, like our ports in the Delta, was often attacked with mortar or rocket fire.

William H. "Chip" Ostenberg IV. Photo courtesy
William H. "Chip" Ostenberg

The most memorable part of my time in Vietnam was the friendships, both U.S. and Vietnamese. When I was transferred from the 1097th Medium Boat Company to the 159 Transportation Battalion, moving my gear, I noticed the "Mama san" responsible for the barracks was being threatened by another soldier. I stopped him and, after he left, contracted with her for laundry. Near the end of my first tour, I turned in two sets of uniforms to supply and came back to the States for thirty day leave, awaiting my next tour. When I returned to Vietnam and went to supply to get my new uniforms, the supply sergeant told me he didn't have any uniforms for me. I never understood why until someone told me they thought he was selling stuff on the black market. Anyway, I told Mama San I only had two sets, so I would wear each for two days to allow her to wash and iron them. A day later, when I returned after duty, there were three sets of uniforms with all the patches and rank. Mama San had gone to the black market and paid for them for me. She, and other friends, made serving an honor.

Soldiers in Vietnam. Photo: U.S. Army

I remember making the decision for the second Vietnam tour, and then a third tour, having a required three-year service obligation: I could be sent back, or even worse, my brother could be sent over to an experience close to Hell. I couldn't seem to write Mom to tell her I had signed up for the second tour. Instead, I came home to surprise her. She was a girls' housemom at the Principia Upper School, and, as it worked out, they were having the prom. Mom was a chaperone, and I had the honor of escorting her in my Class A uniform. She said I look very handsome, but mothers always say that.

Back in Vietnam, we were told that if the war was lost, those we worked with would be killed, along with politicians, teachers, and anyone who worked with the Americans or their allies. I thought the war could be won if the Vietnamese could be protected; however, I learned that there was always someone with his own agenda. Like all members of the military, we took an oath to defend the Constitution, and that also means that protesters had the right to demonstrate. However, I felt the war would continue because the Viet Cong would just hold on until America quit. I didn't realize how that would affect me later in life. Toward the end of my third tour, we received a rocket attack for the first time during the day. I was wearing my flak jacket and steel pot, received wounds in my arms, and after the attack there was a large dent in the helmet. I decided not to do a fourth tour and went home. There is a lot I don't remember about my time in the Army in Vietnam. But I stayed connected.

My military experience in Vietnam occurred between my high school and college years at Principia. I graduated from the Upper School in 1964, entered the United States Army in 1967 and left active duty in 1970, returning to Principia and graduating from the college in 1973. I entered the U.S. Army National Guard in the Engineers in 1982, serving as recon sergeant, and later platoon sergeant of Third Platoon, B Company, in the 113th Engineer Battalion (Combat Light). In 1986 I transferred to the U.S. Army Reserves in the Engineers serving as Direct Support Supervisor—863rd Engineer Battalion (Combat Heavy, First Sergeant—652nd Engineer Company Assault Float Bridge Ribbon, Engineer Sergeant Major (Korea & Pacific Rim, Central & South America, and Middle East)—416th Engineer Command, and finally Command Sergeant Major—863rd Engineer Battalion (Combat Heavy), and 1st Group, 1st Brigade, 85th Division. I returned to Active Duty as Task Force Command Sergeant Major—1st Brigade, 85th Division. When I reached maximum age, I retired from the United States Army in 2005, thirty-eight years after joining in 1967 to answer the call during the Vietnam War.

CHIP OSTENBERG served three consecutive tours in Vietnam between 1967 and 1970, continued service in the National Guard and Army Reserves, returned to active duty in 2003-2005, and rose to the rank of command sergeant major, the highest enlisted rank in the Army and the senior enlisted adviser to the commanding officer. His numerous military jobs were in various transportation and engineering companies, battalions, and commands, primarily part of the Army Corps of Engineers. In Vietnam he was in the 1097th Transportation Company (Med Boat), a part of the 9th Infantry Division Mobile Riverine, and then the 159th Transportation Battalion, as Non Commissioned Officer in Charge of the Operations and Security sections, stationed at Vung Tau and Delta Ports, serving in III and IV Corps. [Administratively South Vietnam was divided into four corps: III Corps extended from the northern Mekong Delta to the southern Central Highlands of South Vietnam; IV Corps was headquartered at Can Tho in the Mekong Delta.] Ostenberg's service medals included the prestigious Legion of Merit Military Ribbon; Meritorious Service Medal; multiple Army Commendation, Army Achievement, other meritorious service ribbons; and Global War on Terrorism Service Ribbon.

Ostenberg's distinguished military career was not unique in the Ostenberg family. His father was a pilot in the U.S. Army Air Corps in World War II, serving in North Africa and Europe (he was a war detainee in Portugal), as well as in the China-Burma-India Theater of operations, where he flew the Hump into Burma. Nearly one thousand men and six hundred Air Transport planes were lost over the hump, a dangerous 530 mile route over the Himalayan Mountains by means of which allied forces supplied Chinese forces in the war against the Japanese. Family tradition continued when Command Sergeant Major Ostenberg's younger brother Rob (also an author in this volume) served as an infantry platoon leader in the Army in I Corps, Vietnam, decided to remain career military, and rose to the rank of major general.

William H. Ostenberg also had multiple Principia connections. He attended the Upper School graduating in 1964, and, following his active duty in the Army, he returned to Principia College and graduated in 1973. There he was a member of Rackham Court East (the same house affiliation as his father and younger brother) and majored in business and economics with a minor in computer science. Ostenberg also managed the "Odd Job Crew," a team of students and campus workers providing labor to Principia College residents needing help with the maintenance of their properties. Armed with experience from his upbringing on a ranch in Colorado, as well as his maintenance and leadership experience in the military, Ostenberg was asked to manage the crew, and if a student did not have a necessary skill, "the sergeant" would teach him. Ostenberg's sister Susan and brother Rob were also Principians, graduating from the Upper School in 1962 and 1965 respectively, his brother Rob continuing on to the college (C69). As previously noted, after the death of his father in 1967, Ostenberg's mother served Principia as an Upper School "house mom" in the girls' dormitory.

Ostenberg's active business career has included property management and home construction, computer work as a system analyst and programmer, and research and development in the steel industry. Now retired, Ostenberg lives in Crown Point, Indiana, with his wife Rae Ann Kirkendorfer, a Principia College graduate of 1972. Their son William H. Ostenberg V attended Principia Upper School (US95) and College (C99) [deceased in 2004 leaving a wife, Heather Harriman Ostenberg, and daughter, Olivia Love Ostenberg]. Command Sergeant Major Ostenberg's daughter Leah was also a graduate of Principia College (C01). She is now married to Dr. Joshua Stender, PhD They have a daughter Lilah Isabel Stender.

"On Fire!"

RICHARD E. UPSHAW

The year was 1968; the month was February; and the day was one day after what was later called the Tet Offensive, a now familiar surge by North Vietnamese and Vietcong invading fighters to eject American and South Vietnamese forces from major cities in the northern provinces of Vietnam. I had just arrived at the major airport of Da Nang, Vietnam, in the area known as I Corps. I was amazed at the extent of excitement by the local population, seemingly motivated more by fear than by joy for the efforts of our joint forces. The smell of smoke filled the air, and I wondered, strangely, why this was supposed to be a positive thing for me, a second lieutenant reporting for a thirteen-month tour of combat duty in this far-off land of rice paddies and thick jungles full of monkeys and pythons.

Richard Upshaw. Photo courtesy Richard Upshaw

As I made my way through the fast-moving crowd, I was shocked to see the face of my ole Principia buddy, Pete Sappenfield, almost jogging to his departure flight for CONUS, a term I later learned to be an acronym for the States… Continental United States. What a delight it was… a big bear-hug from us both— him having completed his tour of duty flying the A-6 Intruder attack jet aircraft, and me just fresh into my duties as a CH-46 Sea Knight transport helicopter pilot. Oh, how we cherished the moment… but both of us way too much in a hurry to get to our destinations.

U.S. Marine CH-46 Sea Knight Transport Helicoptor

I'll never forget the combination of joy, as well as anguish, I felt in my heart, knowing that Pete had safely completed his combat assignment, and mine had just commenced. Both members of the "Lords of East"— Rackham Court East[36] back at Principia—Pete a year ahead of me, teammates in all three sports of football, basketball, and baseball. Pete was the very Marine who had lured me into officer training at Quantico, Virginia, so I could serve my country flying the outrageous beast of all jet aircraft, the F-4 Phantom! Little did I know that the scuttlebutt[37] was that the lifespan of Marine helicopter pilots in Vietnam was eight days! No way that I would get to F-4s; choppers, here I come!

---

36 Rackham Court East was a men's residence hall at Principia College, then essentially a fraternity; more recently the house has served as a freshman dormitory and periodically housed other student residence groups.

37 Military gossip.

We had some brief words, and Pete was on his way home. I was off to what was called Marble Mountain, a Marine air facility just to the east of Da Nang, and right on the shoreline of the South China Sea. I was pleased to find my way so easily to the military bus that escorted me over to Marble, but certainly *not* so pleased to discover my first combat flight assignment the very next day!

Richard Upshaw. Photo courtesy Richard Upshaw

The mission was an emergency extract of South Vietnamese troops from an airfield about twenty miles to the south of our base, a place called Thống Đức. At the time, I had a total of thirty-four flight hours logged in the CH-46 from my training back at New River, North Carolina. Here, I was a copilot flying into a hot zone with enemy .50-caliber machine guns on both ends of the runway surrounded by hostile Vietcong, commonly known as "Gooks" to my Marine comrades, but also simply called "Charlie." This was my very first mission in the war between the Communist North Vietnamese, and the freedom-loving, democracy-pursuing South Vietnamese.

We arrived at a devastated airfield that had been over-run by the Viet Cong; the air controller directed us to an area just to the northeast of the airfield. I'll never forget my aircraft commander, First Lieutenant Paul Moody (we called him Mumbles, because you could barely understand his mumbling responses over the radios); Mumbles smoothly spiraled our bird down between the trees, and we softly touched down. "What a beautiful approach!" I thought. As copilot, I stared at the instrument panel, hands and feet close to the controls in case Mumbles took a round and needed me to take over and get us out of there. Additionally, as I just learned on this mission, my radios were turned off so I could concentrate on my duties and not be distracted by the three radios blaring in our ears—the FM radio between our wingmen, the UHF from the air controller, and the intercom among our crew chief, gunner, and pilot.

Richard Upshaw returns to the cockpit, August 6,
2009. Photo courtesy Richard Upshaw

After touch-down, I lowered the ramp at the rear of the aircraft, and the ARVNs (Army of Vietnam) scrambled on board. Then, Mumbles slowly but steadily lifted us out of the landing zone (LZ) and carefully circled back around to the left to remain directly over our departing LZ, a routine such that, should we take a disabling hit from one of those enemy .50 calibers, we could sit back down safely into the LZ we had just departed. Then, suddenly, Mumbles started back down, without any indication to me as to why the hell we were going back down. Of course, with my radios turned off, I couldn't have heard him explain anyway! After another carefully controlled soft touch-down, we lifted off again, and headed back to the ARVN's camp. Just why Mumbles set us back down, I had not a clue. I only remember just being extremely grateful that we made it out, back to base, and safely home... our home at Marble!

Over the next thirteen months, I flew over 740 missions, into and out of hot LZs, flying in and out of Marble Mountain, based aboard ship (USS *Tripoli*) for three months flying missions up and down the coast of I Corps, and then back inland to the Phu Bai air field about halfway between Da Nang and the DMZ. Needless to say, I had many exciting and dangerous encounters of incoming enemy fire, only once being forced to vacate my damaged aircraft on the ground. But that very first mission is one I'll never forget.

Jump forward four decades. We're at our squadron reunion in Reno, Nevada, and I'm sharing my golf cart with none other than Staff Sergeant Bob Riner, the very crew chief aboard our chopper on that first mission of mine into Thong Duc Airfield. Was I surprised... as was he! As we made our way around the golf course, I asked Sergeant Riner, "Why in the hell did Mumbles set us back down into that hell-hole? — .50 calibers streaming by all around; close air support firing rockets back at the enemy; smoke everywhere!"

You'll never believe what Riner said.

"Captain, we took a round in our right main landing gear, and I reported to Mumbles that our *tire* had been hit!" Well, he thought I'd said, *'We are on Fire!'* So he set us back down and screamed, *'Are we still on fire?'* So, I screamed back, *'Hell no...Let's get the [blank] outta here!'*"

It took me forty years to learn the answer. I was so bubbly grateful to have survived my very first mission flying into hot LZs, that I never once asked Mumbles why he set us back down into that zone. Can you imagine what I now scream at Mumbles every time we reunite for our squadron reunion?

"No, Mumbles, *'tire,'*... not *'on fire!'*"

DICK UPSHAW flew helicopters in Vietnam assigned to Marble Mountain, Da Nang/Phu Bai. It was demanding duty about which he writes herein, describing his first assignment. A captain in the Marine Corps, Upshaw attended Officer Candidate School at PLC (Platoon Leaders Class) in Quantico, Virginia, went on to flight school at Pensacola, Florida, and received further specialized training at the Marine Corps Air Station, New River, North Carolina, transitioning to the CH-46 helicopter, the aircraft he would fly in combat in the Republic of Vietnam. During his thirteen active months of combat from February 1968 to March 1969, Upshaw earned thirty-seven Air Medals with Combat V, as well as the Vietnam Service Medal. In addition to ten months flying the CH-46 helicopter, first at Danang and last at Phu Bai, Vietnam, Upshaw also flew in between for three months aboard USS *Tripoli* (LPH-10), an amphibious assault ship, all included in the squadron designated HMM-265. Just prior to his discharge in 1970, Upshaw served as athletic officer of squadron HMM-162 in Santa Ana, California.

Born in Deming, New Mexico, in 1944, Richard Upshaw was raised in California, living in the town of Imperial at the time he decided to travel in 1962 to Principia College for his undergraduate education. He majored in history, was a member of Rackham Court East and during his senior year helped establish a new campus men's residence hall, Highland Hall, serving as the house's first president. Throughout this time, Upshaw was establishing himself as one of the school's most remarkable athletes lettering four years in football, four years in baseball, and three years in basketball. Upshaw and his wife have two sons and a daughter. His second son Ron graduated from Principia College in 1993, twenty-seven years after his father, following two of Upshaw's nephews at Principia (in the college classes of 1985 and 1987) and two decades before another generation graduated from the college: Upshaw's grandniece (C11) and grandnephew (C13).

Upshaw continues to support activities of interest to Christian Scientists, serving recently as chairman/president of "A Brighter World Inc." which produces feature commercial films. The first project was entitled "The Healer" and related the story of Mary Baker Eddy's life and ultimate success over the "Next Friends Suit" [see *ABrighterWorldInc.org*, and *thehealerfilm.com.*] For forty years since his own years at Principia and subsequent active duty in the Marine Corps, Upshaw has managed a successful Taco Bell franchise and remains an active businessman and restaurant owner living in Heath, Texas.

Royal Thai Army guard standing watch on the
construction of a bridge being built on "Friendship
Highway" — a new road from Bangkok north to the
Mekong River. Intended eventually to meet the Ho
Chi Min Trail. Near Raum Chit Chai (Sakon Nakhon),
1971. Ink drawing. Photo courtesy Glenn Felch

Post-draft Drafting: An Army Artist at Work

GLENN FELCH

PROLOGUE

It was a courageous decision in the spring of 1968: to head straight into grad school knowing that college graduates were a prime target for military service in Vietnam. It seemed that most of my peers were enlisting as officers, in part to avoid what looked like guaranteed assignments as infantry soldiers. However, I was definitely not the military type, and, having received a full tuition scholarship and paid assistantship to a university in Ohio, I thought the risk was worth taking.

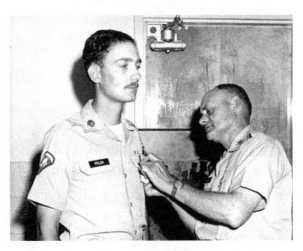

Sp5 Glenn Felch being awarded the U.S. Army Commendation Medal for service as a member of Army Art Team XIII and as a driver for the Command Office at Fort Bliss, Texas. June, 1971, award presented by Colonel P. J. Maline, Deputy Commander of Ft. Bliss. Photo: U.S. Army, courtesy Glenn Felch

An important note: I never thought of myself as a "draft dodger," even as I presumed to understand those who "skipped town" to avoid the draft. I simply did not know how I could serve the military in a way compatible with my temperament and skills. My prayers were all variations on this theme: "If needed, You will fit me to the right task."

Ink sketch by Army Artist Sp4 Glenn Felch, family on
a khlong in central Thailand, 1970.
Photo courtesy Glenn Felch

I

About two months into my first quarter as a graduate student (Fall, 1968), I received my draft notice. Effective immediately. The school of art chair obtained a deferment for me until June, based upon my contract with the school to teach two required general education classes each quarter, affecting some 180 students for the year. So I was not inducted into service until June, 23, 1969, having just barely completed an MA degree, with two years more yet to earn my MFA. Quite honestly, I didn't think I'd ever be "making art" again. As I stood in line at the induction bureau, the overwhelming feeling was that two years as a draftee were going to feel like two years in a penitentiary. There was one bright spot on that first official day of being "processed": midway into the day the single line of inductees split into two lines, forking left and right. Left was the U.S. Army. Right was the U.S. Marines. No line jostling permitted. I went left.

Army Artist Sp4 Glenn Felch sketching "en plein air" in central Thailand, 1969-70. Photo by fellow artist Sp5 Kenneth Grissom, Army Art Team XIII, courtesy Glenn Felch

There was also one fleeting moment of pride: if only coach Crafton[38] could see me now. Didn't several of his football players who went down with me to St. Louis for our pre-induction physical two summers ago receive the coveted 4-F 'unfit' classification while I was stamped with the dreaded 1-A 'prime specimen' approval? Wasn't my athletic fame based on a particular Sunday afternoon, when playing left field in a highly charged intra-mural soft ball game, I made the fatal decision to chase after my hat in the wind rather than catch the pop fly that gently soared my way at the same time?

I marveled that an hour in basic training seemed like a day: A day that would never end. Fort Polk, Louisiana, in the summer is a memorable place. I could run a comfortable mile when I started my basic training exercises. By the end of the "cycle," I could barely

---

38 James Crafton, athletic director and football coach at Principia College.

make it to the finish line. And neither could my good friend-in-misery Private Murphy. We were the two "17-year troops" having both earned our MA degrees. Anything that went remotely wrong during our sweltering training was blamed on us. We "collected" more than our fair share of push-ups in penance. Of course, it didn't help to have names that drill sergeants loved to boom out: "Where's our jinx team, Murphy & Felch?" If it wasn't for a handful of sympathetic high school kids and a contingency of Cajun troops (I could speak French, and this was helpful to them), I would never have made it through M-14 rifle range training, gas-mask harassment, and hand-to-hand combat drills.

Ink sketch by Sp4 Glenn Felch, Army shipyard in a port
in Bangkok, Thailand, 1970. Photo courtesy Glenn Felch

The next most significant memorable event occurred on the day of graduation from basic. I pointed out to my CO that with all due respect I could not attend the parade ceremonies because my orders stated that I was to be picked up by a taxi and taken to the airport right in the middle of the commencement march and formation. (My orders, which were at least two weeks late in coming, were for assignment to Missile School at Redstone Arsenal in Huntsville, Alabama. Everyone else was going to Advanced Infantry Training located on the other half of Fort Polk.) Thus, for a few final hours in Company B, this PFC "17-year-man" was untouchable.

Sketch of radar truck by Sp4 Glenn Felch in Korat, Thailand, 1970. Photo courtesy Glenn Felch

For seven months I was educated in electronics, specifically the art of repairing Redeye and Shillelagh surface-to-air missiles. I was also promoted to the rank of corporal and assigned to lead a platoon. Then, after completing this very cerebral stint, I was once again the odd troop out. But this time my orders sent me to Fort Bliss, Texas, as "excess personnel," while all my platoon buddies were sent to Korea where they filled out their military obligation. I was heart-broken. I had bonded strongly with my squad, and for months thereafter I sorely missed being with them.

"Morning Inventory." Ink sketch by Sp4 Glenn Felch.
Photo courtesy Glenn Felch

At Bliss I was slow to embrace my new assignment—learning how to drive very large, olive drab troop buses. Then one day I found myself being interviewed to serve as a chauffeur to the command post officers—one general, two colonels, one major, one captain, and one sergeant major. I believe I secured the assignment when the ranking colonel asked me, "What would you do if you had a sixteen-year-old son who was failing all his classes and about to be kicked out of school?" After a measurable silence I replied, "Well, sir, if I recall correctly, Winston Churchill flunked out of school before becoming prime minister of England." The most challenging part of this chauffeuring assignment was keeping the official cars polished from the effects of both frequent sand storms and a colonel who loved spitting chewing tobacco out the rear window. I loved placing the general's star flags on the front bumper, and being ordered to run red lights in downtown El Paso if we were late for some function.

In my "off" duty hours, I prepared a portfolio of drawings and paintings with the intent of submitting these to the chief of staff's office in the Pentagon. While in basic training I had seen a notice posted outside the PX [post exchange] announcing that applications were being accepted for Army Art Team XIII, temporary duty in Thailand. I tore the flyer off the board and had been carrying it around in my duffle bag for eight to ten months. The application deadline was such that I had just enough time to accomplish this enterprise—although I had told none of my officers about it. Then, notification of my acceptance was received at headquarters, and to my relief the "brass" were in total support of the assignment. "We'll manage without you, somehow," they said. This was a fitting conclusion to my first year as a draftee.

I I

For the second year of my service as a draftee, I painted pictures and produced drawings, first in Thailand, as one of a team of four soldiers whose backgrounds were similar to mine. We had the distinction of being assigned to the first ever "non combat" team whose mission was to record only peaceful aspects of the Army's presence: building roads, distributing aid to civilians, recording bucolic landscapes unscarred by war. I came to love the design potential of motor pools filled with all sorts of trucks; ports in Bangkok defined by rusty ship hulls with massive anchors; ornate temples punctuated with saffron-robbed monks; street markets arrayed with all kinds of food fare and sometimes dozens of "wild" monkeys; as well as vast fields filled with barrels of oil as far as the eye could see. We traveled all over the country returning periodically to our official studio in a shack on the Army base in Korat, situated within a few feet of a chain-link fence that separated us from the U.S. Air Force base. We never became comfortable with the roar of jets and bombers taking off at all times of the day and night, especially as Thailand was supposedly a neutral country. One upbeat, completely unexpected encounter occurred one Sunday afternoon when I was doing a watercolor near that chain-link fence. After being aware that I was being silently watched for a prolonged time, I turned around to see fellow classmate and artist from Principia, Jimmy Clark, who was then serving as a pilot in the Air Force.[39]

We did have a few dangerous moments, including a near capsizing calamity in the bay of Sattahip when our ancient, undersized, fishing-turned-excursion boat tried to outrun a sudden typhoon. Our otherwise "can-do" local Thai "captain" threatened to abandon ship leaving us to decide for ourselves whether or not to jump overboard and swim to a shore we could not see. Our lieutenant refused to let any of us jump and my post became ballast on the starboard rim of the bow. We eventually made it back to our dock which was only minutes away from being washed ashore. For those cold, wave-beaten hours "at sea" we were "Navy Seal Art Team XIII" although no medals were awarded for our versatile bravery in the line of duty.

On the other hand, throughout our days we never needed to carry weapons, and we often wore civilian clothes.

Following a gala exhibition in the Dusit Thani Hotel in Bangkok, with the USARSUPTHAI (United States Army Support Thailand) command officers in attendance, all our artwork was sent to the Office Chief of Military History in the Pentagon, where last I knew,

---

39 Jim Clark writes, "I well remember the day I rode a bike from the air base at Korat, Thailand (where I was stationed as a USAF pilot flying EC-121 reconnaissance planes) over onto the adjacent Thai army base and came across Glenn sitting under a tree painting a watercolor of the base fire station."

it rotated on-and-off the walls and has been used for various military publications.

The military has relied upon artists to record its activities since Continental Army days. During the Vietnam era the armed services forthrightly recognized the worth of artistic viewpoints to the complex fabric of the American story.

Ink sketch by Sp4 Glenn Felch, Temple compound at Takhli, Thailand, 1970. Photo courtesy Glenn Felch

My final months in service were also pleasant. Upon return from Thailand, the special services personnel at Fort Bliss requested that I continue as an army artist recording the activities at Fort Bliss and at White Sands missile range. This met with the approval of the commanding officers upon one condition: that I chauffeur if there were ever an emergency need. That happened only once when Werner Von Braun came for a visit. Otherwise, I was left to my own devices and assigned my own vehicle. This assignment included such things as recording war games in the desert dunes between Forts Bliss and Hood; searching for design variety to relieve the monotony of the desert post; and painting an "official" artwork for the command office. (I did two: one that satisfied my feelings about the Vietnam War, and one that celebrated Army pride at Bliss. All of the other artwork ended up in the post's Replica Museum).

I ended up staying a week longer in service than I was supposed to, missing my eagerly anticipated ETS (Estimated Termination of Service)[40] date by over a week! This "contribution" enabled me to mat and frame much of the Bliss-Sands artwork for a final exhibition.

Ink sketch by Army Artist Sp4 Glenn Felch, joint
Thai-U.S. police station, 1970. Photo courtesy Glenn Felch

Military service juxtaposes some of life's most contrasting moments. How did one make sense of the emphasis placed on physical fitness measured by one's performance in the "low crawl" course but overseen by a platoon sergeant who weighed nearly 300 pounds? Or the status of warrant officers suspended within a world of non-coms and commissioned personnel? Or post-wide mandatory "police calls" in a desert that blew candy wrappers into oblivion but firmly fixed tumbleweeds in the treads of tanks? Or the paradox of a platoon

---

40 This was the day I lived for — 23 June, 1971. To this day, I always eat an extra dessert on the 23rd of every June.

formation at reveille, during which a "lifer" sergeant unknowingly watered plastic rose bushes, with a platoon formation at taps, in front of those same rose bushes, listening to a heart-breaking rendition of "Amazing Grace," played for a fellow recruit killed that same day in a training exercise?

EPILOGUE

Perhaps a final note should be rendered to what may have been the most anxious moment of my two years as a draftee. It was during our first gathering as a platoon of fresh recruits, still dressed in our "civies" (because there were no uniforms available for us yet), sitting in a military-style circle on hard, dusty ground outside our barracks in Fort Polk. A cadre of drill sergeants was rummaging through our duffle bags and disposing of extraneous items, mostly "unauthorized" literature. We were told that any troop brave enough to challenge a sergeant's choice of items for the burn pile could do so by standing up, asking for "permission to beg," identifying himself with a series of military numbers, and stating his case. My tiny, travel set of Christian Science books had been tossed upon the "to burn" pile.

I do not remember exactly what I said, but I did stand up and more like a camp counselor railing at a camper who was likely to jeopardize a team's chance to win an event, I "begged" (declared) my case. (Perhaps it was more like a civilian making a case for these childish army games to cease.) My books were returned and remained a conspicuous, well-used part of my "gear" for the next two years.

GLENN FELCH was an artist throughout his life, and when he was drafted into the Army in 1969, it was not long before the military noticed his talents in art. Setting aside his initial training as a Redeye and Shillelagh missile technician, the Army assigned him duties as an army artist. Thus, following boot camp at Fort Polk, Louisiana, further training for seven months at Redstone Arsenal at Huntsville, Alabama, and an assignment as a chauffeur for the command post at Fort Bliss, Texas, Felch took up his sketch pad, pencil, pen, and ink and traveled to USARSUPTHAI (United States Army Support, Thailand) at Korat, Thailand, for a temporary tour of duty as an army artist—one of four soldiers assigned to the Army's first *non-combat* art team. There Felch created drawings, pen and ink sketches, and watercolors of both peaceful military subjects and civilian environments; his artwork became part of the military's permanent art collection and archive, including original work in the Office Chief of Military History (OCMH) at the Pentagon and in the Replica Museum at Ft. Bliss. Felch's performance resulted in his receipt of a good conduct medal and U.S. Army Commendation Medal, prior to his discharge in 1971.

Like others of his generation, Felch's father had served in World War II, flying fifty-two missions as a B-25 pilot in New Guinea. Glenn was born soon after the war, in February 1946, in New Rochelle, New York. He had moved from Connecticut to Homewood, Illinois, by high school age, and was living in Perrysburg, Ohio, by the time he came to Principia for his college education, graduating with a bachelor's degree in studio art in 1968. Felch was a member of Rackham Court West, and served on his house governance board. Among his "seemingly endless" art-related contributions during his college years were drawings and paintings for Rackham West, a portfolio of drawings and folk art featuring Elsah, and the creation of a mural in the stair hall of an historic Elsah village home of a college history professor. Felch followed his undergraduate training as an artist with MA and MFA degrees from Bowling Green State University in Ohio. He married another Principia artist, Judith McCreary (C67), and both husband and wife became leading faculty members at Principia College from 1969 (Judith) and 1973 (Glenn) to 2007. The majority of these years were spent in the studio art department. Felch has a daughter and a son, Anna and Daniel, both educated at Principia from pre-school into their high school years. The Felches spent recent retirement years at their home and studio in Ellsworth, Maine, just close enough to Deer Isle and other coastal communities to inspire their creative energies. Glenn passed on in July, 2016, as this anthology was being completed.

"Scramble At Phan Rang," A National Guard Heritage
Painting by William F. Phillips. Photo courtesy of the
National Guard Bureau

Colorado National Guard at Phan Rang, Vietnam

SID HUBBARD

My name is Sid Hubbard. I was a member of the Colorado Air National Guard which consisted of a squadron of F100 Super Saber jet fighters. Many of our pilots had Korean War experience and were also commercial aviation pilots. A high percentage of the enlisted men in the Guard were college graduates and some had post-graduate degrees as well. As a result of the *Pueblo* crisis in North Korean waters in 1968, President Lyndon Johnson activated four National Guard units across the country in case military action was needed in Korea. The Colorado Air Guard was one of the four. I was driving to work listening to the *Pueblo* crisis developments on the radio when I heard that our unit had been activated. I made a U-turn and went directly home, got into my Air Force uniform, and reported to the air base. That was my last day of work for the Weyerhaeuser Company. It was a bit of a shock to my wife and me, but somehow I managed to go from salesman to soldier in a few hours.

While the Korean/*Pueblo* crisis was front page news, we spent a couple of weeks of intensive training for our military mission. But as the *Pueblo* crisis seemed to wind down, we expected to be deactivated. Instead, we were given seventy-two hour notice to prepare to be stationed overseas. The defense department did not want it widely known that National Guard troops were being sent to Vietnam, so our orders only said the destination was the Far East and no return date was given. After a long flight we landed at Phan Rang Air Base in the Central Highlands area of South Vietnam and stayed there for eleven months.

I was a munitions specialist: I helped to fuse, load, and arm (and de-arm) the bombs, missiles, and guns for the jet fighters. We would load the planes, usually at night, and then be at the end of the runway to remove safety pins and install 20mm rounds into the machine gun chambers as the planes prepared to take off. When the planes returned, we reversed the process so the planes would be safe before they returned to the parking area.

Although we became regular Air Force men after activation, we kept our identity by wearing "Ski Colorado" pins on our uniforms. We had our share of enemy attacks on the base, particularly on the flight line, but our tour of duty occasioned nothing close to the intensity experienced by many of the Marines and Army soldiers. We lost two pilots and planes in combat missions and three other planes were destroyed in mortar and rocket attacks on the flight line.

One of the good things about the team's going into and coming out of combat from the same geographical area (Colorado), and the general familiarity with each other from weekend drills and two-week summer sessions, is that we found more support from knowing each other than individuals typically experience who rotate into units made up of personnel from all over the country. Moreover, back home, Dick and Joie (Carter) Power (C63), who lived near Denver, provided tremendous support to my wife Doni (Doni Ellison C63) while I was overseas.

When I left for Vietnam, Doni and I had one daughter, and we were expecting another. Aside from seeing Doni in Hawaii for rest and recovery (R&R), during my Vietnam tour of duty we were only able to talk to each other a couple of times via ham radio relays. I would say "hi, how are you?" then "over," and Doni would say "fine, how are you doing?" then "over." It was nice of the volunteer ham radio operators to provide this service. When I came home, I got to meet my new four-month-old daughter Audrey, and I got reacquainted with our two-year-old daughter Vallee.

When our unit arrived back at Buckley Field near Denver, early in the morning, all were greeted by our wives and other family members, and the governor of Colorado (John Love) was there as well to greet all of us. The planes in our squadron did a "fly over" Denver before they landed. There was a lot of press coverage, and generally we were made to feel like heroes. In fact, a picture of Doni and me was picked up by Associated Press, and friends and relatives around the country saw the picture in their newspapers. When we drove home that early morning, there was a banner across our garage door which had big letters saying "Welcome Home Sergeant Sid" and it was signed by all the neighborhood kids. I still have the banner. The neighborhood where we lived had many Catholics, and I learned later that many of them kept burning candles for me for a safe return — pretty nice of them.

Welcome Home (Sid and Doni Hubbard). News clipping, collection of Sid Hubbard

Generally, I felt the community made me feel good about my service and in many ways showed their appreciation. Moreover, a clear benefit I enjoyed upon my return was the GI bill. I was able to go to graduate school at the University of Colorado and earn my Master's Degree in business, thanks to this help. On the other hand, I am aware that this warm homecoming was not commonplace for all soldiers returning home. I, too, had a taste of the other viewpoint from the Vietnam era. In one of my first classes at the graduate school, a guy sitting in front of me wore a Levi jacket with an image of the Viet Cong flag displayed conspicuously on the back. Welcome home, soldier!

SID HUBBARD served as staff sergeant with the 120th Tactical Fighter Squadron of the U.S. Air Force. Following boot camp he was assigned to Buckley Field (Air Force base) in Denver, Colorado. When orders to Vietnam came, Hubbard was sent to Phan Rang, an air field used by the Japanese during World War II, by the French during the French occupation of Indochina (ended in 1954), and then abandoned. As the war in South Vietnam expanded, the United States moved engineering and construction materials to the airfield in 1965 and developed the airport to accommodate U.S. and Vietnamese Air Force fighter and helicopter combat units. Hubbard arrived with his reserve unit in 1968, serving as a weapons mechanic.

This was a far cry from the California home town of his youth, Palo Alto (Hubbard was born in San Jose in 1943), and while Stanford University was nearby, when Hubbard grew to college age, he decided to attend Principia College in Illinois [C65]. There he majored in history, lettered in football, track, and baseball, and was selected captain of both football and track teams. He served his "fraternity" house, Rackham Court East, as freshman head, responsible for the residents' first-year orientation and membership initiation. Hubbard is married to Doni Ellison of Principia's college class of 1963, and his brother Taylor was in the Upper School class of 1963. The Hubbards have two daughters, Audrey (who attended Principia's Upper School for a couple of years) and Vallee.

Hubbard earned an MBA at the University of Colorado and after the military pursued a career heading his own structural contracting company, Hubbard Structures, Inc., a one-time subsidiary of his father's lumber yard. Based in Redwood City, California, the company is involved with heavy-timber construction for commercial buildings, including, notably, the expansion of the Monterey Bay Aquarium. Hubbard also served as president of Placerville Industries Inc. a mining company, and he and his wife own a horse ranch in Grass Valley. Active with the YMCA, especially in the late 1980s, Hubbard served as president of the YMCA of the Mid-Peninsula (Silicon Valley). He was also president of the Construction Employees Association of Northern California. During the 1990s Hubbard served on the city council of Los Altos Hills and was elected for two terms as the town's mayor. Now retired, he is busy with property management, and recreational activities including golf, tennis, and hiking.

Son Tay POW Raid

MIKE KNEELAND

Shortly after arriving on Yankee Station on board USS *Ranger* (CVA-61) in about October 1970, we learned of a large offensive that had been kept secret. We only knew that we needed to be ready for a massive, night airstrike. The rumors were that "we were going up north," although the U.S. was not bombing North Vietnam at that time. The mention of combat flights into North Vietnam brought chills. We were well aware that most A-6 crew members lost in Vietnam were shot down up north. Many of my previous squadron's crew members were either MIA (Missing In Action), KIA (Killed In Action), or confirmed prisoners in the Hanoi Hilton, that dreaded prison where most of the POWs were incarcerated.

The flight crews on board the carrier were all checked for their recency of experience and other qualifications for night combat. Those flight crews selected to participate attended a large, secret briefing. We only knew that a majority of the Navy's available aircraft would fly up into the area around and east of North Vietnam. Deck [Deskin Waters], my B/N (Bombardier Navigator), and I manned a tanker A-6 that night.

The night was busy with many planes in the air. Because of scheduling, Deck and I were diverted to Da Nang instead of returning to the carrier. Upon returning to the carrier the next morning, we learned that a massive but futile effort had been made to rescue American POWs in the Son Tay POW Camp. While the U.S. Navy aircraft from several aircraft carriers flew a diversionary maneuver east of North Vietnam in the North China Sea, the Air Force launched a massive flight of helicopters and fixed-wing aircraft from Thailand to the west. The helicopters were supposed to land in the Son Tay POW Camp, extract the prisoners and return them to U.S. protection. For several months, air intelligence photos had shown extensive POW activity in this camp. When the helicopters landed, there were no prisoners in the camp. They'd been moved. As we learned in many other experiences of our involvement in Vietnam, leaked intelligence ruined the mission.

The day after the raid, Deck and I were briefed to get ready for an immediate departure for Saigon. Only our CO (commanding officer), the ship's CO, and some intelligence officers knew about our mission. Since I held a Top-Secret Courier clearance, I was authorized to transport Top Secret documents. All of the naval intelligence from all the participating ships in the raid needed to be flown to Saigon. Three, large, well-secured cardboard boxes were loaded into the avionics bay of our A-6. Since our flight was scheduled for a time of day unusual for regular combat flight operations, we received a lot of questions and ribbing as we were positioned on the catapult and the ship was turned into the wind to launch only our aircraft. Our instructions were to get the Top Secret packets to Saigon and to ditch the aircraft in very deep water in the event we were unable to complete the mission due to any aircraft malfunction. We launched.

The flight to the Tan Son Nhut airbase near Saigon was routine. But when we landed, several Air Force cars approached the plane, and we found ourselves surrounded by men armed with machine guns. Air Force personnel helped us unload the three boxes and place them in the locked compartment of the vehicle in which we rode, and under guard we were transported to the Tan Son Nhut intelligence compound. There the three boxes were transferred to the Air Force intelligence officers who gave me receipts for the Top Secret materials. These three receipts were the only Top Secret receipts that I saved as souvenirs among the many Top Secret receipts that I was issued in my Navy career. Previous Top Secret receipts were more routine. I believed that these receipts were extremely important, and the possession of them might later be needed to prove my actions. Fortunately, they were never required to support my successful passing of this top secret material to its proper destination.

We returned to the carrier rather unceremoniously, and landed during a normal combat flight recovery period. By then, our squadron mates knew our mission and they were no longer concerned that we had received special privileges. Some, no doubt, suspected we were given some extra R&R, which was hardly the case!

In the years since, I have learned a lot about the Son Tay POW Raid. At the Oshkosh Air Show, Deck and I met William A. Guenon Jr., an Air Force officer who flew in one of the supporting C-130 Hercules aircraft and who wrote *Secret and Dangerous: Night of the Son Tay POW Raid*, a book about the operation. There are several other books written about the Son Tay POW Raid. Had that raid been successful, it would have given everyone a huge boost in morale. Alas, reliable intelligence can be the recipe for potentially significant military action and contribute to victories large and small, but leaked intelligence will spoil the brew.

Hey GI, Want Buy Money?

JAMES H. ANDREWS

On the night of December 31, 1970, I was in Saigon, asleep in my room in a small, French-style hotel that the Army had acquired to house junior officers. The usual 10 p.m. curfew had put a damper on New Year's Eve merrymaking. I was jolted awake by weapons fire. Thinking that the Viet Cong had staged another surprise attack like the deadly Tet offensive in 1968, I staggered to the small balcony outside my window. All around me, tipsy GIs with M-16s were filling the sky with red tracer rounds, creating a spectacular New Year's fireworks display. Of course, they were heedless of the fact that those rounds would descend somewhere, probably on the tin-roofed shantytowns of rural Vietnamese who had fled for safety to the capital of their war-torn country.

I was a first lieutenant in the Army's Military Intelligence branch, stationed at U.S. military headquarters. I was assigned to the Combined Intelligence Center, Vietnam (CICV, pronounced sick-vee), where I commanded a team of analysts who compiled detailed information about all enemy activity throughout South Vietnam. We used the information to brief newly arrived senior officers on Viet Cong and North Vietnamese military operations in their sectors of responsibility.

My desk was next to that of my "Vietnamization" counterpart, a South Vietnamese captain who seemed to have no need of training by me. He spoke no English, and my Vietnamese was limited to the usual GI argot, so we communicated in French (thank you, Ned and Paula Bradley).[41]

From time to time, I would fly to liaison meetings with G2 (intelligence) officers at Army division headquarters around the country, including bases at Nha Trang and Pleiku.

---

41 Ned and Paula Bradley were Professors of French at Principia College.

Saigon was fully pacified by this time, 1970-71, and on the occasional afternoon off, I could explore the city without carrying a weapon. I armed myself only during trips away from Saigon. Even in the well-guarded capital, though, the war could seep in under the door. One night a bomb exploded in my quarters, killing the duty officer and two other American occupants. The so-called satchel bomb was hidden beneath a desk near the entrance where the nighttime duty officer kept vigil. The small suitcase was probably carried into the building by one of the Vietnamese cleaning women.

1st Lt. Jim Andrews outside the Combined Intelligence
Center, Vietnam (CICV), Saigon, late 1970.
Photo courtesy Jim Andrews

Still, Saigon was the rear echelon, where danger commonly meant having to cross one of the teeming city's chaotic avenues. Some awkward moments came when former classmates from my Infantry OCS training company at Fort Benning, Georgia, would contact me about bedding down in my room during trips to Saigon, either to pick up supplies or en route to R & R flights. These men, usually infantry platoon leaders, would arrive from the field in their faded, dusty fatigues, to be greeted by me in my starched fatigues and shiny boots and escorted to the mess hall where I ate three square meals a day. *C'est la guerre.*

1st Lt. Andrews at his parents' home in Denver, CO,
after his return from Vietnam, June, 1971.
Photo courtesy Jim Andrews

Principia friends I encountered in Vietnam included Greg Arthur, John Glen, and Mike Kneeland, and I worked down the hall from Doug Voorsanger. On Sunday mornings, Doug and I met — sometimes alone, sometimes with others — to conduct Christian Science church services.

As background for a memorable experience, I should explain that upon arriving in Vietnam, all U.S. military personnel were required to exchange their American greenbacks for funny money called "military payments currency" (MPC), which could be used in the PX and in servicemen's clubs. For transactions in local shops and restaurants, we could purchase Vietnamese *piasters* at authorized currency bureaus, at an official exchange rate. It was prohibited to transfer MPC to Vietnamese nationals, although there was a thriving black market.

To thwart the black market, once or twice a year the military authorities would abruptly invalidate all outstanding MPC and require U.S. service personnel to exchange the invalid scrip for newly designed bills. The timing of these irregular invalidations was top secret.

One evening, as I was walking from the mess hall through city streets to my billet, a Vietnamese man stepped out from the shadows with a whispered offer. This was an almost daily occurrence, so I wasn't alarmed. Usually these small-time operators offered girls, drugs, or contraband, or they wanted to buy MPC at a favorable exchange rate. This time, however, the furtive crook wanted to *sell* me MPC. I brushed him off and continued on my way, puzzling over the proposed transaction.

I didn't connect the dots until, two hours later, orders came down invalidating the current MPC and advising Americans to exchange old scrip for new as soon as possible. The fellow who approached me was desperately trying to unload his MPC before it became worthless.

Given the obvious porousness of our security around the currency exchange, I found myself wondering if there was anything that Vietnamese networks didn't know about our military plans and operations.

Though military life obviously has its challenges, I found much to value in my Army experience and learned lessons that have remained with me for more than forty years. And while my service can't be likened to that of men who saw combat, I'm proud to have served my country in this way and to have performed with what I tried to make my best effort.

JIM ANDREWS is a 1968 graduate of Principia College with a graduate law degree (JD) from the Stanford Law School. Like his brother John, Jim's education at Principia was that of a "lifer"; he started at the school in kindergarten, graduated from the high school in 1964, and earned a BA degree at the college in 1968. Jim was a history major, member of the same residence hall at college as his brother (Buck House), and served as the college men's organization president his senior year. A fourth generation Principian, Andrews served on the school's alumni board from 1991-94 and on its board of trustees from 2008-12.

Jim Andrews did not follow the military paths of his paternal grandfather, father, and brother, who were all Navy men, but served instead in the U.S. Army infantry. With special training in military intelligence, Andrews was stationed for one tour in Saigon, Vietnam. Awarded the Bronze Star and Army Commendation medal, Andrews was discharged in 1971 at the rank of first lieutenant. After the military he pursued a career in law and journalism, and is now retired. Married to a Principia alumna, Rebecca Eichar, Andrews lives in Williamsburg, Virginia. Their son Garner and two daughters Lisa and Sarah graduated from the Principia School [high school] in 2008, 2005, and 2003, with Sarah graduating from Principia College in 2007, a fifth generation Andrews at Principia.

Franke and Warner: The Prin Network in Wartime Vietnam

STEVE WELLS

Many spouses of Principians know the phenomenon all too well. Your Prin spouse knows people everywhere, yet even if you went to a much larger school, you seldom run into anyone from those days. Here's a tale that illustrates how I found this to be true during the war in Vietnam.

On leaving Navy Officer Candidate School, I was among a group who joined the Navy's Explosive Ordnance Disposal [EOD] teams. About thirty of us spent the next year going from one school to another while traveling to Florida, Alabama, and Maryland. With me in this group was my Prin classmate, Dick Hammer. In the training group one year behind us were Roy Kussmann and Rick Halladay. The others in my group had all graduated from much larger schools, including Ohio State, Yale, Stanford, and Auburn. Every new location found Dick and me meeting up with others having a Prin connection. Since the others in our training group never seemed to know anyone in town, our Prin network became something of note and increasing notoriety.

Once we completed training, most of us were sent to Hawaii for later assignment to teams operating throughout the Pacific. The frequent contacts with Principians continued unabated. Mostly by word of mouth, we knew who was where, and we worked at keeping in contact. This effort among Principians was unique and very special. Alums of other schools simply did not do this.

When I was sent to the small island of Yap in Micronesia, I met up with Don Bliss Jr. doing his Peace Corps service. When onboard a supply ship on Yankee Station, our crew always sent over my personal phone line to ships coming alongside, because they knew there would be someone on the other ship I'd want to talk with. Often that was Pete Van Vleck or another airdale. My last deployment was to a team in the Mekong Delta, and while there I had the pleasure of taking Roy and Rick on water skiing excursions up and down the river! They often came for visits from their bases closer to Saigon.

EOD bomb disposal. Steve Wells (l) and GMT1 Gary
Fellingham (rt). Photo courtesy Steve Wells

The best story came when I was deployed to that team in the Mekong Delta, yet it involves me only indirectly. One of the men who'd been with me the prior two-plus years was Bob W. who'd graduated from Hamilton College.

My memory has Bob somewhere in the Mekong Delta getting shot at. He got on the radio and broadcast a plea for help. Something like, "Anybody out there that speaks English?" My Prin classmate and fellow Westie,[42] Bill Franke, replied. Bill was skipper of a Navy Swift Boat patrolling nearby. Bill said something like, "Where are you? If I can, I'll swoop along shore and not stop. You guys jump onboard, and we'll get out of there fast." Bob and his team did just that, and once they were safely lying on the deck, Bill asked who they were and

---

42 Member of residence hall Rackham Court West at Principia College.

what they were doing alone out in the boonies? They replied they were Navy EOD. "Oh," Bill then said, "EOD? Do you know...?" Bob suddenly interrupted and said, "If you are from Principia, then stop the boat, and I'll take my chances onshore!"

Recently by email, Bill confirmed this sea story. He wrote, "There was just so much going on. Strangely, my most vivid memory, other than the actual pick up (which I can picture because I was the guy pulling your guys on board), were the feelings I was experiencing. I was totally exposed, with lots of bullets flying around. I remember, almost abstractly, thinking how random and impersonal it all was... they were either going to hit or miss, and there was little I was going to do about it. Further, I was worried about being pulled over the side, which was not a good thing when you were wearing fifty pounds of gear, and were as lousy a swimmer as I. But I do recall asking someone if he knew you guys and his response. I was pretty busy at that point in time, with all of the associated noises, so communication was pretty restricted."

Clearly, we're still in touch, and the network continues to work its magic.

Looking back on those years, I see how my Navy experiences changed my life, and the work we accomplished as teams and the leadership lessons I gained remain among my proudest accomplishments. EOD work is inherently defensive; every job given to us was an opportunity to get someone out of a dangerous predicament, and conversely, I never was forced deliberately to endanger another. That was for me a very satisfying way to serve my country, honor my father (a career Navy man), and participate directly in the biggest story of my generation.

EOD also gave me the chance to learn how to scuba dive and "play" with amazing tools and explosives. While Navy EOD techs today have even more cool stuff (robots, bomb suits, ground piercing radar, and sophisticated diving rigs), I got to spend three months diving among the coral reefs of the Yap, Truk, and Palau archipelagos cleaning up WWII remnants. I got to dive in Hong Kong harbor and Subic Bay, and hang with the Australian Harbor Clearance divers on the beautiful beaches of Vung Tau. I carried an ID card that said, "Due to the urgency of the mission, the bearer of this card is to be given highest priority for transportation," which meant I could easily fly around Vietnam and see the country, no questions asked. I spent six months in the company of one of the most accomplished cumshaw practitioners in the Navy, and as a result, during my time in the Mekong Delta we ate very well and lived in an exceptionally comfortable hooch.[43] My team mates were extraordinary characters, often larger than life. Some remain my friends to this day.

Those days were certainly not all fun and games. However, as is often the case, the events I remember and memorialize in my collection of sea stories, are the very good times. There is much good to remember. Brotherhood among my fellow Principians tops that list.

---

43 Cumshaw: military slang for obtaining goods by irregular means (cutting corners re. standard procurement procedures, exchanging favors, calling in debts, etc.), i.e., stocking supplies more efficiently than individual supply personnel, a ship, or a base could execute through regular channels. Hooch [or hootch]: while hooch can refer to alcoholic beverages (booze), a hooch, as used here refers to a thatched hut or any improvised living quarters.

A Mirror Sign

RICHARD HAMMER

1969

The Cua Viet river
Ran fast here that day, but
The body had been caught
By a branch on the sand bar.

With legs still in the water,
Moving, seeming to kick.
Seeming unwilling to be
Swept away, just yet.

Lost in a fire fight
The night before while on patrol.
Having been hit and falling off
The fast moving PBR.[44]

Now found, with vacant eyes
And white, wrinkled skin.
Locals watch from some distance,
The checking for possible booby traps, and
Then placement in the dark zippered bag.

This is not death's signature.
A now abandoned shell.
But a mirror sign
That there is more to life
Than this.

---

44 The PBR reference is to Patrol Boat River. These craft were used by the Navy
to keep the waters open for supply ships from the coast into Quang Tri, the
headquarters for the Marines in I Core area.

RICHARD HAMMER was an explosive ordinance disposal [EOD] officer in the U.S. Navy assigned to Oahu, Hawaii, serving two tours in Vietnam, with later service as an intelligence officer. His assignments took him to Yankee Station off Vietnam and to DaNang/Cua Viet in country. Cua Viet was the furthest north of the Navy bases in Vietnam and for most of the war was under constant attack from mortars, rockets, and ground forces by the North Vietnamese Army (NVA). Skirting the Demilitarized Zone [DMZ], the base provided fuel, ammunition, supplies, construction materials, and administration in support of Marine and Army combat forces. Following Hammer's years of active service (1966-69) he remained a Navy reservist, was called up for a year and a half active duty for Desert Storm, and retired at the rank of commander in 1993 after twenty-six years of service. After a period in business, Hammer retired, and currently enjoys teaching yoga in Cape Coral, Florida.

Hammer graduated from Principia College in 1966 with majors in business and biology. He was a member of Rackham Court East and was selected as an inaugural member of a new house organization on campus initially nicknamed Club 212. A native of Indiana, where he was born in 1944, Hammer returned to his home state to earn an MA degree at Indiana University. He has one son, Michael.

Carrier bridge

It's All in Who You Know

WILLARD M. (BILL) HANZLIK

During 1969-71, I was an officer aboard the aircraft carrier, USS *Ranger* (CVA-61), joining the ship shortly after being commissioned an ensign following Officer Candidate School in Newport, Rhode Island. The ship was on station in the Gulf of Tonkin off the coast of North Vietnam when I reported. For the next two years, I served in the navigation department, spending most days (or nights) on the bridge, driving the ship as officer of the deck. During my service on *Ranger*, the ship deployed twice from Alameda, California, to Vietnam for nine-month tours.

Shortly after joining *Ranger*, I encountered two other Principia College graduates on the ship, Dave Jones (C'66) and Mike Kneeland (C'66). Both were pilots attached to the air wing, and to discover that there were three Prin grads among 5,000 men on a ship in Vietnam was almost a homecoming.

During my second cruise to Vietnam, I was contacted by Principia biology professor John "Doc" Wanamaker with news that his brother, Ernie (who had lived in Asia since graduating from the College) wanted to meet me in Hong Kong when my ship visited there. Upon learning the ship's Hong Kong schedule, I contacted Ernie, who extended an invitation to a party at a friend's home on Victoria Peak.

By then I was a lieutenant (junior grade), and I arrived at the party (by taxi) wearing a dress white uniform. The party was held in an expansive and elegant apartment overlooking the harbor, and was crowded with Americans who were gathered, it turned out, in my honor.

Shortly after my arrival, a black sedan flying an American flag drove up and delivered another Naval officer. It was the captain of USS *Ranger*, Captain Joseph P. Moorer, the brother of the then Chief of Naval Operations, Admiral Thomas H. Moorer. It turns out that Admiral Moorer was a friend of Ernie Wannamaker!

As the evening ended, I wondered how to call a taxi to return to the dock, where I would wait for a water taxi to the ship, anchored out in the harbor. After most guests had departed, Captain Moorer asked if I would join him in his return to the ship. Could I decline? The black sedan drove us to the dock where the gleaming mahogany and brass captain's gig awaited. We rode across Hong Kong harbor on a beautiful, star-filled night to the ship.

Carrier quarterdeck. Photo by Robert M. Craig

My boss at the time, a commander, was a career officer and a true "nervous nelly," always concerned that protocol be properly followed and that nothing happen to sully his career. As fate would have it, the commander was waiting at the top of ship's gangway to greet the captain, who arrived to a smart salute from the commander. And then, behind the captain, emerging from the gig, was Lieutenant Hanzlik, to the visible dismay of the commander. He hesitated for a moment, and then also saluted me smartly.

The world changed following that night. For the rest of the cruise, the commander was extraordinarily accommodating and respectful, and I enjoyed an unusually close friendship with the captain.

WILLARD HANZLIK followed in his older brother's footsteps in several ways: both graduated from Principia College, both were residents of Brooks House South, both joined the Navy and served aboard USS *Ranger* (CVA-61), and both went to Vietnam, Willard for three tours. Williard was (almost to the day) eight years younger, born in June, 1946. Like his brother, he went to Newport to Officer Candidate School and was assigned as a deck officer to USS *Canberra* (C-70). *Canberra* was one of the first guided missile ships in the U.S. Navy, a heavy cruiser commissioned in 1943, returned to combat service in Vietnam, and during Hanzlik's tour aboard was in her final years before being decommissioned in 1970. Hanzlik transferred to the carrier *Ranger*, serving as navigation division officer and officer of the deck underway. With multiple Vietnam tours, Hanzlik's service was recognized by the Vietnam Service Medal and Navy Achievement Award. Following his Navy career, Hanzlik earned an MBA at the University of Virginia and pursued a career in investment and private equity.

Hanzlik's Principia associations involve "multiple nieces and nephews and in-laws" who attended the school, as well as his brother and sister. Willard graduated from the college with a major in business in 1968, and twenty years later he began another twenty years of service on the school's board of trustees (1988-2008). He served on Principia's investment committee as chairman of the Fred van Eck Support Foundation for Principia, a Dutch entity that owns, on behalf of Principia, a manufacturing company named Cordstrap BV (producers of strap, cordlash, buckles, and dunnage bags used to secure freight in transit). Married for over thirty-five years to Principia College [C70] alumna Corde Helms (now deceased), Hanzlik has two daughters, Lucie and Christie, both graduates of Principia College and Lucie an alumna of Principia Upper School as well. Hanzlik describes his life today as retired "sort of."

The Weapons on Either Side of the Books

STEVEN OSTENBERG SPAULDING

I was drafted into the Army in Los Angeles in 1965 and promptly went to Fort Knox, Kentucky, for basic training, advanced individual training, and college-option officer candidate school. Military training would have been a shock to the system under ordinary circumstances, but it turned out that Fort Knox was experiencing a major attack of spinal meningitis, and we were kept in quarantine from other training companies. Fear was rampant: I later heard that six of the draftees that came from Los Angeles with me passed on. My two most abiding memories of my training were the metaphysical support I received from my family and Christian Science teacher during this time and, later on, my conviction that one of the reasons I was able to complete everything successfully was that I had been significantly "toughened up" by four years of Principia football with coach Crafton![45]

My MOS (military occupational specialty) was armor (operating tanks), but I received my commission as a quartermaster officer from Fort Lee, Virginia, which resulted in my being assigned to the directorate of supply of the 506 Field Depot at Saigon, Vietnam. In August, 1967, we spent about thirty hours travelling from Oakland, California, to Tan Son Nhut airfield outside Saigon, sandwiched in a modified commercial aircraft. I expected to arrive into some sort of war zone, so I was quite bewildered when, after processing in at the airbase, we were loaded onto a bus and driven for about an hour into Saigon on the main highway which teemed with civilians on bicycles, carts, wagons, cars, and every other conceivable means of transportation. I was very uncomfortable, especially since there were no U.S. military personnel with us, and none of us on the bus were armed. As it turned

---

45 James Crafton, athletic director and football coach at Principia College.

out, travelling unarmed around Saigon became the norm for the next four to five months.

Saigon was the destination for most of the military cargo shipped into South Vietnam. Cargo was offloaded from ships at two locations: Saigon Port and New Port. My assignment was to oversee a platoon of men who 24/7 determined where to send each item coming off a ship for storage at numerous locations in and around Saigon. Sometimes, especially in the case of weapons or food, the cargo was escorted by U.S. military police [MP]; otherwise it went on unescorted civilian trucks (and you could often see portions of it for sale on the street the next day). My method of transportation, which was very uncomfortable at first, was in an open Jeep, driven by a Vietnamese civilian who spoke no English (I spoke no Vietnamese other than a little slang I picked up), unarmed, and completely vulnerable. I had elected to live on the depot, which was on the Saigon river, instead of at a hotel in the Cholon district of Saigon as I felt very unsafe in those situations, a feeling that was borne out in 1968. My "sacrifice" (said with apologies to my fellow soldiers in the field) was that there was no air-conditioning or clean or hot water for showers. As it turned out, most of the senior personnel lived in hotels in downtown Saigon, about a thirty-minute drive from the depot. So, for several months I drove around Saigon and Long Binh (a satellite depot location), urban locales as busy with people as Times Square.

All this changed on the night of January 30, 1968, when the Tet offensive was launched by the North Vietnamese and Viet Cong. I was awakened in the early morning by shouting and the sound of machine gun fire coming from helicopters on the other side of the river firing into downtown Saigon. We had no idea what was happening, but clearly the situation had changed. The next day we helped rush a shipment of weapons and body armor to the U.S. Embassy as they were still fighting the VC who had attacked. For the next month there was no traffic in or out of our depot without MP escort, and the senior officers were stuck downtown. We were normally commanded by a brigadier general and numerous high-ranking officers, but we had only a captain and several second lieutenants during this period.

(Not sure if this was good or bad!) Anyway, once we slowly began to move out from the depot, we only drove in two Jeeps, armed to the teeth, with only United States personnel. My men were in several firefights but suffered no casualties.

Steve Spaulding conducting Christian Science services in Saigon. Photo courtesy Steve Spaulding

Two personal experiences stand out to me. First, several months after Tet, I was being driven by one of my troops to Long Binh with a briefcase containing payroll for wounded troops in a hospital. On the way, we encountered a monsoon rainstorm and my driver lost control of the Jeep, and we went off the road, flipping and landing into a barbed wire apron. We both had jumped out of the vehicle, and I landed on the rocks and gashed open my knee. My driver was unhurt. It turned out we had an Army ambulance behind us who stopped, picked me up, and took me to a hospital. When the doctor took a look at me, she said I had severed several cartilage and needed to have an operation to repair them.

I asked her if she knew what Christian Science was, and, when she said she did, I said I would like to handle it through Christian

Science treatment. She was a captain and outranked me, so I wasn't sure if I needed her agreement, but she shrugged and said, OK, if that is what I wanted to do. She cleaned and bandaged the wound and gave me some crutches. My driver found another Jeep, we finished paying the troops, and we returned to Saigon before dark, always a priority! My communication home was by letter and audio cassette, and much prayerful help was forthcoming. Within two weeks I was walking and jogging normally, and the healing has been permanent! Absolute proof that Christian Science heals!

A second experience was entirely different. I was a wartime minister for The Mother Church[46] and in mid-1968 they asked me to conduct a Christian Science Sunday service in downtown Saigon. Things had settled down somewhat, so I agreed, and, on Sunday, I checked out a Jeep and headed into the city, trying to be very alert to being followed. I was able to find my destination and pulled into the building courtyard, again trying to be aware of my surroundings. The context was striking: I walked into the apartment with a briefcase in one hand filled with the Bible, *Science and Health with Key to the Scriptures*,[47] a Christian Science hymnal, and *Quarterly*,[48] and dressed in flak jacket and steel helmet and carrying in the other hand an M-16 rifle, .45 pistol, and grenades. Using the desk as my "readers' platform," I placed the weapons on either side of the books. Recalling this scene has always amused me! The congregation was mostly French and Vietnamese, and I read in English, but I still felt these gatherings in Saigon were a special service, certainly for me!

Throughout my military experience, I focused on Mrs. Eddy's statement, "Whatever it is your duty to do, you can do without harm to

46 The First Church of Christ, Scientist, Boston, Massachusetts, and world-wide headquarters of Christian Science.

47 Mary Baker G. Eddy, *Science and Health With Key to the Scriptures* (Boston: The Christian Science Publishing Society, first published 1875), is the Christian Science text book.

48 The *Christian Science Quarterly* publishes weekly Bible lessons, studied daily by Christian Scientists, and read Sundays at Christian Science services world-wide.

yourself,"[49] ironically (or should I say meaningfully?) the very same message that independently served William Donaldson [see Donaldson's essay herein entitled, "Whatever it is your Duty to do…"]. I truly felt that the strength of that statement kept me safe during the Fort Knox meningitis siege. Even more so, in Saigon: after Tet, we spent many nights manning the perimeter of our depot, having been alerted about possible attacks; yet after one year of standing guard and much traveling away from the depot, not once did I shoot at anyone, nor did anyone shoot at me! I was so grateful to return home essentially unscarred by war.

 **STEVE SPAULDING'S** major in French at Principia College most likely focused his attention more on the Loire Valley than on French Indochina, but not long after his graduation he found himself assigned to a one year tour in Vietnam, where he served in the U.S. Army in Saigon. His cousins Rob and Chip Ostenberg would serve in the military, as would his brother Clark. After initial training at Fort Knox, Kentucky, Spaulding was assigned to Fort Lee, Virginia, and in August, 1967, went to Vietnam to serve in the directorate of supply department, 506 Field Depot, Saigon. Spaulding received the Bronze Star in recognition of his service and was discharged in 1970 at the rank of first lieutenant.

Born in 1942 in Port Chester, New York, Spaulding lived in Bel Air, California, at the time he traveled to Elsah, Illinois, to enroll in Principia College. An accomplished athlete, Spaulding lettered each of his four years in football and golf. He served the Christian Science College Organization as first reader and was a member of the Starlight Chorale. His residence hall was Rackham Court East. Both of his parents attended Principia College; his father was also an alumnus of the Upper School. His three brothers, Tuck (US63 C67), Clark (US64 C68), and David (US69 C73) followed suit, attending the upper school and college. Married to Carolyn Witt, Spaulding has three sons, Mike (US87), Christopher (US89), and Jeff (US89 C93), all three educated at the upper school and Jeff attending the college. Spaulding graduated from Principia College with a BA

---

49 Mary Baker G. Eddy, *Science and Health With Key to the Scriptures* (Boston: The Christian Science Publishing Society, first published 1875): 385. Used courtesy of The Mary Baker Eddy Collection.

degree in 1963, and his career since the military has been mostly in commercial real estate, from which he is now retired. Between 2007 and 2015, he spent eight years as a director at High Ridge House, a Christian Science nursing facility in Riverdale, NY. Currently residing in Bridgeport, Connecticut, Spaulding enjoys time with his grandchildren and remains active at church.

"Whatever it is Your Duty to Do..."

WILLIAM K. DONALDSON

My account is more church testimony than war monologue and is offered in that spirit. In the fall of 1966 I transferred to Principia College from an ivy league school. By December of 1968 I had accumulated enough credits to graduate with a BA in religion and philosophy. I told the academic office to mail me my diploma, and I headed home to the suburbs of Philadelphia to face my local draft board. You see my draft board had a problem meeting their monthly quota of inductees for the Pentagon. Eighty-six percent of their eligible candidates were in college safely garrisoned by their II-S status. Hence the local board was happy to see me come through the doors. So I volunteered for the draft. Their only question was, "Would you like to spend the Christmas holidays with your family?" To which I replied, "Of course, yes."

I entered the U.S. Army in January of 1969 and was sent to Fort Bragg for basic training. In retrospect, it wasn't one of the brightest decisions I'd ever made. North Carolina winters are cold and wet. I did eventually graduate from basic after a month's medical leave for contracting "double pneumonia."

While in basic, I took a battery of tests, and I was told I qualified for officer candidate school. I knew the fatality rates in Vietnam for second lieutenants assigned to (or leading) infantry units. I said, "No thanks; what's next?" I was directed to fill out what the Army calls a wish list. Looking at a list of potential Army careers, I chose "chaplain's assistant" as my most inspired choice. Instead, the Army chose "military police officer," better known as 95 Bravo.

I was directed next to Fort Gordon, Georgia, for eight weeks of police training. Nothing particularly astonishing happened there.

If you are "law abiding," it is not a difficult transition to become "law enforcing." One surprise did occur at this juncture, however: I acquired a new nick name among my colleagues. They decided I should henceforth be known as "Deacon Bill" since it had been duly noted that I attended chapel twice a week. Upon graduation, I was ordered to report to the 57th MP Company at West Point.

Does the U.S. Military Academy have a police problem? No, but during the football season they have a horrendous traffic problem parking cars and buses on a campus never designed for 20,000 visitors. I had been stationed there but three months when a remarkable thing occurred as we were preparing for the Army-Air Force game. It was a pleasant fall morning, and I had been to the library at West Point to read my Bible lesson-sermon. I was walking down the hill to my barracks near the Hudson River when a powerful intuition overcame me which simply said to my consciousness "South Vietnam." Initially, I thought it was a suggestion of fear, but the only way I found peace was to respond to this angelic warning by saying, "If I have to go, I will go."

Six weeks later, a police sergeant in our barracks stood on a chair and shouted, "We've received some forty-five orders for Vietnam." Our company strength was a little less than 200. As each name was called, he simply said, "South Vietnam." When he got to my name, he said, "West Germany!" You can imagine the accusatory looks I received, but much as I welcomed the good news, it just didn't feel right that I was the only one so designated for a different assignment. A few minutes later, my own sergeant said to me words like these, "Not to burst your bubble, Bill, but you're headed to Vietnam with the rest of us." Then the correction seemed right to my spiritual intuition, and I was at peace. I reckoned if my Heavenly Father was so merciful as to give me a "heads-up," then He would be present to protect me whatever the Army dished my way. That angelic warning, and the inferences I drew from it, served me well for the next thirty years when I had police assignments in the States far more dangerous than my subsequent war experience in Vietnam turned out to be.

In December of '69, I reported to Long Binh in the III Corps area and was assigned to a combat MP unit whose duties were principally rear-echelon. Working alongside my South Vietnamese police counterparts gave me a new perspective. Many of them had served more than ten years in a civil war and lost valued family members. Their outlook had a sobering effect upon any spirit in me that tended to regard this matter as a one year adventure.

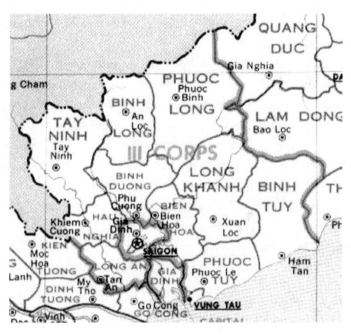

Map of III Corps Tactical Zone, South Vietnam.
Photo: Central Intelligence Agency

My most interesting criminal case started out rather innocently. At 0200 hours three "eighteen wheelers" approached my exit gate to a supply depot fully loaded with construction materials, and the trucks seemed to have the proper paperwork. The time for such a departure was unusual but not unprecedented. But I noted they were not part of a convoy. And each GI driver was slightly intoxicated and in a celebratory mood. The requisitions appeared to be in order, but something didn't "smell right." When one of the drivers admitted to me that he was flying home later the same day and was in a holding company awaiting his flight, I called for my supervisor. The soldiers were placed under arrest. The three men later made a full confession to a C.I.D. (Criminal Investigative Division) unit. The trucked materials were to have been delivered to the black market in Saigon. The drivers were to be wired stateside their percentage of the ill-gotten gains. The masterminds of the ingenious scheme were South Korean nationals employed by the Army's logistical team who had dreamed up this fraud. It was speculated later that perhaps the Viet Cong were going to use the stolen construction materials to buttress tunnels in the III Corps region.

To summarize, I was grateful not to have been present during the Tet Offensive of '68. I was also grateful not to have been plagued with PTSD [post-traumatic stress disorder] nor exposed to Agent Orange.[50] After eleven months I was sent home "harmless and unharmed" in time for Christmas, and I was given an honorable discharge with a good conduct medal to show my folks. I went on to make a career in law enforcement in two metropolitan areas, New York City and Boston. In 1999, I retired with the rank of police lieutenant. My life's story attests well to the statement found on page 385 in *Science and Health* by Mrs. Eddy: "Whatever it is your duty to do, you can do without harm to yourself."[51]

---

50 PTSD [post-traumatic stress disorder] is a disorder in which a person has difficulty recovering after experiencing or witnessing a terrifying event. Herbicide Orange (HO) or Agent Orange was one of the highly toxic herbicides and defoliants used by the United States military during the Vietnam War, circa 1961-71.

51 Mary Baker Eddy, *Science and Health with Key to the Scriptures* (Boston: The Christian Science Publishing Society, first published 1875): 385. Used courtesy of The Mary Baker Eddy Collection.

WILLIAM K. DONALDSON pursued a career in police work both during his military enlistment and after his discharge. A specialist four in the Army, Donaldson served a tour in Vietnam in 1969-70 working as a combat MP (military police) in Long Binh, the largest U.S. Army base in Vietnam. Located near Biên Hòa Air Base and sited some thirty-five kilometers from Saigon, Long Binh was a major Army base of 60,000 personnel in 1969, a logistics center, and the major command headquarters for United States Army Vietnam (USARV). It was the largest U.S. Army base outside the continental United States. Donaldson returned home with the Vietnam Service Medal, National Defense Medal, and Vietnam Campaign Medal. He then shifted his law enforcement career to become an urban police lieutenant in Boston and New York City, serving on the civilian police force for thirty years.

Born in 1946 in New York City, Donaldson studied philosophy at Principia College, graduating in December, 1968, an early graduate of the class of 1969. A member of Brooks House North, Donaldson was active in intramural sports participating on his house's basketball team. Immediately after graduation, he joined the Army, went to boot camp at Fort Bragg, North Carolina, was stationed briefly at West Point, and then was sent to Vietnam attached to the headquarters troop command, USARV.

Brothers

STEVE SANDBERG

"Unique" describes my Vietnam experience. It begins with a hug and kiss from my college sweetheart (whom I had recently married) as I board a Boeing 707 for the twenty-plus hour flight from Travis Air Force Base, California, to Tan Son Nhut air base, Saigon, Vietnam, along with 180 others headed to the 'war zone.' Upon landing I was issued two sets of olive green fatigues, a cap, and a pair of jungle boots. Then on to a Huey Helo for the one hour ride to Binh Thuy, headquarters for HA(L)-3 [a Navy "helicoptor attack light" squadron], and then one more hour flight to DET-One, based aboard a U.S. LST ["landing ship, tank," an amphibious transport ship) anchored in the Gulf of Thailand. Welcome to the Mekong Delta, Yankee boy.

From the LST [I recall USS *Garrett County* (LST-786) and USS *Jennings County* (LST-846)], my rotating one-day-on, one-day-off, flight schedule launched me to Seafloat, the floating barges anchorage adjacent to the southernmost village in South Vietnam, Nam Can. From there the Navy's Operation Solid Anchor began. Our mission was to provide overhead gunship aerial coverage for the Navy's brown-water Swift Boats and Navy Seals as they patrolled/inserted the rivers and canals of those southernmost rivers and canals. They were looking for Viet Cong and North Vietnam Army regulars, who were supposed to be in the jungle forest for R&R [rest and relaxation], down from north of the DMZ—or so the stories went. We didn't encounter too many brown uniform-clad locals; however there were a lot of "black pajama"-attired folk carrying weapons of all sorts!

DET-One, HAL-3 had ten detachments spread out in the Mekong Delta south of Saigon. Each detachment had two Huey (H-1) helicopter gunships armed with two 7.25 rocket pods (controlled by the pilot), and an M-60 machine gun fixed mounted controlled by the copilot. Two door gunners each carried an M-60, firing them from side cargo doors. A detachment had eight pilots and eight crew rotating on/off, with most flights occurring during daylight hours. But at night 'on call' crews stood ready to 'scramble' launch, if called upon to support night-time Swift Boat Seal activity.

Two of the individual Air Medals I received were awarded for separate flying missions in which our help encountered hostile fire. One was a night-time evacuation of a Seal team whose mission had gone bad. The Seals had encountered a large number of enemy and need to be air lifted out of the jungle. We landed in the jungle, took them aboard, and "hastily departed" from an area where we were not welcome by local VC inhabitants. Most of the Mekong Delta was considered "hostile" Viet Cong territory, and while one might have taken hostile fire or simply flown on support missions over "bad guy territory," the region in general was hostile and air medals accumulated. A mission was a single flight, and so many single flights then equaled a "strike flight." Most of my time in country was in the Mekong Delta, so. I received thirty-three strike flight Air Medals for missions during my year (June 1968 to July 1969) in country.

It was aboard an LST on which Principian Doug Dixon, XO, and I reunited. And of course, Bill Franke was aboard Seafloat as captain of a Swift Boat. Our encounter on the river (Bill's and mine) has been described in an earlier chapter establishing the truism that from our Midwestern college you can run, but you cannot hide, from "all" those Principia grads.[52]

After six months down south I was entitled to a week of R&R. Mine took me back on a helo to Binh Thuy, then on to Saigon, and once again onto a Boeing 707. This time I was headed east to Honolulu, Hawaii. There she was, my college sweetheart, ready with a hug and a kiss. We headed off to a luxury hotel on Waikiki Beach, as far away from the war as I could get. Other duties called: when you see your wife in a bikini, six months pregnant, a different sort of valor requires digging a hole in the beach sand so that she can lie tummy down in the sand. We also discovered the Hawaiian muumuu, the original maternity dress for before, during, and after pregnancy.

---

52 See "Help in the Line of Duty," in Part I of this anthology.

After a week, I was back aboard that Boeing 707 and up, up, and away again to South Vietnam. Upon landing this time, I returned to HA(L)-3 HQ where I remained to fly logistic missions to the ten detachments that were scattered throughout South Vietnam. The accommodations at DET-one and HQ were a far cry from those on Waikiki Beach, but neither were they like *Apocalypse Now* and *Platoon* images. After a flight to SeaFloat, I typically returned to the LST for a shower, dinner in the officers' mess, served by Navy stewards on table cloths with heavy silverware and china, and then we might attend a shipboard movie — reel to reel — all in the air-conditioned spaces of the ship, and finally, I was off to bed, sleeping on a bunk with sheets and blanket and "inconvenienced" because the A/C sometimes gets too cold at night! At HQ, you got the three meals in a mess hall, slept in your own room, and went to your office, although not all were air conditioned. You wore those olive green fatigues a lot when not flying and wearing a flight suit. And so it went for the remaining six months: a regular routine with daily flights to the detachments throughout South Vietnam, usually ending up back at HQ.

Unless, that is, your helo has mechanical trouble and you have to spend a day out in the jungle waiting for spare parts to arrive. Or something really unique happens, as when I landed aboard a Navy support supply ship anchored up one of the many canals that the French built, and was informed that I was the proud father of "a baby boy, mother and child doing well." I immediately rushed to the ship's supply store: "Do you have any Hersey candy bars — with *nuts* — I've just had a baby boy, and I don't smoke cigars!" Leave it to the Surface Navy Supply logistics to provide what you need when you least expect it. She was six months pregnant when I last saw her! How time flies when you're having fun in the Mekong Delta. Time for another R&R: war is hell; off to Hong Kong for a week, same old Boeing 707 flight.

The finish line is getting close now, with only three months to go. The logistics flights continue with regularity, the flight time adding up to over 1600 hours for the twelve months. The flights down to DET-One reiterate that you're still trying to win over the locals' hearts and minds, even if the Agent Orange has pretty much de-foliated the forest from which the locals make their living, turning trees into charcoal which the Vietnamese float up the canals and river to Saigon.

Finally, my orders came: I was to depart from Cam Ranh Bay just south of the DMZ aboard another of those Boeing 707s. I left from Binh Thuy by helo to the base up north. After a night on that 'freedom plane,' along with 180-plus other guys, we were heading home. Once off the ground we heard the landing gear go up, and a loud cheer echoed through the plane. In twenty-plus hours we landed at Fort Lewis, Washington. There, on the tarmac, stood that woman ready with another hug and kiss.

Webster defines unique as "being without a like or equal; unmatched; single in kind or excellence; sole." Was my experience unique or typical? I am not sure how many of the original 180 passengers aboard my flight *to* Vietnam, a year ago, or aboard subsequent 707 flights to southeast Asia, remained in South Vietnam never to be greeted, as I was, upon returning home. The Vietnam Wall in DC speaks volumes about those who did not make it aboard a return 'Freedom Flight.' There is a bond among those who went to that remote country to serve in some capacity, a bond that few knew could even exist before our duty took us there. The other day, I met a man who was wearing a baseball cap lettered with "Vietnam Vet" and the ribbons associated with that "conflict." When he was told I had been there too, he hugged me: "Brother Welcome Home" were the few simple words out of his mouth. I think, for me, the word describing our shared experience was "unique" after all. We were brothers, for sure!

STEVE SANDBERG served for thirteen years on active duty as a "regular Navy'" officer attached to various Navy squadrons, staffs, and commands. His father had been a Navy Supply Officer during World War II, so the Navy seemed a natural fit. Sandberg completed flight school in Pensacola, Florida, in June, 1967 and as a designated helicopter pilot, he was ordered to San Diego, serving one year in helicopter anti-submarine squadron eight (HS-8), before being ordered to HA(L) 3 for a one year tour of duty in Vietnam. Following Vietnam, Sandberg returned to San Diego to serve as an instructor pilot in HS-10 squadron. Three years later, Sandberg was ordered to CVW-11, Air Wing Staff, to serve as an administrative officer aboard USS *Kitty Hawk* (CV-65). Then, in 1976, Sandberg was sent to Washington DC to attend a one-year post-graduate school (Naval Intelligence) after which he was off to the Pentagon and the Joint Staff, where he served his last year of active duty as executive assistant in The Office of the Chairman, Joint Chiefs of Staff, at that time General David Jones, U.S. Air Force.

Sandberg resigned his regular officer commission in August, 1980, and (now a lieutenant commander) became a "weekend warrior," joining a naval reserve unit for fourteen years, before retiring at the rank of captain in 1994. Serving in various staff positions, Sandberg was assigned to one of the naval reserve units in Washington DC that supported the Supreme Allied Commander Atlantic.

For his exemplary service as a helicopter pilot in Vietnam, Sandberg received two individual action Air Medals and thirty-three strike flight Air Medals, as well as the Vietnam Cross of Gallantry. His military duties took him to Binh Thuy, Gulf of Thailand, Saigon, Cam Ranh Bay, Yankee Station, Japan, Hong Kong, Singapore, South Korea, Guam, Hawaii, London, West Berlin, Madrid, and Brussels.

Born in 1943 in Kansas City, Kansas, Sandberg attended Principia from eighth grade through college, graduating with a degree in business administration in 1965. He would later earn a master's degree from Central Michigan University. Successful in athletics at Principia, Sandberg lettered three years in football and four years in baseball. A member of Buck House, Sandberg was a leader in campus governance, serving as Men's Organization president his senior year. He noted with tongue in cheek that among his extracurricular activities were observations of the submarine races viewed from atop the campus bluffs overlooking the Mississippi River, (a euphemism for the school's "lover's lane"). He was successful in this endeavor as well, marrying his college sweetheart, and C65 classmate Suzie Loomis. Fifty years later she confesses she plans to keep

Sandberg around to see how he turns out. The Sandbergs' two children spent a couple of years in the mid 1980s at Principia Middle and Upper Schools.

Following his active military service, Sandberg has pursued a career as a stock broker. He enjoys boating and traveling and lives in Austin, Texas.

Swift Boat On Patrol, CosDiv 11, the Ca Mau Peninsula

WILLIAM E. FRANKE

As I commenced writing this account, I sat at a desk in a hotel room in Ho Chi Minh City (formerly known as Saigon). I peered through a window overlooking the Saigon River and saw below the statue of Tran Hung Dao, the revered Vietnamese general who on three separate occasions in the thirteenth century repelled Mongol invasions of what is now Vietnam. It is ironic that I received the email from my good friends Robert Craig and Steve Wells asking that I tell of my 1969-70 tour of duty in Vietnam, just as I was departing for that country forty-eight years later on business. As I conclude this article, I prepare to travel to San Diego, site of both my training and a memorial to those who served with me in Vietnam "still on patrol," where I will attend the change of command ceremony for my nephew, who will be assuming command of an *Arleigh Burke*-class destroyer.

Candidly, despite our strong friendship, I was reluctant to accept their request. But, perhaps it is time. If not now, when?... And for what greater reason than the request of two friends and fellow sailors, one an accomplished and respected historian? I will give it my best shot, in the process seeking to explain anecdotally enough to provide a true appreciation. While relating accounts from my perspective, I do not do so for myself, but for those amongst us who did not return... men alongside whom I served... men who are honored every two years at memorial services attended by the surviving "Swiftees" over which I typically preside.

Further, the reader must appreciate that there are dozens of stories that could be told, from which I have selected a few in order to be responsive. I understand that the archives of the division to which I was primarily assigned record some 110 firefights with combatants during my tenure. There are stories with each such incident, in which men far more heroic than I could ever hope to be distinguished themselves. When men are trying desperately to destroy each other, or when we are forced to take these military vessels, boats often heavily damaged from combat, into the notoriously rough Gulf of Siam, dramatic things happen, ... each of them potentially a life or death circumstance... with my unavoidable involvement in the command role that I played. That is reality... and reality, within limits, is what I have been asked to provide.

During the Vietnam War, I served as a commissioned line officer in the United States Navy, on active duty for three years and on reserve status for an additional three years. A "line officer" or "officer of the line," upon which command authority is bestowed, is rooted in Navy tradition; the term references the 18th- and 19th-century British Royal Navy strategy of deploying warships in line formations to maximize the effectiveness of their weapons, from which the counter tactic of "crossing the T" evolved. (Crossing the T was first used by the Japanese fleet against the Russians in the 1905 Sino-Russian war, with devastating impact upon a far superior force, which in turn led to the anarchy in Russia from which Lenin ultimately rose to power.)

After several months training at the Naval Base in Coronado, California, I served a year in Vietnam, the first of my two assignments while on active duty. I lived aboard a river patrol boat (a "Swift Boat") as the commanding officer (actually, the Officer in Charge, which is the designation used for non-commissioned naval vessels). Further, on many combat missions after the first few months, I also served as the Operational and Tactical Commander (OTC) of the mission. As OTC, in addition to my own boat, I commanded up to twelve other boats, air support of generally two Seawolf helicopter gunships, a reconnaissance helicopter, and occasional off shore gunfire support. Depending upon the mission, we might embark up to a division of Vietnamese marines. We also were frequently called upon to support

Navy Seal Teams. We operated exclusively in the rivers and canals of the Mekong Delta and the Ca Mau Peninsula.

But first, I must start with not one, but three confessions relating to incidents during my military service pre-dating this tour to Vietnam.

Swift Boats PCF-23. Photo courtesy William E. Franke

Confession Number One: I am probably the only Naval Officer in the history of the United States Navy that did not know how to swim, nor even float! While at OCS, I had a buddy, another midshipman, take the test for me. When I showed up for Swift Boat training, however, the Navy ordered me to take it again! I flunked and spent two very long weeks with two chief petty officers who were assigned to teach me to swim... and not very nicely. It was ugly.

Confession Number Two: Although accepted into Officer Candidate School, before my report date, I received a draft notice to report to the U.S. Army on an earlier date. It's nice to be wanted. I got the draft notice late on a Friday afternoon. I called my recruiter, who could only give me a general phone number at the Navy Department. At about six p.m. that Friday night, I called that number. Out of the thousands of people who worked in the Navy Department, and at this late hour on the start of a weekend, the person who answered the phone was the very person who was frantically typing the list of people who had been accepted for the next OCS class, scheduled to report on the following Monday at 0600 hours. Upon hearing of my predicament, without asking anyone, that sweet lady simply erased my name from the April report date list and wrote it in for the March report date list. I left the next morning in order to report on time.

Later, the Army came to get me (rivalries), but our base commander was a sports fanatic, and I had had a great basketball game the prior weekend, so he refused to turn me over, and I became a sailor instead of a grunt.

Confessions Number Three: This confession relates to liberty, the scourge of every sailor. After I knew I was headed for Vietnam (for which I was a volunteer), I visited two Principia College mates, Bill Bollinger and Jay Anderson, in Washington, DC; this was a problem in that DC was well beyond the distance permitted by my liberty. Bollinger, as he drove home from DC, was hurriedly driving me to an airport in Philadelphia to catch the last flight to Newport when we were stopped by a radar speed trap. Knowing that I was in serious trouble if I missed this flight, I jumped out of the car, slammed my midshipman's cover (hat) on my head, and announced in the sternest of voices to the officer walking to the car that it was a matter of national security that I get to the airport in Philadelphia in order to make my ship as I was the cryptology officer. I suppose one could argue that position, except for the cryptology part.

Have you ever played telephone, where each subsequent recitation is even more emphatic than the last? Well, this police officer called his desk sergeant, who called the chief of police, who because it extended beyond their jurisdiction called the Pennsylvania highway patrol. By that last call, I must have been characterized as James Bond because...I realize this appears far-fetched, but I swear that it was true…I got a siren-screaming, lights-blaring, tires-peeling ride to the Philadelphia airport… even to the point of a screeching halt in the middle of an intersection at the Pennsylvania state line where a waiting highway patrol car had blocked oncoming traffic, waiting to drive me the balance of the trip. I was real glad none of those guys knew what a cryptologist did. I still remember Bollinger sitting in his car, staring in disbelief as we screeched off… being handed the speeding ticket.

I made the flight, but it was clear that I was the cause of the delay. As I ambled down the aisle, I saw my company commander, a lieutenant in the Navy, who didn't know whether to chew me out for being out of bounds and for causing him to be late in leaving or just to laugh. He must have been related to that little old lady at the Pentagon, because he simply shook his head and let it ride. Once again, I was destined to be a sailor and not a grunt.

Swift Boats PCF-40.
Photo courtesy U.S. Naval War College Museum

A Swift Boat was a twenty-seven-plus-ton, fifty-foot-long vessel armed with three Browning fifty-caliber and up to an additional three M-60 machine guns, an 81-millimeter mortar, and an almost always malfunctioning automatic grenade launcher. It carried a crew of six enlisted (including one Vietnamese sailor) and one officer. On my crew, the Vietnamese sailor was sixteen years old, two of the U.S.

sailors were seventeen, two were eighteen, and my leading petty officer was nineteen years of age. I was the old guy at age twenty-two. Because the fleet was losing so many of its officers in this duty, I was one of a few ensigns assigned to Swift Boats straight out of Officer Candidate School.

PC-38 Riverine. Photo courtesy William E. Franke

A Swift Boat had, at least on paper, a top speed of 27 knots, which is about 21 miles per hour... as my leading petty officer stated, about the speed we drive through a school zone. One cool fact, however, was that we gained enough skill in handling these boats that we could surf waves with them, thereby achieving speeds up to about 38 knots; this worked really well in transit... if the wave was going our way! Adjusting our speed to catch a wave as it was breaking, we could then further adjust the speed of the boat to keep on top of it, literally surfing the wave... just as with a surf board, except this was a twenty-seven-ton surf board. It was pretty exciting having that twenty-seven-ton boat sticking out into the air up to five feet ahead of the wave and some twenty feet above the trough in front. (You did not want to go any further, however, because you could fall off the wave forward and into a disaster.)

A Swift Boat could never be confused with a luxury cruiser. Except when we were able to barter with local fishermen for fresh fish and vegetables, we generally ate C Rations, or "Sea Rats," which had literally been packaged for combatants during World War II. (The only exception was a fresh candy bar inserted into the Sea Rats package, coming from a company in St. Joseph, Missouri, owned, as I recall, by the family of Kim Kimbell, a classmate at Principia College. But, those candy bars were generally long gone before they made it to our boats.) We heated the cans of food, generally pork and beans, by burning C-4, a plastic explosive. (C-4 requires an electrical shock to explode.) The sulphur content of the C 4, however, destroyed any taste the food might have left after some thirty years in a can... probably not a bad thing. The "facilities" were a bucket with a line tied to it, or in our case two buckets one of which was painted pink to designate it as the Officer's Head. Our bunks had foam rubber mattresses covered in plastic that were so hot to sleep on, especially during the day inside a baking cabin, that you would wake up every hour or so as the sweat pooled around your nostrils to the point that you were inhaling it. We showered when it rained... tracking a rain squall in the Gulf of Siam with our radar long enough to strip down, lather up, and then, hopefully, rinse. (That ritual was quite a sight: up to a hundred skinny, pasty white, shivering sailors running about naked on the fantails of the boats.)

Nor could a Swift Boat be characterized as seaworthy. These boats, originally designed to transport personnel to offshore drilling platforms in the Gulf of Mexico, had been modified to carry as much armament as possible, markedly raising the center of gravity and hence making them extremely vulnerable to heavy seas. While patrols going into a canal were not pleasant, to a man we all felt that fighting thirty-foot swells for hours in the pitch black, on a boat tossing so violently that the helmsman had to be tied down, was our greatest fear. Soon after my arrival in Vietnam, while attempting to deliver the mail to a "tin can" (e.g. a U.S. Navy destroyer), a boat was lost at sea when waves crashed through the gun tub (which was seventeen feet above the water line); water rushed into the cabin and sank the boat with all hands.

In Vietnam, the original 102 Swift Boats were divided into five divisions, ranging from Da Nang in the north down and around the coastline to the Cambodian border on the opposite coast. Other than those boats in Da Nang who encountered some combat along the border with the north, the "action" was in Coastal Divisions 13 (Mekong Delta) and the feared Black Cat division, CosDiv 11 (the Ca Mau Peninsula).

Upon arrival in country, I was initially assigned to CosDiv 13, which was charged with denying the enemy the use of the rivers and canals of the Mekong Delta, the only viable means to transport the tonnage of supplies, equipment, and men required to wage war at this scale, by the bad guys. The Mekong Delta is roughly a fifteen thousand square mile area (about the size of Maryland and Delaware combined), with hundreds of miles of interconnected rivers and canals meandering through marshlands and farm lands. It was, and remains, the bread basket of South Vietnam, with most of the produce for that nation grown there.

The South Vietnamese government was in control of the Mekong (at least during the daylight hours), with patrols there generally undertaken solo. Depending upon your assignment, a Swift Boat could end up a couple hundred miles from base, spending up to six weeks on your own. As a consequence, the crews learned to forage from local resources.

I can give you some sense of the nature of duty in CosDiv 11 by describing my first patrol in that division.

After an indoctrination mission of about twenty hours (where I manned a machine gun on the mission that Nebraska Senator Bob Kerry's Seal Team was inserted, and where he was critically wounded), I was sent out alone with my brand new crew (with whom I had trained in Coronado) to patrol the Sông Cổ Chiên.[53]

On the first day of our first patrol, a calm, but clearly stressed, skipper, patrolling the sector immediately upstream, called for assistance. I arrived to find his boat surrounded by some twenty sampans, with several little old Vietnamese ladies incomprehensibly and excitedly hollering in unison. Regretting that I had left my ceremonial sword in the states and therefore ill prepared to repel boarders (just joking), I nonetheless went on board his boat, after weaving our way through many sampans, to discover that these ladies had brought a young girl on board who was in labor, seeking the assistance of the Americans. Oh boy... what do I do now? As the senior officer (everybody was senior to me), the other skipper pulled rank and told me he would get on the comms to a doctor at the medevac hospital and relay to me the instructions for the delivery of a baby... which he did... and, much to my amazement, I did as well... finally extracting from the birth canal a puffy eyed baby girl. What a dichotomy! I was there to wage war, but my very first act on my first patrol in Vietnam, was to assist in the delivery of life.

That same day ended with another twist, one whose irony was not discovered for twenty five years! At about two a.m. we got another call, but this call was not calm. It was from an Army advisor whose words we could barely comprehend with all of the static and heavy weapons fire in the background. His Vietnamese compound had been overrun by North Vietnamese Regulars. He sent out a distress signal

---

53 Sông Cổ Chiên is the Co Chien River (a tributary of the Tien River) that flows 82 kilometers northwest to southeast from Vinh Long city and into the East Sea.

(I think it was in fact called "Broken Arrow"), a code word for which there was a standing order to cease all other missions and come to the aid of an American in imminent risk. The only problem was that to do so we had to transit at high speed a very narrow, winding canal controlled by the enemy, a shallow waterway where at any moment we could run aground. We got underway, at the fastest possible speed. I can remember the huge wake our twin 490 horsepower diesel engines churned up astern in such shallow, restricted waters, a canal as narrow as fifteen feet, with constantly exploding, massively high, spouts of water as the wake hit the uneven shoreline. The canal was so narrow that on a few occasions, on turns, our propellers dug into the bank. We came around a bend to encounter a wooden foot bridge across the stream that had been knocked down to block passage: we rammed through it (much to the consternation of our gunner's mate in the peat tank, or bow, of the boat). We arrived on site, set up a defensive parameter as best we could, and fired into the compound every single mortar round (but one) that we held, having first warned our allies to hunker down. The attack was blunted, and the American and his troops retook the position.

Why did we not fire the last round? Because it became lodged in the mortar tube due to the excessive heat from firing so many rounds so fast (the tube became slightly warped). We knew we were exceeding limits, but we had no choice. Each round had nine bags of black powder, each about the size of a brat, affixed around the base, attached at both ends by a tiny thread that often tore away when a round was inserted. We feared one of those bags of black powder had torn lose, not at all uncommon, and was now touching that extremely hot mortar tube. If so, it would soon detonate, causing massive destruction. There are not a lot of places to hide on a fifty foot boat if that round cooked off, especially in that this particular round was a "willie pete" or white phosphorous round.

We quickly exited the fire zone, returning to the middle of the river in our patrol area. At that point, with the balance of the crew as far forward as possible, and after we had poured water down the tube to prevent that cook off, my gunners mate inverted the mortar, hitting the tube against the stanchions supporting it, until the mortar round slowly edged out and into my waiting arms as I lay directly beneath the mortar tube. I held that unstable round in the exact same way that I had held that little baby just a few hours earlier, except this time I slowly slid to the side of the boat and gently dropped the round into the river. I might add that I was wearing so much flack gear... all of it stinking after years of constant use by endlessly sweating sailors... that I looked like the Michelin man.

Sometime later, the advisor we rescued came to our base to thank me, but no one knew what he was talking about. I was never very good at term papers in college, or after-action reports in the Navy. Because I had only been in the base for a short time before being transferred to a new division, and because I never got around to writing that after-action report, few even knew who I was... or of the incident.

The episode continues... fast forward twenty-five years... I am leaving the first reunion of the Swift Boat Sailors Association with my own baby girls... two daughters, then ages twelve and nine. A very pretty young lady runs up to embrace me, crying that, but for me, she would have never known her father. The Vietnamese advisor we had rescued had come to our reunion with his daughter, born while he was on that tour in the Mekong Delta, to find me at this first reunion. Yet another baby girl, touched that day—what a world we lived in! I was humbled.

On my first patrol, I delivered a baby, engaged in an extended fire fight to save an American advisor, struggled to free a blazing hot mortar round lodged in our mortar tube, and along the way got entirely too close to a B-52 airstrike, all in about twenty-four hours.

After about two months at CosDiv 13, I was called in by the division commander, a great guy from Buffalo, New York, and told that I was being transferred to CosDiv 11... the feared Black Cat Division. I still remember that sixty second conversation, and all of the anxieties and emotions that surged, upon being given the news. We were to get underway the next a.m.

The transit to CosDiv 11, commencing 7 May 1969, took three days. We steamed to the very southern tip of Vietnam and then came back around and up through the Gulf of Siam to Phu Quoc Island, which was about seventy nautical miles due west of Vietnam's border with Cambodia. During this time, other than refueling stops, we were alone, without even an ability to raise U.S. forces on our comms.

Mike Solhaug (left) and Bill Franke (right).
Photo courtesy William E. Franke

At the last refueling stop alongside an LST, we arrived just as the CosDiv 11 boats were returning from a mission. Arriving just ahead of them, we stood with the other sailors from the "T", watching for them to come out of the dense foliage of the shoreline. At first, we saw their wake from the powerful diesels… then we heard the familiar drone of those diesels. Finally, they came closer for us to see five boats in a line. Then, just as a flight of aircraft peeling out of formation, the boats left formation one at a time to come alongside.

As the boats got nearer it was clear that men were down… lots of them… seriously wounded boys, many still teens, being frantically attended to by fellow sailors who had obviously become very skilled at treating trauma and horrific injuries. As they tied up alongside, corpsmen from the ship went to work. I tried to help, but I felt totally inadequate and rejected by the somber boat crews who looked at me as an unknown interloper. It was a new world… one hell of a long way from the bluffs of the Mississippi in more ways than simple miles. These men of CosDiv 11 were unlike others… they were on the knife's edge, living purely upon adrenalin… faced with raw survival for themselves and their shipmates. I saw then how ill prepared we were… that we had to earn our stripes and get up to their level of intensity and instincts, or simply not survive. It was a somber introduction to the Black Cat division.

My good friend and roommate from Coronado, Mike Solhaug (a graduate of St. Olaf College in Minnesota and a great guy), was one of the skippers. Our crews, having trained together in Coronado, were close. After the wounded had been cared for, and the boats handed over to the LST crews for necessary repairs, we got together with the "Haug" and his crew members. They had changed… while they remained our friends, they were withdrawn, often times distant. I at first attributed that to exhaustion, but I soon learned it was from far more complex reasons.

Later that evening, the LST was replenished, with sailors forming a chain gang to transfer food goods across the nest of Swift Boats. Opportunity knocked….our crew members got into the line and, as the supply officer was looking elsewhere, tossed aside two five gallon

containers of strawberry ice cream and a gallon of what we thought
were peaches, which other crew members then hurriedly hid. Those
peaches turned out to be raspberry concentrate. It made for a decent
desert, but to a man we spent the rest of the night sicker than dogs,
since we had felt compelled to finish all ten gallons. To this day I
cannot eat strawberry ice cream.

CosDiv 11 was assigned the western side of Vietnam from the Cambodian border down to and including the Ca Mau Peninsula. This
area included the U Minh Forest, which is the largest mangrove forest
in the world outside of the Amazon basin. Because of my interest in
history, this forest held special significance to me. In 1952 500 French
Legionnaires parachuted into the middle of this forest, with the objective of sweeping to the south on a mission to destroy the bases and
depots of the Viet Minh (the predecessor to the Viet Cong). This force,
comprised mainly of Senegalese Legionnaires (considered amongst the
most hardened) was never seen, nor heard of, again. They simply van-
ished. Two decades later, in various subsequent combat situations, we
captured arms stamped as issued to Legionnaires, always assuming that
many such arms were from that 500-man force twenty years earlier.

This area was completely controlled by the North Vietnamese
Army, which had an estimated 30,000 troops in the area (along with
a further estimated 50,000 Viet Cong, e.g. the citizen soldiers). It was
their sanctuary, their base of operations that contained munitions
depots, hospitals, command centers, training facilities, etc. It was from
this region that they waged war in the Mekong Delta with impunity.

A division of Swift Boats, three helicopters, and a Seal Team, along
with a few other basically stationary combat units assigned to strategic
sites, were relocated there, with the mission of conducting surprise
assaults along the rivers and canals to disrupt and destroy enemy positions during the days and setting up ambushes at night.

As you can quickly surmise, the numbers were not very comforting.
Basically, about 160 sailors on twenty-four boats (with generally fewer
than eighteen operational at any time) along with a Seal Team, both
of which were supported by two Seawolf helicopter gunships, were
pitted against 30,000 truly hardened North Vietnamese Regulars and

another 50,000 part-time Viet Cong. We had the advantage of surprise against a fairly dispersed force, but that was the only advantage… and it was short lived as we came rumbling up a canal aboard noisy boats. Our mission was to prod the hornet's nest, hopefully by surprise, causing as much destruction as we could, and then get back out before we were stung too many times! It was never contemplated that we would defeat this massive force… we were simply to cause them so much damage that they were forced to turn their attention away from the Mekong and toward us. Candidly, I felt then, and remain of the same opinion today, that, as isolated as we were on a tiny little island, we were sent there with the conclusion that we were expendable… an acceptable cost for the damage that command thought we would inflict.

Riverboat in Vietnam. Photo courtesy William E. Franke

And so, the mission, the tactics to accomplish the mission, and the lifestyle in CosDiv 11 were dramatically different from many, perhaps most, other arenas in the conflict. There were no movies… no USO shows… nothing to serve as a distraction. We went out on combat missions virtually every day and every night… perhaps as many as three hundred of them during our boat's time at the Ca Mau Peninsula. The missions were short, generally lasting less than ten hours during the day and another four hours at night, with the boats transiting down a river or a canal to attack a target. Other than that, we slept in one hundred plus degree temperature and in sheer emotional and physical exhaustion. That is all we did.

It was personal: the North Vietnamese Regulars, by monitoring our comms, knew who the skippers were, even down to their names. They taunted the skippers… targeted them on the missions… offered bounties on their heads. They likewise targeted the Vietnamese serving with us. One of the Vietnamese learned that his mother and two daughters had been viciously victimized and murdered. The Vietnamese sailor on my crew, a wonderful young man, knew his father and brother had been killed. That, in turn, made it personal for all of us. It became our private little war, far more intense, fought in an obscure, impossible-to-get-to region, inside of a much larger war, with both sides slugging it out on a daily basis, and with no rules.

Due to this intensity, one of the memories that I shall never forget was the hour leading up to a typical mission in CosDiv II… not all missions but far too many. It started with the pre-mission briefing, generally around four a.m., where the mission was announced and the boats were assigned a position in the line. The high-risk positions were the lead boat of both waves and the trail boat, which was often targeted in an effort to block the channel in order to prevent the boats from escaping a kill zone. Those positions were reserved for the most seasoned officers.

After the briefing, the officers retired to their respective boats, insuring that all necessary precautions had been undertaken. When I was the OTC, however, I relied upon my chief petty officer to undertake this review while I made my rounds of the boats, making sure that all boats were squared away—patched up from earlier mission damage. More significantly, however, I took the measure of the men….looking into their eyes and measuring their capacity to handle the stress of the day. It was a foolish man who held no fear. Fear was not the issue… it was how you handled it. And that was what I sought to assess.

There was incredible tension during this time. Even though most of the sailors were in their late teens to early twenties, there was no horsing around, no idle banter. Everyone was quietly, solemnly, undertaking their duties. On my first mission, for example, I saw the seasoned guys buttoning the collars of their shirts, a confusing gesture in such heat. I later found out why: when red hot shell casings, from the machine guns manned in the helicopter gunships that hovered a few feet above the boats, fell amongst the men, any casing that fell into a man's shirt with an open collar caused severe burns. And it literally rained fire on some missions. My college friend Steve Sandberg was often the pilot of one of those Seawolf gunships hovering above my boat to provide as much protection as he could. Steve was a brave, brave man… totally vulnerable to a well-aimed B-40 rocket.

The embarkation scene would culminate with a signal from the OTC to fire up the engines, generally indicated by a raised arm twirled about, a signal awaited by one hundred men on the edge. The ensuing noise and action is never to be forgotten once experienced… the eruption of 24 diesel engines, rumbling noisily as they settled down… the aluminum flaps of their exhaust manifolds flapping frantically against the hull… the cocking and loading of sixty to seventy machine guns… pins on mortar rounds pulled, with rounds loaded into the mortar tubes… and last-minute radio checks nervously, and probably needlessly, undertaken. The last of the flak jackets, helmets, small arms, grenades, and medical supplies were passed around. Lines were cast away, with the rubber tires used as fenders between the boats stored as the engines accelerated to provide power to the twenty-seven tons of boat. It was about as tense as it could get. I will never forget the sheer enormity of those departures and mission moments.

I need go no further than my first mission in the Black Cat division to illustrate this tension, as well as to provide context to the reservations initially made about writing this article. That inaugural mission was into the Rach Duong Keo (a name I will never forget), a relatively narrow river on the eastern coast 172 miles southeast of Saigon. We carried with us the 6th battalion of the Vietnamese marines, assigned with the mission to destroy a munitions assembly and storage facility.

The previous time on this river, our division had lost one of the Swift Boats (the 43 boat), with four others severally damaged. More significantly, we lost five men, including Don Droz, skipper of the 43 boat, with 46 sailors or marines suffering wounds. Knowledge of this recent experience intensified the tension we felt as we prepared to re-enter that canal. In recounting these episodes, I feel compelled to mention the loss of those men. To fail to do so would be a disservice to their sacrifice for our nation.

In this morass of evil, one further incident at Ca Mau will always remain with me, an experience I can only describe as spiritual. While we spent most of our time on the boats, we occasionally tied up alongside an LST anchored in the Gulf of Siam. On one such occasion, at about four a.m., I was awakened by a sailor because a typhoon had suddenly hit us, with one of the nested boats (whose skipper had been medevaced) sinking from damages sustained that day. I can remember coming on deck, shocked at the severity of the storm, seeing the nest wildly gyrating in massive swells that had so quickly developed. The several sailors standing watch on the boats, none yet twenty, were clinging on to whatever they could get hold of. There was no time to delay… the nest was in grave danger. I climbed down the "Jacob's" ladder (the same rope ladder as depicted in war movies of World War II and utilized by marines disembarking ships to hit the beaches). I was in my skivvies, drenched and shivering in the downpour; I waited in the pitch dark for the swell of a wave to lift the boats up to me on the rope ladder. After letting a few swells pass to get the timing and distance, I picked my moment and jumped about six feet to the deck of the closest boat. Once on board the nest, I got the damaged boat underway, to prevent it, should it sink, from tearing away the cleats of adjoining boats and causing them, in turn, to sink. Ultimately, we got a P-250 pump on board and pumped out the seawater. Unfortunately, the damage was severe, with the pumps barely able to keep up. The seawater came dangerously close to the batteries and the air intakes for the diesels. Realizing I had little alternative because we would otherwise eventually sink in those heavy seas, I went over the side (tied to a line) to find and temporarily patch the breaches in the hull.... a pretty stupid thing to do in pitch dark in the middle of a typhoon....especially if you still didn't know how to swim.

What was most memorable about the incident, however, was what followed....the seas were horrific, with massive swells of seawater looming some thirty feet above the decks of the boats. While in the trough I was reminded of the movie where Charlton Heston as Moses parted the Red Sea. Returning to my boat, we fought the ocean all day, constantly jockeying our twin engine speeds to keep the seas directly to our stern so that we would not broach and sink. We were constantly guarding against waves breaking atop our boats, which would have simply collapsed under the hundreds of tons of water. It was chaos, with the twenty some boats after fourteen hours scattered over a ten square mile area.

With no one in sight, and in the midst of these incredible waves and black skies, a monster wave broke directly astern of the boat, with seawater pushing up the flaps on the exhaust manifolds, allowing seawater to rush up the manifold to flood and kill my engines. Because we had sustained damage on the prior mission, with our generator destroyed, we had no battery power to restart the diesels. The next swell would clearly broach us, causing us to sink miles from the closest boat, and with no shoreline in sight.

I will simply never be able adequately to describe what happened next. There was not a next swell. Rather, there was a quicker-than-instantaneous transition from turbulence to the calmest of seas... so calm that I saw the ripples moving out concentrically from a shell casing I threw into the sea in order to challenge my utter disbelief.

Those who know me know that I am not a religious person. It was my junior year at college before I found out what the beautiful building on the bluffs with the steeple was. But, I can attribute this instantaneous transition, one where my crew and I looked at each other in exhausted disbelief, to no possible earthly cause. Were it not for this incomprehensibly instantaneous change in weather conditions and the stilling of the surrounding seas, neither I nor my crew had more than another few seconds of life remaining. To this day I think of it often, and I remain transfixed by the event.

During my tour, I frequently encountered Principia graduates. On one occasion we were dispatched to pick up an EDT team that, as I recall, was being overrun by the bad guys. It turned out that these men were from the same group as Steve Wells. I had very little time to chat, but I was able to relay my regards to him. Steve had a tough job in Vietnam. I have a lot of respect for what he did. [See Steve Wells's essay, "Franke and Warner" in this volume]

The most amazing story, however, had to do with an incident that just happened to occur, as I later discovered, on the Saturday of Homecoming at Principia College. Having sustained damage from underwater mines detonating under my boat, I was ordered to transit to a repair facility three days up the coast of Vietnam. I had a two boat escort to get me out of the river. We were ambushed, with several injuries, and one of the boats was also disabled in the kill zone. Part of this story was related in an article first published in my alma mater's alumni magazine and retold here [See "Help in the Line of Duty"]. I can confirm the remarkable coincidences of that day and its course of events.

Once we were able to clear the ambush with the disabled boat, and it was evident we were unable to call in medevac helicopters (both because of the remoteness of our site and in that we were still in the kill zone, continuing to receive small arms fire), we were forced to use the helicopter gunships to get the injured men to safety and treatment. As the tallest and by then the most seasoned, I was the natural candidate to lift the men into the hovering helicopters, the blades of the copters perilously close to our whip antennas. As I did so, (and at six foot six considering myself an inviting target as I stretched to lift/ shove six often unconscious sailors into those gunships), I looked up at the pilot of one of the two Huey gunships, a young naval officer who was totally concentrating on keeping the skids of his copter close enough to me to get the men in, while not so close as to hit those whip antennae. The pilot was Steve Sandberg, once again coming to my aid. He flew off of an LST on which another Principia alum, Doug Dixon, served as the Executive Officer.

Because the incident involved wounded sailors, the senior naval commander in Vietnam, Admiral Zumwalt, was briefed on the incident, with the briefing being undertaken by Rick Halladay, another naval officer and Prin graduate I knew at college.

Finally, because one of the boats sank, a diving crew was sent to refloat that boat. The diving officer was Rick Alt, another man I knew both in high school and college, and the brother of CNN journalist Candy Crowley. As several have already noted in this volume, it is a small world.

The last thirty days of my tour, I was taken from the boats. I had pushed my luck long enough, being one of the longest surviving skippers. (The average survival amongst skippers was about three and one half months... I was on my tenth month). I was ordered back to the base, some two hundred miles to the north off Phu Quoc Island where I was to supervise the repair of a replacement APL or barrack ship for the division. (The original one had almost been sunk when a sailor, while on overnight guard duty, threw hand grenades so close to the ballast tanks of the APL that he ruptured them). Those who know me will also get a laugh out of the fact that I was also assigned duty as the division chaplain.

There are so many other stories....but enough has been told to get an understanding of the duty.

There is a postscript to my duties in Vietnam, a last hurrah. It involves a bucket of paint. In the Navy, exteriors of ships are painted deck gray, and interiors are painted haze gray, a tradition that is "never" violated.[54] We held, however, small quantities of red paint for fire equipment and lines, and white paint for various other limited purposes. Red properly mixed with white with a touch of deck gray makes a very strong pink.

On the eve of my departure from Vietnam, I locked the officers' quarters, and proceeded to have that area painted a bright pink... not part of it but all of it... the walls, floors, ceilings, hatches... all of it. On the morning I left, taking my last ride on a Swift Boat to

---

54 With one notable exception, perhaps: See Craig's essay below, "Interior Decorator for a Warship."

the shore and to an awaiting Australian aircraft, engines warmed and ready for transit to Tan Son Nhut airport for my "freedom bird" flight to the U.S., I gave the keys to those I was leaving in Vietnam. My last memory of them was triggered by their discovery of the décor: their immediate and angry hollering at me as I waved good bye and the Swift Boat quickly picked up speed, their words lost in the drone of the engines. It was my farewell to a great group of men... men who had survived the odds, risen from the forsaken, and along the way earned many, many personal citations for valor as well as for our unit two Meritorious Unit Citations from the Secretary of the Navy and two Presidential Unit Citations from the President of the United States.

And so, there you have it. Others have far more dramatic tales to tell than Swift Boat sailors, still others, far less. But, to all Vietnam vets, what we did individually was and remains less important than the collective answer we gave to a call to duty. We all played the cards we were dealt. All of us were prepared to do what I did....it was just that I got dealt that hand. Most would have done it better, if called upon to do so. But, it was me, and a bunch of other Americans, almost to the man from conservative, Christian backgrounds, who got this call. And, this book tells you how we responded.

WILLIAM E. FRANKE, lawyer and businessman, majored in economics [business administration] at Principia College and holds a Juris Doctorate degree (1974) from Washington University School of Law. He also studied at the London School of Economics and the Washington University School of Business. Franke's extensive experience as a businessman has included business administration of start-up companies, success in real estate and finance, and investments both in the United States and Asia.

In 1968 Franke was commissioned as an officer of the line in the United States Navy. Franke served as officer-in-charge of a river patrol boat as well as operational and tactical commander of a task group, including twelve river patrol boats, multiple aircraft, and some three hundred ground troops. Franke was awarded the Silver Star, the Bronze Star with Combat V, the Purple Heart, and the Vietnamese Cross of Gallantry, among others. His task group was awarded two Presidential Unit Citations and two Navy Meritorious Unit citations. Active since the war in numerous civic and charity organizations, Franke has shown particular interest in organizations dedicated to the protection of children.

Franke is a graduate of both Principia Upper School (US62) and Principia College (C66). His brother and two sisters also attended Principia.

Born in Batchtown, Illinois, Franke was raised in Ferguson, Missouri, and now lives with his wife Ruth Ann (Kassing) Franke in Great Falls, Virginia. The Frankes have five daughters and three grandchildren.

A Tank Is Not a Home

PETER STONE

"A Tank is Not a Home" first appeared in *Afterwords: The Ones We Save*, the December 2013 anthology of the Veterans Writing Workshop, and is used with permission.

Bobby felt he was lucky to be assigned to a tank in an armored battalion, the Cavalry. At age twenty-one he couldn't imagine a better job in the Army. Living and working around an M48 "Patton" was not a bad life at all. That is, if you had to find yourself in Vietnam in 1967.

He liked the way the green exterior hull looked when it was freshly washed and clean. But, also when it was covered in road dust, sand, and dirt. He liked the sounds of the engine roaring and rocks crunching beneath the tractor treads as they rolled on. He liked the smell of the grease on the turret. When the big ninety-mm gun fired its eardrum-shattering "boom," there was a familiar aftersmell of gunpowder that excited his nostrils. His tank had an aura that said "Don't mess with me, I'm comin' through!" He thought it could go just about anywhere.

Although all of the M48s were identical, many were given names and personalities by their crews, such as "Mother Hubbard," "Miss Liberty," "Suzie-Q," and "Dusty Springfield." Bobby and his three crewmates named their tank "Nelly Belle" and spoke of her (and to her) as if she were part of their immediate family. She, and they, belonged to the 1-77th Armored Battalion, along with twenty-three other tanks assigned to a sector in Quang Tri Province near the DMZ.

Nelly's driver was Taylor, an impish red-headed twenty-two year old. The gunner, Ferretti, was a stocky, dark-eyed soldier with the look of a street thug. Their TC or tank commander was ten-year veteran Sergeant Baynard, a puffy faced farmer from Tennessee with a seriously receding hairline and an unusual fear of sunburn. Bobby himself served as the loader. Besides loading the ammunition, he was responsible for maintaining all of the guns.

Bobby liked to ride up on Nelly's back, or walk alongside during slow movements. He and Ferretti had a running argument: Bobby felt that it was safer to be outside because if they hit a land mine everyone inside would "buy the farm" almost certainly. Ferretti contended that being outside made him vulnerable to a sniper or Viet Cong ambush or NVA[55] patrol. He preferred the protection of being inside "Mama Nell" except when it became unbearably hot.

Taylor was the craziest of the bunch. At nightfall he opened the top hatch and stuck his head out and howled at the moon. TC Baynard told him he would get it shot full of holes some night, but Taylor continued whenever the moon appeared.

Ferretti felt compelled to respond to each and every comment made by anyone else. TC Baynard called him "the Answer Man." Ferretti began with the words, "Here's your ____" and grabbed at his crotch while he smirked at whoever had spoken. If Bobby said he needed to clean his gun, you could be sure Ferretti would reply "Here's your gun!" Or, if Taylor mentioned that the mess tent was serving cheese fondu for lunch, Ferretti would immediately come back with "Here's your fondu! Right here!" Crude as they were, Ferretti's responses were reassuring to Bobby simply because they were so predictable.

One day Taylor announced a game of "Water Buffalo Spotting." In Taylor's rules whoever first spotted a water buffalo got one point. If the water buffalo was actually working—pulling a plow through a rice field—it was worth two points. A dead water buffalo was five points. And finally, if a crew member actually touched a water buffalo it counted for ten points. More than once the tank veered off the road toward a rice field and what looked like two desperately insane-looking figures jumped out and raced toward a large beast of burden standing in a nearby paddy. Local farmers stared and scratched their heads, at a loss to explain or understand any of it.

---

55 North Vietnamese Army

Soon it became an important part of their daily routine. Points were officially tallied and posted on Nelly's front panel every Monday morning. On November 1st the score stood: Taylor—64; Bobby—59; Baynard—45; and Ferretti—30. They decided the winner as of New Year's Day would get a one-month exemption from fueling, lubricating, and washing Nelly.

In early November the North Vietnamese launched a series of major engagements that became known as the Border Battles. The 1-77th Battalion met the enemy at Con Thien and Khe Sanh in Quang Tri Province. There was intense fighting that included infantry, air support, and the Cavalry—the irreplaceable tankers.

Nelly Belle was up on the front line at Khe Sanh when the attack began. She and her crew blazed through the enemy line and took out an NVA truck-mounted machine gun and two supply trucks; then turned east to the Marine air base and helped to stop an assault on the air field. Bobby was topside manning the machine gun when a bullet from nowhere pierced his right hand. The force knocked him to the ground, and he lost consciousness.

He awoke in a field hospital with a crude bandage on his hand. He had no feeling in it, but after an hour the local anesthetic wore off, and it hurt like hell. Next morning he was medevaced to the hospital ship USS *Repose* ten miles off the coast. There he underwent a surgical operation that took less than an hour, and began several days of rest and recovery. After six days he felt he could return to duty and rejoin his crew and Nelly Belle. He was released a day later and returned by helicopter to 1-77th Command, now located at Dong Ha. His hand with its fresh white bandages looked like an oversized marshmallow.

As they approached Dong Ha, Bobby smiled as the chopper flew over a rice field with two water buffaloes in it. Both were hitched to plows. Bobby became even more anxious to rejoin the guys. He was worried that TC Baynard or Ferretti might have surpassed his score by now. He guessed the guys would give him a big round of slaps on the back and butt when he rejoined them. Maybe a punch or two on the arm. But no firm handshakes just yet, he hoped.

From the landing pad Bobby went straight to the base commander's office, reported for duty, and requested orders to rejoin his unit. After a half hour a clerk with PFC[56] stripes and a name badge that said 'Leonard' approached and asked him to state his name, rank, and serial number. Another twenty minutes passed, and Private Leonard returned and ushered Bobby into the adjutant's office.

The adjutant stood up and returned Bobby's salute after he entered the office. He looked Bobby straight in the eyes and said "You'll be sorry to learn that your crew is no longer intact. The tank hit a land mine less than thirty minutes after you were wounded. Sergeant Baynard and Private Ferretti were killed. Private Taylor is recovering from head injuries in the field hospital in DaNang. You'll wait here at the air base until you're reassigned to another tank crew in the 1-77th Battalion." Bobby felt numb. He didn't say a word, but stood motionless. The adjutant continued "I'm sorry to bear bad news. You'll have a day or two to digest it here on the base. Private Leonard here will show you to your temporary quarters. Your new orders should be cut within forty-eight hours. Meanwhile, morning colors are at 0700 hours and breakfast is at 0715."

Bobby did not hear a word after "… hospital in DaNang." He was unaware of leaving the office and of how very slowly he scuffled the fifty yards of dirt road to the hooch where his temporary bunk was located. Private Leonard did not hurry him. Bobby stowed his duffle bag under his bunk and sat on the edge staring at his knees for a long time. After awhile he looked up and realized he was alone. He felt chilled. He felt like he might have to vomit. Thoughts raced through his head. In one brief moment in that adjutant's office the focus of his world was gone. Gone for good. As he waited in that unfamiliar place, he thought to himself how much he really hated tanks. What could be worse than being the enemy's favorite target? He decided that tomorrow he would request a transfer to an infantry unit.

As he sat there the screen door slammed and a young Marine pilot entered the hooch carrying a portable radio blasting at max volume.

---

56 Private First Class.

He saw Bobby and winked at him as he waived a casual greeting. Bobby sat motionless, but he recognized the song, so familiar it was etched into his brain. It was The Animals singing, "We Gotta Get Outta This Place."

LIEUTENANT PETER STONE served aboard USS *Valley Forge* (LPH-8) attached to Amphibious Squadron 5 during his active duty in the Navy (1967-69). Home-ported in Long Beach, *Valley Forge* operated in 1968 and 1969 in the Gulf of Tonkin, Coastal DMZ, and DaNang, the latter a coastal port located 85 miles south of the 17th parallel separating North and South Vietnam and home to the busiest airport in Vietnam during the war. Commissioned just after World War II as an *Essex*-class carrier, *Valley Forge* launched the first air strikes against North Korea during the Korean War, was re-designated an attack carrier (CVA-45) in 1952 and, by 1954, an anti-submarine warfare support carrier, and again, in 1961, was retrofitted, mostly internally, and reclassified as an amphibious assault ship. During the Vietnam conflict, *Valley Forge* maintained a landing force of marines. During 1968 and 1969 the ship's helicopters transported troops and supplies ashore during search and destroy missions near the DMZ, and *Valley Forge* provided medevac support evacuating wounded marines back to the ship for medical treatment; for this latter role the ship became known as "Hero Haven." Assigned to the ship during this period, Stone received the Vietnam Service Medal, was recognized with the Vietnamese Campaign Medal, and was awarded the Commanding Officer's Commendation.

Born in Mount Vernon, New York, in 1942, like others of his generation, Stone was older than the ship he served on. Both required adapting to changing conditions, and this history and business administration student from Principia College (C64), fresh from his MBA at Washington University ('66), soon found himself serving as combat information officer aboard an amphibious assault ship off Vietnam. His literary contributions to this volume of Vietnam memoirs present themselves as short stories, but they are essentially autobiographical and dramatize events Stone witnessed. A member of Brooks North residence hall at Principia College, Stone served his house as social head, lettered in both varsity football and baseball, and was a member of the school's debate team and campus newspaper. Married to Kitty Smith, a Principia College alumna (C67), Stone has a son, Kevin, who graduated from Principia College in 1994, and a daughter

Vivian whose degree is from Washington University in St. Louis (1998). Stone's post military career has been in management consulting in the field of freight transportation and logistics. From 1994 to 2008 Stone served as Chairman of the Commission on Human Rights. Now retired and living in White Plains New York, Stone remains active with church activities, with the Philippine "Sister Church" Project, and with being a grandfather to twins.

No Rest Elsewhere

ALLEN G. ORCUTT

[editorial assistance by John K. Andrews Jr.]

Before I departed for Vietnam, my friend and former WW II South Pacific Marine, David Rennie, shared with me a Latin inscription he had seen on the battle-dented breastplate of a suit of armor in a Scottish castle. It read *Nulla Quiat Alibi*, "No Rest Elsewhere." That constantly sustained me during thirteen months in-country. There would be no rest elsewhere for me, I realized, but in doing my duty—upholding the honor, camaraderie, and trust shared by fellow warriors, in this case Marine Corps pilots.

Danang, September 29, 1968

And then we were there. Standing on hot marston matting, respectfully awaiting east-bound Marines who wore faded utilities and engineered smiles. No one, I mean no one, was taking pictures. We were listening to the war over our shoulders.

The balance of that first day found five fresh lieutenants headed south to Marble Mountain Air Facility just west of Danang. This is where our individual cathartic experience would finally transform us over the next several days into the "paid professional killers" as prognosticated in the now-famous Pensacola Navy flight school welcoming remarks to new pilots.

Rudy, Paul, Mickey, O. B., and me, Ork, checked into our new squadrons to discover our status as the latest FNGs (Effing New Guys). We had a lot to learn including getting checked out in the aircraft tactical and emergency procedures, maps and terrain, radios, friendly and unfriendly fire.

For months we had been training to fly the CH-46 Sea Knight. This training took place in the classroom, on the flight line, and from aboard the LPH aircraft carrier.[57] No detail was too small in our transitioning to this helicopter. The checklist for preflight, starting and takeoff included over 100 items and procedures. Every pilot knew them without exception. Even though all the items were committed to memory, both the HAC and H2P (aircraft commander and copilot) read each item aloud and responded aloud. If the aircraft needed to be shut down during a mission, it was always made ready for quick departure.

In the first months, the copilot was the designated rear ramp control officer. This was one of the responsibilities the FNG could get right during his first few days. H2Ps always did the preflight inspection and were also responsible for night maintenance turn-ups. In addition they were an important part of the squadron's twenty-four-hour standby to fly emergency medevac and to fly mortar watch overflight of the base facility.

The squadron duty officer made nightly rounds to awake those flying night or early morning missions. The operations duty officer was a senior captain who made all of the squadron flight assignments for the coming day. Our squadron was HMM 164, part of the Marine Air Group 16 and the 1st Marine Air Wing.

Our leader was Lt. Col. Dick Trundy. It didn't take long for us to learn how fortunate we were to have this man as our skipper. He was always up front and ready to fly the missions at hand. We had six majors, five captains, eighteen lieutenants, and, of course, an executive officer to keep everyone in line.

Crucial to every flight were the enlisted aircrew: crew chief, corpsman, and gunner. They kept the aircraft flying, with fifteen out of twenty-plus birds ready to fly on a busy day. Once airborne, the crew chief and gunner would man the two .50-caliber machine guns, and the corpsman assisted when needed. They always worked well together.

Good examples surfaced daily. Senior noncommissioned crew chief J.J. Jones was standing near the transmission when rounds struck. J.J. quickly stepped out into the rear ramp as the aircraft departed and

---

57 LPH, or landing platform helicopter, carriers are aircraft carriers converted for helicopter operation only.

held his finger over the hole that was instantly spraying hot hydraulic fluid. Everyone present knew the consequences of losing transmission oil in flight, especially J.J. No rest elsewhere when choices were no longer choices—especially on the field of battle.

Hill 55, October 11, 1968

Transitioning to a combat squadron was more than adjusting to the details of a hostile environment. It was also more than following orders and advice given by the experienced crew members. It was the most dangerous for a new and inexperienced pilot, or a distracted one, and for that reason they were not put on the flight schedule during the first (or last) days of their tour.

This was the time for FNG's like me to fine-tune our aeronautical skills and draw on our innate horse sense in solving problems when under fire. Few new pilots could shoot a good autorotation into a spiraling approach to the landing zone from 1,500 feet. You can bet, however, that they were paying attention, especially at night. Most of us actually learned the way by lightly riding on the flight controls whenever the zone was hot.

Those days in early October were hot and overcast, but we were flying just the same. Most of our squadron aircraft were southwest of us near Charlie Ridge and the Vietcong-owned village of Thoung Duc. Crews there were reporting heavy fire.

Two more CH-46s were going to be needed, as the situation was going from bad to worse. Just when I stepped into flight operations, they got word that two aircraft in the vicinity of Hill 55 had been involved in a midair collision.

A flight of four CH-46 crews had been resupplying Marines near Hill 55. The fourth bird, piloted by Willy Hale and Jeff Renaud, had just asked the last two passengers to get off and board the next aircraft. The pilots were probably working the weight and balance charts because both passengers promptly debarked.

Airborne a moment later and making a steep lift, both pilots saw a windshield full of rotor blades suddenly ripping into each other. Within seconds, at about 400 feet the other, previously unseen helicopter from a different squadron burst into flames and plummeted nose down into a river bank. As the front blades came off, the CH-46 began violently falling end over end with the crew chief hanging onto starboard door attempting to jump at the right time. It didn't happen.

For those watching the accident occur, time seemed to freeze as both aircraft fell to the earth and disintegrated in a magnesium fire. Other aircraft quickly landed and retrieved the bodies of the passengers and crew.

William T. Hale—Bill to his family, Willy to all of us who flew with him—was my closest friend in the Marines. Losing him that way, so senselessly, just a matter of days after we got to the war, hit me hard. That and the ominous silence from Sandy, my wife at the time, from whom there were no letters week after week since our parting in San Francisco when I deployed, were like a dark cloud over my thoughts all the time.

I took some of it out by jotting little scraps of poetry in a notebook I kept by my bunk. One piece went this way:

In Memory of William T. Hale

Ole Willy
Didn't mind being called Bill Tom,
As a matter
Of fact
He was "much obliged" to handle anything
Predictable or distasteful
Except October 11, 1968.
"Hey bubba, how ya doin'?"
He'd say
With his long arm on my shoulder.
Yep, I can't recollect
Any
Time he wasn't agreeable to help
Everybody else or me.
And if I were to tell you of the
Lessons

He never knew he taught me with
His
You can't upset my peace of mind attitude
You would love him
Too

Several of us also wrote letters to Willy's mother, Leola Hale, in Big Spring, Texas. I still have her reply. She told me of the last conversation they ever had: "Just before he caught his plane I said, 'Bill, is there any way on earth you could back out?' He said, 'Back out! I wouldn't miss this for the whole world!' We buried him with a great deal of pride, for he was doing what he felt he must. He loved flying and told me over and over, 'I can fly and fly well.'" It's true. Willy could fly very well. But war makes no allowances for that.

Dodge City, November 20, 1968

I had spent the better part of the evening of November 19 with my fellow pilots outside our hootches[58] watching the mortars and rockets land down near the flight line. Somehow, Charlie always seemed to know first when we had a big mission the following day. This day was no exception.

I awoke before dawn to the shaking and shouting of the squadron duty officer in my hootch telling me that I was to fly in today's mission, Operation Meade River. Things don't get too much worse than that so early in the morning.

Major Wilson was the aircraft commander, and as the copilot in the lead bird of fifteen aircraft from our squadron, I knew I was in for a very busy morning and afternoon.

Meade River turned out to be a cordon operation in an area just north of Go Noi Island, a densely populated region of villages and rice paddies which our grunts had nicknamed Dodge City because of the many fire fights and booby traps encountered in that region. We were delivering seven battalions of Marines into this giant ring.

---

58 See glossary, "hooch"

Major Wilson and I were in Spanish Fly 1-1, which turned out to be the lead aircraft of seventy-three helicopters that were in position to deposit all the battalions at approximately the same time. This would be the largest Marine helicopter assault operation of the war to date.

Allen Orcutt in flight.
Photo courtesy Barbara and Allen Orcutt

Offshore on USS *Tripoli* (LPH-10) and other ships, Marines were climbing aboard our birds for the strike on Dodge City. There were nearly 50 CH-46s and CH-53s prepared to carry our troops into the landing zones. We were escorted by more than ten Huey gunships. Our landing zone location was in the northwest corner of the cordon ring. We had already discussed the landing zones set aside for each of the aircraft in the operation. Major Wilson initiated the approach and motioned for me to "ride along" on the controls in case either of us was hit by ground fire.

The first part of the approach was smooth; not until we were within 500 feet of the landing zone did we receive fire. Our crew chief, gunner, and corpsmen all made sure that the grunts were off-loaded as quickly as possible, while up in the cockpit we were scanning the area to confirm the best departure route.

After lifting up and barely out of the zone, we flew west at treetop level and started our high-speed climb to 1,500 feet amid heavy ground fire. Shortly after arriving at our holding position, the command and control of aircraft asked for a volunteer crew to return to the landing zone and pick up several emergency medevac Marines near a burning HMM 265 aircraft that had been shot down.

We immediately volunteered since we had been the first aircraft in and out of the zone and could easily start our next approach into the area where the other bird was down. Our approach and touch-down were much faster this time since we were receiving a significant increase in the amount of ground fire from off our nose through to the right side of the aircraft.

But we couldn't leave until all of the Marines were loaded, both wounded and KIA [killed in action]. I made the mistake of looking back into the cargo hold that was full of dismembered body parts all of which were receiving rounds as we waited for everyone to get aboard.

When all the crew and injured were on board, we lifted up and again began a high-speed climb up to the altitude over 1,500 feet. We flew directly to USS *Sanctuary* (AH-17), a hospital ship steaming off the coast of Vietnam awaiting casualties.

When we got close to *Sanctuary*, Major Wilson extended his hand and thanked me for my help in making the mission a successful one. Looking back over the years, I felt that he did a very good job under very heavy fire conditions.

Meanwhile, back at the cordon, the 2nd Battalion 7th Marines had found themselves that afternoon in a mess with a very difficult Communist bunker complex near the part of the stream that we called the Horseshoe. There would be many days of fighting remaining. But for now our job was to refuel and stand by. The major and I looked at each other and both of us said, "Let's go home."

Go Noi, April 2007

Willy Hale's last day was about my worst day in Vietnam. I wanted to see where it happened. It never occurred to me I'd also meet an eyewitness and experience a moment of grace. But I did.

It was almost forty years after my initial visit to Vietnam that I was able to make my first return trip with Development of Vietnam Endeavors, the DOVE Fund—a veterans' humanitarian project. We especially wanted to visit the area around Go Noi Island south of Danang, since everything I had read pointed to this specific area as the one in which my friends had lost their lives in that midair collision.

My wife, Barbara, and I were packed into a small Volkswagen microbus along with a driver and interpreter. I asked the driver to take us to the Go Noi area. I remembered this village from all the reports that came out of the collision, and I wanted to get as close as possible to it before striking out on foot.

After we had walked around the village for perhaps twenty minutes, a gentleman about sixty-five years of age came out of one of the houses to greet us and to ask if there was any way he could be helpful. The man's name was Mr. Houng.

I asked our interpreter to relay to him the reasons for our visit and the timing of the original accident in 1968. To our surprise, Mr. Houng immediately nodded his head when asked the question again about the mid-air collision. He said, talking to the interpreter, that not only was he aware of the accident, but he had actually watched the whole event as it occurred.

A few minutes later, Mr. Houng invited us into his home to meet with his family and have a cup of tea. The Houngs were a very cheerful and delightful family. When asked about losses in his family during the war, Mr. Houng indicated that his wife's family and his brother had all been killed at that time.

We talked through the interpreter for about thirty minutes as we sat in Mr. Houng's house with the pictures and memories of his loved ones long since lost. I put my hand on his shoulder and told him how sorry I was that this war ever occurred.

Mr. Houng's response was unhesitating and direct. "I do not blame you or other soldiers who fought in this war. It is the Vietnamese and U.S. senior statesmen and politicians that we must all look to, to shoulder the blame for this unfortunate experience." We traded names, addresses, and greetings before leaving. I hope to have another opportunity to meet them again.

ALLEN G. ORCUTT, a captain in the U.S. Marine Corps, served as a helicopter pilot with a tour of duty in Da Nang, Vietnam. Both his father and both grandfathers had been in the military, his father serving with General George Patton in World War II and his grandfathers serving in World War I, one of whom saw action at Belleau Wood. Neither shared their experiences, although their portraits in uniform hang in a place of honor opposite Allen's desk; as Allen noted, their memories are "deep within." In the spirit of their dedication and service, Allen has published three volumes of poetry, the most recent of which is entitled *No Rest Elsewhere*, proclaiming "there is no rest elsewhere than to uphold the honor, camaraderie, and trust shared by fellow warriors, in this case Marine Corps pilots."

Following Officer Candidate School at Quantico, Virginia, in 1966, and flight school in Pensacola, Florida, in 1967, Orcutt arrived in Vietnam in 1968, the year of the Tet offensive, and "the worst for helicopters, pilots, and crews." He served as operations officer and aviation safety officer, completing his active duty in 1970. For Orcutt, *Nulla Quiat Alibi* [No Rest Elsewhere] was the motto of a warrior elite at war.[59] In addition to the Vietnam Campaign Medal, National Defense Service Medal, and Meritorious Unit Commendation, Orcutt's military service was recognized with an Air Medal, Combat Action Medal, and the Vietnam Cross of Gallantry with Palm. Since his time in the military, Orcutt served as Director of Corporate Relations, U.S. Chamber of Commerce.

Born in Augusta, Georgia, Orcutt grew up in Oklahoma City and attended Principia Upper School (US62) where his older brother was a member of the high school class of 1960. At Principia College [C66], Orcutt was a member of Buck House, joined Prisoc (the soccer club) with his friend, Buck House brother, and future submariner John Andrews, and majored in history. He married Barbara Floria Orcutt and has one son and three daughters. After his retirement, he lived in Glenwood Springs, Colorado, until his passing in late 2015.

---

59 Although the Latin source and accuracy cannot be verified, *Nulla Quiat Alibi* became the operative motto of Allen's war experience and later his civilian life, "absolutely central to Allen's life for fifty years," his best friend testifies.

Carrier landing approach.
Photo from *Intrepid 1968 Cruisebook*

PART VI:

At Sea

Carrier elevator from hangar bay to flight deck
Photo by Robert M. Craig

The 1967-68 Vietnam Cruise of Air Wing 15 (CVW-15) Aboard *Coral Sea* (CVA-43)

BARRIE L. COOPER

On the rare occasions since the 1960s that I've discussed my Vietnam service, I would recall only one or two events in isolation, but my reminiscences went no further than that. I have never, until now, made the effort to chronicle these experiences as a thread of related events unfolding over time. Revisiting these events has been an act of self-discovery, certainly revealing, indeed cathartic for me. I made four cruises to Vietnam, but the first was the most eventful, and my retrospective account of the 1967-68 Vietnam cruise of Air Wing 15 (CVW-15) aboard *Coral Sea* (CVA-43) is the most I can expect readers to bear in a single sitting. The retelling of the remaining experiences must await another day.

The Roots of Commitment

Why did I join the U.S. Navy? Well, I had uncles who served in the Navy during World War II, and one had a wonderful gift for telling "sea stories" about his Navy experiences. For the uninitiated, sea stories are mostly true tales of one's maritime experiences, but with elements of the story often embellished, either to make a point, or to create an exciting, or funny, or [pick any adjective] tale. In addition to being enjoyable, my uncle's sea stories filled me with wonder about naval service, and had a significant impact on me. I became certain that one day I would join the Navy.

My uncle may have been good at telling sea stories, but I confess I've never been good at it: to the extent that tales were "tall tales," I fell short because deceiving people makes me uncomfortable. Everything I've written below is as true as my recollections and researched records will allow. I hope the following account of my experiences will shed some light on what it was like to serve on an aircraft carrier during the Vietnam War.

Two Years of Preparation

Even before I graduated from Principia College in June 1965, I raised my right hand on February 8 and committed to the Navy. In July, I headed for Newport, Rhode Island, and entered Officer Candidate School (OCS) on July 17. My sea-story-telling uncle had suggested to me that the future of the Navy was below the surface. But conventional submarines were yesterday's technology, and were being decommissioned. The alternative was nuclear submarine service. But in those days, acceptance into the program required a successful personal interview with Admiral Hyman Rickover, the father of the nuclear submarine program. He had veto power, and he was a notoriously difficult, cantankerous, and capricious interviewer. OCS candidates in particular were unlikely to meet his approval, because he seemed to view them with disdain. Sometimes, he would just look at an interviewee and dismiss him. So I ruled submarines out.

When I learned about Naval Aviation, I decided it was the route for me. Being somewhat nearsighted, I was steered away from pilot training and toward becoming a Naval Flight Officer (NFO), a general classification applied to any officer aircrew member other than a pilot. I completed OCS, earned my commission as an ensign on November 19, 1965, and then began nearly a year of additional training, earning my NFO wings in October, 1966. There were a number of categories of NFOs, and I was elated at my selection to become a Radar Intercept Officer (RIO). That meant I would be a "backseater" in the McDonnell F-4 Phantom II Mach 2 fighter, the Navy's newest fighter aircraft. (I recall touring the McDonnell plant in St. Louis while at Principia, viewing early F-4s under assembly.)

I received orders to the F-4 "replacement" (i.e., transition training) squadron, Fighter Squadron 121 (VF-121), at NAS Miramar in San Diego, exactly where I hoped to go. If we were to fight a war, I wanted to be, and felt obligated to be, a part of it: most Navy squadrons deploying to Vietnam were from the west coast. After completing transition training, I was assigned to VF-151, also at Miramar. In preparation for the cruise, we underwent additional squadron and air wing training. Air wings deploy as a unit aboard aircraft carriers, and ours, Air Wing 15 (CVW-15), was scheduled to deploy aboard USS *Coral Sea* (CVA-43). At the time, an air wing consisted of two fighter (VF) squadrons, three light bomber, or "attack," (VA) squadrons, an airborne early warning (VAW) squadron, together with a number of smaller units, or "detachments" from larger squadrons, that performed various essential functions, such as reconnaissance and airborne refueling. Air wings today have much the same makeup.

F-4 carrier landing. Photo by S. M. "Pete" Purvis

On paper, the primary mission of fighter squadrons is to engage enemy aircraft in air-to-air combat, while attack squadrons have an air-to-ground mission, which usually means dropping bombs. In reality, during Vietnam, F-4s also dropped bombs, because the air-to-air threat in Vietnam was often secondary. The attack squadrons aboard *Coral Sea,* on my first cruise, were two squadrons of A-4E Skyhawks (the Skyhawk was sometimes called the Tinker Toy, because of its small size and relative simplicity), and one squadron of A-1 Sky-raiders. The Skyraider squadron aboard *Coral Sea*, VA-25, was the last ever piston-engine propeller-driven combat aircraft to deploy aboard an aircraft carrier. Being around the A-1s and their pilots was highly enjoyable, like going back in time to WW II or the Korean War. In fact, partly because the original Navy designation for the A-1 was AD, its unofficial nickname became the SPAD, recalling the WW I French biplane with that name. Calling it the SPAD captured the aura of the A-1 as an echo of the past. A-1 pilots played up this aura with aplomb, with many wearing scarves or ascots with their flight suits.

Heading West

We departed for the western Pacific (WESTPAC in Navy lingo) aboard *Coral Sea* on July 26, 1967, to join other U.S. aircraft carriers in fighting the Vietnam War. One of those carriers was USS *Forrestal* (CVA-59), which arrived on "Yankee Station" just two days before our departure. Yankee Station was the term for the steaming area in the Gulf of Tonkin off the North Vietnam coast where aircraft carriers operated. But on July 29, our third day steaming west, and *Forrestal's* fifth day of operations, she encountered a terrible disaster. Preparing for the first launch of the day, *Forrestal* had a large number of aircraft positioned on the flight deck awaiting startup. Heat from a poorly positioned piece of aircraft support equipment caused a Zuni rocket to fire from under the wing of an F-4 into an external fuel tank of an A-4. The impact caused the tank to rupture and some bombs to drop into the fuel, which began to burn. It didn't take long for the bombs to explode, and the involvement of other aircraft and ordnance in the conflagration. Ultimately, this resulted in a chain-reaction inferno, killing one hundred thirty-four and injuring many more. In the A-4 that was initially hit, or perhaps the one next to it (accounts differ), was Lt. Cdr. and future Arizona U.S. Senator John McCain. Reacting quickly, he could see what was about to happen and scrambled to safety below the flight deck before ordnance started to explode and aircraft began to burn.

This incident proved to have a large impact on *Coral Sea*. *Forrestal's* combat cruise was now done, after just five days "on the line" (actually, four days and a disaster), because it would require many months for repair, and there was no aircraft carrier available to take her place. This placed an extra burden on the other aircraft carriers then operating on Yankee Station, and, of course, on us when we arrived there a few weeks later. It also led to another occurrence of significance in which I was involved tangentially, as my narrative will explain below.

USS *Coral Sea* CVA-43. Photo U.S. Navy

After brief stops in Pearl Harbor, Hawaii; Yokosuka, Japan; and Subic Bay, Philippines; on August 25, *Coral Sea* headed toward Yankee Station. Unfortunately, only one day out of Subic, we threw a propeller blade, which resulted in severe vibrations and rendered our carrier unable to conduct operations. As a consequence, we had to steam back north to Yokosuka, where the U.S. then had (and still has) a major ship repair facility. We were placed in dry dock, and a propeller was "borrowed" from USS *Midway* (CVA-41) as a replacement. Three weeks later, we were able, finally, to join the fight, though the prop was not a perfect fix. Although historical accounts do not mention it, there was still a noticeable vibration when the ship cranked up to full power, and we were told the reason was that the blades on the replacement prop had a different pitch than the other three props. When turning into the wind to launch aircraft, the ship experienced continued vibration, which, together with the ship's fifteen degree heel (temporary lean due to the ship's turn), could cause a drinking glass to walk its way across the table and onto the deck (floor) if you didn't catch it in time. In the larger scheme of things, of course, this was more an irritation than a problem.

Coral Sea's Far East Cruise 1968 patch.
Photo by S. M. "Pete" Purvis

Living aboard an aircraft carrier, especially an older one like *Coral Sea*, involved tight berthing quarters. Enlisted quarters were especially tight with bunks stacked three high and with very little storage space for personal items. Officer spaces were better, but "officer's country" still had limited space. Staterooms for air wing officers were on the deck immediately below the flight deck, so the already inadequate air conditioning was further taxed by the heat generated from hot-burning jet engines on the steel flight deck just a few feet above. Because I was one of the most junior officers on my first cruise, I lived in a bunk room with seven other junior officers. I don't remember the bunk room dimensions, but my best guess is that it was around fifteen by eighteen feet. But that included four double-deck bunks, as well as desktops and drawers for personal belongings, leaving little space to move around.

One other factor intruded on our bunk room, not only on the available space, but also on our physical comfort and peace of mind.

That factor was the hard to ignore catapult. Running directly by the junior officers' bunk room was the housing for one of the steam catapults that launches aircraft from the flight deck. Not only did this equipment add even more heat to the bunk room, it made it difficult to concentrate or sleep. During launches or when flight deck personnel were testing the "cat" (called "firing no-loads"), the bunk room was not only noisy, but when the catapult hit the bumper at the end of its "throw," there was a violent shake in the bunk room. If you were sitting in your bunk, your head would bounce off the *bulkhead* (seagoing lingo for wall), and the whole bunk room would shake.

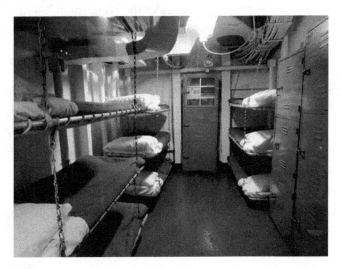

Bunk beds aboard an *Essex*-class carrier [USS *Intrepid* CVS-11]. Photo by Robert M. Craig

Getting My Sea Legs

Once back from Yokosuka and now on Yankee Station, our first few flight missions were against weakly defended, low-threat targets, allowing us to acclimate ourselves to combat operations. I remember that the first target that my regular pilot, Lt. Cdr. Samuel M. "Pete" Purvis, and I were assigned was the Tam Da pile driver, of all things. I have no idea what military significance, if any, our mission against the pile driver had. Other early targets appeared to be of similar insignificant strategic or tactical value, usually consisting of rudimentary bridges so small that they were not only difficult to find, but also difficult to hit. As a result, our post-flight debriefings to intelligence officers would result in reports indicating that we had "cratered the approaches," a euphemism for saying we missed the bridge, but may have pockmarked the dirt road at either end.

Fighter aircraft also flew a lot of Barrier Combat Air Patrol (BARCAP) missions, which consisted of flying a racetrack pattern parallel to the North Vietnam coast to protect ships on Yankee Station. BARCAPs were far enough away from the carrier that we were passed off to a cruiser farther north to be under their operational control. This cruiser was designated as the PIRAZ (Positive Identification Radar Advisory Zone) ship, and its radio call sign was always "Red Crown." BARCAPs could be characterized as boring, even stultifying, because the enemy had very little that presented a threat to our operations. As a result, the flight consisted of one to one-and-a-half hours of "boring holes in the sky," as we used to say, usually in a combat spread formation, two to three miles abeam one another. About the only time these flights would get interesting, or dicey, was when our assigned altitude had solid clouds, causing us to have to fly "in the goo." When this was the case, the wingman would usually fly in a three- to five-mile trail position behind the leader, using our air-intercept radar to maintain position.

BARCAPs aside, we soon began to operate against targets that were more highly defended and with more strategic significance. Defenses usually consisted of a mix of SAMs (surface-to-air missiles; all SAMs then in Vietnam were SA-2 Guidelines, which looked like telephone poles as they darted through the sky), small-to-medium caliber AAA (anti-aircraft artillery, "triple A," or "flak" as we called it), and small arms (hand-held weapons). SAMs were enough of a threat that, to be defeated, they had to be acquired visually and maneuvered against to defeat their electronic tracking. Failure to see the missile and maneuver effectively could cause serious or fatal damage to the aircraft and its occupants. Avoiding small arms fire meant staying above 3,000 feet or so. Countering AAA generally meant trying to avoid the altitudes that small and medium caliber artillery fuses were set to detonate. You could usually see AAA detonations, so we would try to avoid these altitudes (though you could still be hit by an unexploded shell). Following these rules sounds simple, but there were many competing stimuli demanding our attention, such as avoiding other friendly aircraft; heeding the signals of cockpit electronic warning gear; monitoring other cockpit signals; setting various flight and ordnance switches; occasionally engaging enemy aircraft; and, of course, flying the airplane. These elements meant that aircrews had to be hyper-alert. Still, a modicum of skill and prudence was generally enough to keep the aircraft and aircrew safe, and most downed aircraft I was aware of either disregarded procedures or failed to see and react to a threat.

SAM over Vietnam. Photo by S. M. "Pete" Purvis

During the cruise, the airplane I was flying in was hit only once, by small-caliber triple A. The shell entered the airframe just ahead of the tail and exited through the exhaust, exacting only minimal damage. The following photo shows me after that flight, pointing at the entry point of the round. Behind me you can see the tail of an

AIM-7 Sparrow missile and the 600-gallon centerline tank. If I recall correctly, that flight was part of a large air strike (or "Alpha Strike") flown against a target near the port city of Haiphong. "Alphas" might consist of thirty or more aircraft.

Barrie L. Cooper pointing at wound from small caliber
enemy fire. Photo by S. M. "Pete" Purvis

During Alpha Strikes, fighter aircraft often had the combined mission of Flak Suppressor/TARCAP (target combat air patrol). As Flak Suppressor, we would accelerate ahead of the main strike force and drop our ordnance first, with the intent of causing the AAA gunners to take cover rather than fire their guns, thus making it safer for the attack aircraft to drop their bombs a few moments later. Then after dropping our ordnance, we would assume the TARCAP role. This meant climbing above the remaining strike force to protect them against possible attacks by North Vietnamese MiGs (so called because they were Soviet-made fighters designed and manufactured by Mikoyan Gurevich), usually MiG-17 subsonic fighters and/or MiG-21 supersonic fighters. Sometimes, if the MiG threat was believed to be significant, carriers would also launch one or more sections (two aircraft) of MIGCAP, which were tasked to roam free, and engage any airborne MiGs they might find.

It was on an Alpha Strike that, in avoiding SAMs and heavy flak, we "pulled" 9.3 Gs (that is, while maneuvering against triple A and SAMs, we turned so tightly that the aircraft was subjected to a G force 9.3 times the pull of gravity). This, of course, meant that we also felt 9.3 Gs in the cockpit, usually enough for someone to black out (lose consciousness) or gray out (lose peripheral vision and/or visual acuity as a precursor to blacking out), but our adrenaline was pumping so hard that we never felt it. Aircrews are aided in countering the Gs by an anti-G-suit, more commonly just called a G-suit, a piece of garb that might remind you of cowboy chaps. Enclosed in the G-suit are inflatable bladders wrapped around the waist and legs. A tube is plugged into a receptacle in the aircraft when strapping into the cockpit, and when the aircraft makes a hard turn, the bladders inflate progressively, depending on the number of Gs pulled. This keeps the blood from pooling in the legs and belly area, and counters the tendency to black out or to gray out.

Although the pilot has a G meter recording the G forces in the front cockpit, I didn't realize we had pulled that many Gs until after the flight. Because that exceeded the G limit for the aircraft, it had to be inspected to ensure that there was no structural damage. Most combat aircraft at the time had G limits of 6½ to 7 Gs, and subjecting an airframe to more than the limit would shorten the service life of the aircraft, based on records kept for every aircraft.

Fender Bender

When operating at sea, every week or two, combatant ships rendezvous with supply ships of various sorts, for underway replenishment, or what the Navy calls UNREP. These ships provide fuel for the ship and aircraft, ship parts and supplies, food, and other consumables and perishables. Once the providing and receiving ships have established position, lines, cables, and hoses are passed across the space between them to make the transfers. This is an exacting operation, in which ships must steam alongside one another at exactly the same speed and heading, sometimes for as much as an hour, and even minor deviations in heading or speed by either ship can cause problems, or even worse, a collision. This is exactly what happened to *Coral Sea* on October 10, when we collided with USS *Mt. Katmai* (AE-16), damaging both ships. Aboard *Coral Sea*, both starboard aircraft elevators were damaged and knocked off their tracks. The damage was severe enough that it would have to be repaired in port. However, probably because the United States was one aircraft carrier short of its full complement on Yankee Station during this time, due to the *Forrestal* fire, *Coral Sea* couldn't be spared to leave Yankee Station until its next scheduled in-port period.

Even though we couldn't leave the line, we were not able to operate with our full complement of aircraft. With two of our three aircraft elevators out of commission, our ability to reposition aircraft for launch and maintenance was severely reduced. During flight operations, when an aircraft is expected to be *down* for more than a few minutes (that is, when it is not flyable due to a mechanical, structural, or electrical/electronics problem), or when it is scheduled to undergo periodic maintenance, it must be moved to the hangar deck on one of the elevators so maintenance crews can work on it and bring it back to an *up*, or flyable, status. With only one of three elevators operable, aircraft positioning became a logistical nightmare. The only way to avoid gridlock was to fly a number of aircraft back to NAS Cubi Point, the Naval Air Station across the bay from Subic Bay Naval Station. This freed up enough space for us to operate until we could get to port and have the elevators repaired. One of the pilots flying an aircraft back to Cubi was my regular pilot, Lt. Cdr. Purvis.

Suffering Losses

One of the reasons we had to remain on the line in late 1967 was that we were tasked to fly missions against some of the most heavily defended targets of the war. On October 23 and 24, we flew a number of Alpha Strikes against Phúc Yên, a heavily defended MiG base near Hanoi. On the strike the morning of October 24, our commanding officer, Cdr. Charles "Chuck" Gillespie and his RIO, Lt. (jg.) Richard

"Dick" Clark, were hit by a SAM. Official reports indicate that they were tracked by two SAMs. Gillespie avoided one, but the second disabled his aircraft. Cdr. Gillespie ejected and was held for five and a half years as a prisoner of war. Eyewitness accounts indicate that Dick Clark did not eject. One report indicated that he was slumped over in the rear cockpit, so he may have been disabled by the SAM blast. However, another report indicated that two parachutes were seen from that aircraft. I am unable to determine which was correct.

Cdr. Gillespie's wingman, Lt. (jg.) Robert "Goose" Frishman, with his RIO Lt. (jg.) Earl "Loose" Lewis, descended in an attempt to maintain visual and radio contact with Cdr. Gillespie after he ejected. In this effort, probably because they were flying slowly and at a low altitude, Frishman and Lewis, too, were shot down. All except Lt. (jg.) Clark became prisoners of war (POWs). Cdr. Gillespie and Lt. (jg.) Lewis were released with most of the POWs in 1973, but Lt. (jg.) Frishman, whose right arm was shattered when his aircraft was hit, was released early, in August, 1969, probably a combined propaganda and humanitarian effort by the North Vietnamese.

We were told that Lt. (jg.) Frishman's early release was approved of and condoned by the other POWs, who wanted him to spread the word in the U.S. of the brutal POW treatment. However, back in the U.S., most in the Naval Aviation community shunned him, believing that his acceptance of early release indicated moral weakness, and that it worked to his personal benefit while other POWs were still suffering. For a while, Frish was assigned to the Bachelor Officers' Quarters (BOQ), probably just to give him something to do, because the job entailed minimal work and responsibility. I went over to the BOQ and visited him once, but he seemed somewhat distant and reserved, and I had to conclude that he was depressed, not the outgoing, jocular, fun-loving person he had been before being shot down.

I was part of the final strike of the October 23-24 Alpha Strikes on Phúc Yên, flying with Lt. Cdr. Joe Coleman while Pete Purvis was in Cubi Point. The SAM and triple A activity continued to be heavy, although fewer SAM firings were reported than on the earlier Phúc Yên Alphas, probably because the North Vietnamese inventory was depleted. We were on the wing of another squadron aircraft, but due to evasive maneuvering in the target area, we lost sight of our leader while delivering our ordnance at one end of the runway, and were forced to egress from the target alone, without the mutual protection provided by flying with another aircraft. We made it back to the North Vietnamese coast (going *feet wet*, in Navy parlance) without incident, and Joe's relief was evident, as he keyed the microphone on strike frequency and announced, "OK, God, I've got it now!"

The next evening, an incident occurred below decks in an ordnance storage area that might have had consequences as terrible as the *Forrestal* fire. While ordnance personnel were performing tests on Zuni rockets in the ordnance spaces, one of them "cooked off," or exploded, starting a nasty fire. For a while, it appeared that the fire might spread out of control, but due to quick action by emergency response personnel, employing carts with two new firefighting technologies (called light water and Purple K powder) that *Coral Sea* obtained just as we left for the cruise, the fire was doused with only moderate damage. No one was killed, although nine men were injured. It was apparent that the new substances helped *Coral Sea* avoid major disaster.

October 26 was our last full day on the line before leaving for repairs and some rest and recreation (R&R) in Subic. On this day, I participated in the last Alpha Strike of that line period, attacking the Kim Quan ferry crossing, two miles south of Hanoi. This strike was coordinated with aircraft from USS *Oriskany* (CVA-34), which was to follow us by a couple of minutes in attacking a thermal power plant just to the north of our target. As our aircraft rolled in on the target, we surprisingly met little AAA or SAM resistance. But our attack must have stirred up a hornet's nest on the ground, and when the *Oriskany* strike aircraft arrived, the AAA and SAMs erupted, causing the loss of two of *Oriskany*'s aircraft.

Recall that John McCain had been a pilot on *Forrestal* in July, 1967, when the flight deck erupted in fire and explosions, forcing *Forrestal* to limp home, ending its deployment after only five days on the line. However, McCain was determined to earn his spurs as a combat pilot. Two months earlier, in May, his father, John S. McCain Jr., had been promoted to a four-star admiral and became Commander in Chief,

U.S. Naval Forces, Europe. Lt. Cdr. McCain probably benefited from his father's seniority in the military in securing a vacant pilot billet in an A-4 squadron aboard *Oriskany*. Moreover, it is not surprising that *Oriskany* had unfilled billets, because its air wing kept losing aircraft left and right, so much so that we called her "the plane-a-day *Oriskany*." (It took a bit of hubris for us in VF-151 to use the term, given that we had just lost two aircraft and four squadron members, and would lose more aircraft and aircrews later on; so there may have been similar derisive aphorisms directed toward us.)

As a result of his reassignment to *Oriskany*, John McCain wound up flying on the same multi-carrier Alpha Strike that I was on, but by the time the strike group from *Oriskany* rolled in, the AAA and SAM sites had come alive, and McCain was one of two pilots shot down that day.[60] He was destined to spend five and a half years as a POW, subjected to brutal treatment. Although some claimed (including McCain himself) that he received less severe treatment than other POWs for propaganda reasons, I believe that his father's high rank and position resulted in his receiving *harsher* treatment than might otherwise be the case. I remember talking with others in our squadron ready room immediately after the flight, and we all believed then that John would be subjected to especially brutal treatment for the very reason of his being the son of an admiral. Indeed, less than nine months later, on July 4, 1968, his father was appointed CINCPAC (Commander in Chief Pacific), essentially the most senior military leader of the Vietnam conflict.

Weather Rears Its Ugly Head

When *Coral Sea* finally left Yankee Station, on October 27, 1967, for Subic Bay, the crew members were more than ready for some R&R, and the ship was ready for its own "R&R" (although the latter would be repair [of the elevators] and replenishment). Unfortunately, after only five days in port, we had to put to sea ahead of schedule on November 3 to avoid the wrath of Typhoon Emma. While at sea,

---

60 McCain reported aboard *Oriskany*, September 30, 1967; less than a month later his plane was shot down on his twenty-third bombing mission, October 26, 1967.

we rescued some Chinese sailors aboard a Liberian flagged freighter that had been battered by the storm, and dropped them off in Hong Kong. We then returned to Subic to complete the elevator repair.

By the time we got back to Yankee Station the second week in November, the monsoon season had set in. This meant that overcast skies or broken clouds pervaded areas with high-threat, high-value targets, so we were severely limited in our ability to conduct operations. Often we would launch aircraft for Alpha Strikes, and they would proceed toward the target, only to have the strike leader cancel the Alpha because of bad weather en route to, or at the target. The strike formation would then break up, and sections (two aircraft) or divisions (four aircraft) would be "diverted" to attack pre-designated alternate targets. These secondary targets were less heavily defended and of lower strategic value than the primary target, because they were farther south, but they usually had better weather.

Occasionally, the weather would be satisfactory, or at least marginal, and it was the strike leader's call whether to carry out the strike. An Alpha Strike on November 16 was emblematic. Returning aircrews said that the strike should never have been flown. Although the cloud cover to and from the target area was "broken" (mostly cloudy), the strike leader, Cdr. David Sperling, executive officer (XO) of VA-155, with fudged mental calculus and, perhaps, visions of glory, elected to continue the strike anyway. There were clouds below the strike formation, so it was very difficult to see and react to the defenses below. As a result, an aircraft from our squadron piloted by Lt. Cdr. Paul Schultz with RIO Lt. (jg.) Tim Sullivan was hit by a SAM that they saw only at the last second, and were unable to maneuver in time to avoid it. Both had to eject and spent the next five and a half years as POWs. Our squadron in particular was bitter about this needless loss, and someone coined the derisive moniker "All-Weather Sperling" to describe the strike leader. But as events often transpire in the Navy, he was elevated only a few days later to become squadron CO. He was ultimately awarded another stripe to his epaulets before Paul and Tim were released, retiring as a Captain.

More Losses

One of the aircraft carriers on Yankee Station during this time was USS *Intrepid* (CVS-11). From the early 1950s until 1974, the assigned missions for aircraft carriers were either "attack" (which were designated CVAs, and included some small carriers, all midsized carriers like *Coral Sea*, and all of the newer, larger carriers) or "anti-submarine warfare" (ASW, designated as CVSs, all of which were smaller, older carriers). As the designations suggest, the attack carrier mission was air-to-air and air-to-ground, and the ASW mission was to pursue enemy submarines. However, because of the demands of the Vietnam War at the time, there was a need for more attack carriers than available, so *Intrepid* was temporarily refitted to perform the attack role (though it retained its CVS designation). The problem was that she lacked the space for a full complement of fighter aircraft, so *Coral Sea* and other attack carriers were sometimes tasked to supply fighters to protect *Intrepid* Alpha Strikes.

Therefore, on November 19, we "loaned" two aircraft to *Intrepid* as TARCAP for one of their Alpha Strikes, the lead aircraft flown by Lt. Cdr. Claude Douglas "Doug" Clower with Lt. (jg.) Walter O. "Walt" Estes as his RIO, and Lt. (jg.) James E. "Jack" Teague as his wingman, accompanied by RIO Lt. (jg.) Theodore G. "Ted" Stier. During the strike, one of the aircrew members saw two MiGs, and they turned to engage, but another section of MiGs attacked from behind and below. While engaged with the first section of MiGs, they were ambushed by the second section, which went unnoticed until they approached a firing position astern, and both F-4s were shot down. Official records state that they all initially became POWs, citing the fact that the North Vietnamese made public the IDs of Walt, Ted, and Jack (I don't know why Doug's ID was not made public), but I have found no evidence that Walt or Jack ever actually reached a POW camp. Doug and Ted were released five and a half years later, but the fate of Walt and Jack remains a mystery. An online statement by Ted states that he saw only one parachute from Doug's plane, and another online narrative states that Doug saw only one parachute from Jack Teague's aircraft. In 1973, when Doug and Ted were released, I was assigned to escort Walt's parents in San Diego as they sought to speak with Doug, but I was not told what information they were able to glean. Whatever they were told, it had to be devastating to them.

Just six days after we lost these aircraft, a flight deck tragedy occurred aboard *Coral Sea*. During the start procedures for a launch on November 25, Cdr. William H. "Bill" Searfus, CO of VA-155, had manned his aircraft for a flight, but wished to swap aircraft with his wingman, whom Cdr. Searfus was giving the opportunity to lead the flight. (It is preferred that the flight leader launch first, so the other aircraft can join him. The flight deck locations of the aircraft when spotted generally determine their launch order.) He climbed in the other aircraft, but we don't know whether he had strapped in. While other aircraft were being taxied forward for launch, one of them, an F-4, was momentarily stopped with its main landing gear resting against one of the arresting cables. When not being used to arrest landing aircraft, these cables are left in place, but the tension is relaxed so that the wires rest on the deck. If an aircraft is stopped directly against the wire, it requires quite a bit of power for the aircraft to taxi over it, because an arresting wire is $1\frac{1}{4}$ to $1\frac{1}{2}$ inches thick. In addition, because the carrier is by now steaming into the wind, there may be 30 to 40 knots of headwind. In this case, as the F-4 added power to get over the wire, the blast blew under the wings of CDR Searfus's aircraft, lifting it up and off the deck and over the fantail (the furthest aft part of the ship), impacting upside down in the water. Either because Cdr. Searfus was not strapped in, or because one wing lifted so quickly, he was not able to eject. The impact with the water made it impossible to open the canopy and almost certainly disabled him as well. Neither he nor the aircraft was recovered. This was especially tragic, because Cdr. Searfus was seen as an excellent leader, and was well-liked by everyone who knew him. With this loss, Cdr. "All Weather" Sperling was elevated to CO.

A Brief Respite

With all the difficult and terrible things that had happened aboard ship, we needed a diversion to brighten things up. During the Vietnam era, Bob Hope almost always came to Southeast Asia on a USO tour before and during the holidays. After performing at numerous bases in Vietnam, Thailand, and other locations, Hope and his troupe visited USS *Ranger* (CVA 61) and then, on December 22, landed aboard *Coral Sea*. With Hope was an all-star cast, among them the reigning Miss World Madeleine Hartog-Bel, actress Raquel Welch, singer and actress Barbara McNair, actress and dancer Elaine Dunn, Phil Crosby (Bing Crosby's son), comedian Earl Wilson, and bandleader Les Brown. Brown's Band of Renown, however, was left ashore because members couldn't fit on the C-2 Greyhound carrier onboard delivery (COD) aircraft that flew the Hope troupe aboard). Raquel visited our squadron ready room, and asked a few questions (questions she may have been briefed to ask). I can say that she was as beautiful in person as she was in photos. In 1967, she was considered an emerging starlet, having appeared in a small number of films, but only a few years before, she had graduated from a La Jolla High School in San Diego, and for a while was a weather forecaster on a local television station.

Bob Hope's USO shows of this period are preserved in abbreviated form in a 1½ hour YouTube video of Hope's 1967 Christmas tour, which includes a montage of excerpts from shows at the sites he visited. Aboard *Coral Sea*, Hope did a stand-up routine, and the troupe performed for the crew on the hangar deck, but only about 90 seconds of the *Coral Sea* show is shown in the video, beginning at about the 54 minute mark.

You Call This a Cease Fire?

Late in 1967, Pope Paul VI declared New Year's Day 1968 to be a day of peace, and both the U.S. and South Vietnam agreed to a truce. The Viet Cong also agreed to a thirty-six hour ceasefire, but that didn't stop them from attacking a U.S. position about fifty-five miles northwest of Saigon near the Cambodian border, killing twenty-three

Americans and wounding 153. Farther north, the U.S. wanted to see what North Vietnam was doing during the ceasefire. In furtherance of that goal, *Coral Sea* was scheduled to fly photo reconnaissance missions on New Year's Day. On one of these flights, Pete Purvis and I flew as photo escort on a photo reconnaissance mission flown by Lt. (jg.) Jay Miller, one of the pilots in our RF-8 photo detachment, VFP-63, Det. 43. The purpose of the Photo Escort mission is to protect the photo aircraft, which is armed only with cameras. As the escort, we usually maintain a position above and behind the photo aircraft, inside a half mile. Although Jay was merely taking photos, the North Vietnamese opened fire on him, and all of a sudden he was engulfed in flak bursts surrounding his aircraft. Amazingly, he was not hit, and he quickly made a maximum G turn to starboard to evade the flak. I have a photo from his belly camera with him in that turn, and there were flak bursts throughout the picture. Jay told us after the flight that the AAA was not a complete surprise, because gun control radar had "lit up" the sensors in his cockpit. But it came as a complete surprise to us, because we had absolutely no cockpit indications of AAA radar activity, even though we were probably only 200 to 300 yards away from him. Later during the flight, we turned south so Jay could get photographs of Route 1, which connected North and South Vietnam from one end to the other. Filling the highway, we saw hundreds of North Vietnamese trucks bumper to bumper, all heading south, surely loaded with weaponry and supplies for the North Vietnamese Army and the Viet Cong fighting us in the south.

Little of significance occurred aboard *Coral Sea* the rest of January and early February, because this was still monsoon season in the north. Most of our flights by this time were sent to South Vietnam to work with airborne forward air controllers (FACs) directing our efforts. To enable our bombing, the FACs would mark the position of enemy troops, ordnance, or supplies with white phosphorus ("Willy Pete") smoke and call us in to drop bombs on, or a certain distance from, the marked positions. These flights were an effort to interdict North Vietnamese and Viet Cong movements and activity along the Ho Chi Minh Trail and in other critical areas of South Vietnam. The low flying FACs could see the effects of our efforts, and when we had expended all of our ordnance, they would assess our effectiveness with an estimate of the percent of the target destroyed.

International Incident

While we were flying these humdrum missions, an international incident was unfolding far to our north. On January 22, USS *Pueblo* (AGER-2), a small, lightly armed, intelligence (i.e., spy) ship, operating in international waters off the North Korean coast, was surrounded by North Korean patrol boats, fired upon, and captured. Its entire crew of eighty-three was interned. Because this was the first American warship to be captured since the War of 1812, it was certain that the Navy would respond with a show of force. We learned shortly after the *Pueblo* capture that all aircraft carriers on their way to or from Vietnam would be tasked to spend time conducting air operations in the Sea of Japan near Korea. Right after the capture, it is my recollection that there were always two carriers on patrol in the Sea of Japan. We realized that, unless the crisis was resolved, we would also spend time there, an area bordered on the east by Japan and on the west by North and South Korea, and farther to the north by what was then the Soviet Union. More on this below.

The Chase

The pattern of flying BARCAPs and attacking minor targets was interrupted for Pete and me the night of February 8. When aircraft carriers are conducting flight operations, they normally fly a twelve-hour flight schedule. The twelve off-hours are necessary for squadron personnel to maintain and repair aircraft. To do this, aircraft are constantly being moved between the flight deck and the hangar deck, so the ship is still a beehive of activity, even without flight operations. Aircraft are continually re-spotted for maintenance purposes, and then as time for the first launch approaches, spotted for the next day's flight operations. Also, when conducting combat operations, ordnance is brought to the flight deck to be loaded on aircraft. During the twelve hours when there is no scheduled flying, the carrier must maintain an effective defense posture in order to defend itself and the accompanying ships from airborne threats. This posture is maintained by having one aircrew from each fighter squadron stand a watch strapped in an aircraft able to launch in 5 minutes. Fittingly, this watch is called the Alert 5. It is typically backed up by another aircrew in flight gear in the squadron ready room, called the Alert 15. Should the Alert 5 crew be launched, the ready room crew becomes the new Alert 5 crew in their place.

Launching the Alert 5 can really get the adrenaline pumping, or as we might put it, increase the "pucker factor." Why? Well, in the first place, an Alert 5 launch is not that common. You usually spend your two hours lounging in the cockpit, shooting the breeze or catching a few Zs, or perhaps once during your watch, starting the aircraft to check out the flight and weapon systems. So when you actually have to launch, you must undergo a real mental adjustment. Your ability to go through start-up and preflight check procedures smoothly and with professionalism is a reflection on both the aircrew and the squadron.

Second, as you're scrambling to prepare for launch, the eyes of the captain, people on the bridge and in primary flight control (PriFly), and flight deck personnel are on you and no one else. Third, you are about to be launched to face a possible imminent threat, often one about which you have very little knowledge. Finally, if it's nighttime, you have the added anxiety of a night catapult launch. When the catapult tosses you into the black night, being accelerated from zero to 150 knots in about 3 seconds, it's disorienting, no matter how many times you've done it.

All of this is enough to jack up anybody's pucker factor. Starting the aircraft, completing all preflight checks, and taxiing to the catapult for launch, all has to be accomplished in 300 seconds or less. Meanwhile, other things are happening. The ship is accelerating to full speed and making a hard turn into the wind, and the launch crew is readying the catapult for launch, creating a sense of urgency and activity. This is in contrast to the normal start routine, in which the preflight checks, taxi, and launch occur in a careful, deliberate, unhurried manner, spanning 20 or 30 minutes.

On the night of February 8, as Pete Purvis and I manned the Alert 5 aircraft, we already knew that there was MiG activity south of Hanoi. Two MiG-21s were flying in a north-south racetrack pattern, between 50 and 100 miles or so south of Hanoi. The MiGs may have been conducting training, such as air intercepts, but any time MiGs are airborne, they must be considered a threat. Already airborne from *Coral Sea* was a section of BARCAP aircraft, part of the last launch and recovery of the day, but because they were near the end of their flight, they had insufficient fuel to engage the MiGs.

That was the scenario we were presented with that night. All of a sudden, we heard on a flight deck loudspeaker "Launch the Alert 5!" Start-up, taxi, and launch actually went smoothly, and we joined up with the other Alert 5 aircraft from our sister F-4 squadron. Their radar was marginal, with a search capability but no ability to lock onto another aircraft, so we assumed the lead. We were sent north and given a new radio frequency to check in with Red Crown. Our controller informed us that the MiGs were still flying their north-south pattern, and our controller told us, "We're going to go get 'em." My immediate thought was "What you mean 'we,' kemosabe?"[61] Down there on the PIRAZ ship sat our controller, sending us into hostile action, and the greatest danger he faced was the possibility of getting zapped if he spilled his coffee all over the radar controls. Nevertheless, we were eager to engage, if possible, because at night, MiG-21s have minimal offensive capability. Their rudimentary airborne radar had only about a twelve-mile detection range and a six-mile head-on firing range, and their radar missile used a primitive beam-rider guidance system.

We were vectored toward the southernmost MiG, with our wingman in trail. The MiG was at a fairly high altitude, perhaps

---

61 *Kemosabe* refers to the name, of uncertain meaning, by which Tonto referred to the Lone Ranger in the popular *Lone Ranger* radio and television series, and the subsequent "what do you mean 'we'" jokes derived from its familiar use. Some have argued *kemosabe* is Apache for "idiot," although the more benign translation of the word of unknown etymological origin is "faithful friend" or "trusted scout."

25,000 feet, and with our trusty APQ-72 air intercept radar working beautifully, I easily got a contact at forty-four miles, and locked him up at forty-one miles. I think he was heading south when I first gained contact, but the moment I locked on, he began a rapid turn starboard toward north to head back to Hanoi. Using the radar's computation of the best intercept solution (based on the airspeed of the interceptor and the airspeed and heading of the target) we turned starboard to about northwest for the intercept. Because we had accelerated in full afterburner as soon as we were vectored, we were already above the 375 knot maximum speed for jettisoning the centerline fuel tank, which would have reduced drag and allowed us to accelerate faster and to a greater maximum speed. As we began to close on the MiG, it was apparent that our intercept heading would take us directly over Thanh Hóa, a large city south of Hanoi that was heavily defended by multiple SAM sites. Because we would be flying at high subsonic or supersonic speeds, I think Pete was highly concerned that such speeds would prevent us from maneuvering effectively to counter a SAM launched against us. As a result, we altered our heading to skirt Thanh Hóa to the east, which lengthened our track to catch the MiG.

By this time, we had accelerated beyond Mach 1 (faster than the speed of sound) and had closed to about nine miles astern, which was reasonably close, but still out of the range of either our Sparrow or Sidewinder missiles. At this point, our radar telemetry indicated we were closing on the MiG at a rate of about fifty knots, but all of a sudden, this became an opening speed of 100 knots, a clear indication that the MiG had also broken through Mach 1. Obviously, we now realized we weren't going to catch him, because we were near our maximum speed. By this time, we were only about twenty miles south of Hanoi, so we decided that discretion was the better part of valor, and broke off the chase, heading for feet wet.

Coral Sea knew that we would need fuel after the chase, so a KA-3 tanker had been vectored west so we could rendezvous with him to refuel off the coast. (Actually, operating doctrine and prudence dictate that aircraft carriers ensure that tanking assets are airborne any time other aircraft are flying.) While an F-4 can fly for nearly 3 hours at maximum endurance cruise settings, if it is flown in full afterburner, it can burn all its fuel in about 25 minutes, even with a centerline fuel tank that adds about 30 percent to the fuel load.

SAM site (aerial). Photo by S. M. "Pete" Purvis

After we had refueled, we were informed that we would not be able to return to the carrier, because the aircraft had already been spotted on the flight deck for next morning's first launch. To move and re-spot the aircraft would be prohibitively disruptive and labor intensive, so we were directed to "bingo" (divert) to a South Vietnamese airfield. Normally, we would land at Da Nang air base, which had primarily Air Force and Marine units as tenants. Da Nang was at that time the busiest airfield in the world, based on daily takeoffs and landings. However, on this night, Da Nang was ruled out, because clouds were at one hundred feet with quarter-mile visibility, below F-4 landing minimums of 200 feet and half-mile visibility. That being the case, we headed to Chu Lai air base, in 1967 still a small Marine base, about fifty-five miles south of Da Nang. As it turned out, the weather at

Chu Lai was near minimums as well, and we broke out of the clouds at about 250 feet above ground level. That was close!

Once we landed and made arrangements to have our aircraft refueled for the next morning's flight back to *Coral Sea*, we discovered that they had minimal facilities for accommodating transient aircrews. There were beds or bunks available for only three of us. And guess what. Because I was the junior officer in the flight, I was the odd man out, and wound up having to sleep in a bunk belonging to a Marine who was on watch that night, not the most pleasant eventuality. At any rate, the following morning we prepared to fly back to *Coral Sea* only to encounter an additional delay. When we tried to taxi out to take off, it had already gotten hot and steamy, and one of our main landing gear sank into the blacktop on the transient flight line. The F-4 was a lot heavier than the A-4s and other aircraft usually seen at Chu Lai. At about 49,000 lbs. with full fuel, our F-4 could not take off until a crane was summoned to hoist us free. Before long we were on our way home to *Coral Sea,* mixing in with other aircraft landing at the end of their flight.

There is an ironic, but I think humorous, further outcome of our MiG chase. A week or so after returning to the ship, I discovered that I had a case of the crabs. There could be only one explanation for this, and that Marine's bunk was it. Before the bingo to Chu Lai, I had been aboard ship for 3½ weeks, and I was the only one sleeping in my bed. So my night in that Marine's bunk was the only time I could have caught the crabs. I'm not above self-deprecating humor, but how many people do you know who can say they chased a MiG but caught the crabs?

A Brush with China

Perusal of a map of southeast Asia shows that the Gulf of Tonkin is a sheltered arm of the South China Sea, bordered on the west by North Vietnam, on the north by the Chinese mainland, and on the east by Hainan Island, also part of China. Recall that in 1968, we did not have diplomatic relations with the People's Republic of China, choosing instead to recognize what was then called Nationalist China on Taiwan Island as the legitimate government of China. We did not take the first steps to establish diplomatic relations with the People's Republic of China until 1971, with Secretary of State Henry Kissinger's secret trip to China in July, followed by President Nixon's historic visit the following February. Technically, China was the enemy, because it was then an ally of North Vietnam. When we would visit Hong Kong, which was then still a British colony and a regular stop on every WESTPAC cruise, we were prohibited from entering any facility that was designated as Chinese Communist owned or managed.

With this as a backdrop, on February 14, six days after our MiG chase, an incident occurred involving China and *Coral Sea* that at the time we thought might become a major international incident. Pilots were ferrying two unarmed A-1s back from NAS Cubi Point to *Coral Sea*. At that time, pilots were free to plan their own navigation and fly their own route to Yankee Station. However, these two aircraft drifted too far north, flying close enough to Hainan Island that the Chinese launched fighter aircraft, shooting down one of the A-1s, piloted by Lt. (jg.) Joseph P. Dunn. The pilot of the other aircraft avoided visual detection by hiding in the clouds, and eventually made his way to Da Nang, and then back to *Coral Sea*.

Because of the incident, *Coral Sea* (and, I think, the other carriers on Yankee Station) reacted by putting all of the A-4s and A-1s below in the hanger deck and all of the fighters on the flight deck, armed only with air-to-air missiles. It looked to us as though we were preparing for war with China. Had we inadvertently set in motion World War III? We were all briefed on Hainan's air order of battle (AOB, the number and location of combat aircraft on the island), and learned that there were hundreds of MiGs at various bases there. It seemed a real possibility that we might have to launch and fight these massive numbers of Chinese fighters, even though we were horribly outnumbered. However, after a couple of days of steaming around in this heightened state of alert, the mood eased, and we resumed normal combat operations. My last combat flight on this cruise turned out to be on February 20, after which we steamed for Subic Bay and then to Yokosuka.

Climate Change

As mentioned above, we had learned we would probably have to spend time in the Sea of Japan as a show of force because of the *Pueblo* capture. As a result, *Coral Sea* and its personnel would need to be prepared for the cold weather. For aircrews, that meant we would need protection from the wintry weather and the Sea of Japan's cold waters should we have to eject. At that time, before the days of wetsuits, aircrews flying over cold water had to wear a bulky suit to insulate them from the cold. I don't know the formal name of these suits, but we not-so-affectionately called them "poopy suits." They were very uncomfortable, and wearing one made you feel like the Michelin Man. Upon donning one for the first time, I was immediately grateful that, unlike our east-coast F-4 brethren, who flew out of NAS Oceana, Virginia, we at Miramar didn't have to wear poopy suits during the winter. Unlike the Atlantic off Virginia in winter, the water temperature along the southern California coast, in the Tonkin Gulf, and in other locations we flew never got cold enough to warrant wearing poopy suits.

Because *Coral Sea* had not expected to operate in cold waters during this cruise, aircrews had not been issued poopy suits, so they now had to be ordered. This job fell to squadron maintenance personnel. The particular maintenance folks responsible for the ordering had the long-winded rating name of aircrew survival equipmentmen, but everyone still referred to them as parachute riggers, the rating name until 1965, or even more briefly, parariggers or just riggers. Obtaining poopy suits for most of the aircrews proved to be no problem, but getting one for our CO, Cdr. Bobby D. Willard (who replaced Cdr. Gillespie as CO when he became a POW) was another matter. Commander Willard was a short fireplug of a man, which made it difficult to find a poopy suit to fit him. But of course, it would not do for the CO to be sans poopy suit. The branch officer for the riggers at the time was Lt. (jg.) William "Bill" Pellegrini, and although the riggers were under his charge, he did not order poopy suits himself. Nevertheless, the CO's wrath fell on Bill, possibly because Cdr. Willard didn't see him as the most diligent of branch officers. As we were already steaming north toward Japan, with Cdr. Willard still without a poopy suit, I overheard him telling Bill in the back of the ready room, "Pellegrini, if you want to salvage what you have left of your fitness report, you *will* find me a poopy suit!" Well, magically, Pellegrini's parachute riggers *did* manage to find the CO a poopy suit, and the crisis passed.

As it turned out, by the time we arrived in the Sea of Japan in early March, international tensions had quieted down, and Pete and I flew only eight times, over a period of nine days, with two of those flights into and out of NAS Atsugi, Japan, for a couple of days R&R. As I recall, the stay was most welcome and relaxing.

Heading Home

Upon steaming out of the Sea of Japan, *Coral Sea* enjoyed a most pleasant surprise when it stopped at the small Naval base in the Japanese port of Sasebo. At the time, Sasebo was notable for its bucolic, peaceful ambience, and the local populace was friendly and welcoming. It was a nice way to close out the cruise. After a few days, we returned to Yokosuka on March 19, restocking with supplies and fuel one last time before the ship left on March 27 for San Francisco Bay, arriving on April 6. Even if they put into Pearl Harbor for only a day to refuel, my calculations indicate that the *Coral Sea* must have averaged at least 25 knots (about 28 mph) for the transit. That's really moving.

However, for lucky returning aircrew members, including me, there was a program called Magic Carpet, which allowed us to fly back to the United States. I think later flights used military aircraft, but for this flight, we flew from Tokyo to Los Angeles on a commercial flight, intermixed with quiet, prim, courteous Japanese passengers. You can imagine how well they mixed with a bunch of boisterous Navy aircrew just finishing a combat cruise. Many of the crewmembers were drinking and carousing up and down the aircraft aisle. (Yes, in those days, all commercial aircraft had only one aisle.) Some of the Japanese passengers appeared to be scared out of their wits! Upon landing at LAX, I'm sure they were overjoyed to rid themselves of the Navy reprobates they had been cooped up with in an aluminum tube for ten or eleven hours.

One last incident punctuated the end of the cruise. We changed aircraft at LAX, and those of us based at NAS Miramar made the short flight there. Climbing out of LAX after takeoff, the pilot had to make a violent maneuver to avoid a midair collision, which shook everybody up, and sent belongings flying. We were understandably glad to arrive at Miramar in one piece.

Reflection

Arrival at Miramar enabled me finally to close the book on my first cruise. I was glad to be home, but it was more relief than elation. Any happiness was tempered by the fact that our squadron lost five aircraft and ten aircrew members, nearly one third of the squadron's pilots and radar intercept officers, a terrible price to pay. I am reminded of George Patton's observation that "it is foolish and wrong to mourn the men who died. Rather we should thank God that such men lived."[62]

Although I had learned a lot, as an Air Wing 15 flight officer aboard *Coral Sea*, I still had a lot to learn, and three more Vietnam cruises to learn it. In the end, looking back with the perspective of fifty years, my thoughts today accord with the words of the British philosopher John Stuart Mill, published a century before the Vietnam conflict: "War is an ugly thing, but not the ugliest of things: the decayed and degraded state of moral and patriotic feeling which thinks that nothing is *worth* a war, is worse. ... A man who has nothing which he is willing to fight for, nothing which he cares more about than he does about his personal safety, is a miserable creature who has no chance of being free, unless made and kept so by the exertions of better men than himself."[63] Former comrades in arms, my Vietnam-era brothers who believed there was a call to war worthy of personal response and service, periodically gather proudly as Vietnam vets, and share their stories. The recording of the experiences of my three other Vietnam cruises will have to wait for another such day.

---

62 George S Patton Jr., speech at the Copley Plaza Hotel, Boston Massachusetts, June 7, 1945, reported by William Blair in The New York *Times,* June 8, 1945, p. 6.

63 John Stuart Mill, *The Contest in America,* Boston: Little Brown and Company, 1862: 31.

BARRIE L. COOPER joined the Navy upon graduation from Principia College in 1965 and went to the Navy's Officer Candidate School in Newport, Rhode Island. Two of Cooper's uncles had been career Navy (enlisted) and other relatives had enlisted in the Navy and Army Air Corps during and after World War II. Following commissioning, Ensign Cooper served on active duty until the end of the Vietnam War in 1975, discharged as a lieutenant, and then continued in the Navy Reserve for an additional six years retiring at the rank of commander. He served on multiple tours in Vietnam [Yankee Station], operating on two cruises with Fighter Squadron 151 [VF 151] (1967-69) and two cruises with Fighter Squadron 111 [VF 111] (1973-75) both aboard USS *Coral Sea* (CVA-43). He was an assistant quality assurance officer, then supply officer with VF 151, and on his 1973-4 cruise, assistant maintenance officer, and finally aircraft maintenance officer in 1974-5. He was awarded the Air Medal (fourteen strike-flight awards), as well as the Navy Commendation Medal, Navy Achievement Medal, and Vietnam Service Medal. After active duty, during his time in the Naval Reserve, Cooper was an engineering technician at the Naval Air Rework Facility at the Naval Air Station, North Island, California (1975-78) and from 1982-1999 served as personnel research psychologist at the Navy Research and Development Center, San Diego. He would go on to earn a PhD in industrial-organizational psychology in 2003 from the California School of Professional Psychology. Subsequently he was appointed an adjunct professor at National University and Alliant International University, San Diego (2004-11), and from 2011-14 continued as an associate professor there.

Born in 1943 in New Orleans, Cooper was raised in Shreveport, Louisiana, where he was living when he decided to attend Principia Upper School as a boarding student his junior year, the high school that his older sister Connie had attended as a junior and senior in the late 1950s. Barrie would go on to Principia College earning a bachelor's degree with a combined major in economics and business administration. He would later earn an MBA at San Diego State University in 1984. A member of Rackham East residence hall, Cooper participated on his house team in intramural touch football and softball and sang in the college choir his senior year. He later married Martchen Dickson-Cooper (they have no children), and is now retired living in San Diego. Cooper spends his time reading biographies, books on history, and studies of current affairs. He enjoys race walking, and remains busy conducting and reviewing research on team effectiveness.

SEA LOG ENTRY... USS *Walker* ... Sea of Japan ... May 10, 1967

NORMAN BLEICHMAN

You'll never guess who we bumped into today—the Soviet navy! I kid you not. Here's what happened.

It was an otherwise beautiful day at sea. I was a Naval Supply Officer aboard the USS *Walker* (DD-517), a *Fletcher*-class destroyer, built during WWII with a projected useful life back then of only a few years. Now, almost 25 years later, she was still afloat, smartly keeping up with the newer cruisers and frigates, running plane-guard for the carrier USS *Hornet* (CV-12) while it was launching aircraft. We were part of a task force conducting antisubmarine warfare exercises in the Sea of Japan.

As a supply officer, I was not privy to—nor very interested in—the strategy and tactics involved in this type of screening duty. That was all to change in the blink of an eye. A Soviet Kotlin-class destroyer *Besslednyi* (DD-022) entered our maneuvering space, attempting to harass the carrier, make it change direction, and thus curtail the launch cycle. *Walker*, using accepted rules-of-the road tactics was in the process of heading off the intruder, when the unthinkable occurred. Pulling up aft close along our starboard quarter at moderate speed, the Soviets apparently neglected to take into account the physics of the situation, specifically the mutual pull between our two vessels. And so, the inevitable collision occurred. The damage was minor—their railings scraping against ours. But we both came full stop, remained dead in the water, and pointed our guns (5″ 38s) downward toward the deck.

During this time our entire crew was at General Quarters. My battle station was in the crypto room, a tiny, dark space with what was then state-of-the-art encrypting and decrypting gear—all mechanical wheels and gears, nothing digital in those days. We sent the required status reports to those needing to know, but I frankly have no recollection of any specific information or instructions coming in. What I do remember is that I was suddenly summoned to the bridge by my CO. He knew I had taken some Russian language courses in school—three quarters worth at Principia College—and asked me if I remembered enough to send a message to the other ship which was now floating a mere 30 yards away. Honestly, the only two phrases that came to me were "Peace in the world" and "Where's the bathroom?" The captain wisely chose the first one. I can only assume it was effective, as no further aggression occurred. At least not *that* day.

Norman Bleichman & USS *Walker* (DD-517). Photo
courtesy Norman Bleichman

Yes, if this weren't dramatic enough, the very *next* day, an eerily identical scenario unfolded, this time with a Krupnyy-class destroyer (DDGS-025). Same intended interference by them, same defensive tactic by *Walker*, same law of physics, same result [*crunch!*]. This time, however, *Walker* received a proper souvenir—a wooden panel from their motor whaleboat fell aft on our deck. (My CO has that framed and hanging in his living room to this day.)

Soviet Kotlin-class destroyer *Besslednyi* (DD-022).
Photo courtesy Norman Bleichman

Needless to say, the novelty of the first day's events was replaced by the potential seriousness of this second day. Would there be a cumulative effect? Retaliation? Escalation? Thankfully, no. From what I could tell, admirals and chiefs of staff were brought into the discussion, and some tension-easing and face-saving occurred at a very high level. When we pulled into Sasebo, Japan, a few days later for minor repairs, the media was there in force to interview our CO. It was big news—in fact, we made the front page of the New York *Times*—right hand column, above the fold. And it's quite possible, with the news cycle being what it was in those days, the story could have had longer legs, were it not that the Israeli Six-Day War happened within weeks and completely dominated the headlines.

Our "fifteen minutes of fame" lasted perhaps a little longer than that. And of course the details of those few days linger on and comprise some of the more indelible memories of my military service. Incidentally, the motto of DESRON 22, the destroyer squadron to which *Walker* belonged, was "Ready for Sea." We may not have been ready for those particular incidents, but in retrospect, I feel we responded with class, grace, and even a little panache.

"Peace in the world."

NORM BLEICHMAN is currently a Christian Science practitioner and recently served as Second Reader at The Mother Church, the First Church of Christ, Scientist, in Boston, Massachusetts. Born and raised in Los Angeles, he has lived (until recently) in New England since 1987 when he began serving as Managing Editor of *World Monitor Magazine.* He has worked for several departments of the Church in communications and media production, including the Committee on Publication, the Clerk's Office, and office of The Writings of Mary Baker Eddy (now called the Office of the Publisher's Agent). He has also been involved in producing The Mother Church Annual Meeting, a yearly gathering in Boston of the Church members of the international Christian Science community. Bleichman now lives in Santa Fe, New Mexico.

A 1965 graduate of Principia College, Bleichman was a business major in college, a member of Brooks North residence hall, and social head of first his sophomore class and later his fraternity house. His mother, Shirley Minkus, graduated from Principia College in 1939, and his daughter Emilyjane attended the Upper School from 2000 to 2004. He and his wife Bonnie Padgett, a member of the college class of 1966, also have a son, Benjamin. After graduation from Principia and active duty in the military (1966-69), Bleichman pursued a career as a script writer for television, an advertising copywriter, and a video producer.

After receiving his commission from Officer Candidate School in Newport, Rhode Island, and attending Navy Supply Corps School in Athens, Georgia, Bleichman was posted to San Diego and Pearl Harbor (where his ship USS *Walker* was homeported), and he served in Vietnam at the Naval Supply Depot, Cua Viet. Cua Viet was a trans-shipment point for supplies routed to Dong Ha, the capital of Quang Tri Province. The Navy's northernmost base in Vietnam, Cua Viet was arduous duty, due to both enemy fire and a harsh physical environment marked by winds and rains of winter monsoons. Shoals outside the river mouth endangered ships that were transporting supplies to Cua Viet from Da Nang, the largest city in the south central coast of Vietnam and located ninety nautical miles to the south. Bleichman served as supply officer, disbursing officer, and crypto officer, and his service in Vietnam was recognized by the Vietnam Service Medal.

"They've Seized The *Pueblo*"

JOHN K. ANDREWS JR.

"Attention all hands. Man your battle stations. I repeat, man your battle stations." Commander Bob Gavazzi's voice blared from the ship's announcing system into every part of USS *Bonefish* (SS-582). It was early 1968, and I was the newest of eight officers aboard our diesel-electric submarine on clandestine surveillance patrol in the Yellow Sea between Korea (and beyond it, Japan) to the east and China to the west.

Topside, as we could tell through the periscope, it was a bright winter day with choppy seas; features of the Chinese coastline were visible some miles to the west. But none of the ninety of us on board had been up in the sunshine for many days now, and it would be another six weeks before *Bonefish* could finally surface and our watch-standing would move from the cramped, sweaty control room to the fresh breeze up on the bridge.

Invisibility, a submarine's unique advantage on the naval chess-board, was imperative for us just then, because our boat was where she had no business being, as far as the Communist Chinese and the neighboring North Koreans were concerned. Though snorkeling outside the recognized twelve-mile boundary of international waters, we were far inside the fifty-mile territorial waters those hostile regimes claimed. To see and to listen (electronically and by sonar) but not to be seen or heard—that was our mission from ComSubPac.

I happened to be on watch that morning—January 24, 1968—when the skipper's order to battle stations shocked the ship awake. "This is the captain speaking," Gavazzi went on. "We have just received a fleet radio message that USS *Pueblo* has been fired on by North Korean vessels, boarded and seized, and she was taken into Wonsan harbor under escort.

"It appears Bonefish is the closest U.S. military asset of any kind, air or naval, to North Korea. Pending further orders, we could be in a shooting war with their naval units at any time. I intend to fight our ship, and I will look to every one of you to do your utmost. We must do everything we can for the *Pueblo*—everything," Captain Gavazzi concluded.

A commissioned officer for less than nine months and at sea for just nine weeks, I was as green as any young ensign could possibly be. In the skipper's voice over the crackly 1MC speakers, I heard a note of grim urgency that he had never used before. Battle stations on a submarine were for the World War II era, my father's days on USS *Archer-Fish*, with six war patrols against Imperial Japan. Such was not the role of subs in Korean fighting during the 1950s, or today, in the Vietnam conflict of the '60s.

But now out of the blue, on a routine intelligence patrol, expecting to confront no one in anger and to be confronted by no one, this could be "it." Battle stations. A shooting war! *Pueblo*, we knew, was on the surface in these same disputed waters to do much the same kind of electronic snooping that *Bonefish* was doing submerged. That could be us taken captive.

And for our captain, there was a personal dimension as well. Commander Lloyd "Pete" Bucher, *Pueblo*'s skipper, had been a submariner. At the sub base in Yokosuka, Japan, earlier in January, Gavazzi and most of our wardroom had attended a farewell party for his old friend, the night before *Pueblo* left port on her first mission since being rehabbed and put back in commission as AGER-2 the previous year.

Junior as I was and stuck with the "dirty duty" in port that night, I had missed the party—and with it the opportunity to learn that Lt. Edward Murphy, Bucher's executive officer, was a fellow Principian. He had graduated in 1960 as a classmate of my friend John Boyman, who would go on to become president of Principia College, and Murphy was well acquainted with Egil "Bud" Krogh (C'61), himself a naval officer in the years before Vietnam and later a colleague of mine on Nixon's White House staff. Only much later did I learn of Ed Murphy's Principia connection. His firsthand account of the *Pueblo* incident, including eleven months of brutality as a North Korean POW, is given in Murphy's book *Second in Command* (Holt, Rinehart, and Winston, 1971). He now maintains the website *PuebloExec.com* and continues to do public speaking on lessons of the ordeal.

USS *Pueblo* (AGER-2) off San Diego,
California, 19 October 1967

But back to those tense hours on the 24th of January. Honestly, the details have faded. I didn't keep a journal of my time at sea (wish I had), and it's been a long time. Ask me about the Denver Broncos' season, or the coming matchups in Colorado elections. On those I know chapter and verse.

We probably stayed at battle stations for three or four hours. Lt. Cdr. Jack Renard, our XO, paced nervously and thought aloud about options. Lt. Jim Finlen, weapons officer, saw to the making ready of torpedoes. Lt. Dick Marlin, engineering officer (and my boss: this humanities major was, woe betide, the ship's assistant engineer), calculated battery life should we have to go deep and go quiet.

The waiting and the wondering were excruciating; I remember those even more than the gnawing dread in my stomach. But most vividly I can still feel the sense of helplessness as we imagined the humiliation of a proud U.S. Navy ship and the maltreatment of her shocked crew, and realized with growing finality that there was nothing that we on *Bonefish*, at least, could do. Nothing but chafe with frustration, and pray.

In any case, hostilities involving us would have only been part of a general eruption of war with the Norks, not a specific rescue attempt. Wonsan, near which the seizure on the high seas had occurred, was on the east side of the Korean peninsula, and our patrol area was across the land mass on the west side. After a time, the men and officers of *Bonefish* stood down from battle stations; the routine of underwater life resumed for us through February and into March, until our eventual return to Yokosuka.

It's now known—of which we obviously had no idea at the time—that command authorities in Pearl Harbor and Washington initially moved an aircraft carrier, scrambled planes, and even launched rescue boats toward Wonsan. But they ultimately decided not to push it, lest more harm should come to the *Pueblo* hostages. Anyway, President Lyndon Johnson's overriding priority just then was the war in Vietnam, where the Tet offensive was to rock U.S. forces only a week later—and LBJ's own political string, to everyone's astonishment, would itself run out on March 31, when he renounced another term.

To relive that hair-trigger day at periscope depth in the Yellow Sea is to remember how much I learned about leadership and life from my commanding officers on *Bonefish*. Bob Gavazzi, though that day was the closest he ever came to targeting a torpedo on the enemy, was a happy warrior as well as an inspirational skipper. His watchword, I learned upon joining the wardroom, was: "If it doesn't feel good, you're not doing it right." Beneath the joking innuendo about sailors on liberty, this was a message of esprit and elan—and Gavaz lived these to the full.

Bob's successor in command of SS-582, shortly after we returned to Pearl Harbor from that Westpac deployment, was Cdr. Jim "Doc" Blanchard, who had been a football star at Annapolis. Doc not only coached our boat's flag football team in the Sub Base Pearl league, he quarterbacked us to win after win. The Old Man, in this case, was still young enough to evade the blitz and throw touchdowns. What a boost for the competitive morale of our crew in all things afloat and ashore.

On the other hand, to study again the pursuit, subduing, surrender, and captivity of the *Pueblo* — defiantly on display in North Korea even to this day as a museum of the treacherous Yankee dogs — is to have a troubling reminder of our nation's military fecklessness over the past generation or two. Not only did the United States arguably misplay Korea, Vietnam, Iraq, and Afghanistan in grand strategy, but the incident off Wonsan also foreshadowed other American tactical humiliations — from Desert One under Carter and Khobar Towers under Reagan, to Mogadishu under Bush, the USS *Cole* under Clinton, and most recently, Benghazi under Obama.

Not since our parents in the Greatest Generation defeated Hitler and Tojo has the United States truly won a war. America must not become "a pitiful, helpless giant," warned President Nixon in 1970, soon after I was released to the inactive reserve. Have we? It's a haunting question.

But in the perspective of our own small college, I take heart from the century-long tradition whereby young men and women whose ideals were formed by Scripture, Mrs. Eddy, and Mrs. Morgan keep stepping up to wear the uniform, to serve, and if necessary to sacrifice. I'm grateful that Principia began as a military school, where my grandfather could be a cadet before heading off to the U.S. Naval Academy and World War I. That his fourth son, my dad, was a submariner and raised me to be one. That our nephew, son of a Principian, is at West Point today.

I'm grateful that the same pocket Bible I studied at sea in 1968, a gift from my wife and C'66 classmate, Donna, was with me when we revisited Pearl Harbor in 2013 and took our grandson through the WWII submarine *Bowfin*, moored there as a memorial. Inscribed on the flyleaf in her handwriting is God's promise from Isaiah 43:2: "When thou passest through the waters, I will be with thee." And I always felt He was.

JOHN K. ANDREWS JR. was a third-generation Navy officer whose grandfather graduated from the Naval Academy in 1914 and whose father was a World War II submarine officer. Andrews's initial training at the Navy's Officer Candidate School in Newport culminated in his commission as a naval officer in April 1967 achieving the rank of lieutenant at the time of his discharge in 1969. Following his father's footsteps, John become submarine qualified, serving as assistant engineering officer and then supply officer aboard USS *Bonefish* SS 582. *Bonefish* was home based at Sub Base Pearl Harbor, with cruises to U.S. Pacific coast and to WESTPAC, including offshore Vietnam.

Born in Allegan, Michigan, Andrews spent most of his youth in St. Louis, Missouri, where his family enrolled him at Principia and where he became a "lifer," educated from first grade through high school at Principia's Lower, Middle, and Upper Schools, and from 1962-1966 at Principia College. He was part of the historic and extended Andrews family at Principia: both his parents and paternal grandparents were Prin graduates, an uncle was on the college faculty, another uncle served as college president, and other of his ancestors included the dean of the college faculty during the 1930s, and (prior to World War I) the school's first housemom. Continuing a long Andrews tradition at Principia, John Kneeland Andrews Jr. excelled in academics, athletics, and other collegiate activities. He served as president of Buck House (his college residence hall), as well as freshman head of a newly formed student residence (Highland Hall). He was on the drafting committee for the college's honor code. In athletics, Andrews earned varsity letters each of his four years on the track team. In addition, he helped initiate and develop Prisoc, a soccer club on campus, serving as co-captain for three years, and when the sport was recognized by the athletic department with full varsity status, Andrews earned a letter in the sport his senior year; he returned briefly after his graduation to coach soccer before beginning his active duty in the Navy. In academics, Andrews double-majored in political science and business administration, and in 1966 graduated first in his class. As a budding political scientist, Andrews served on the steering committee for Principia College's prestigious Public Affairs Conference which attracts scholars from major universities nation-wide to discuss current affairs and develop white papers on issues of contemporary interest. Andrews would later serve the Nixon White House as a speech writer, served as President of the Colorado Senate, and is currently Vice President for public policy, Colorado Christian University. In 2011 Andrews published *Responsibility Reborn: A Citizen's Guide to the Next American Century.* He is married to Principia alumna Donna D'Evelyn (C66); the Andrewses, who live in Centennial, Colorado, have one son and two daughters.

Carrier flight deck. Photo by Robert M. Craig

TLIMS

MIKE KNEELAND

It was mid March of 1971. Deck [Deskin Waters], my bombardier/ navigator [B/N], and I had been flying visual and all-weather bombing missions in an A-6 from the deck of USS *Ranger* (CVA-61) for about five months. While the carrier landings and combat flying never became routine, the events of most missions happened as expected. But not this time.

Prior to each mission, we would receive a twenty- to thirty-minute brief from the intelligence department about the intended target, including anti-aircraft positions and expected fire, the agencies with which we would work, and the frequencies on which to contact them. My kneeboard would be filled with writing.

I always saved a small square in the top right corner of my kneeboard for the initials TLIMS to remind me that "The Lord is My Shepherd." While some others used the 91st Psalm, the 23rd was most familiar to me and frequently brought comfort. I had used it before getting into combat, but now it became my daily companion.

On this March night the weather conditions were particularly rough. It was rainy and windy as we preflighted the plane and prepared the mission. We always got wet and uncomfortable during this pre-flight process but getting into the plane and getting the heat blowing inside the cockpit helped dry us out and become more comfortable. This night seemed rather ominous. Our target was a petroleum storage area in Laos.

As the catapult fired, launching us into the air, the inertial navigation system failed. The attitude indicator rolled over on its side. I immediately turned my scan to the backup gyro, gained a safe altitude, and raised the landing gear and flaps. We called ship operations, reported our situation, and requested our options. We were told we could either drop our bombs in the sea or continue on and "buddy-bomb" on the other aircraft that was launched for a similar target. We usually carried twenty-two 500-pound bombs. Deck and I decided that our job was to deliver these bombs to their target and that we would press on.

Mike Kneeland and his bombardier/navigator, Deskin Waters ("Deck"). Photo courtesy Mike Kneeland

We were told to contact the other A-6 that had launched just before us. George, the other pilot, gave me his radial and distance from a known navigation station, and we proceeded towards his position over Laos at about 25,000 feet. I could see the anti-collision light of George's A-6 from many miles away. I slid in under his right wing and assumed a comfortable position that I had taken many times in day, night, and bad weather conditions.

We discussed our projected actions to the target. We would make two passes at the target, releasing half of our bomb load with each pass. I would fly on George's wing using his A-6 formation and position lights for reference. There was also a slight bit of moonlight that night lighting the top of his aircraft. During buddy-bombing, the lead aircraft uses the aircraft electronic bombing system to release the bombs on target, and the second aircraft with the inoperable bombing system releases its bombs simultaneously with the lead aircraft. This was a maneuver we'd performed many times.

As we dropped closer to our release altitude of 3,500 feet, there were breaks in the clouds, and the anti-aircraft fire intensified. George came on the radio and announced, "I'm sorry, Mike, but I am going to have to turn off all outside aircraft lights since they can see us, and we are taking heavy fire." He arranged for Ray, the B/N, to turn up his map light inside the cockpit for an additional position reference. I had flown lots of night formation in the clouds but this was a new challenge. I tucked in as close as possible in order to see the relative motion between the aircraft. We had just a few feet of wingtip separation.

As we approached the target, the anti-aircraft fire became very heavy. We knew that this was an important target. Deck no longer had a radar system to watch so he was looking outside the cockpit and narrated the scene. At one point he stated, "Wow, I can see these tracers coming up under the wing and exploding over the top of us." I couldn't take my eyes off the lead aircraft for a second, but at this point a tracer came between the two aircraft and was readily visible even to me.

Months before, on our first night mission, Deck and I were looking out over the area into which we would be flying. It was a clear night, and we could see the tracers miles away leaving a graceful arc into the sky and exploding like the 4th of July fireworks. We were quite impressed with the pretty sight until Deck looked at his map and exclaimed, "Oh, &%&@#, that's where we're going." It was one of the few times that I ever heard Deck use rough language. That night we flew directly down into that line of anti-aircraft fire.

It seemed like a long approach, but George finally gave the familiar "Get ready," then "Standby, standby, standby, Hack!" We could feel the 500-pound bombs leave the aircraft. The clouds below us lit up a bright orange as those bombs ignited the petroleum products below. I was relieved as we pulled off the target, but then realized that we had another pass to make before our mission was complete. The second pass was similar although I do not remember the anti-aircraft fire being as intense. Many times during heavy anti-aircraft fire, especially during extended bombing runs, I felt like I was passing through a tunnel. I could always see a light at the end, but the experience was harrowing. That night I "walk[ed] through the valley of the shadow of death."[64] It was an experience that was indelibly burned into my memory.

A-6 in flight. Photo courtesy Mike Kneeland

I was grateful as we left the target for the last time, but the job was not over: we still had a night carrier landing in rough weather to complete our mission. When low visibility conditions existed, the

64 "Yea, though I walk through the valley of the shadow of death, I will fear no evil: for thou *art* with me; thy rod and thy staff they comfort me." Psalms 23: 4.

A-6 was "talked down" to the carrier by a radar controller in a "carrier controlled approach." We were allowed to descend to weather minimums of one hundred feet above the water and a quarter of a mile visibility before we could transition to a visual approach to the carrier and land. At our approach speed, that gave us roughly seven seconds to transition from instrument flying to seeing the carrier and hitting the deck. In the years since, I have heard that several astronauts who were naval aviators, when asked about the hardest part of their astronaut career, quickly reply, "night carrier landings." Those night carrier landings were never routine.

I was very grateful to get aboard USS *Ranger* that night in March, 1971. It was always good to be back home, debriefed, fed, and showered, but this night had been intense, and I had learned a lot. I discovered more about my capabilities both as a naval aviator and as a student of Christian Science. Indeed, the many lessons as a Christian Scientist, learned both before and during my Principia experience enabled me to survive my combat tour on USS *Ranger,* and I am grateful to know with confidence that TLIMS.

Vietnam Recollections

B. DUDLEY COLE III

In the mid-1960s, I was attached to Small Boats, stationed at the amphibious base on Coronado Island, California, where we trained with *Nasty*-class PT (Patrol Torpedo) boats.[65] Our Small Boats motto was "Give me a fast shallow draft boat because I intend to go in harm's way."

Later I was stationed in Da Nang as commanding officer of a UDT (Underwater Demolition Team) base from which covert operations, such as "agent handling," were initiated against North Vietnam. Agent handling means capturing village citizens for questioning regarding activities of the Viet Cong. Our tactics included dropping off UDT teams for clandestine operations in the Tonkin Gulf in basket boats stowed aboard the PT boats. The captured citizens were then returned to their villages in basket boats after questioning.

The PT boats operated in convoy, single file, three boats at a time under "ENCOM Sierra," which meant there were no communications, lights, nor radio transmissions. During attack mode one night, a PT boat's gyro compass malfunctioned, which caused the boat to fall behind. In an effort to catch up with the other two PT boats, the helmsman increased speed, and at a speed of 40 knots, the boat collided in the dark with the boat ahead, seriously damaging the stern, approximately 200 yards off the coast.

As a result, the boat was taking on water, but did not completely submerge. The attack phase was interrupted in order to rescue the crew in the Tonkin Gulf, and, accordingly, the mission was aborted. There was no loss of life on that mission. The next day, in accordance

---

65 The Coronado Naval Amphibious Base was established during World War II and later became the West Coast home of the Navy SEALs (the Navy's "Sea, Air, and Land" Teams. *Nasty*-class fast patrol boats were built for the U.S. Navy between 1962 and 1968 intended for "unorthodox operations" during the Vietnam War, typically action by Special Forces.

with standard operating procedures, a U.S. jet was scrambled off the aircraft carrier USS *America* (CVA-66) to bomb the damaged boat and prevent military secrets from falling into the hands of the North Vietnamese. In spite of such setbacks, PT boats continued to interdict enemy guns and supplies that were being transported via the Tonkin Gulf, action that diminished the fighting capability of the Viet Cong.

Overall, PT boats were fast, were reliable, and performed well. At the time, Norway constructed the double-planked mahogany boats. The twin 1800 horsepower Napier Deltic engines were manufactured by Rolls Royce. We discovered firsthand that the double-planked mahogany was unsatisfactory for lengthy deployments, since the mahogany hulls became waterlogged and required dry docking on a regular basis. As the commanding officer of this evolution, I recommended future PT boats be constructed of a more durable material, and I was glad to learn that subsequent vessels were constructed of aluminum in Berwick, Louisiana. I was awarded the Navy Commendation Medal for meritorious service from 10 June to 24 November, 1966.

I then attended destroyer school in Newport, Rhode Island, and subsequently I was assigned to USS *Furse* (DD-882) where I served as engineering officer (1968-70). My duty as chief engineer was to manage maintenance and repair issues. The ship was manned by a competent crew, and we had no problem with procuring spare parts and technical assistance. *Furse* deployed to Vietnam during the summer and early fall of 1968. I am reminded of an incident while conducting close-in shore bombardment aboard *Furse* off the coast of North Vietnam. The ship was hit by return fire from a North Vietnamese shore battery, penetrating the dash hangar deck located on the stern. The dash hanger is an aluminum hanger located on the after deck of destroyers used to house a remote control helicopter used for anti submarine warfare. The shell damaged the hull above the waterline but did not explode on the dash hanger deck. My general quarters assignment was on the stern. After the explosion, the captain called urgently on the intercom. I expected him to inquire about damages and possible injuries to the crew. Instead, he inquired about damage to his valuable antique rug, which he had recently purchased during a layover in Hong Kong and stored on the hangar deck. For a moment I felt like Mr. Roberts [Henry Fonda] or Ensign Pulver [Jack Lemmon] standing watch over Captain Morton's [James Cagney's] palm tree. My CO's antique rug was unharmed, and the damage control team immediately corrected the damage to the hull, enabling *Furse* to continue on its mission.

After the deployment and on our return state-side to San Diego, *Furse* (which was a WWII-vintage ship) travelled through the Panama Canal. As I recorded on the USS Furse website,[66] "Although we were out of the war zone, we faced a final challenge." The fresh water of Chagres River and Gatun Lake "killed the barnacles on the ship's hull, causing an unexpected leak beneath the #4 boiler." We had to improvise quickly, "creating a breathing apparatus from a gas mask and pump, which allowed a crewman to swim under the hull and put a temporary plug in the leak."

As I shared on the *Furse* website history, "My memory of my Vietnam experience includes moments of fear as well as camaraderie with fellow sailors. There were also moments of humor and enjoyment." I never could have predicted that on a beach in southeast Asia, I would take a break from the war to catch passes from Annapolis grad Roger Staubach, who would later return to the United States to become a star quarterback for the Dallas Cowboys. Lives cross in the strangest places.

CAPTAIN DUDLEY COLE, at twenty-three when he joined the Navy in 1958, was of a slightly older generation than most of the Principians in this volume who were born during or soon after World War II and who joined the military in the late 1960s during the Vietnam era troop escalation. Born in 1935, Cole enlisted in the Navy six years before the Gulf of Tonkin resolution authorizing the president to increase military presence in the southeast

---

66 http://www.ussfurse.org/Ships%20History.html

Asia region. Cole went to boot camp at Great Lakes, Illinois, and then (1958) to Officer Candidate School in Newport, R.I., commissioned an ensign in 1959. Six years later, U.S. combat troops were heavily deployed in Vietnam, bordering areas of Laos and Cambodia were being bombed, and Cole found himself serving two tours in Vietnam where American action reached a peak in 1968. Cole's duties took him to Da Nang and to the Western Pacific with additional service in the Middle East. He was engineering officer aboard the destroyer USS *Furse* (DDR-882), which earned a Navy Unit Citation with Combat "V." Discharged in 1972 at the rank of commander, Cole continued service in the naval reserves. His son and namesake, B. Dudley "Bo" Cole IV served in the U.S. Marines.

Born and raised in West Palm Beach, Florida, (where he still lives in retirement), Captain Cole graduated from Principia Upper School in 1953 and Principia College in 1958 with a major in economics. At the college, he was athletic head of Buck House, was a member of the track team, played softball, and was active in the drama club. Married for more than fifty-five years to Mary Campbell (US56, JrC 58), Captain Cole has three children (all Principians), Calisa (US78), Bo (US79), and Cheryl (US82, C86), as well as nine grandchildren. Cole's parents were also Principians, B. D. Cole Jr attending the Upper School and Cole's mother Edna Bremer attending the junior college. Captain Cole's business career after the military was in insurance. Post-retirement, he has enjoyed competitive masters swimming and triathlons. During the past four decades, Cole was active in civil organizations, serving as president of both the local Rotary Club and the Association of Retired Citizens, serving on the board of directors of his local chamber of commerce, active in his church, and serving as vice president of his insurance agency.

USS *Ranger* (CVA-61).
Photo: U.S. Navy National Museum of Naval Aviation

The Hot Poop
With Uncle Hanz

RAYBURN HANZLIK

In December, 1965, I embarked with my squadron on the aircraft carrier USS *Ranger* (CVA-61) in Alameda, California, for a nine-month deployment to Southeast Asia. I was an air intelligence officer with Heavy Attack Squadron Two (VAH-2), one of eight squadrons in the air wing aboard *Ranger*. The ship's mission was to provide aerial combat support to the U.S. ground war in South Vietnam.

Shortly after *Ranger* arrived in the Gulf of Tonkin in January, 1966, the United States began air strikes on North Vietnam, with *Ranger* aircraft among the first to fly these highly perilous missions, which continued over the next eight months. Daily (or nightly) we flew 100+ missions, launching and recovering sorties of aircraft every ninety minutes over fifteen hours. Pilots departing and returning in each of these "cycles" required briefings and debriefings by intelligence officers.

My assignment was primary briefing officer, with responsibility to impart timely intelligence to the pilots just prior to their missions. Since World War II, these shipboard briefings were usually conducted in a classroom setting, with the briefer addressing seated pilots, using charts and maps as briefing aids. At the beginning of *Ranger*'s operations, we employed this traditional arrangement, briefing pilots in the intelligence center. But this was a busy, cramped facility, with pilots coming and going for briefings and debriefings, and not an environment conducive to quality briefings.

The idea came to brief the pilots in their squadron ready rooms using the ship's new closed-circuit television system. Each ready room had a monitor (as did the ship's captain and other operations facilities), which was used for routine announcements. By employing this system for briefings, pilots could stay in their ready rooms until time to man aircraft, getting timely intelligence information without trekking to the intelligence center.

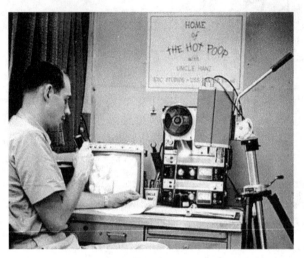

Ray Hanzlik Broadcasting an Intelligence Briefing.
Photo courtesy Ray Hanzlik

At first, the briefing format was unchanged. I continued the usual stand-up presentation, but in front of a camera instead of an audience of pilots. While this was an improvement, detailed map and chart information proved difficult to read on a monitor. We soon changed the format, with the camera now focused only on information cards (assembled in a notebook). Cards were kept updated for each briefing subject, such as search & rescue information, location of downed aircraft, surface-to-air missile sightings, etc. The ten-plus-minute briefings consisted of flipping through and discussing the stack of cards, with the camera broadcasting each card to all the monitors on the secure system.

With ten briefings a day for sixty-day periods of operations (with short breaks every two months), the challenge was to keep the pilot's attention. So I took a cue from Johnny Carson and made briefings more of a late night TV production, employing music, graphics, and humor. The Tijuana Brass provided background music (and became the signature sound of the program), and the cards were spiced with photos of pin-ups. The briefings were named *The Hot Poop with Uncle Hanz* and became known as the *Uncle Hanz Show*. They soon were a must-see event, with pilots watching who had no immediate mission. And the biggest fan was the ship's captain (who particularly liked the pin-ups).

Intelligence Briefing Information Card.
Photo courtesy Ray Hanzlik

Word of the *Uncle Hanz Show* got around the fleet in WestPac, and officers from other ships visited *Ranger* to see the briefing system in action. Our test project on *Ranger* eventually resulted in the introduction of closed circuit television briefings on other ships in the fleet.

The Hot Poop with Uncle Hanz. Photo courtesy Ray Hanzlik

Besides the satisfaction of being part of this breakthrough for shipboard intelligence briefings, I was awarded the Navy Achievement

Medal and received orders to the Pentagon as an admiral's aide. My new boss (Rear Admiral Henry Miller) pinned the medal on me after reporting to him for duty in the fall of 1966.

Postscript

In August, 1969, three years after *Ranger* returned from our deployment, my brother Willard (C'68) reported aboard the carrier. He served two years as an officer of the ship, which returned twice to Southeast Asia for combat operations in the Gulf of Tonkin during his tour. [See, "It's All in Who You Know" by Willard Hanzlik]

 **RAY HANZLIK,** son of a World War II Naval aviator, served in the Navy from 1963 to 1968. Following graduation from Officer Candidate School in Newport, Rhode Island, Pre-Flight School in Pensacola, Florida, and the Air Intelligence Training School in Denver, Colorado, Hanzlik was assigned to the Naval Station, Roosevelt Roads, Puerto Rico, as base Air Intelligence Officer (1964-65). Reassigned in late 1965 to Heavy Attack Squadron Two in Whidbey Island, Washington, as the unit's Air Intelligence Officer, Hanzlik deployed with his squadron aboard USS *Ranger* to Vietnam for operations in the Gulf of Tonkin. Following this Vietnam tour in late 1966, Hanzlik was selected as Personal Aide/Flag Lieutenant to Rear Admiral Henry Louis Miller, the Navy's Chief of Information at the Pentagon, where he served until discharged in 1968. For his Vietnam combat service, Hanzlik was awarded the Navy Achievement Medal in addition to the Vietnam Service Medal and Navy Unit Commendation Medal.

Hanzlik was born in 1938 in Los Angeles, raised in Vista, California, and came to Principia Upper School as a boarding student in 1954 (class of 1956). He attended Principia College, where he graduated in 1960 with a BS degree and double major in mathematics and physics. A resident of Brooks House South, Hanzlik served on his house governing board and campus fire crew, lettered in varsity football and golf, and was secretary to the men's athletic director. His sister, Ann, graduated from the Upper School two years after Hanzlik and attended the College for a year. His younger brother, Willard, also an author in this collection of memoirs, graduated from the College in 1968.

Hanzlik attended graduate and law school at the University of Virginia, where he earned MA and JD degrees. His post-Navy career included serving on the Nixon and Ford White House staffs, practicing law in Washington, DC, running for the U.S. Senate in California in 1980, and administering a Department of Energy regulatory agency during the Reagan Administration. He presently manages the lobbying firm he established in Washington. Married to Marilyn Burnap, an Upper School classmate, Hanzlik has a daughter and three sons, all of whom attended Principia. The Hanzliks recently moved to Leesburg, Virginia.

Flying Down the Throat of a SAM

MIKE KNEELAND

SAMs (Surface to Air Missiles) were long, rocket-propelled missiles which, when launched, used radar in order to track and destroy an airborne aircraft. When the SAM exploded, it usually completely blew up the plane. SAM's were launched from Fan Song Radar trailers that were deployed to North Vietnam from supporting countries (reportedly the USSR), and they were also usually operated by individuals from those countries. These Russian SAMs were responsible for a large percentage of the downed aircraft over North Vietnam, and they were feared by all flight crews.[67]

Our A-6's had avionics equipment onboard that gave crews both an aural and a visual report of radar signals. These radar signals could be guiding anti-aircraft guns, could be from already launched SAMs, or could be from other aircraft simply looking at us with their radar. The visual indication was a small scope which delineated the direction and strength of the radar signal. The aural indication was a demodulation of the radar signal which filled our headsets with different clicks, buzzes, and tones. We learned to identify the various radars by their aural signature. We also had a large, red light located next to the bombsight that indicated if a SAM radar site had locked on us, if it had launched a missile, and if the missile was guiding on our aircraft. The red light would first light steadily, then flash, as the missile came toward us. The

---

67 In 1960 Francis Gary Powers's U-2 reconnaissance aircraft was shot down by an SA-2 missile over the Soviet Union. Seven years later, John McCain piloted his carrier-based A-4 Skyhawk to his assigned target in Vietnam, waited too long to take evasive action against an incoming SA-2 (preferring to fulfill his bombing mission) which he did seconds before the SAM knocked the right wing off his plane. McCain was forced to eject, injuring himself, and parachuted into Hanoi's Trúc Bach Lake from which he was dragged out and taken prisoner by the North Vietnamese.

noises got increasingly loud and ominous as the missile got closer. That loud warble in your headset really informed you that something was greatly wrong and that you'd better take immediate action.

1985 artist rendering of a Soviet missile system [here, a later use of SA-12s against U.S. F-16 Falcons], U.S. Army. Photo: Defense Intelligence Agency

In the spring of 1971 there were several SAM sites north of the DMZ that had been particularly threatening to U.S. planes. Our Commanding Officer was asked to eliminate one of these SAM sites. He chose Deck, my B/N (Bombardier/Navigator), and me for his wingman on the mission to target the SAMs. Deck and I were both single and considered more expendable.

Our armament for this mission was limited: only two Standard ARM (Anti-Radiation Missile) missiles each. These 1,400 pound missiles were rocket-propelled and guided to the SAM launching site by "flying down the throat" of the SAM's guiding radar signal. The Standard ARM warhead included high explosives inside a band of thousands of small metal fragments that, when exploded inside the radar site, rendered the site incapable of being rebuilt. Other types of bombs might damage the launching trailer, but much of the wiring could be salvaged. A Standard ARM was like a huge grenade and damaged the equipment beyond restoration.

North Vietnamese SAM crew in front of SA-2
launcher. Photo: U.S. Air Force

The procedure used in launching the Standard ARM was to fly over the SAM site until you received a "lock-on" from the radar. Once the SAM was launched, you immediately pulled the aircraft nose down, aimed towards the site, and launched the Standard ARM which then rode the radar signal to its destination, the threatening Fan Song Radar site. You then had to deal with the SAM that was already accelerating towards your aircraft, reaching speeds of Mach 3.5 (three and one-half times the speed of sound).

If you turned away too quickly, the SAM could track you and hit your aircraft. If you waited too long, you got hit. The trick was to wait until you thought you were about to be hit and pull hard. Because the SAM was, by then, traveling over Mach 2, the A-6 could easily outturn the SAM when it was maneuvered to a flight path 90 degrees to the SAM's route of flight. We were supposed to pull 6 G's (six times the pull of gravity), but some pilots exceeded 9 G's when that SAM was coming. Those who pulled away too soon probably aren't here to tell about it. One pilot from my first squadron waited until he thought the SAM was near enough, and it flew over the top of the cockpit before the pilot pulled his A-6 away. He could see the fins and exhaust of that SAM as it accelerated across the top of his canopy! I'm sure those were two very startled crew members!

A-6A Intruders over Vietnam, 1968. Photo: U.S. Navy

The preflight briefing went as expected. The SAM site had been active and threatened our aircraft; it needed to be eliminated. We briefed and waited for the launch command. Then, just as our time for launch arrived, air intelligence came in and reported that the targeted SAM site was now obscured by clouds. We wouldn't be able to attack it. Another crew would get a chance at that SAM site another day when the weather improved. I never learned if that SAM site was eliminated. Such was the case in the Vietnam war. Events happened so quickly that you were soon into the next mission or challenge with little time to think about the results of the last.

I was relieved to be released from the tension and anticipation, and I've always wondered what that mission might have entailed. We were almost certain to have been shot at with those deadly SAMs. Evading them would have been a real life or death scenario. It certainly would have been one of the more challenging flights among those I took in the Vietnam theater.

Being hit by a SAM would have exploded the plane. If we had been able to eject safely after the SAM's impact, we would have descended by parachute either onto the land or water. A water landing was preferable since you had a better chance of getting plucked from the sea by U.S. forces before being caught by the North Vietnamese. Parachuting onto land almost certainly meant getting caught. Your best option then was to be only beat up enough to make it to the Hanoi Hilton. Some men parachuted safely but never survived the trip to the POW camp. I'm grateful that I always returned to my ship, and finally returned to the Good Old U.S. of A.

Scott Schneberger, 1973, boarding a VAQ-134 squadron EA-6B
Prowler while stationed aboard USS *Constellation* (CV-64).
Photo by Lt. Tom Harnish, courtesy Scott Schneberger.

Homeless Aboard a Floating City, Population 5,500

SCOTT L. SCHNEBERGER

I'm not saying that conditions aboard an aircraft carrier in 1973 off the coast of Vietnam were anywhere nearly as challenging as conditions, say, in a Marine Corps bunker ashore at Khe Sanh. But I will say that conditions were worse than Hollywood movies portrayed. Okay, maybe that's not saying much, but when you're living onboard a carrier for nine months it can seem very challenging. Here's why.

Living Quarters

A 1973-era aircraft carrier had eighteen decks and levels (floors); eight levels above the hanger bay and ten decks below the hanger bay. I spent almost all my working hours on the 03 level (third floor above the hanger bay) right below the flight deck. My stateroom was on the fourth deck; seven floors below where I worked. No, there were no elevators—except for airplanes. And the stairs between levels weren't stairs; they were steep ladders with slightly wider steps than your step ladder at home. That was quite a trek going from stateroom to office and back, especially carrying things.

But that was minor compared to the temperature. My stateroom was immediately above one of the engine spaces with boilers for powering a 1,000 foot long ship with a crew of 5,500. Which was fine in the cold waters off California, but when we arrived in the warm waters off Vietnam, my stateroom become unbearable. Medically certified uninhabitable. In spite of two air conditioning vents putting out pretty cold air, the floor was 128 degrees Fahrenheit; the room air temperature was 114F. I could keep my clothes there and change, but I was not allowed to work or sleep there. Moreover, there was not *one* unassigned bunk in a stateroom to be had. Not one. After spending a night in the infirmary, sleeping on rubber sheets in a room that had a drain in the center of the floor, there was only one solution: hot-bunking.

Carrier hatch and ladder view down.
Photo by Robert M. Craig

Essex-class carrier air conditioning.
Photo by Robert M. Craig

I hot-bunked for about eight months. That is, I rolled into someone's bunk that they just rolled out of either because they were on duty, they had flown a plane to shore temporarily, or they were on vacation. For sanitary reasons, I usually slept in my clothes. And most of the time when I got up in the morning I didn't know where I'd be sleeping that night. All day as I worked I'd be asking around the various air squadrons for a temporarily empty bunk. As a result, in the flight jacket I wore I carried my toothbrush, toothpaste, electric razor, and a flashlight. I was basically a homeless Lieutenant Junior Grade.

"Officers Country" stateroom area.
Photo by Robert M. Craig

Officers stateroom barracks. Photo by Robert M. Craig

Water

Gotta have it for washing, drinking, and preparing food. Near those engineering spaces below my stateroom were bilges and various tanks filled with aviation gasoline, jet fuel, fuel oil for the boilers, salt water for ballast, distilled water for boilers and catapults, and drinking water. My ship, USS *Constellation* (CV-64), was not a brand new ship. Over the years of pounding through waves and launching and recovering jet aircraft, the tanks began to lose their integrity and start to leak. The key problem was not salt water encroaching the drinking water tanks; it was jet fuel or kerosene leaking into them. I remember many light-hearted times in staterooms using cigarette lighters to light the blobs of kerosene floating on top of tap water drawn from a sink. Water flambé. It tasted terrible with most toothpastes. Clothes laundered in water with some fuel oil came out a shade of gray; those washed with water containing some salt water came out gritty. Very few people drank water with their meals.

 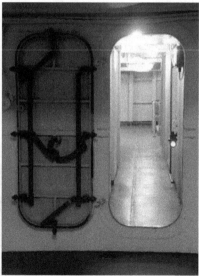

Officers Head (left), watertight door.
Photo by Robert M. Craig

Hallway Hurdles

One of the ways to localize emergencies (flooding, fire, fumes) is to have air- and water-tight doors and hatches throughout a ship. Normally left open, during an emergency they can be swung closed (doors) or dropped (hatches), then "dogged" or tightened shut with rotating bars along the edges. The hatches normally have a consider-ably raised lip, and the door frames are about a foot off the deck and, with rounded "lintels," dropped down similarly from the overhead (ceiling).

Drop hatch. Photo by Robert M. Craig

When travelling from one compartment to another, normal-height people swing one leg up and over the lower rim while simultaneously bending their head down to avoid the upper rim (and head gashes). Now picture doing that little double-ended hurdle jumping every twenty to thirty feet walking around a 1,000-foot long, 250-foot wide ship (on the 03 level). All day long during work, with the ship moving. Getting exercise at sea on an aircraft carrier turned out not to be a problem; in spite of large quantities of grossly-greasy foods three or four times a day, I lost over 20% of my weight during the cruise — I believe just from hurdle jumping water-tight doors.

Noise

Imagine a house made entirely of steel — walls, floors, and ceilings. Now imagine that steel house with eight massive, roaring boilers in the basement bolted to that steel shell. Imagine further that that steel house is filled with hundreds of electric motors and pumps. And then imagine jet airplanes taking off with a roar, and landing with a thud, on the steel roof. It was very noisy inside our aircraft carrier, and it was very noisy all the time. So noisy that the floors and walls vibrated, generating more noise. Add to that the seemingly endless flow of 1MC (loudspeaker system) announcements throughout the ship concerning duty watches, housekeeping routines, operations, emergencies, and drills.

Forecastle. [both anchor chains and steam catapults were adjacent to officer country]. Photo by Robert M. Craig

The saving grace was getting used to the noise and eventually not noticing it; the downside was when it stopped or changed pitch. One night, totally sound asleep, I awoke with a start and sat up in bed at full alert — something was terribly wrong. The ship had had a total electrical failure, all machinery had shut down, and the *quietness* woke me! Fancy being wakened by *no* noise. That happened fairly often during the cruise.

Fire

Steel is also a very good conductor of heat. Think of a fire and how quickly combustible-level heat could travel through a ship made entirely of steel, like a frying pan on a stove. Other than being holed like *Titanic*, fire is the worst nightmare of a sailor. The irony is that the ship is floating in cool, fire-fighting water; the danger is surviving the fire by filling the ship with water and sinking. Adding to that concern are enormous tanks of volatile fuel and compartments filled with high explosive weaponry for guns and aircraft. *Constellation* had a horrific fire many years earlier during construction, and had another many years later at sea. Fire drills and fire alarms on an aircraft carrier are not taken lightly.

Electricity

Steel is also an amazing conductor of electricity, especially when it's floating in a sea of very conductive salt water. Electrically speaking, it's highly "grounded." Long before three-pronged plugs and outlets became the norm in houses, they were mandatory aboard steel ships. Handling a faulty plug or electrical device, while standing on a steel deck floating in sea water, could be highly debilitating. And don't forget all those tanks of volatile fuel and compartments of high explosives. Sparks were to be avoided at all times.

Floating Target

There was a war going on at the time, and we were launching air strikes every day in ninety-minute cycles of servicing airplanes, putting weapons on them and fueling them, positioning them on the flight deck, launching them, preparing for aircraft recovery, and then safely landing them on the flight deck after they had expended their ordnance against enemy forces. To the enemy, we were therefore a highly significant target, especially since only one aircraft carrier was positioned off North Vietnam (at "Yankee Station") and one off South Vietnam (at "Dixie Station"). While it was unlikely that the

North Vietnamese could successfully launch a strike against us, it was not inconceivable using surprise or unconventional warfare. (Think Pearl Harbor.) And we were very big and easy to find, with nowhere to hide. While it wasn't something we mentally dwelt on, the thought of an attack was always there.

On the Other Hand

On the other hand, we did have (most of the time) staterooms with bunks and sinks, hot showers, flush toilets, dining facilities, a store with most of the things you would need, movies, electricity for our gadgets, and a magnificent view of the ocean and stars from eighty feet high on the flight deck. And to top it off, about every thirty days we sailed into some exotic port (or not so exotic) for rest and relaxation. The Navy, perhaps facetiously, called our Vietnam deployment a Vietnam *cruise*. Perhaps we were a cruise ship, or at least a floating "hotel/office" that went from port to port. Hollywood got that part correctly. And that's what we reminded ourselves when we drank kerosene-laced water, dogged down hatches during fire drills, ate food that was mostly powdered, canned, or re-constituted, plugged our ears during aircraft recovery, and wondered about those compartments filled with high explosives. An aircraft carrier wouldn't earn even one hotel star, but that's not why they're built.[68]

---

68 Photos in this essay are from USS *Intrepid* (CVS-11) an earlier Essex-class aircraft carrier than the *Constellation* (CV-64) on which Schneberger served (*Intrepid* cruised to Vietnam three times); hatches, watertight doors, officers' staterooms, heads, etc, as Schneberger describes, are comparable.

SCOTT SCHNEBERGER served for twenty years on active duty in the Navy, retiring in 1990 at the rank of Commander. His grandfather was a naval aviator in World War I, and during World War II his father was in Eastern Air Lines's Military Transport Division (M.T.D.) operated by the Army for the duration of the war. Pilots and staff wore uniforms and had equivalent military rankings. They flew daily flights from Miami-San Juan-Port of Spain-Georgetown-Belem-Natal-Ascension-Accra in Eastern DC-3s then Army C-46s.

Serving as Intelligence Officer ashore and afloat, Scott Schneberger was assigned to numerous ships and shore facilities throughout his two decades of service, including duty in the Mediterranean as well as at Yankee Station off Vietnam. After his discharge, having already earned an MS graduate degree at the Naval Postgraduate School, Schneberger received a PhD from Georgia State University. He went on to serve as a professor and from 2008-2013 Dean of Academics and then Provost at Principia College, his alma mater. He now serves on the Principia Board of Trustees.

Born in Evanston, Illinois, in 1948, Schneberger grew up in Illinois, departing from Arlington Heights, Illinois, to Elsah in 1966 to attend Principia College. A residence of Rackham Court East, where he served as freshman head, Schneberger was also elected president of his sophomore class. He majored in political science, and graduated in 1970, embarking, immediately after college, on his twenty-year career in the Navy. He married Cosy Scholet (C73) and has a daughter who graduated from Principia College in 2006. Now retired, Schneberger and his wife split the year between their house in Austin TX and their cabin in the Adirondacks NY.

"Sailboats [after Feininger]" painting (and later menu
cover) by Robert M. Craig. Photo by Robert M. Craig

Interior Decorator for a Warship

ROBERT M. CRAIG

"Ah-h-h, an *artiste*!"

Duty on *Intrepid* during 1969-70 was hardly heroic and involved a not inconsiderable amount of time in dry dock, including six months in Philadelphia and several months later in Boston. Three earlier deployments to Vietnam over the recent past two years had involved heavy duty wear and tear on the ship and considerable rehabilitation was needed and performed in Philly. World War II battle experience had earned the ship the nickname "The Fighting I," but now, spending extended time in dry dock, she was called the "Dry I." Serving aboard a ship in dry dock provided further opportunities during the evenings to attend concerts and other events in a great city, and for someone interested in architecture to continue using weekend liberty hours to tour building sites. Time was well spent in Philadelphia and Boston, both of which have notable architecture, and Philly was close enough to Ocean City, Maryland, for me to see family weekends and go to the beach. But there were also periods on board with little to do, so I took up a former hobby from college and painted a few watercolors. One day, as I was putting the finishing touches on a painting, my boss, a full Commander in the Supply Corps, happened by and said, "Ah-h-h, an *artiste*! I think I'll move you from S-4 disbursing and make you food service officer in charge of S-2."

When I asked him what the S-2 division and food service operation had to do with being an artist, he said, "Chief Robert Dunlap in S-2 division has just spent almost all of our $10,000 rehab money on a %%^# load of decorative junk, and I think you may be the only one on this ship who can figure out what to do with it all." The decorative panels, drapes, light fixtures, "art work," and "you won't believe the miscellaneous" was intended to improve enlisted recreational space, especially the mess decks, second class lounge, etc. "The chief has bought fake Tiffany ceiling lights for God's sake, a truck load of stuff—mostly from K-Mart I think, and no one knows quite what to do with it all." And then the chief Supply Officer dropped the bomb: "We need an interior decorator for this quarter-century-old warship, and you're the closest I can come up with, so you're it."

My present colleagues in the College of Architecture at Georgia Tech, where I have taught for the past 40 years, would be amused to learn that one of my first jobs as a designer was to serve as an interior decorator for a 1943, *Essex*-class, still-on-active-duty, aircraft carrier, dolling up the mess decks with an inherited assortment of odd bits and pieces purchased by a chief petty officer who had gone on an uncontrolled shopping spree. The career-Navy old salt was guided solely by what can only be considered an eclectic and less-than-bourgeois aesthetic taste. There must have been a blue-light special at K-Mart, because when I inventoried the array of "stuff" already purchased for the ship, it boggled the imagination. My designer inventory and palette would include the aforementioned plastic domed Tiffany-style hanging lamps; red and white peppermint striped canvas; drapery material in three patterns (bright orange and black, modern autumnal, and forest green country scenes with a woodsy Currier and Ives character); Frederic Remington prints with a collection of spurs, toy pistols, bridles, Jesse James wanted posters, and miscellaneous lengths of rope mounted on bright orange panels that would have made Home Depot executives happy[69]; plastic ivy; paste-on brick facing; an "old wooden" bucket; various tree limbs and sapling trunks stripped of bark (just begging to become Western corral posts) and other miscellaneous lengths of rough-hewn wood; ice cream parlor chairs and small round tables; and only about ten per cent of the rehab budget left over.

---

69 Although Home Depot would not be founded until 1978, the company's trademark orange would have been considered compatible to Dunlap's orange panels.

I was introduced to two large mess deck compartments, a couple of narrow gangway [corridor] spaces, a small second class lounge compartment, and told to "have at it." The S-1 division [requisitions] was at my disposal to supply paint and anything else I'd need. Assuming that the nineteen-year old enlisted S-1 "storekeeper" on duty in the supplies division might be aesthetically challenged, I asked with some hesitation, "What colors of paint do you have in stock?" His answer reminded me of Henry Ford's comment in selling Model T's when Ford said that a customer could have any color he liked, so long as it was black.

Butterscotch Room, USS *Intrepid*

"Colors?" the S-1 duty seaman offered helpfully. "Hey, lieutenant, we got lots of battleship gray."

"That's all?"

"Of course not; that's for outside the ship. We also got gallons and gallons of pale pea green which goes on all the interior bulkheads, although some are authorized to be painted haze gray too, or even just white."

"I'm familiar with the Navy's standard, double-barreled palette," I responded, "haze gray outside, and for the inside: the ubiquitous pale green..."

"Fighting I" panel, La Cucaracha "tangerine room" USS *Intrepid*. Photo by PH2 B. L. Mack, January 10, 1970

"I don't know whether we got any of that *you-bick wa-tous* green, just this here pale green."

I refused to be defeated, and, as the duly-appointed *Intrepid* "*artiste*," I was determined to break Navy tradition. The first thing I had to do to spruce up the mess decks was to change the colors. Since nearly every interior surface within the ship was painted pale green, including my targeted mess decks and enlisted men's recreational spaces, I asked myself, *How can the sailors escape from the sameness of it all? Emaciated pea green was everywhere you looked..*

"Which one ya want, lieutenant?" the S-1 clerk concluded, "gray or green?"

"Neither," I said, "I want some pizzazz. Dig deeper in your storage locker and find some bright red and yellow."

"No poss-ee-bla! All we got is gray and green."

"Son, have you ever seen damage control stations around the ship, with hanging fire hoses and fire extinguishers?"

"Yeah, but..."

"What color are the glass-faced storage boxes?"

"Red."

"Fire engine red, to be more precise. And have you ever been on the edge of the flight deck, or stood at the edge of one of the ship's three aircraft elevators, the ones that lift F-8s and A-4s from the hangar bay to the flight deck?"

"Sure."

"What color are the caution stripes at the edge of the opening"

"Yellow and white, sometimes yellow and black, I think"

La Cucaracha "Tangerine Room" USS *Intrepid*.
Photo January 10, 1970

"That's bright 'caution yellow' to be precise. Now somebody on board *Intrepid* paints these yellow stripes and red fire boxes periodically, and it's not by using battleship gray and pale green paint. Dig deeper in the hold and find me every can or red, yellow, black, and white paint you have and bring the whole lot to the mess decks with a large garbage can. This interior designer is about to mix some mean-assed paint colors!"

An hour later, wheeling a large palate of paint cans across the mess deck, the S-1 sailor shouted with delight, "Hey, Lieutenant, sir, I found it all and some blue as well."

Imagine that: Navy blue in the Navy! I muttered to myself.

"Great! Now let's see what Jim Green's color wheel and primary color charts taught me in color theory art class."

"Who's Jim Green?"

"My college art teacher. All you need is cyan, magenta, and yellow with black and white to adjust hue."

"Huh?"

Orange panels (hiding ventilation ductwork) and the new tangerine walls. Photo January 10, 1970

"Primary colors: fire engine red, caution yellow, and good ole Navy blue. Now, we can mix red and yellow to get orange; mix yellow and blue to get green; and mix blue and red and voilà! You got purple, and then just add white or black—even haze gray—we can create just about any color in between…"

"Jeez, lieutenant, you wouldn't paint the mess decks purple, would ya?"

"No, that would be too cheerless. This isn't Queen Victoria's mourning ship after the loss of Albert."

"Huh?"

"Oh, never mind."

"Well what about orange?" The seaman was starting to look sea sick. "Gosh, lieutenant, mess decks shouldn't be orange." Then, with a little mischief in his own eye, he added, "Hey, is that why you wanted the fire-box red paint and the caution-line yeller?"

"Why not? We gotta find some place to use those bright orange panels that Chief Dunlap bought—the ones with the spurs and rifles and wanted posters attached. I think I'll mount the panels against the vertical exhaust shafts so we can hide ventilation ductwork and mechanical systems… then we'll paint all the adjacent bulkheads pale tangarine, and then…"

"Whoa, lieutenant, pale tangerine? They're gonna lock you up and throw away the key."

"Let's see how much we can paint before they do, eh sailor? Grab that garbage can and start dumping in white paint, and ask your buddy to start stirring while I pour in small bits of yellow and red."

"What about the overheads? They're full of pipes and runs of vent ducts and wires and are uglier than sin."

Casrep Café and Underway Replenishment. Detail of a photo by
PH2 B. L. Mack, January 10, 1970

"We'll paint them too, and in the next compartment… let's see… we'll paint the overhead jet black, to hide all that piping and create a night sky."

"What ya gonna do with the Tiffany chandeliers?"

"That "night sky" compartment over there will become a sidewalk Parisian café– more like a courtyard patio, and with a black overhead, and a peppermint striped awning over a brick faced store front, we'll concentrate all the Tiffany lights in there and with the ice cream parlor chairs and round tables it'll look like you're in an outdoor sidewalk café. What'ya think?"

"I think you're nuts"—err, sorry sir"

"Do you think you can get someone in S-1 to build me an octagonal wishing well?–Chief Dunlap bought an ole wooden bucket, and I have to put it somewhere."

French Café, USS *Intrepid.*
Photo by PH2 B. L. Mack, January 10, 1970

So we started pouring white paint into the large garbage cans, mixed in the red and yellow as another sailor brought over a hideous orange patterned set of drapes that Dunlap had bought on sale, and the S-1 sailors awaited for another "Voilà" from the *artiste*. Two more dabs of caution yellow, and then the recipe seemed right—"Voilà… No, I stand corrected: Olé!"

"Olé?"

"Yes, if that second space is to be the French Café, this larger one will be Spanish, "We'll call it 'La Cucaracha' and hope no one has a Spanish dictionary.

"I can make you some signs," one of the S-1 sailor's buddies offered.

"Great, we'll hang oval signs from the overhead, use painted wood with a border of glued-on metal chain, and that will use up any excess decorative brass chain after hanging the Tiffany lights next door"

"You going to redo the ship's store in there?" another sailor asked pointing to the future French Café?"

"We'll reface the gedunk storefront in brick, put it under a peppermint striped awning, and call it "Underway Replenishment"—maybe envision a sidewalk area around the wishing well and call it the "Casrep Café."[70]

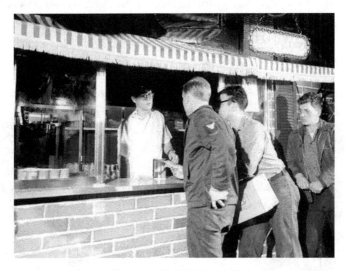

Gedunk store, "Casrep Café" [*Intrepid* ship's store at the edge of the "French café" mess decks]. Photo by PH2 B. L. Mack, January 10, 1970

"What are ya gonna do with all those 4 foot lengths of bark-less tree trunks?"

"We'll make 'em into corral posts for the Western Room, hang the pictorial country drapery to hide the bulkhead, paint the overhead with that blue paint you got…"

"Sorry, sir, the blue is Navy blue–real dark."

"That's what the white paint's for," and I started dripping blue into another large can of white paint in search of sky blue.

"Hey, this is cool…"

---

70 CASREP is a Navy acronym for casualty report. A gedunk (or geedunk) bar is the canteen, snack bar, and sundries store of a large ship of the U.S. Navy.

"... and we'll tie the rope lengths as lassos, hang them from corral posts, and then... how 'bout we play some Willie Nelson over the intercom system?"

"What intercom system? We haven't got an intercom system, except for "general quarters" announcements from the bridge, and I don't think the ole man'll let you play Muzak over the ship's system." Then the parts division sailor started mimicking the ship's captain: "Now hear this! Now hear this! We interrupt this program to bring you—General Quarters! General Quarters! This is Not a Drill! Man your Stations!... and we'll be right back after this commercial."

Wishing well in the French outdoor café

"Very funny! No, we'll set up our own parallel intercom for the mess decks. We have $1,000 left over in the rehab money. I'll buy speakers and get the ship's electricians to hide them in the black painted overheads; we'll set up a control panel in the supply office, and we'll make tapes for dinner music: Willie Nelson in the Western Room and Edith Piaf for the French Café."

"Edith who?

"How 'bout Charles Aznavour, Maurice Chevalier, or arias from Puccini's La Bohème? [another blank stare] Well, never mind, pour in a bit more blue."

And thus the *Intrepid* mess decks were transformed by an "interior decorator for a warship," a parts-division sailor and a hand full of his buddies from S-1, a team of S-2 cooks and scullery messmen, and a couple of electricians. A "butterscotch room" was the controversial result of a left-over batch of mismatched paint, and a galley passageway turned out a bit more earthy than intended, but the bright tangerine room brought the sought-after and distinctly noticeable pizzazz. The "La Cucaracha" Room, was full of orange panels with the Frederic Remington cowboy sketches and "Wanted" posters to whet one's appetite for the adjacent Western Room with its corral posts and hanging lassos. The stainless steel salad bar, colorful beverage station, butterscotch overhead, and bright (very bright and totally unmilitary) tangerine bulkheads sought to transform a drab mess hall into a flashy food court.

Western theme of "Blue Room" [2nd class petty officers] USS *Intrepid*. Photo by PH2 B. L. Mack, January 10, 1970

But the French Café, as Chevalier himself might say, was *magnifique*. At one end: the Underway Replenishment "gedunk" store, brick faced with bright sidewalk red and white striped peppermint awning. In the center, a brick faced, ivy clad wishing well, complete with "ye olde hanging wooden bucket," the whole on wheels due to the necessity to clear a path for bombs during general quarters. Someone among the mess cooks was always assigned "wishing well duty." When general quarters sounded, he rushed to the wishing well, unhooked it from the deck, wheeled it to a corner of the compartment, and re-hooked it safely out of the way. Ice cream parlor chairs

and tables were whisked aside like the parting of the Red Sea, and a hatch opened at one corner of the mess deck's "café" compartment where ordinance was stored. Munitions division sailors wheeled the bombs across the French café to an elevator where they were lifted to the hangar bay and mounted on awaiting planes. On the third deck, the scene appeared like something out of *Dr. Strangelove*,[71] but every man, from

Ordnance on way to aircraft. Photo from *Intrepid 1968 Cruisebook.*

mess cook to food service officer, had his job. When "general quarters" ended and "all clear" was sounded, the wishing well was

hooked back in place, tables and chairs returned, the Tiffany lights sparkled, and Edith Piaf started singing again, "La Vie en Rose."

At some time during the transformation of the mess decks, the thought crossed my mind that what we were doing might not be the norm for a military warship at sea, and in the minds of hard-nosed salts, a tangerine room on an aircraft carrier, let alone a French Café, might represent just cause for disciplinary action. Might someone hear about this beyond *Intrepid* itself? Aboard ship, the improvements were the subject of meal conversations for weeks. A few no doubt thought the new Food Service Officer needed a section 8 (psychiatric discharge), but most thought it was cool. So we ratcheted it up a notch and instituted International Nights, with exotic menus — same Navy

---

71 *Dr. Stangelove, or: How I Learned to Stop Worrying and Love the Bomb* was a 1964 British film by Stanley Kubrick starring Peter Sellers. Among the more bizarre events in the film was the cataclysmic ending scene with Slim Pickens riding like a bronco buster a falling nuclear doomsday bomb, cowboy hat in hand, and yelping "Yee-Ha-a-a-a." As the nuclear blast marks the end the world, Vera Lynn is heard singing, "We'll Meet Again."

Food Service cartoon. Photo from *Intrepid 1968 Cruisebook*

Menu planning meeting, S-2 division. Author at center; Senior
Chief Robert W. Dunlap to author's right; Chief D. A. French
(holding pen) far left.

food, but up-scaled marketing. The theme rooms were matched with standard Navy-recommended two-week rotation menus rearranged each day as "southwestern night" or "French," "Spanish," "Italian" or even "American" Night, with meal choices in the cafeteria line conforming. "Mystery meat" became boeuf bourguignon, tacos and enchiladas were accompanied by Spanish and Mexican decorations (and Herb Alpert's "Tijuana Brass"), and a plain spaghetti and meat balls platter was replaced by Fettuccini Milanese or, (with a few peas, egg, bacon, Parmigiano-Reggiano, and Alfredo sauce instead), the offering was "Carbonara." With a French Café, a revamped "haute cuisine" menu, and gaudy tangerine walls, we were a veritable cruise liner ready for war. "Why not enter the Ney Award competition?" we soon concluded.

Menu planning meeting, S-2 division. Author (holding pie card) conversing with Senior Chief Robert W. Dunlap

The Navy was already reputed to have some of the best food among the military services [even western barbeque beats field rations in tins], and the *Intrepid* mess decks decor would certainly stand out in any food service competition. The Ney Award is given annually to the best food service division in the entire fleet, with competition in four categories: large and small shore facilities, and large ships and small ships afloat.

So *Intrepid* entered the Ney Award competition with gusto. During each round of judging, we watched visiting inspection officers, mouths agape and with glazed eyes, pass through the rehab'd mess decks in complete disbelief, complimenting the chefs, bakers, and all their enlisted crew (these were no mere Navy cooks or scullery S-2Ms now; we were international chefs!). And when the Ney Award inspection reports came in, one round after another, *Intrepid* was still in the running. Before each inspection, the chief petty officers worked hard with the enlisted to clean all preparation and provision storage areas, hone their serving skills, master procedures, and encourage everyone to bring home the prize. As we entered the semi-finals, I suggested that we dispense with soap and water, and for the "behind the scenes" spaces use, instead, our left over buckets of white paint: we'll re-paint all food-prep and kitchen areas gloss white, to match the "white glove" inspection—the storage and preparation spaces looked as clean as a baby's skin. Equipment was polished, uniforms pressed, and when the final inspectors, real top brass this time, prepared to come aboard for the last stage of the competition, I asked the leading S-2 chief petty officer, "You ever do any ice carvings?"

For special occasions, *Intrepid* bakers prepare cakes
beyond the ordinary. Photo: author's collection

"Hell, No" the old salt said.

"Neither have I. I'll meet you in the freezer in thirty minutes. Bring some knives, chisels, rags, and warm water."

We had no idea what we were doing. Nonetheless, the chief created a large-handled basket made of ice and an ice sailboat, whose gunnels were filled with cocktail sauce and whose ice rails were lined with jumbo shrimp—shrimp standing "at attention" like white-uniformed sailors manning the rails. The ice sail stood about two feet high, while still in the freezer—less and less, as it stood on the hors d'oeuvres table melting, but for the inspection team it was formidable. I tried to carve an elegant swan, but concluded that its thin curved neck of ice might melt before the inspectors arrived, so (forced to keep the neck clumsily thick), I turned the partially carved ice block around, reshaped the swan neck into a squirrel's tail, sat the animal up positioned so that the squirrel was holding a box of nuts in his claws, and called it quits. We brought our several ice carvings to the third deck and quickly changed clothes, to greet the inspectors.

Ice carving (basket) for Ney Competition, USS *Intrepid*.
Photo: author's collection

The brass had no doubt been warned about the French Café, but ice carvings were completely unexpected. When the competition was over, *Intrepid*'s food service operation was declared #1 among large ships afloat world-wide, and took third place internationally among all categories, shore facilities as well. That watercolor that had gotten me this job as Food Service Officer in the first place was printed as the menu cover for the June 18, 1970, meal served for the final Ney Award Inspection. It was a performance worthy of *cordon bleu.*[72]

Ice carving (sailboat) for Ney Competition, USS *Intrepid*

Honorable Discharge

During this same period, as my Navy commitment was drawing to a close, I had applied for graduate school, and was accepted in both of the two new programs offering PhDs in the history of architecture, Columbia and Cornell. My fellow supply officers joked that it was about time I learned something about good design. I was not due out of the Navy until the summer of 1971, but an "early release" program was offered reflecting President Richard Nixon's efforts to wind down the Vietnam War and to release from duty early those non-career military personnel, especially the more expensive officer ranks, who applied with good reason to be discharged a few months prior to their normal date for discharge. Both doctoral programs were to begin in the fall of 1970, a few months after the Ney Award but 9 months *before* I was due to be discharged from the Navy. I stalled, by suggesting to both Cornell and Columbia that I would need financial assistance in order to attend, and in the meantime I applied for an "early release."

---

72 Le Cordon Bleu, founded n Paris in 1895, is the world's largest and most renowned school of culinary arts, gastronomy, and hospitality management, with some twenty schools on five continents.

Soon after, *Intrepid* was engaged in NATO operations in the Caribbean, somewhere off Guantanamo Bay, Cuba, and in the middle of this operation, I received a message to come to the bridge immediately because the captain wanted to see me. I wondered if this had something to do with the tangerine mess decks, or perhaps the captain did not have a sense of humor concerning naming the space "La Cucharacha."

"You Lt. (jg.) Craig?" he said, looking over his shoulders and trying not to be distracted from his primary task of steering the ship.

"Yes sir"

"This just came for you; I guess we'll be losing you soon."

"Losing me?" Visions of a transfer so they could repaint the mess decks, or worse, a section eight!

News clipping, mothballing *Intrepid* (December 5, 1973)

I read the teletype: "Cornell University offers full university fellowship for academic year 1970-71. Stephen Jacobs sends." Wow, I'm in (but I was not yet out!). Let's hope the "early release" comes through. Indeed, soon thereafter, I received word that my commissioning date qualified me for an early release, so I would be able to make the fall doctoral class at Cornell. I had served the Navy long enough, and besides, I suspected the captain had put all remaining paint on board under lock and key. I would leave *Intrepid* in August, 1970, and return to civilian life.

Since renowned architect Richard Meier was among a long list of noted graduates from the architecture school at Cornell, I decided, as the interior decorator for a warship, I'd keep a low profile at Cornell.

The French Cafe, the tangerine La Cucaracha, and the Western Room on *Intrepid* did *not* become a part of my curriculum vitae. And when *Intrepid* was decommissioned in 1974, the year after I received my PhD, it appeared to be the end of an era. The ship was gutted, removing all portable equipment and furnishings, including stripping the mess decks and erasing all evidence of the French café and its auxiliary tangerine and sky blue compartments. The noble ship with the unorthodox mess decks was being readied for mothballs.

POSTSCRIPT: *INTREPID* SEA, AIR, AND SPACE MUSEUM, NEW YORK

Ah, but there is always a postscript. Years later, during a meeting in Chicago of the board of directors of the Society of Architectural Historians (SAH) on which I then served, it was announced that the editor that SAH had recently named for the society's book series, *Buildings of the United States*, needed to resign because he had just accepted a new job in New York as curator of a museum there. John Zukowsky had been curator of architecture at the Art Institute of Chicago and was a noted scholar of Chicago architecture, and I presumed the museum in New York, where his new job was, must be the Metropolitan Museum of Art, or the Guggenheim, or maybe the Museum of Modern Art. It was a year later that I discovered Zukowski was chief curator of the *Intrepid* Sea Air and Space Museum. A decommissioned *Intrepid* had been saved in 1982 from a permanent embalming in mothballs, brought back to New York as a ship museum, docked at the West 46th Street pier 86, and is today a National Historic Landmark.

I bumped into Zukowsky a year later at an architectural history conference and casually mentioned that I had heard he was working as a curator on "my old ship." His eyes opened widely, as though he were Sir Henry Stanley just encountering Dr. Livingston in the middle of a jungle.

"*Your* old ship?"

"Yes, I served on *Intrepid* in the late 1960s," I told John, "I lived on board for two years and…" He looked at me with new interest:

no longer a colleague in architectural history: suddenly, in his mind, I was an historic resource.

"What can you tell me?" he asked, having no idea what was to follow.

"Oh, nothing much," I teased him. "But wait 'til I tell you what I did to the mess decks." I started to grin. "I converted one of the mess compartments of the carrier into a French Café with ice cream parlor chairs and ivy-clad wishing well, and we played Edith Piaf songs over the intercom." I was on a roll. "We ditched the standard military green always used for interiors, and painted the main mess deck compartment tangerine. "The 'Butterscotch Room' was a mistake — leftover paint, but the Western Room was…"

He interrupted me, with a slap on the back, and said, "You ole dog, you're pulling my leg."

"No, I really did. I'll send you pictures."

Soon after my scrapbook arrived in New York, I had a message from John: "Come to New York to consult. We're putting them back"

"You're putting what back?

"The mess decks"

"You're doing what?" I asked John. "Now you're pulling *my* leg."

"No I'm not. As chief curator I'm in charge of all exhibits and a major focus is the sailor's life aboard ship. We want to reconstruct at least part of your mess decks, just as you redesigned them in 1969-70, draperies and corral posts and all."

"You want Chief Dunlap's God-awful orange and black draperies back?"

"Yes!" And like a decorative arts curator at Winterthur,[73] Zukowsky set out to find "authentic" 1960s K-Mart curtains in identical bright orange and black patterns in order to reinstall them in an historically correct recreated food service area on the third deck. Parts of the Western Room would be rebuilt… but then Zukowsky interupted

---

73 Winterthur Museum of Decorative Arts in Wilmington, Delaware, is one of the country's premier collections of historic period rooms, exhibiting Henry Francis DuPont's collection of American furniture and decorative arts, displayed in rooms moved to, or reconstructed in, the museum.

himself and said, "But we have a problem. Since the ship was gutted in 1974 during decommissioning, we don't know how much reinstating we can do... we're not even sure *where* the French Cafe originally was, so can you come to New York to show us?"

"Mais bien sûr, Monsieur." I said with a French accent.

So off we went, my wife Carole and I, for a weekend in New York, touring *Intrepid* again for the first time in over thirty-five years. It was a bitter cold December day. The ship had been moved to New Jersey for the museum overhaul, and as I worked my way through the empty third deck compartments that I hadn't visited for almost four decades, I found myself in the former tangerine room, clinically white now, the entire interior stripped of fixtures and white-washed from mothballing. The scrap book photos I had sent John were spread around an eight-foot table in what I immediately identified as the La Cucaracha compartment! Zukowsky thought we were in the former French Café space.

"No, that's through there," I said pointing.

He looked confused, but then said, "Well, that's why we brought you to the ship."

So we walked into the next compartment aft, carrying an early 1970 color photograph of the French Café; I stood in the exact spot where the photographer had stood in 1970, and I "consulted." Zukowsky stood behind me looking over my shoulder at the historic photo.

"See, the peppermint striped awning was over there," I said pointing. "Behind that wall was the ship's gedunk store– the wishing well would have been here, with a "wishing well" sign hanging from the overhead above it..."

And then we both froze. There, hanging from the overhead steel, with several links painted hard-fast to the ceiling surface, was the K-Mart chain from which the wishing well sign had swung, those many years ago. It was just a few inches of chain, sprayed over with thick white paint, as were all interior surfaces of the carrier when its decommissioning, decades earlier, gave the graveyard-ed ship its final coat of white wash. Ever since, the chain had been hiding in the antiseptic uniformity of the Navy's "ubiquitous" mothball color throughout: this fragment was now an archaeological relic of Craig's French Café. You would think Zukowsky had discovered King Tut's tomb! He removed the chain with a reverence I could not resist deriding. "It's K-Mart, John, not Lalique." But it was *evidence* that the French Cafe was here!

Mess decks behind glass: restoration of the western
corral, 2014. Photo by Robert M. Craig

Two years later I returned to New York to give a lecture on board *Intrepid* detailing my role in the 1969-70 mess decks remodeling, and to see the progress of John's reinstallations. The corral posts were back with their lassos and sky blue overhead, the butterscotch p-way was as unorthodox as ever, red and white checkered table cloths were set with Navy-issue stainless steel compartmentalized trays, but, alas, no French Café yet, although I continued to nudge the curators to "bring back Piaf."

"We need that compartment space for the boy scouts and school trip lunches," the curators claimed, justifying their banal "food court" transformation there. "And ice cream parlor chairs and Tiffany chandeliers simply wouldn't last a week when 150 kids are having lunch after several hours of running all over the ship."

"You think sailors toting 500 pound bombs during general quarters is child's play?" I would counter, trying to point out that the French Café had withstood "battle stations" alerts and "general quarters." I continue to hope the museum will bring back the French Café. It was, as the French would say, *la pièce de résistance*. Perhaps we need a write-in campaign.

But I was treated like royalty that day of my lecture, as the curators took me back to the third deck, eager to show off what they had done to restore my mess decks. There it was, an exact replica of Chief Dunlop's orange and black curtain, exactly matching the photograph from my scrapbook (which the museum had framed and put on the adjacent display wall to show that the curtain was "authentic").[74] Gaudy, but authentic! The western palisade fort posts were back, and the museum has since installed an interactive kiosk that visitors can access, including a mug shot of yours truly, the 1969-70 *Intrepid* [pun intended] Food Service Officer who is to blame for the Western Room, and the ghost of Edith Piaf.

Current plans are to open, soon, the ship's restored food service office, which in 1969, and for several years, was "command central" for the intercom piped-in music, including, by the way, Frank Sinatra

---

74 On a return trip to New York in 2014, I noted that this photo from my scrapbook was affixed to a placard which reads, "Renovating *Intrepid's* Mess. Sailors aboard a Navy ship could get tired of looking at endless steel walls. *Intrepid's* unique mess deck décor offered a friendlier environment for eating and socializing. During the Vietnam War, the Navy provided funds for improving shipboard living spaces. While *Intrepid* was in dry dock in 1969, Food Service Officer Robert Craig oversaw the redesign of the mess deck. Craig and his staff decorated spaces in Western and café themes using materials collected from yard sales. They blended standard naval paints to create custom colors. A sound system played themed music, as well as popular hits. Today, the mess deck reflects these unique designs. On *Intrepid,* second class petty officers ate their meals here in the second class mess. During the 1969 renovation, the second class mess was redecorated in a Western theme. Stockade fencing and wagon wheels suggested a ranch in the American West. The light blue paint evoked the Western sky and earned the space its nickname, the 'Blue Room.'"

singing his new hit "I Did It My Way." In that small office aboard the "Fighting I," international night menus were planned, and castanets, bouzouki music, and mandolins transformed the ambiance of the third deck. Significant to me, this small office was the scene of the crime that day when I painted a small watercolor of sailing ships, and the senior supply officer reassigned me to duty as interior decorator for a warship.

Restored mess decks. *Intrepid* Sea, Air, and Space Museum, 2014. Photo by Robert M. Craig

The Ramirez Trophy

PETER STONE

"The Ramirez Trophy" first appeared in *Afterwords: In Remembrance*, the January 2013 anthology of the Veterans Writing Workshop, and is used with permission.

Ramirez did not appear to be a happy young man. He was something of a loner. I guess you might say, "Who could blame him?" When I first saw him in February of 1968 he was 8,000 miles from home, and we were shipmates serving aboard the helicopter carrier USS *Valley Forge* (LPH-8) off the coast of Vietnam. He held the rank of "fireman apprentice"—the lowest possible rung on the ladder of success. And, he was in B-Division, a "snipe" who worked in the ship's engine room where it was miserably hot, deafeningly noisy, and without ever a trace of daylight. Three decks below the surface, the smell of fuel oil and grease was so prevalent that snipes actually got used to it. They reached a point where they were unaware of it—but any deck hands that dared to go down into the bilges might choke on the stench. The snipes also got used to the chief engineer's snarling and screaming orders while on watch. It made for a harsh existence.

I saw Ramirez from time to time when he came up for a coffee break or a smoke or just some fresh air on the hangar deck or the fantail. Sometimes on the mess deck during chow call. He didn't talk much. His division officer was Kevin Dunn, my roommate and friend. On occasion Ramirez needed to ask Kevin for permission of one type or another, and knocked on the door of our stateroom. He was ultra-respectful, and while he addressed Kevin as "Mr. Dunn," he always called me just "Sir." Ramirez was a good sailor and tried to keep everything squared away. As far as I knew he had never been on report.

For a diversion from the tensions of war Kevin and I started a volleyball league. We began by forming two teams—his from B-Division snipes and mine from my OI-Division radarmen. We held a tournament on a Sunday afternoon with the winner of best three out of five games declared the champions. Then we challenged all comers from other divisions starting on the following Sunday. We got permission from the XO[75] to use aircraft elevator–A on the forward flight deck as our sports arena.

Ramirez was on the B-Division team along with seven others. He was a natural athlete, but stood only five feet, eight inches tall. Three of his teammates were big, black guys, and they were inseparable buddies. They formed an intimidating front wall on the court, and all three were scoring machines. Two other members of the snipe team were over six feet tall and also were close friends. Ramirez, the only one with a Hispanic background, got along with everyone but always seemed to be on the outside looking in. After a game he often would cool off by walking the length of the hangar deck alone, stopping on the fantail to stare out at the Gulf of Tonkin for long periods.

During the games we lowered the elevator ten feet to form a perfect volleyball court with enthusiastic fans and onlookers standing or sitting up above on the edge of the flight deck looking down on the players. There was loud, not always polite, cheering from the various division groups—radiomen, signalmen, aircraft mechanics, medics, deck apes, and so on. My radarmen held the distinction of second place for a brief time, losing to Kevin Dunn's snipes in the initial tournament. Then, by the time the cruise ended, we finished in tenth place in a field of eighteen. B-Division went undefeated.

Volleyball became so popular on the "*Happy Valley*" that Captain Payne began officiating the coin toss at the start of every Sunday afternoon game. I was always impressed at the sight of the Old Man in full dress uniform standing in the center of Elevator-A as it slowly descended to volleyball depth with its high-pitched whirring engine noise. He had his yeoman play a tinny recording of the national

---

75 Executive officer, second in command of the ship.

anthem over the 1-MC loudspeaker system at the start of each tournament. Then, after the coin toss to determine first serve, he would raise his bull horn and loudly proclaim "Let the tournament begin!" followed by wild cheering and arm waving from above. Sometimes the players had an extra challenge when high seas caused the ship to pitch, roll, and yaw; especially during monsoon season. There were times when all twelve players on the court lost their footing and were rolling on their backs on the deck.

One Saturday afternoon the ship arrived in Subic Bay in the Philippines for five days of R&R and replenishment. Going ashore on liberty some of our crewmembers met a group of Australian sailors from the missile cruiser *Canberra* and challenged them to a volleyball match aboard our ship. Foolishly, they accepted. Next day two-thirds of our crew gave up the opportunity to go ashore in order to watch the big match. Our champions from B-Division slaughtered the Aussies, who accepted defeat good-naturedly. Virtually everyone then went ashore to celebrate at the enlisted men's club, officer's club, or in the town of Olongapo. Kevin and I were both on watch and so did not join them.

An hour later Ramirez appeared on the quarterdeck and asked Kevin for permission to switch duty with another shipmate who wanted to spend the evening ashore. Kevin granted the request and asked Ramirez why he wasn't going ashore himself. I noticed he called Ramirez by his first name, Esteban. His response was impressive. He said that he never really enjoyed getting drunk with his shipmates; and also that he did not want to socialize with women he considered prostitutes. He pulled out a photo of his girlfriend and showed it to both of us in turn, remarking that she was the only girl who interested him. Both of us asked her name, and he smiled as he told us "it's Livia."

A week later, back in Vietnam, off the coast of Quang Tri Province, I received an honor I had been hoping for. I was invited by the ship's Navigator to go through a training course to become Officer of the Deck, Underway. Once qualified, I would be able to take command of the entire ship from the bridge during four-hour watch periods. That is, unless and until relieved of "the conn" by the captain. With study and practice I passed the test in six weeks and was qualified in mid-April. During that time we all underwent the "Tet Offensive" when the North Vietnamese Army (NVA) launched a determined, sustained effort to overrun American positions in the northern half of South Vietnam. We launched five all-out amphibious assault missions to counter the enemy's thrusts.

Volleyball was all but forgotten for the months of March and April. I did not see Ramirez or any of the champion B-Division volleyball team for weeks. Movies for the crew were suspended for most of the evenings that spring. We did not visit any ports, except Da Nang. No one aboard received any mail from home during the disruptive six-week period. It was a strain on everyone. Tensions mounted and fist fights broke out on the mess deck almost daily. Dozens of marines who launched from our ship were killed in the operations, which instilled a solemn mood over everyone aboard.

One afternoon in early May I crossed the hangar deck and saw Ramirez standing against the outer bulkhead looking out at the Vietnamese coast in the distance. He was holding a piece of paper, probably a letter, and staring out at the water. I said "Hello" but he did not answer or look in my direction. I didn't stop to talk as I was hurrying to go on watch up on the bridge.

That day I was assigned the 1600 to 2000 watch as OOD.[76] We were steaming at a lazy twelve knots along the coast five miles from shore. Kevin had preceded me as OOD on the noon watch, and I relieved him of the conn a bit early—around ten minutes before 1600. He said he wasn't tired and stayed on the bridge to keep me company for a couple of hours.

We talked about major league baseball, Italian versus Irish food, whether a "Huey" could lift a truck, and a few other topics.

When the sun began to set, he said, "See ya later," and turned to go below decks to the wardroom for dinner. The boatswain's mate of the watch, Schreiber, turned to me suddenly with a grimace. He grabbed his headphones and mouthpiece with both hands. Then,

---

76 Officer of the Deck.

in his high-pitched voice, he shouted "Portside-aft lookout reports, 'Man overboard!'" I gave an immediate order to Schreiber, "Tell the lookout to mark the spot with a life ring and keep his glasses trained on the man in the water!" Then to the helmsman, "Left full rudder and steady up at 240-degrees!" And another to the engineman, "All engines back FULL!" All three replied, "Aye, aye, Sir!" and responded accordingly. Another urgent report came from Schreiber, "Sky-aft lookout confirms, 'Man in the water off the port quarter!'"

Kevin remained on the bridge to back me up. It was getting dark fast, and with a heavy cloud cover there was no moon. His wrinkled forehead and squinted eyes told me Kevin was seriously worried. Thus far my training had served me well. I was not in doubt as to what to do, but was uncertain how successfully I could pull it off. I knew there were no other ships in the area closer than fifteen miles from our position. That is, at least thirty minutes away, so we were on our own.

Sky-aft lookout reported he was continuing to keep his glasses on "Oscar" (the name always used for an unidentified man in the water). I continued counting off five minutes and then gave an "All engines ahead one-third!" The 900-foot long ship heeled sharply to port as it made its emergency turnabout. Feeling the movement, the navigator rushed from his stateroom and appeared on the bridge. His face was stern but calm. He watched silently as I told Schreiber to sound "All hands to quarters!" to get a muster and find out who was missing.

The captain also called up to the bridge on the sound-powered phone. I apprised him of the situation, and he answered "Very well," and within two minutes appeared on the bridge, himself. I told Schreiber to "Summon the boatswain and have him standby to lower a lifeboat off the starboard side amidships." Again, I heard his high-pitched voice give the expected "Aye, aye, Sir."

Within six minutes I ordered, "All engines back Two-thirds!" Then two minutes later, "All engines Stop!" The ship came to a stop at almost the exact spot where the first report had come in. Starboard-aft lookout reported seeing the life ring twenty yards from the ship. We had done it! For a moment I felt pride in successfully pulling off a near-perfect "Man Overboard Maneuver." But, this was not just an exercise. It was for real.

Another sailor climbed the exterior ladder and entered the bridge. He was Fireman First Class Jeffries, a tall black man from B-Division. He spoke softly into Kevin's ear. Kevin's face dropped its expression and went pale as he turned and told the captain and all of the bridge watch, "It's Fireman Esteban Ramirez." I felt a brief surge of optimism that our maneuver was a good one, and gave us an excellent chance of rescuing Ramirez even though the seas were high.

Then Kevin approached me and said in a low voice that apparently Ramirez had jumped overboard intentionally. There was a delivery of mail via helicopter from DaNang that morning, and Ramirez received a letter from home. He had been in a good mood earlier, but after reading the letter he spoke to no one for the rest of the day. He spent hours on the hangar deck staring at the water. He served a four-hour watch in the engine room and then did not return to the B-Division berthing space. He skipped evening mess call. He was last seen going back up to the portside of the hangar deck alone. As Kevin explained this all of us on the bridge guessed what that letter had been about. I think everyone of us felt empty and awful. With an involuntary shiver, I felt like my body temperature had dropped ten degrees. Then I shook myself and returned to the task at hand.

Darkness was closing in fast. I told Schreiber to "Have the deck watch man all the searchlights on the starboard side." The reply came quickly. "Starboard-aft lookout reports spotting Oscar forty yards off the starboard side. Two more life rings are in the water." Then the sad follow-up report: "Man overboard has pushed a life ring away and is swimming away from the ship." A minute later the boatswain and his crew had lowered the lifeboat and headed for Ramirez' position. With his radio the boatswain confirmed to us on the bridge that Oscar was swimming away from the ship, and it was now dark. There was a tense silence as we on the bridge awaited further news.

Fifteen minutes went by, and the boatswain radioed again. He spoke slowly, "Bridge, this is the boatswain. It's pitch dark, we can't see him, and he don't want to be saved. We've given it all we can. Request permission to return to the ship."

No one on the bridge spoke for what seemed a long time. Finally, the navigator stepped up close to my ear and said, "You'd better respond to the boatswain." I responded "Aye, aye, sir," and radioed the boatswain telling him to return aboard and thanking him for his efforts. Then, realizing I was calling off the search, I suddenly felt my throat contract like I was going to cry or choke. Fighting back the urge with clenched teeth, I heard the Old Man say, "May his soul be at rest with the Lord."

Next morning I awoke around 0730 and went to stand watch in Combat Information Center. Kevin went down to the engine room for his shift. Nothing much happened. We met in the wardroom at lunch time, but couldn't find many words to say to each other or to anyone else. After lunch I went to the captain's cabin and asked for five minutes of his time. I asked him if it would be appropriate to have an investigation of the crew's morale — especially those serving in the engine room — to prevent potential tragedies like last night's event.

He replied "As commanding officer I am responsible for the morale of the crew; and I am very concerned with that responsibility. But, no one can really get inside the head of another man and predict what he will do and why. We're not in the business of orchestrating a pleasure cruise. We are a warship. We must train every man to do his duty and instill discipline to keep him doing it to the best of his ability. One of the hardest realities of life in the Navy is that during tours at sea, relationships are sometimes abandoned by a girl friend or even a wife back home. And, a man far off at sea has no way to influence or change it. If he's tough enough, he'll learn to live with it and move forward. Fireman Ramirez saw no way out for himself, but that does not mean he was weak or not a good man. We can try to understand his state of mind, and we will remember him. But, we cannot honor his self-destructive decision in itself. Suicide aboard ship is not unknown, but we must keep it from being popularized. I hope that girl back home can learn to live with the outcome as well."

After a few weeks the Sunday afternoon volleyball games resumed. But, the team from B-Division retired and did not play again. I had the ship's metal shop craft a trophy and presented it to Kevin with all the men of B-Division in attendance. It bore an inscription "USS *Valley Forge* Volleyball Champions," and below it, "In memory of Fireman Esteban Ramirez."

Still on patrol. Photo by Robert M. Craig

PART VII:

Still on Patrol

I Joined the Corps

ROD CARLSON

I joined the Corps…

To be a Marine
to be something
to be a pilot
to go to Vietnam
to count the days
to go home
to put the past to rest
to move on but
to never move on
to see their faces
to sob
to remember going
to Vietnam
to be a pilot
to be something
to be a Marine.

Flight deck. Photo by Robert M. Craig

Sightseeing over Laos

MIKE KNEELAND

As we neared the end of our cruise, the missions became more routine, and the combat missions seemed less stressful. It was the spring of 1970. Most of us had already earned our Ranger Centurion patches for having made at least 100 carrier landings on USS *Ranger*. While the night carrier landings never became routine, the day combat missions and day carrier landings had become rather customary. This all changed one day.

The sky over Laos was always a deep blue. The cotton-white clouds contrasted so beautifully against that pollution-free sky. Below there was a triple-canopy of deep-green vegetation. That meant there were three layers of vegetation between the ground and the sky. The rivers, waterfalls, and karst ridges added an unmistakable beauty. Those tall trees rivaled any we'd seen back in the United States. There was very little sign of human life below. It was very easy to get lost in all the magnificence of the surroundings.

The half-hour flights to and from the target gave us plenty of time to watch and discuss that beautiful scenery or anything else that was on our minds at the moment. The cockpit was rather quiet with only the slight scream of the jet engines punctuated by the occasional radio chatter or ECM (Electronic Counter Measures) tones in our headset indicating that an enemy radar or SAM (surface to air missile) had locked on our aircraft.

As we pulled off the target from our last bombing run that day we were chit-chatting with the FAC (Forward Air Controller) who was in his plane below. These FAC's became intimately familiar with their area and enemy emplacements. They were stationed in Thailand, and we on the carrier, but we visited with them every day when we came in-country to drop our bombs on their designated targets. Through our radio conversations we came to feel quite comfortable communicating with them.

This particular spring day provided another trip over that picturesque countryside. As our day's mission concluded, we indulged in
a little chit chat with our FAC; we conversed about the area and its
beauty, and he described some of the impressive features to be seen
on our trip home. He told us that we could follow the river south,
find a pretty waterfall, fly over some interesting valleys, and experience
other sights worth seeing. It sounded so serene. So we embarked on
our adventure. Since our scheduled landing time at the carrier was
still a while away, it would be more fun to sightsee than to orbit in
the sky over the ocean awaiting our arrival time onboard USS *Ranger*.
Instead of immediately climbing to 25,000 feet after pulling off the
target, we stayed low, about 3,500 feet and above small-arms fire, and
proceeded on our sightseeing venture.

The FAC was right. There was a beautiful river, a waterfall, some
pretty karst ridges, and all that beautiful vegetation below. Deck, my
Bombardier Navigator (B/N), and I were just having the greatest time
touring the Laotian countryside when the sky in front of us suddenly
exploded with white antiaircraft fire. We were caught completely off
guard! We were in the wrong place!

I immediately went to full power and began vigorously jinking in
order to avoid being hit. Jinking is a maneuver where you randomly
change the heading of the aircraft to avoid having the guns below
"track" you. If you fly in a straight or predictable line, the antiaircraft gunners can shoot to the spot in front of your aircraft, and
their antiaircraft fire will intercept your line of flight. They were not
taking prisoners in Laos so, if you were shot down, you had to evade
and escape until you were plucked from the jungle. The flight crew
members that were captured were usually executed.

It was an intense few minutes as we violently jinked back and
forth in an attempt to keep from being shot down. Your sense of time
is always expanded during frightful moments like that. The whole
episode probably only lasted a minute or so. We made it free of the
area of fire and resumed our trip home across South Vietnam and back
to USS *Ranger*. The rest of the flight was uneventful. After landing on
the ship, we breathed a sigh of relief and discussed how we wouldn't

be as complacent next time. It was too easy to let the beauty below obscure the fact that there was a war going on, and the gunners on the ground were trying to keep us from flying home.

For the rest of the cruise we were always a little more careful. The view was just as grand, but we observed it while maintaining our constant jinking to avoid being hit by antiaircraft fire and becoming a casualty of war. About a month later, my Vietnam tour ended, and in another three weeks I was home, but it might have been otherwise. On that day of sightseeing over Laos, I learned to be always vigilant and never to assume. It was just one of the many lessons I learned in Vietnam and for which I am very grateful. I grew up a lot in Vietnam.

Forty-five years later I can still envision that beautiful, lush countryside, the waterfalls, and all the beauty below. And I can vividly remember seeing those antiaircraft shells exploding in front of the aircraft. I remember, because that was the day that we almost didn't make it home.

Retirement Speech

WALLY WETHE

June 25, 1997
Ceremonial Lawn
Bolling AFB, DC

(Referencing the heat of the day)
"Reminds me of my time in Mogadishu."[77]

Ladies and gentlemen, let's have some fun. If I were giving a briefing, as I have done many times in my career, we'd start with a time check. Coming up on 0958 and ten seconds. Five, four, three, two, one, hack! This briefing will be three minutes long, in accordance with 11th Wing instructions and in mercy to my family, friends, and everyone else here today. Actually, paying attention to the time is an important part of a military job. I remember my ninety days of officer training school like it was yesterday. They made a big deal out of time there, and I never had enough. And then there was pilot training down in Texas. They called it the year of fifty-three weeks and in the first of those weeks, I wondered if I would make it.

The first jet I trained in was the T-37, a tiny little plane with engines so small and shrill it was referred to as a six thousand pound dog whistle. On my first few flights my instructor pilot reminded me about time all the time. He once told me, "Wethe, you are so far behind the airplane, I think if it crashed, you wouldn't get hurt!" But I caught on pretty quickly, and a couple of weeks later, while we were taxiing toward the runway for takeoff, he told me to pull over and stop. "I think you're ready to fly this thing alone," he said, and

---

77 Largest city in and capital of Somalia, located on coastal Banaadir region of Indian Ocean and famous for Delta Force's "Black Hawk Down" battle in October, 1993.

he got out, much to my amazement. I was the first in my class to fly solo in an Air Force jet. Time flew by on that ride and the succeeding twenty-eight years have flown by too. I couldn't begin to tell you all the great times I have had in the Air Force, and all the great stories; I guess I'll have to write a book about it. I'm grateful that I spent my entire career helping people all over the world. Wherever I landed, people were glad to see me, because as an airlifter, in command of a Lockheed C-130 Hercules, I was usually bringing in food, mail, and, for some, a ride out. I was combat ready, but I was never required to kill anyone or even fire a shot in anger. I thank God for that.

I also have a few other things to say. Thanks to my wife who stuck by her ghost of a husband during those early years. Thanks to my kids who have made me truly proud to be a father. Thanks to my parents and to my relatives, who by example taught me my core values. Thanks to all my friends here today. I think even some of my Sunday School students may even be out there. And thanks to my co-workers over the years who were so professional and to my fellow servicemen and women who will carry on in defense of this great country of ours. Thanks everybody. It has really been a high flight.[78] Ladies and Gentlemen: this briefing—my portion—is now concluded.

> Oh! I have slipped the surly bonds of earth,
> And danced the skies on laughter-silvered wings;
> Sunward I've climbed, and joined the tumbling mirth
> Of sun-split clouds, — and done a hundred things
> You have not dreamed of—Wheeled and soared and swung
> High in the sunlit silence. Hov'ring there
> I've chased the shouting wind along, and flung

---

78 "High Flight" is a poem written by John Gillespie Magee Jr and well known to military fliers. Magee, born in Shanghai, China, in 1922 (his father was American and his mother originally British), came to the United States in 1939, won a scholarship to Yale, but enlisted in September, 1940, in the Royal Canadian Air Force, and was sent to England in July, 1941, for combat duty. He composed "High Flight" in August or September and sent the poem to his parents. A couple of months later, four days after Pearl Harbor, Magee's plane collided with another plane over England, killing Magee at the age of nineteen. He is buried in Scopwick, Lincolnshire.

My eager craft through footless halls of air...
Up, up the long, delirious, burning blue
I've topped the wind-swept heights with easy grace
Where never lark or even eagle flew —
And, while with silent lifting mind I've trod
The high untrespassed sanctity of space,
Put out my hand, and touched the face of God.

Wounded Bird

PETER STONE

"Wounded Bird" first appeared in *Afterwords: From War and Home*, the September 2011 anthology of the Veterans Writing Workshop, and is used with permission.

All across the Gulf of Tonkin the heat was up to a balmy 98 degrees again with no hint of a breeze. The amphibious aircraft carrier USS *Valley Forge* (LPH-8) had been involved in five combat assaults during eight months off the coast of Vietnam. But now, for the past six summer weeks, she repeated a daily routine of slow patrol rectangles two miles off the DMZ providing supplies and medevac services to the marines on the beach and in-country. Lieutenant-Junior Grade Dave McCann was feeling uncomfortable from the heat, but even more from the tedious, long days of inactivity aboard ship. Like all his shipmates, he had not received any mail for six weeks. No communication from home and nothing to do was a strain on everyone's temperament.

On this lazy afternoon, around 1600 hours, a general announcement broke the monotony. Dave was in the ward room when he heard "Now hear this! Medevacs inbound. Ten minutes. Medevac Team-Alpha standby on deck." It was a call for Dave and his team of sixteen enlisted men to scramble to the flight deck with stretchers ready to carry the wounded and battle-weary marines to sick bay as soon as their choppers landed." Dave looked at his watch as he took position at the head of his team amidships on the starboard side of the flight deck. They were ready and standing in formation within four minutes of the call. Then his eyes started scanning the western horizon.

Ten minutes passed. Team-Alpha remained in position but no inbound helicopters in sight. Fifteen minutes — still nothing. Then, after twenty minutes, Dave was among the first to spot two CH53

"Sea Stallion" helicopters flying directly toward the ship. One about fifty feet aloft and the other beneath the first, just ten feet above the water's surface. The first bird landed on the forward flight deck, and immediately half of Dave's team extracted four wounded marines and hustled them below to sick bay.

The pilot jumped out onto the deck, raced up to the bridge, and informed the captain that the second helicopter had taken hostile fire and been damaged and could not gain altitude. Also, their radio was knocked out. Word spread quickly and all hands in the area hurried to the port side of the hangar deck where they watched the disabled chopper circling several times, trying to gain enough height to land on the flight deck. Dave could hear loud cheering from hundreds of sailors down on the hangar deck, all encouraging the pilot of the damaged chopper. It sounded like a packed baseball stadium urging the home team on while trailing in the bottom of the ninth inning.

The cheering became louder as the pilot desperately pulled back on the stick in effort to gain altitude, but Dave could see that it was not going to be easy. He wondered nervously how many wounded were aboard and what their fate would be. He heard the cheering sailors who had learned the name of the pilot, Bill Judson, break into a rhythmic chant of "Go, Billy, Go!" This went on for a full half hour with Judson attempting short approaches, long runs, and circular spirals—anything to try to make the flight deck, fifty feet above the water.

Dave could not resist shouting encouragement, along with hundreds of sailors and marines. He glanced down at the hangar deck and noticed dozens of onlookers' cameras appear, taking hundreds of photos of the tense scene. He felt his voice give out from the cheering shouts.

After the chopper's first five attempts, Dave's heart sank a bit when he saw the copilot jettison a dozen large canvas bags in an effort to lighten up. The bags floated for a couple of minutes before sinking into the deep, and the cheering aboard ship suddenly died down for a brief moment. In clear view the bags had 'FPO' emblazoned on them—that is Fleet Post Office in DaNang where the birds had taken off before being diverted to their Medevac mission. Six weeks worth of mail from home was being tossed overboard to try to save the marines. Realizing it was the right action Dave starting cheering again, louder than before. So did everyone else.

But, he saw that the helicopter, unable to lift itself, now had its landing struts and belly in the water—still maintaining an upright position with its large rotor blades whirling noisily. She was about 100 feet from the ship's port side. The force of the rotors made a rimmed bowl in the water's surface. Dave and everyone sensed that this was a dangerous moment. Once the pilot cut the engine, the bird would sink quickly and not straight downward but would likely tip over sharply as she went down. He knew the rotors would be lethal guillotines for anyone jumping out of the chopper's cabin in the direction where the rotors hit the water.

A surge of hope came over Dave as he saw a lifeboat lowered into the water with the ship's boatswain and four crewmen aboard. He saw them swiftly row alongside the chopper and extract three wounded marines, leaving only the pilot and copilot. More cheers went up as the rescue boat returned, and the wounded were lifted onto the ship and taken to sick bay.

Dave returned his attention to the chopper and saw the copilot jump into the choppy water with his life jacket in place. He swam toward the ship until he was safely away from the helicopter and turned and waved an all-clear signal to his pilot.

Dave held his breath as the pilot cut the engines and the damaged Sea Stallion lurched to its starboard side and quickly sank beneath the waves. No sign that the pilot had escaped. A dead silence came over everyone watching. Dave saw the last glimmer of green metal structure disappear into the deep. He took a deep breath and then held it so as to measure how long Judson could stay underwater without drowning. After a full minute he took another breath and felt devastated. He still saw no sign of Judson.

But, then in a jubilant moment there he was! Judson in an orange life jacket flailing and coughing in the water was the greatest thing

Dave could have hoped for. The cheer that went up from the ship was deafening.

Within a few minutes Bill Judson climbed aboard and was greeted with a bear hug from Mike Carberry, his copilot. Then scores of shoulder hugs, pats on the back, and slaps on the butt from a happy group of onlookers. Dave found himself rushing over to them. He and several others instinctively lifted Judson and Carberry onto their shoulders. Dave felt no weight at all from that happy cargo as they carried them across the deck towards their quarters where dry clothes awaited.

More than a year later Dave found himself in a restaurant in Yokohama with a shipmate, Jim Berghoff; both full lieutenants by now. They entered, removed their shoes, and were shown to one of the tables separated by bamboo curtains. Both men sat cross-legged on benches only six inches off the floor. A few feet away a doll-like young woman in a silk kimono was playing the Japanese koto. With her constant smile, she reminded Dave of a Nishi doll he had bought in Yokosuka and sent stateside to his niece back home.

After ordering steaks and shrimp tempura, Dave watched through a slot in the curtain as four U.S. servicemen were being seated at the next table;—a marine officer with wings above his shirt pocket and three enlisted marines. He noticed the three grunts offer warm handshakes to the officer in turn as they sat down. He could hear their conversation through the thin bamboo curtain.

"It's a beautiful tradition," one of the grunts said, and Dave guessed he was raising his saki cup as he added, "Here's to all you bird pilots who have pulled our asses out of the fire!" As the other marines chimed in "Here's to all of 'em," Dave's thought instantly flashed to Bill Judson and Mike Carberry and that tense afternoon off the DMZ. He pulled back the bamboo curtain, stood up, leaned over, and extended his hand to the group, saying "Here's to all you guys." The surprised marine pilot smiled, raised his cup toward Dave, and simply responded, "*Semper Fi*!"

Richard Hammer. Photo courtesy Richard Hammer

Richard Hammer's EOD team at Ca Viet, 1969.
Photo courtesy Richard Hammer

Memorial Day 2003

RICHARD HAMMER

The call was given:
support the nation's cause.
In righteousness and honor
we stood up
and carried forward
the pride-filled banner
of youthful strength and resolve,
seeking to test
the adventure in us
and fate.

I do not recall the dark hour,
the failure to Love,
named differently,
that had brought us to this distant land,
where we could justify Law of Conflict acts
titled atrocities elsewhere.

But this day,
the thought is of my brother.
He, too, answered the call,
and now tastes earth's sweetness.

Training Pilots Off Corpus Christi

ROBERT M. CRAIG

The conversation had somehow drifted to the war, although I hadn't noticed how. We were biding time, exchanging social niceties with people we had just met, and recalling past excursions with members of the semi-professional architecture society who were gathered for our periodic field trip. Each time we gathered to investigate sites somewhere new in the state, there were many fellow tourists I did not know well; some were first-timers. Repeat excursionists often compared houses or sites from past tours, and stood ready to laugh at some organizational misstep or gaff, including offering imaginative excuses why our host had not yet arrived. If the truth be known, as today's weekend travelers began to gather, I didn't know most of the group at all. I had attended several previous "vernacular excursions," and knew that what we all had in common was an interest in architecture, or if that word was too high style, we loved run-down old buildings. That was all we knew about each other until that day when we spoke about the war.

The two dozen or so people gathered were member of Vernacular Georgia, an informal organization of curators, students, historic preservationists, and architectural devotees who met periodically somewhere in the state of Georgia to particulate in a casually organized excursion to tour vernacular sites — old mills, historic and sometimes abandoned houses, hundred-year-old farms, public buildings under restoration [behind the scenes tours], renovated or rebuilt forts, camp revival tents, tabby ruins, and any number of decrepit building sites typically not architect-designed, but simply commonplace objects of folk or vernacular or roadside culture, a culture fast disappearing. Organizers never knew who, or how many people, would show up;

they merely announced the meeting place and time, and the tour proceeded, often moving from historic site to site by a convoy of automobiles resembling a British car rally.

Flight Recovery off Vietnam. Photo by Robert M. Craig

That particular day, we were in Marietta, Georgia, waiting for the host to open a pre-Civil War house, and a typical group of interested "vernacularists" had showed up: wall paper specialists, architects investigating historic mantelpiece profiles or window trim, a few locals simply curious about the organization, and just plain tourists who liked to visit old houses. And yet, with all that interest in history and half-ruined buildings, the conversation that day had turned to the war. We were not scheduled to attend a mock battle at a Civil War site, recreating some encounter of Union and Confederate troops during the Battle of Atlanta or Sherman's March to the Sea. Nor had we recently toured some revolutionary era fort or colonial battle site near the coast. The war that curiously had become the topic of casual discussion thirty-five years after it had ended was the Vietnam War.

Someone in the group had mentioned that he had served in the military, a comment prompted, in passing, by a remark on an otherwise unrelated topic. While one or two in the group were not yet born when newspaper headlines spoke of the Tet offensive or the Fall of Saigon, at least half of the gathering of excursionists were in their sixties, and it was likely that some of them had earlier been drafted or maybe even had been to Vietnam. Someone had trained at Fort Benning in Georgia, or flew out of Warner Robbins Air Force Base nearby, and, before I realized it, I had been pulled into the conversation to mention that I had served on the carrier USS *Intrepid* during the 1960s.

"Did you go to Vietnam?" someone wanted to know, as the group's only knowledge of me was that I was an architecture professor at Georgia Tech, and somehow the equation of "old prof" and Vietnam didn't compute.

"For a brief time, yes," I responded.

"Were you ever in danger?" a young man wanted to know.

"The carrier *was* off Vietnam when I reported aboard in 1968," I responded, and I immediately sensed a new respect from the gathering tour group, simply because I had served. "*Intrepid* launched squadrons of planes flying sorties into Vietnam, but I was not a pilot, and my tour to 'Nam was very short. Most of my time on *Intrepid* was stateside. And yes, a carrier can be a very dangerous place, where accidents can happen."

"Were you ever scared?" I was asked. "And did you ever see anyone killed?"

"I recall no such fear while in the Tonkin Gulf: I guess I assumed that North Vietnam did not have a navy that could threaten us from the sea, and that any air attack was generally protected by our own naval air forces and flotilla of destroyers, cruisers, and the like, all of which surrounded *Intrepid* in fleet formation. The other ships' main task was to protect the carrier. So I guess I was less concerned in Vietnam than I was, for instance, during flight ops in the Gulf of Mexico a year later."

"Why then?"

Other members in our Vernacular Georgia group began to gather around in larger numbers as I explained that for about six weeks, *Intrepid* was assigned to relieve the training carrier USS *Lexington* (CVS-16) operating in association with the naval air training base in Pensacola, FL. *Lexington* served the pilot training program at

Pensacola, and *Intrepid* took over for a brief period in 1969, while *Lexington* underwent some periodical maintenance and repairs. "We sailed into the Gulf, set course for somewhere off Corpus Christi, Texas, I recall, and student pilots learned how to land their planes on a carrier flight deck. It was a bit disconcerting to realize they had never done so before.

"I occasionally went topside to watch, and typically a student pilot and instructor would take off (the student's 'first ever' launch from a carrier), would come around, and then land his plane on the flight deck, not always smoothly. If their approach was too high or low, they were waived off," and I told my listeners that a plane flying only ten or so feet above the flight deck at a speed of 80-100 mph, (waived off at the last minute because its approach was too high for the wire and hook to engage), "now, that was pretty exciting!" The instructor in the plane simply told the student pilot to come around and try again.

Carrier launch. Photo from *Intrepid 1968 Cruisebook*

I then paused, realizing the entire excursion group had gathered around to listen. "One afternoon, a launch went badly. A student pilot tried to abort the takeoff, for what reason I never knew. Presumably sensing something was wrong, the student tried to stop the plane before he ran out of flight deck, but the flight deck was just a few feet too short, and the plane, student pilot, and instructor (it all appeared in slow motion at the end), reached the forward edge of the flight deck and slow-w-w-ly toppled over the bow of *Intrepid* and into the sea. The ship, in such a launching operation, was heading into the wind at about thirty knots, so the carrier immediately struck and ran over the downed airplane. The instructor and student pilot had been ejected into the sea; one lay motionless face down, the other gave a 'thumbs up.'"

Then I explained that in any flight operation on an aircraft carrier, whether launching planes or landing them, a rescue helicopter (and sometimes more than one) is already in the air throughout the launch or recovery operation, so on that day off Corpus Christi, a helicopter was immediately hovering over the downed pilots. "Since one man appeared to be treading water and gave a 'thumbs up,'" I continued to relate, "the helicopter rushed to the second man floating face down and quickly dragged him from the sea, but he had been killed. The helicopter then returned quickly to the other man *but could not find him*."

Searching the seas. Photo by Robert M. Craig

My audience gasped as my voice choked on the last phrase.

And then, a man standing at the edge of the gathering, lean and looking fit, and about my age, stepped slowly forward. His sober, weathered face and almost stoic demeanor with fixed eyes concentrated on me, caused me to pause. He broke the silence and said to me, in a tone that was hard to decipher.

"How did you know about that episode in such accurate detail? That's exactly how it happened."

I looked up at him in amazement, thought about what he had just said, and then I asked him, "How did *you* know that my description was 'exactly how it all happened'?"

"I was the helicopter pilot," he said.

Goodbye to *Intrepid*

JOHN S. KISTLER

In March of 1974 I was attached to a shore command in Lakehurst, New Jersey. I was a young lieutenant flying copilot with a senior commander named Hap Quackenbush in an S-2 Tracker aircraft. We were returning from Norfolk to Lakehurst at 8,000 feet when we passed the mouth of the Chesapeake Bay. It was early evening, and Commander Quackenbush was in the left seat, and he noticed an aircraft carrier moving north up the Chesapeake Bay, paralleling our flight path. Without announcing his intentions, Commander Quackenbush suddenly, but not abruptly, turned the aircraft toward the carrier and announced to Air Traffic Control that he wished to descend to 4,000 feet. With permission from ATC, we veered toward the ship, which we discovered was being towed by a fleet tug. He told me that the ship was USS *Intrepid*. Then, he contacted ATC again to resume our original heading and altitude. I advanced the throttles for the climb and asked the commander a question about *Intrepid*, which I had served on in 1970.

Hap Quackenbush didn't answer right away, and as I looked toward him, I saw that his lower lip and sides of his mouth were quivering. He was crying. A few minutes later he said, "*Intrepid* and I were commissioned the same year, 1943, and I served on her. She was just decommissioned this week. It looks like this year we will both be retiring. In the war, we lost some good men on that ship. I think of them often."

There was no more conversation in the cockpit for the rest of the flight.

College freshman John Kistler decorating Homecoming float, 1964 yearbook. Photo: *The Sheaf* (1964) courtesy The Principia

Intrepid patch. Photo by Robert M. Craig

CAPTAIN JOHN S. KISTLER served as an aviator for thirty years in the U.S. Navy. His squadrons over the years were assigned to six carriers including *Intrepid* (CVS-11), *Wasp* (CVS-18), *Franklin D. Roosevelt* (CV-42), *Forrestal* (CV-59), *Independence* (CV-62), and the super carrier *Nimitz* (CVN-68). He also served two tours from 1978 to 1980 aboard *LaSalle* (AGF-3), an amphibious transport dock converted in 1972 to a command ship with a diplomatic role and home ported in Behrain. *LaSalle* was the Middle East Force flagship; Kistler was officer in charge of HS-1 Detachment One [SH-3 helicoptors]. One of America's main allies in the Middle East was the Shah of Iran who controlled the Persian Gulf, but whose government collapsed with Mohammad Reza Shah Pahlavi leaving Iran in January 1979 to live in exile. Following the Shah's arrival in New York, Iranians attacked and took over the American embassy in Tehran and took 50 Americans hostage for 444 days. *La Salle* assisted in the evacuation of 260 American and foreign national civilians from the Iranian seaport of Bandar Abbas. In 2014 Captain Kistler published *New Moon Rising*, a work of historical fiction, but a book based upon many events in the Persian Gulf during the months prior to and following the fall of Reza Shah Pahlavi in 1979. Kistler notes that "the names of the characters in the story are fictitious, but represent many of the Navy men I sailed with aboard USS *LaSalle* (AGF-3) from 1978 to 1980."

Born in Miami, Florida, Kistler attended both the high school [US 63] and college [C67] at Principia majoring in history before heading to the Naval War College for a second BA degree. At Principia College Kistler was a cheerleader and member of the campus fire crew, sang in the college choir, and worked on the college newspaper. He was a member of Rackham Court West residence hall, whose "fraternity" brothers and future Navy officers (and authors herein) include Rod Carlson, Jim Chamberlin, Robert Craig, Glenn Felch, Bill Franke, Don Huber, Tucker Lake, Steve Wells, and Walle Wethe. The Navy's recruiting slogan, "Join the Navy and See the World" was especially relevant to the future Captain Kistler whose career service took him to Puerto Rico, Spain, Italy, Crete, Greece, Malta, Bahrain, Oman, Iran, United Arab Emirates, Djibouti, Kenya, Pakistan, Southampton, Hamburg, Hawaii, Alameda, San Diego, Pensacola, Jacksonville, New Orleans, Lakehurst, Newport, Key West, Washington, DC, Norfolk, and Quonset Point. Recipient of four Legion of Merit awards, three Meritorious Service medals, and two Navy Commendation ribbons, Kistler retired from the Navy in 1998. He has since been a contractor for the Department of State, U.S. Army, and U.S. Marine Corps, as well as an author. Married to Karen Anderson

(C68), the Kistlers have two sons, John and Eric, and a daughter, Laura (all three graduates of the Principia School [high school]), as well as seven grandchildren. Captain Kistler's middle child and namesake John Anderson Kistler graduated from Principia College in 1994, a third generation Kistler at Principia.

At Peace with My Past

MIKE KNEELAND

During my combat tour flying A6's, I dropped about one thousand 500-pound bombs. The targets were river crossings, truck convoys, truck parks, and petroleum and weapons depots. I also dropped land mines and anti-personnel weapons. I'm sure there was loss of life involved. For many years since, I've had many opportunities to think about the consequences of my actions.

I still vividly remember one of my early missions. I dropped a load of bombs at night on a truck convoy and watched as the bombs exploded and all the truck lights went out. As I tried to go to sleep that night, the thought occurred to me that I probably had killed people that day. It was a life-changing event for me.

We were aware of the brutal torture of our fellow airmen taking place in the Hanoi Hilton. There were no prisoners being taken in Laos over which we were flying. Pilots shot down in Laos were usually tortured to death on the spot. Furthermore, we knew that all the destruction of supplies that we were causing deterred enemy action and was preventing additional loss of life of our fellow Americans serving in South Vietnam. This made it easier to justify our combat actions. We were preventing the spread of Communism into Southeast Asia. Our actions were supported by Australia, South Korea, and other nations who supplied troops and provided supplies for our efforts in Vietnam.

My grandfather and father, both Principians, had served in WWI and WWII respectively. I never questioned the morality of my service. Military service was a duty I owed my country. Prior to graduating in 1966, I enlisted in the Navy's flight program. At that time we had not yet experienced the extent of the opposition to the Vietnam War that would come by 1968, and the nation-changing effects of Watergate lay in the future. The thinking was still, "My country, right or wrong, but my country." We were convinced that we were doing the right thing.

I consider myself to be a devout student of Christian Science. My study of The Bible, including using Strong's Exhaustive Concordance, leads me to believe that the sixth commandment in its original text was "Thou Shalt Not Murder." This is different from "Thou Shalt Not Kill." I do not think that taking another life to save oneself, one's family, or one's country is against the sixth commandment.

If I am wrong about this and destined to Everlasting Punishment, as some would say, I am willing to take whatever awaits me. For I believe that I will be standing shoulder-to-shoulder in Hell with some of our civilization's finest men. This would include all those who have caused a loss of lives in combat, from the earliest days of recorded history, to our forefathers and our fathers who served, as I did, in order to reverse the tide of tyranny on a distant shore. I stand, as well, with all the men and women since, who have fought so that we may preserve the precious freedoms that we have today. I am at peace with my past.

Swift Boat Postscript

WILLIAM E. FRANKE

Every two years, the Swift Boat sailors, who formed an association in large part due to the efforts of my chief petty officer, reunite generally in either San Diego or Washington, DC. Typically, the gathering will number three hundred "Swiftees," with wives and other family members swelling the ranks to close to five hundred.

While ostensibly it is a reunion, in fact, although unspoken, those Swiftees are there to pay tribute to those of our brotherhood "still on patrol."

While there are more sea stories than one could possibly imagine, and lots of hugs and back slapping, the core of the weekend is the Memorial Service held in honor of those men. Even at the banquet, an unoccupied table for two sits discreetly beneath the speaker's dais, complete with a rose in a vase and a bottle of champagne….symbolic of the lives these men should have experienced.

At the Memorial, we honor each of them….calling out their names individually… a process painfully long….followed by the striking of a ship's bell. Full military honors are accorded them, with a Color Guard, a full military salute, and the sounding of taps. It is so beautiful to hear the crystal clear notes of the bugler resonating over the entire San Diego Bay, including aboard the naval vessels nested to the docks. Equally inspiring is to gaze out over the capital in Washington, with taps reverberating down the mall to spill out onto the Capitol grounds.

Often, we are joined by active duty Navy personnel, who attend simply out of respect for a fallen sailor. In that context, age and time in service are without distinction. Even if only in the area, upon hearing taps resonating over the base, they will in reflex come to attention in quiet salute. A fallen sailor, irrespective of what war, is both grieved and honored by all sailors… past, present, and I am confident future.

We are also joined by family members of the sailors being honored. At the last such ceremony, the two younger brothers, along with their wives, of one sailor whose life ended in his nineteenth year were in attendance. It was a special moment for all of us when these two brothers laid the wreath in honor of a long lost sibling.

These men are deserving of such recognition. And they will be so treated for as long as we who returned have the capacity to do so. And, just as we did for those who preceded us, others will pick up that mantle in later years, continuing a tradition that makes the United States Navy so very special.

It has been my privilege, and my honor, to preside over these Memorial Services. It is a duty I take very seriously, spending much time between the services simply thinking how best I can express the significance of their acts of sacrifice for their nation.I owe that to men who will never be blessed, as I have, with the joy of marriage and the holding of my children, and now my grandchildren, in my arms.

I often struggle with it. Why were these men, who selflessly honored the sense of duty their parents and our society imposed upon them, ridiculed and held in disdain for going to Vietnam when others who went to Canada were honored? Where are the values of our nation? The legacy of these sailors, as with all of those who made such a sacrifice for their nation, must be honored, not besmirched.

I end each such service with the same story....because it seems so fitting. It is the story of some unknown member of the British Expeditionary Forces in Burma during World War II who scratched out a message on the surface of a boulder in the few hours remaining before his hopelessly outnumbered and surrounded unit was overwhelmed. It read simply "Tell those back home that we gave our today for their tomorrow."

I, and all of my fellow sailors, recognize the unpopularity of our war. But, to us, it is without relevance. We know simply that our nation made a decision, justified or not, to go to war in the unbearably sweltering jungles of a nation on the other side of the world, and these men, out of our sense of duty, answered that call....and, in so doing, in their minds gave their today for our tomorrow.

That is why I was prepared to tell the story of duty on a Swift Boat.

Before Moving On

ALLEN G. ORCUTT

1969

But wait a minute more,
And try to visualize,
Realize,
That in my eyes
The problems I will face
Will never again be so consistently great,
So persistently
Antagonistic,
So emotionally bereft,
So human,
Though behind me now,
I can say
One more battle is complete,
And I wait a minute more
Before moving on

Brothers. Photo by Robert M. Craig

Sunset and evening star,
And one clear call for me!
And may there be no moaning of the bar,
When I put out to sea…

…For tho' from out our bourne of Time and Place
The flood may bear me far,
I hope to see my Pilot face to face
When I have crost the bar.

EXCERPT FROM "CROSSING THE BAR"
BY ALFRED, LORD TENNYSON

ACKNOWLEDGEMENTS

Anthologies by definition involve many authors in a collaborative effort, and I am grateful for the contributions of those writers gathered here whose accounts sometimes recalled experiences difficult to revisit. Steve Wells initiated the idea that fellow Vietnam veterans attending a 2011 high school reunion should gather one evening at the reunion weekend to share their military experiences—around the fire, so to speak. The idea for a book sprang from that gathering. Both Wells and Brian Morse helped shape the initial character of the anthology and supported my role and autonomy in serving as editor. After Brian's passing, Rod Carlson joined Steve in being available as a small advisory committee to address any issues that might arise in the course of my review of submissions, and to lend advice. In the end, I am responsible for the organization of the book and any editorial errors it may contain.

Jonathan Palmer, president of Principia College, approved the project, and remained in the wings as Vietnam era veteran alumni contributed ideas and submissions for the book. Trudy Palmer and Donna Gibbs assisted with Principia alumni records and with the initial call for submissions. Various archivists responded to questions and provided assistance in archival research and in obtaining photo images, for which I am grateful: Jonathan Roscoe (archivist, Naval History & Heritage Command: Photo Section); Pam Overmann, curator, Navy Art Collection; Kris Impastato, archivist at Principia College, and William Seibert, archivist at the National Archives and Records Administration, St. Louis. At Hellgate Press, book designer Michael Campbell and cover designer L. Redding were generous in their willingness to reflect the editor's preferences regarding layout and design in the book, and publisher Harley Patrick was unfailing in his sincere efforts to respond to our vision for the book; I appreciate his support in this truly collaborative production. My wife, Carole, suggested the publisher and gave me the time to see the project through to completion. I am also grateful for the assistance of Wendy Roth, Melody Baillargeon, Jonathan

Hosmer, Ed Blomquist, Pete Purvis, Nan McComber, Mark Weber, and, of course, our authors.

Each veteran responded to a call a half century ago, and each has again served us all in recording personal recollections of his military experiences. Together, these short memoirs are noteworthy in the association of each author with a small Midwestern college, but they are also representative of the larger military brotherhood of young men and women serving their country during a contentious period, many participating in an unpopular war; in the end, this small group of college-mates are U.S. military veterans documenting a slice of the larger American experience. Both Thomas Carlyle and Ralph Waldo Emerson equated history with biography, and within these pages lies a historical record as biography.[79] Film maker Ken Burns has reminded us that the word "history" contains the word "story."

When Voltaire asked what would constitute useful history, his response was "that which should teach us our duties... without appearing to teach them"[80] [Voltaire, *Philosophical Dictionary*]. This ideal of duty may well lie between the lines for many of our authors, but it is historian Barbara Tuchman who best expressed the rationale for documenting our personal as well as collective experiences as Vietnam era veterans: "The unrecorded past," Tuchman wrote, "is none other than our old friend, the tree in the primeval forest which fell without being heard."[81] I am grateful to each Principian who answered this second call and who contributed essays, stories, and poems to this collection, so that his and her stories would be heard.

---

79 "History is the essence of innumerable biographies," (Thomas Carlyle, "On History," *Fraser's Magazine,* November, 1830, in G. B. Tennyson, ed., *A Carlyle Reader: Selections from the Writings of Thomas Carlyle* (New York: Cambridge University Press, 1984), 57, and "... there is probably no history, only biography," (Ralph Waldo Emerson, *Essays: History,* 1841, in *The Prose Works of Ralph Waldo Emerson* (2 vols) (Boston: Fields, Osgood, & Co., 1870), I: 222.

80 Voltaire, "History," Section 2, in *Philosophical Dictionary.* See Voltaire, *Premium Collection: Novels, Philosophical Writings, Historical Works, Plays, Poems, & Letters (60+ Works in One Volume),* Tobias Smollett, William F. Fleming, and William Walton, transl. (e-artnow), 2016. *info@e-artnow.org.*

81 Barbara Tuchman, "Can History Be Served Up Hot," *New York Times,* March 8, 1964.

GLOSSARY

A-4 Skyhawk: A single seat subsonic Navy and Marine aircraft able to be launched from aircraft carriers; built by Douglas Aircraft Company (McDonnell Douglas), A-4s played a major role in the Vietnam War.

A-6 Intruder: A twinjet, mid-wing all-weather attack aircraft built by Grumman Aerospace, the A-6 Intruder was used by the U.S. Navy and Marine Corps from 1963 to 1997.

abort: Discontinue an aircraft takeoff or missile launch; terminate a mission for any reason other than enemy action.

ace: A military aviator credited with shooting down several enemy aircraft during aerial combat; the qualifying number varies but is usually considered to be five or more. The term is sometimes identified as "a flying ace," "fighter ace," or "air ace." The term was first used by French newspapers, describing Adolphe Pégoud (1889-1915) as *l'as* (the ace), after he downed seven German aircraft in WWI.

admiralty or navy: All vessels in a navy commanded by a fleet admiral, sometimes called admiral of the fleet (five-star level).

aft: Rear or toward the stern of a ship or tail of an aircraft.

Agent Orange: Herbicide Orange (HO) or Agent Orange was one of the highly toxic herbicides and chemical defoliants used by the United States military during the Vietnam War for about ten years after 1961. The Veterans Administration [U.S. Department of Veterans Affairs] recognizes certain cancers, Parkinson's Disease, and other health problems as "presumptive diseases" (related to a veteran's qualifying military service), associated with exposure to Agent Orange or other herbicides during military service, and thus veterans and their survivors may be eligible for benefits.

Airdale/Airedale: Naval aviator or member of the aviation community.

Air Wing: An organizational unit of military fixed and/or rotary aircraft numbering up to about 75 airplanes *See CVW.*

all hands on deck: An order that all members of a ship's crew should report on deck (on main deck or to assigned emergency stations).

Alpha Strike: A term first used in the Vietnam War, an alpha strike was a large air attack by several dozen aircraft of an aircraft carrier air wing.

amidships: Central part of a ship/boat.

ARVN: Army of the Republic of Vietnam; the ground forces of the South Vietnamese military; the larger South Vietnamese military entity was the RVNAF [Republic of Vietnam Armed Forces] including a navy and air force.

AWOL: Absent without leave [absent without permission].

battalion: Infantry unit or armored regiment (of Cavalry squadron) of 300-1,000 made up of two to six companies led by a lieutenant colonel. For larger units, see r*egiment, brigade, division, corps,* and command; for smaller units see *company and platoon.*

black market: An underground economy operating clandestine market transactions characterized by some degree of illegality, often involving improper use of restricted currencies like MPCs or exchange of restricted goods, such as illegal transference of military supplies to civilian use.

boatswain's mate: Navy enlisted personnel rating designating a deck seaman responsible for boat/ship maintenance including deck, rigging, deck equipment, painting, and upkeep of ship's external structure.

booby trap: A device or setup, sometimes baited to lure its victim, which is triggered by its victim and intended to kill, maim, wound, or surprise.

BOQ: Bachelor officer quarters: buildings on U.S. military bases for quartering commissioned officers.

bow: Front end (forward) section of a ship or boat.

bridge: Area of the superstructure of a ship from which the ship is operated.

brigade: A military unit of 3,000-5,000 made up of three to six battalions and two or more regiments and led by a brigadier (brigadier general, brigade general, or one-star general).

brown-water navy: Any naval force capable of military operations in fluvial or littoral environments, especially rivers and tributaries carrying heavy sediment loads from soil runoff or flooding. In Vietnam, the riverine forces (river patrol boats including Swift Boats) operating in the Mekong Delta were largely successful in their efforts to stop North Vietnam's flow of weapons, ammunition, and provisions on rivers and along the South Vietnamese cost during "Operation Market Time" after 1965.

bulkhead: Vertical partition (never called a wall) separating compartments (never called rooms) of a ship.

cache: Often a weapons or provisions cache, a collection of items of the same type stored in a hidden or inaccessible place.

caliber: The diameter of something of circular section; hence, the caliber of a gun refers to the internal diameter of the gun barrel or the diameter of the projectile it shoots; not to be confused with caliper, which is a device used to measure the two opposite sides of an object such as a tree trunk (outside caliper), or the inside of an object [inside caliper].

Cà Mau Peninsula: "The black land" in Khmer language, Cà Mau, at the southwestern tip of Vietnam, is the southernmost of Vietnam's fifty-eight provinces, whose capital is also named Cà Mau. During the Vietnam War, Cà Mau was a stronghold of the Viet Cong's guerrilla activity.

captain's mast: *See mast/captain's mast/admiral's mast.*

CB (Seabee): [Navy] Construction Battalion. Replaced civilian construction companies working for the U.S. Navy from WWII on. International law forbade civilians from resisting enemy attack (doing so classified them as guerrillas, punishable by immediate execution), so skilled military personnel trained in construction trades were formed into a construction battalion known as Seabees to build or repair temporary or permanent military infrastructure wherever needed, and able to drop tools and take up arms as necessary.

Charlie: Military nickname for the Viet Cong; a code word in radio communication representing the letter C; sometimes Charlie is informally used to reference cocaine.

Christian Science: A Protestant religion founded by Mary Baker Eddy with churches world-wide; not to be confused with Scientology, with which there is no affiliation.

CO: Commanding officer.

COD: Carrier onboard delivery.

Color Guard: A detachment of soldiers, sailors, airmen, and/or marines assigned to the protection of regimental colors (flags).

command: The highest military levels led by a four-star general (army command, 100,000 to 200,000 soldiers), five-star general or field marshall (army group or front, 400,000 to one million soldiers), or six-star general (theater or regional command of one-to-ten million troops).

comms: Communications, radios, other transmission devices/hardware.

company: Infantry unit or artillery battery or cavalry troop of 80-150 soldiers (three to six platoons) led by a captain or major (or chief warrant officer).

conn: Command of the ship's movement while underway; as when the captain or another officer relieves the OOD (officer of the deck) of the conn.

Coral Sea: USS *Coral Sea* (CV-CVB-CVA-43), a *Midway*-class carrier originally built with a straight flight deck, its 1943 CVB hull classification indicated its status as a "large aircraft carrier." *Coral Sea* was reclassified an attack carrier in 1952, and modernized with an angle flight deck, steam catapults, and other alterations between 1957 and 1960. Following the 1964 Gulf of Tonkin incident, *Coral Sea* reported for duty with the Seventh Fleet and made several Vietnam deployments between 1964 and 1975.

cordon: A circle or line of military (soldiers, vehicles, aircraft) or police (or other guards) preventing access into or out of an area, camp, or building; as in "the troops cordoned off the village."

corps: A military unit formed of two or more divisions and 20,000 to 50,000 soldiers led by a lieutenant general (three-star general).

cover: Headgear (cap or hat).

cumshaw: Something obtained through unofficial means, including devious and sometimes illegal transactions or bribery. The term derives from *kam siā,* a word in the dialect of Xiamen meaning "grateful thanks," and was heard from beggars in ports prompting sailors to misinterpret the word as meaning a handout. A cumshaw artist was an individual particularly adept at obtaining provisions or goods through sometimes questionable means.

CVS/CVA carrier designation: The hull classification CVS designates an anti-submarine warfare carrier, a small aircraft carrier developed in World War II as an escort carrier whose mission was to hunt and destroy submarines. The CVA classification designates an attack aircraft carrier.

CVW: A carrier air wing (several air squadrons and detachments) operating while embarked aboard an aircraft carrier.

dead in the water: The ship is without power, unable to move.

deck/main deck: Shipboard floor (never called floor), usually numbered, as in "second deck" counting down from main deck of a ship; the main deck is the highest watertight deck of a ship (hangar deck in the case of a carrier).

Delta Force: *See Green Berets/Rangers/Delta Force.*

division or legion: A military unit formed of 6,000 to 20,000 soldiers in two to four brigades and commanded by a major general (two-star general).

DMZ: Demilitarized zone separating North and South Vietnam.

đồng (South Vietnamese đồng): Decimal currency of the Republic of Vietnam (South Vietnam) from 1953 to May 2, 1978 divided into 100 xu (su). The piastre was the currency of French Indochina between 1885 and 1952. The North Vietnamese đồng was introduced in 1946, the South Vietnamese đồng appeared in 1953, each replacing the piaster at par.

EOD: Explosive Ordinance Disposal. Technicians disarm improvised explosive devices in any environment, including underwater.

***Essex*-class carrier:** USS *Essex* (CV-CVA-CVS-9), commissioned December 31, 1942, was the first of twenty-four ships in the aircraft carrier [CV] class to be authorized by the U.S. Congress and is thus the designated class leader. Construction began on April 1, 1941 (prior to Pearl Harbor), but her construction contract was altered and its schedule accelerated for *Essex*'s launch July 31, 1942. *Essex* was later (October 1952) redesignated an attack carrier (CVA) and subsequently (March 1960) an anti-submarine warfare carrier (CVS), but remained part of the Atlanta fleet and saw no Vietnam service. *Essex* was eventually sold for scrap in 1975. During World War II propeller-driven planes were launched from *Essex*-class carriers, whose original flight decks were narrow enough to fit through the Panama Canal.

F-4 Phantom: Employed by the U.S. Navy from 1960-1996, and adopted by the Marine Corps and Air Force, the F-4 was a tandom two seat, twin engine, all weather, long range supersonic jet interceptor and fighter-bomber manufactured by McDonnell Aircraft/McDonnell Douglas. Able to fly at Mach 2.2 speed and at high altitude, the F-4 was used extensively during the Vietnam War for aerial reconnaissance and ground attack; it carried air-to-air missiles, air-to-ground missiles, and various bombs totally up to nine tons of weaponry. Both the Navy and Air Force employed F-4s in their Blue Angels and Thunderbirds flight demonstration teams.

F-8 Crusader: Vought [manufacturer] F-8 Crusaders were "air superiority" single-engine jets able to be carrier launched and fly supersonic speeds. The plane was used by the Navy and Marine Corps principally in the Vietnam War. RF-8 Crusaders were photo reconnaissance planes.

fantail: Aft (rear) end of the main deck of a ship.

feet wet: Flying over water (according to pilot parlance).

firebase/fire support base: A temporary military encampment set up to provide artillery fire support to infantry operating in an area outside the range of fire support from a base camp.

flag officer: A senior military officer of high enough rank to fly a flag to mark the position from which the officer exercises command; in many countries, this term is limited to the navy, (and thus rear admiral and above) although in the U.S. military a general is also considered a flag officer. Sometimes, a junior officer serving an admiral or general as a personal adjutant or aide-de-camp is referred to as a flag lieutenant or flag adjutant. The ship from which the admiral commands is called a flag ship.

fleet: All naval vessels in a general region or ocean (such as the Pacific fleet or the Atlantic fleet) commanded by an admiral (four-star) or vice admiral (three-star).

flotilla: A naval task unit, usually not capital ships but vessels of similar type, commanded by a commodore (one-star) or lower rear admiral; individual vessels are commanded by captains or commanders.

FM: Frequency modulation technology invented in 1933 and used to provide high-fidelity sound in radio broadcasting.

forward: Front of ship (opposite of aft).

forecastle/fo'c'sle: Forward part of a ship below the deck (sometimes a raised deck) often used as crew's living quarters (as well as officers' bunkrooms and staterooms, as described in Schneberger's essay herein). The forecastle can also house anchor chains, ropes, and machinery for lowering and raising the anchor.

g/G force: Gravitational force; a measurement of the perception of weight caused by acceleration: one g is equal to the force of gravity at the Earth's surface, i.e. 9.8 meters per second per second. Continued g forces above about 10 g can result in permanent injury or be lethal to humans.

galley: Food preparation space of a ship (never called a kitchen).

gedunk: Slang term for junk food or sundries; the gedunk store is a large ship's snack bar where sailors can buy candy, chips, and other packaged "junk food." On the carrier *Intrepid,* the gedunk store was remodeled in 1969 as a brick-faced storefront with peppermint striped awning overlooking a sidewalk French café.

general quarters/at general quarters: A shipboard announcement that all hands (everybody aboard ship) must report to assigned battle stations immediately; watertight doors are shut, and security is put on alert (the engineering rooms and bridge are guarded), as crew prepare for an emergency (battle, a storm, dense fog). "Battle stations" is a more specific announcement to don battle gear, ready guns, and prepare for combat: "General quarters. General quarters. All hands man your battle stations."

GI: A soldier of the United States Army or an airman of the U.S. Army Air Force; more generally a member or former member of the U.S. armed forces.

gig: In the military, a demerit; at Navy OCS, a red gig was a demerit; a blue gig was a commendation. The captain's gig is a boat used to taxi the captain, usually from an off-dock anchorage, to shore and back. The admiral's barge performs similar functions for flag officers.

gook: Derogatory military nickname for the Viet Cong; more generally, a derogatory nickname for East and Southeast Asian people; still more generally, a slur referencing any foreigner.

Green Berets/Rangers/Delta Force: The special operations force of the U.S. Army. The primary mission of the Green Berets is unconventional warfare, but also includes counter terrorism, special reconnaissance, foreign internal defense, and direct action which can include hostage rescue, combat search and rescue, and humanitarian assistance. Army Rangers are specialized light infantrymen that perform similar special operations activities. The 1st Special Forces Operational Detachment-Delta is commonly known as Delta Force whose missions include hostage rescue and counterterrorism.

grunt: Military slang, during the Vietnam era, for infantry soldier; a grunt could also be an untrained government or military individual [GRoundUnitNotTrained].

Gulf of Tonkin: A body of water extending from the South China Sea and located off the coast of northern Vietnam, the southern part of the Gulf of Tonkin was the location of the area (a point 190 km east of Đồng Hới,) called Yankee Station) where U.S. aircraft carriers launched strikes during the Vietnam War.

Gulf of Tonkin Incident/Gulf of Tonkin Resolution: The 1964 Gulf of Tonkin incident was the event considered to have initiated the Vietnam War. For many years American military aid, under Presidents Truman, Eisenhower, Kennedy, and Johnson, had supported first the French, and then South Vietnam, in their fight against Communist rebels. U.S.-trained and directed South Vietnamese sailors had been targeting North Vietnamese coastal facilities in bombing raids, while American warships such as the destroyer USS *Maddox* (DD-731) engaged in electronic espionage missions along the coast, relaying intelligence to the South Vietnamese. On July 31, 1964, U.S.-supported patrol boats shelled two North Vietnamese islands in the Gulf of Tonkin, and two days later the destroyer *Maddox* was accosted by three Soviet-built North Vietnamese torpedo boats;

Maddox fired "warning shots" which the North Vietnamese countered with machine-gun and torpedo fire. The American aircraft carrier USS *Ticonderoga* (CV-14) dispatched aircraft to defend *Maddox*. The next day a second destroyer [USS *Turner Joy* (DD-951)] arrived and additional U.S.-supported raids against the North Vietnamese ensued. This was followed by an "ambush" August 2, 1964, of the two destroyers by North Vietnamese boats firing twenty-two torpedoes at the American ships. In retaliation, President Lyndon Johnson ordered air strikes against North Vietnamese boat bases and an oil storage depot, and on August 7, Congress passed the Gulf of Tonkin Resolution essentially giving Johnson a carte blanche to wage war in Vietnam as he saw fit.

Hanoi Hilton: The late 19th century Hỏa Lò Prison in Hanoi was built by French colonists in Vietnam and initially used to incarcerate political prisoners. Later, American POWs were housed here and nicknamed the facility the "Hanoi Hilton." The prison served as jail and interrogation chambers for downed American pilots including Lt. (jg.) Everett Alvarez Jr., who was shot down August 5, 1964, and the future U.S. Senator, John McCain who spent five and a half years as a POW. Here, POWs were tortured, endured unsanitary conditions and poor food, and suffered prolonged periods of solitary confinement.

hatch: Access opening in a ship's deck.

head: Military slang term for a toilet or rest room, typically improvised in the field to be anything from a bucket to a hole in the ground.

Ho Chi Minh Trail: An elaborate logistical system of mountain and jungle paths and trails used by North Vietnam to infiltrate troops and supplies into South Vietnam including, at times, through Cambodia and Laos during the Vietnam War.

hooch [sometimes spelled hootch]: Slang for a thatched hut in Vietnam, a modification of the Japanese *uchi* house, or any improvised living space ranging from a sand-bagged bunker to an improved foxhole. Hooch is also a colloquial term for booze, or alcoholic beverages. In the U.S. South, hooch can refer to the Chattahoochee River.

Huey: UH-1 Iroquois "Huey" is a utility military helicopter used in Vietnam. Introduced by Bell Helicopter as HU-1 in 1959, the Huey developed some twenty variants, and approximately 7,000 were deployed in Vietnam.

The Hump/flying the Hump: Because of high winds and poor weather conditions (and little information about the weather) as well as a lack of radio navigation aids and reliable charts, the Hump was hazardous duty for an airman in World War II. Allied pilots labeled the eastern end of the Himilayan Mountains the Hump, and "flying the Hump" referenced the air transport route of military aircraft flying from India to China, a daily airlift to Chinese forces fighting the Japanese of supplies and provisions operating between April, 1942, and August, 1945, and necessitated by the closing of the Burma Road by the Japanese.

ICBM: Intercontinental ballistic missile.

I Corps [First Corps, "Eye" Corps]: The operational area encompassing the five northernmost provinces in SouthVietnam, including the two major cities of Hue and Da Nang. II Corps (the largest operational area, including twelve provinces extended throughout the central highlands; III Corps included Saigon, ninety percent of South Vietnam's industry, and thirty-eight percent of its population; and IV Corps included sixteen provinces including the Mekong Delta and Ca Mau peninsula.

Intrepid: USS *Intrepid* (CVS-11) was the third *Essex*-class aircraft carrier (and historically the fourth U.S. Navy ship to bear the name "Intrepid"). Following conversion in 1952 to a modern attack carrier (CVA-11), *Intrepid* received steam catapults (first launch October 1954) and a reinforced angle flight deck (1956-57). With these alterations *Intrepid* deployed to Vietnam three times during the 1960s, and set records launching A-4 Skyhawks and A-1 Skyraiders loaded with bombs and rockets with 28-second intervals between launches. Before *Intrepid* left the Tonkin Gulf, she was launching planes at 26-second intervals. *Intrepid* was the last of the *Essex*-class to leave active service, but like *Yorktown* (CV10), *Hornet* (CV12) and *Lexington* (CV16), she survived to become a museum. In 1982 the carrier was towed to New York City, converted to the Intrepid Sea, Air, and Space Museum, and officially designated a National Historic Landmark in 1986.

island: On an aircraft carrier's flight deck, the starboard-side superstructure containing the bridge, radar equipment, etc.

KIA: Killed in action.

Kit Carson Scouts: A creation of the U.S. Marine Corps, Kit Carson Scouts was a program in which Viet Cong defectors to the South Vietnamese cause were trained as intelligence scouts for American infantry units.

knot: One nautical mile per hour (approx 1.15078 mph); 20 knots is approximately 23 mph.

liberty: Naval term for authorized absence from duty, usually for a weekend or less than forty-eight hours.

line officer [officer of the line]: A commissioned officer in the U.S. Navy, Marines, Air Force, or Coast Guard who exercises general command authority and is eligible for operational command (such as piloting the ship as officer of the deck). The primary duties of officers who are not line officers, are authorized within a specialty, normally non-combatant, including chaplains, attorneys, supply, and medical services.

LZ: Landing zone.

Mach [Mach 1, Mach 2, etc]: The ratio of the speed of an aircraft (or body) to the speed of sound in the surrounding air or medium; thus, a jet flying at Mach 2 speed is twice the speed of sound through the Earth's atmosphere.

manning the rail: On naval vessels, manning the rail is a ceremonial stationing of the ship's crew along the rails and superstructure of a ship in order to salute a dignitary or render honors. The custom evolved from "manning the yards" during the era of sailing ships when men stood evenly spaced on the "yards" (the spars holding sails), sometimes giving three cheers to honor a new captain or other distinguished individual. Less formal is the practice of having the crew "at quarters" when the ship is entering or leaving port, although when *Intrepid*, for instance, first arrived at its new home port in 1969, as related herein, the crew manned the rails, standing in dress white uniforms along the perimeter edge of the flight deck.

M.A.S.H. unit: The Mobile Army Surgical Hospital is a fully functional army hospital in a combat zone, but (thanks to the popularity of the television series, M*A*S.*H) it has come to refer more generally to any mobile military field hospital.

mast/captain's mast/admiral's mast: A non-judicial hearing (traditionally convening with the captain standing at the main mast of a naval vessel) in which a commanding officer hears complaints or disciplinary cases involving personnel under his command and disposes of them: the commanding officer can dismiss the charges, mete out punishment under provisions of military law (Uniform Code of Military Justice), or refer the case to a court martial.

medevac: The evacuation, often by helicopter or airplane, of wounded personnel (military battlefield or accident casualties) to a medical field facility, M.A.S.H. unit, or hospital.

Mekong Delta: Region of southwestern Vietnam southwest of Saigon [now Ho Chi Minh City] where the Mekong River [Nine Dragon River] flows into the South China Sea

mess/mess hall/mess deck: Area where military personnel eat, socialize, and sometimes nap although compartments off the mess decks on ships provided sleeping quarters for enlisted personnel.

MIA: Missing in action.

mid rats: Midnight rations: meal served about midnight (0000) for those crewmembers going on or off watch.

MiG fighters/MiG-17/Mig-21: Russian-built jet fighters named for designer and manufacturer Mikoyan Gurevich, the MiG-17 and Mig-21 (examples of which are part of the collection of aircraft on display at Intrepid Sea Air and Space Museum in New York) were supersonic fighter aircraft flown by North Vietnamese pilots during the Vietnam War.

minigun: An M134 Minigun is an externally powered, Gatling-style, six-barrel rotary machine gun manufactured by General Electric capable of firing 7.62 x 51mm ammunition at a rate of 2,000 to 6,000 rounds per minute. The term minigun has come to refer to any externally powered rotary-style gun of rifle caliber. In Vietnam, miniguncds were mounted in the turret and on pylon pods of Bell AH-1 Cobra attack helicopters.

MOS: military occupational specialty.

MP/MPG: Military police/military police group.

MPC: Military payment certificate was a form of currency issued by the Department of Defense (rather than by the Department of Treasury) and used to pay military personnel in certain foreign countries (including Vietnam). MPCs were convertible to U.S. dollars upon departure from a designated MPC zone, and convertible to local currency when military personnel went on leave (although not vice versa). Intended to prevent the dollar from undermining the value of local currencies (and since unauthorized personnel could not legally possess MPCs), the theory was that the system of MPCs would eliminate dollars from local economies. Local merchants accepted MPCs on par with U.S. dollars since they could use the currency on the black market. Periodically and unannounced in advance, MPC banknote styles were changed, with the older style becoming worthless, in an effort to deter black marketers. MPC's came to be considered "monopoly" money, or funny money, usable by soldiers in the PX and serviceman's clubs but whenever required currency exchange days [conversion days of "C-Days"] introduced new styles, all former MPCs were worthless. *See James Andrews's essay herein.* A GI on a military base could be mailed a $100 dollar bill from home, take it into Saigon and exchange it for $180 worth of MPC's, exchange it for South Vietnamese currency at inflated rates, and use (leverage) the low-cost local currency to shop, bar-hop, or buy favors at bargain rates due to the currency manipulation.

NAS: Naval Air Station.

***Nasty* boat/*Nasty* class fast patrol boat:** A group of twenty fast patrol boats built for the U.S. Navy following a Norwegian design, and delivered between 1964 and 1967 for "unorthodox operations" during the Vietnam War (although they remained in service until the early 1980s).

NIS/NCIS: With roots reaching back to 1882 and the establishment of the Office of Naval Intelligence (ONI), by the date of WWII responsibilities expanded to include investigations of sabotage, espionage, and subversive actions of any kind that threatened the Navy. During the Cold War there was a major buildup of civilian special agents, and in 1962 the name Naval Investigative Service (NIS) was adopted. By 1992 the word Criminal was added as the United States Naval Criminal Investigative Service (NCIS), by then under civilian leadership, continued service as the primary law enforcement agency of the United States Department of the Navy.

NVA: North Vietnamese Army.

OCS/OTS: Officers Candidate School/Officer Training School [Navy, Newport, Rhode Island; Army, Fort Benning, Georgia; Marines, Quantico, Virginia; Air Force, Lackland Air Force Base, San Antonio, Texas (now Maxwell Air Force Base, Montgomery, Alabama); Coast Guard, New London, Connecticut].

officers' country: Area aboard ship where commissioned officers' sleeping quarters and staterooms are to be found.

Olongapo City: A city in Central Luzon, Philippines, Olongapo City was adjacent to the U.S. Naval Base at Subic Bay, the largest U.S. Naval installation in the Pacific at the height of the Vietnam War. In 1967 an estimated 215 ships per month passed through Subic Bay. Ramon Magsaysay Drive, between the naval base main gate and Rizal Avenue was lined with nightclubs and teenaged prostitutes, offering cheap beer and other services to over four million servicemen who passed through Subic Bay during the period.

I-A [one-A]: A Selective Service (draft board) classification signifying "available for military service."

I-A-O or I-O [one-A-O or I-O]: A Selective Service (draft board) classification signifying conscientious objector [I-A-O: available for noncombatant military service only; I-O: available for civilian work contributing to the maintenance of the national health, safety, and interest.

IV-F [four-F]: A Selective Service (draft board) classification signifying registrant not qualified for any military service.

OOD: Officer of the deck: the direct representative of the captain, responsible for the ship when the captain is absent from the bridge.

overhead: Top surface of an enclosed space on a ship (under surface of a deck) (never called a ceiling).

PCF (Patrol Craft Fast): *See Swift Boat.*

People's Army of Vietnam (PAVN): The regular North Vietnamese army.

petty officer/NCO: A noncommissioned enlisted officer in a navy (below officers but above ordinary sailors).

piaster: The currency of French Indochina between 1885 and 1952. Piasters were still around in Vietnam during the war.

pilot boat/pilot/maritime pilot: A pilot boat transports a maritime pilot between land and an inbound or outbound ship that the pilot will guide into or out of port. Normally a former ship captain, the maritime pilot is a navigational expert for the given port of call, experienced in ship handling as well as knowledgeable about the waters, tides, winds, and any congestion or danger associated with the harbor or waterway.

platoon: Military unit of usually 26-55 soldiers commanded by a first or second lieutenant; typically sub-groups include sections (12-24 under a staff sergeant), squads or crews (8-12 under a sergeant), cells or fireteams (3-4), or smaller maneuver teams (2-3) led by a private first class.

pollywog or polliwog: A sailor who has never crossed the equator; also known as a slimy pollywog.

port: Left side of a ship; also a town or city with harbor where ships load or unload.

port bow: Front left of a ship or boat.

port quarter: When aboard, facing forward, the left rear part of the ship.

Prin/Principia: An independent, kindergarten-through-college, school for Christian Scientists; the K-12 campus is located in Town and Country, a suburb west of St. Louis, Missouri; the college is located in Elsah, Illinois, overlooking the Mississippi River, about forty-five miles northeast of St. Louis.

PTF: Patrol Torpedo Fast. A *Nasty* Boat; *see also PCF.*

PBR: River Patrol Boat; small and fast (25-29 knots) these boats normally had a crew of four enlisted men and one junior officer commanding.

PTSD [post-traumatic stress disorder]: A disorder in which a person has difficulty recovering after experiencing or witnessing a terrifying event. PTSD among military personnel may result from a physical brain injury caused by blasts during combat. Some thus equate

PTSD with what was once (WWI) called shell shock, although PTSD is generally considered to be more wide ranging.

PX: U.S. Army post exchange (store).

pugil sticks: A heavily padded pole used by military personnel in training for rifle and bayonet combat.

quarterdeck: On a ship, the quarterdeck is the official area for entry (arrival or departure) of personnel, including visitors, while in port and is connected to the dock by a gangplank. It is manned by the officer of the deck (OOD), officially representing the captain, and may occasionally serve official ceremonial arrivals or departures. Where the ship has multiple gangplanks, only one accesses the quarterdeck; the others may serve cargo on- or off-loading, and are manned by a Junior OOD or a Petty Officer of the Watch. While typically amidships today, the quarterdeck was a term historically applied to the part of the upper deck of a ship abaft the mainmast (i.e., in the stern area), including a poop deck when present, and an area usually reserved for officers, guests, and passengers.

R&R: Military term for designated off-duty time for "rest and relaxation" ["rest and recuperation," sometimes dubbed "rest and recreation"].

Ranger: USS *Ranger* (CV/CVA-61) was the first U.S. carrier originally built with an angled flight deck. It was one of four *Forrestal*-class supercarriers constructed in the 1950s (commissioned 1957), and between 1959 and 1973 made seven deployments to the Western Pacific; her service in Vietnam extended from the Gulf of Tonkin incident in 1964 until the cease fire in January 1973.

Rangers: *See Green Berets/Rangers/Delta Force.*

regiment: A military infantry unit of 1,000-3,000 (two or more battalions) commanded by a colonel.

ROTC: Reserved Officers' Training Corps is a group of college- and university-based officer training programs for the U.S. armed forces.

rules of the road: Navigation rules for ships and other vessels at sea to prevent collisions between two or more vessels.

SAM: Surface-to-air missile (ground-to-air missile [GTAM]).

sampan: A relatively flat-bottomed Chinese wooden boat, found along coastal or inland river waterways of Vietnam, frequently used as a traditional fishing boat, and sometimes containing a small shelter for permanent habitation, especially when sampans are used on inland waters.

scuttlebutt: Rumor, gossip, water-cooler chat; term derives from a ship's water "butt," a cask holding daily drinking water and with a hole cut into it (scuttled).

SEALs [Navy SEALS]: A component of the Naval Special Warfare Command, the U.S. Navy's "Sea, Air, and Land" teams, commonly abbreviated as the Navy SEALs, and nicknamed "Frogmen," are the Navy's primary/elite special operations force, established January 1, 1962. Parallel special operations forces of the Air Force and Marine Corps are of more recent date. The special operations component of the Air Force is AFSOC (the Air Force Special Operations Command, established in 1990), which operated prior to 1983 as part of the Tactical Air Command (TAC) and was active between 1983 and 1990 as the Twenty-Third Air Force (23 AF). Its predecessors go back to the lst Air Commando Group of World War II. United States Marine Corps Forces Special Operations Command [MARSOC] was established in 2005, well after the Vietnam War, as a Marine Corps parallel to the Navy SEALS and Green Berets, that is, the Marine Corps's component command of the United States Special Operations Command. *See Green Berets/Rangers/Delta Force.*

shellbacks: Sailors who have crossed the equator and have been initiated into the "Solemn Mysteries of the Ancient Order of the Deep"; also known as Trusty Shellbacks or Sons of Neptune.

Sortie: A combat mission of an individual aircraft, from take off to landing.

Squadron: Military unit in the air force comprised of between 100 and 300 personnel and 7-16 aircraft (three to four flight groups) commanded by a lieutenant colonel or major wing commander. Three to four squadrons make up a group/wing (17 to 48 aircraft and 300-1,000 personnel) and two or more groups/wings comprise a wing/group (48-100 aircraft and 1,000-5,000 personnel). A squadron in the navy is a small number of usually capital ships.

starboard: Right side of a ship or boat.

starboard bow: Front right of a ship or boat.

starboard quarter: When aboard, facing forward, the right rear part of the ship.

STD: Sexually transmitted disease.

stern: Rear (aft) section of a ship or boat.

supersonic [supersonic travel]: Exceeding the speed of sound [Mach 1].

Swift Boat: Officially known as a Patrol Craft Fast (PCF), a Swift Boat was a fifty-foot vessel adapted for combat in Vietnam from aluminum-hulled boats initially fabricated in Louisiana to transport oil- company workers to offshore platforms in the Gulf of Mexico. With the addition of .50-caliber machine guns, 81mm mortars, and other modifications, PCFs were made ready for service in South Vietnam where Swift Boats disrupted North Vietnamese transporting of supplies along the coastline of Vietnam. In 1968 Admiral Elmo Zumwalt Jr. launched Operation Sealords, designed to interdict enemy supply lines throughout the Mekong Delta and Cà Mau Peninsula which meant sending Swift Boats up the rivers and tributaries.

task force: Large number of naval vessels (two or more task groups), created as a temporary grouping for a specific operation, commanded by a vice admiral (three-star), and sometimes called a battle fleet. During the Vietnam War, carrier Task Force 77 launched airstrikes from Yankee Station in the Tonkin Gulf.

task group: Two or more squadrons (usually capital ships) of complementary naval vessels led by a rear admiral (two-star).

Tet Offensive: A large coordinated assault of approximately 80,000 Viet Cong on more than 100 South Vietnamese urban centers in 1968, including an attack on the U.S. embassy in Saigon.

Tonkin Gulf Yacht Club: Nickname for the Navy's Seventh Fleet operating in the Tonkin Gulf, the northwest arm of the South China Sea off North Vietnam. China borders the gulf on the north and east, and Hainan Island borders the gulf on the east. *See Yankee Station.*

II-S status [Two-S]: A Selective Service (draft board) classification signifying registrant deferred because of activity in study.

UCMJ: Uniform Code of Military Justice. *See mast/captain's mast/admiral's mast.*

UHF: Ultra high frequency is the designation for radio frequencies in the range between 300 megahertz (MHz) and 3 gigahertz (GHz), also known as the decimetre band; UHF uses have included walkie-talkies and later personal phones, cell phones, and Wi-Fi and Bluetooth, television broadcasting, satellite communication including GPS, and other applications.

underway: Moving through the water; to get underway is to begin a nautical voyage.

UNREP: Underway replenishment; refueling and restocking a ship while underway by which a supply ship sails parallel to a ship being replenished, maintaining the same course and speed while fuel hoses stretched between the vessels dispense fuel for the ship and aircraft and lines and cables extend from one ship to the other by which transfers of ship parts, supplies, equipment, food, and various other perishables are made. In a military pun, the "French Café" on the mess deck aboard *Intrepid* was nicknamed "Underway Replenishment." *See Craig essay, "Interior Decorator for a Warship."*

USS [ship designation]: Stands for United States Ship.

VF/VFA: One of the oldest designations in the U.S. Navy, in the 1920s VF designated "combat squadron," then "fighting plane squadron" and after WWII (1948-2006) VF signified "fighter squadron [air to air]." The VFA designation indicated a "strike fighter" squadron [air to ground, ,i.e., dropping bombs]. In Vietnam, F-4s in VF squadrons also dropped bombs. The "V" stands for fixed wing aircraft (as opposed to airships or blimps/dirigibles), "F" indicates "fighter," and "A" designates "attack."

Viet Cong [VC]: The National Front for the Liberation of Vietnam, the Viet Cong was a communist political organization with its own army (the People's Liberation Armed Forces of South Vietnam [PLAF]) that fought against the United State and South Vietnamese government forces during the Vietnam War. The organization was dissolved in 1976 after the fall of Saigon and the official reunification of North and South Vietnam under the communist government.

wardroom: Commissioned officers' mess on board a warship; compartment(s) aboard ship where officers eat and socialize.

WESTPAC: The western Pacific.

XO: Executive officer (on a ship, second in command under the captain; on land, the second in command of any army unit (from company to brigade).

Yankee Station: The location in the Gulf of Tonkin from which the U.S. Navy carrier Task Force 77 launched air strikes. During the two periods of greatest intensity of such naval air action (March 2, 1965 to October 31, 1968, and March 30, 1972 to December 29, 1972), there were normally three aircraft carriers "on the line" at Yankee Station, each conducting air operations for twelve hours (0000-1200, 1200-0000, and daylight hours).

yaw: An underway ship twisting or oscillating about a vertical axis often due to side winds and stormy seas.

CONTRIBUTORS

Name, Class, Military Branch, House at Principia, Bio Page

James H. Andrews, US64 C68, U.S. Army [military intelligence], Buck House, 253

John K. Andrews Jr., US62 C66, U.S. Navy [submarines], Buck House, 370

Norman Bleichman, US61 C65, U.S. Navy [Supply Corps], Brooks North, 362

Rod Carlson, C65, U.S. Marines [helicopter pilot], Rackham West, 32

James W. Chamberlin, C66, U.S. Army [artillery], Rackham West, 209

B. Dudley Cole, US53 C58, U.S. Navy [Supply Corps], Buck House, 381

Barrie L. Cooper, C65, U.S. Navy [pilot], Rackham East, 357

Robert M. Craig, US62 C66, U.S. Navy [Supply Corps], Rackham West, 10

William K. Donaldson, C69, U.S. Army [military police], Brooks North, 277

Glenn Felch, C68, U.S. Army [artist], Rackham West, 236

William E. Franke, US62 C66, U.S. Navy [Swift Boats], Rackham West, 306

Thomas M. Gallant, U.S. Navy [photography], Principia dad, 82

Richard Hammer, C66, U.S. Navy [ordinance disposal], Rackham East, 260

Rayburn Hanzlik, US56 C60, U.S. Navy [air intelligence], Brooks South, 388

Willard M. Hanzlik, C68, U.S. Navy [navigation], Brooks South, 265

Steven Heubeck, C66, U.S. Air Force [spec forces grp air], Brooks South, 183

Sid Hubbard, C65, U.S. Air Force [tact. fighter squad], Rackham East, 242

Donald L. Huber, US61 C65, U.S. Air Force [Spec Invs.], Rackham East, 75

John S. Kistler, US63 C67, U.S. Navy [pilot], Rackham West, 467

Mike Kneeland, C66, U.S. Navy [pilot], Rackham East, 37

H. Tucker Lake Jr., C69, U.S. Navy [air reservist, VT-0], Rackham West, 65

David R. Nysewander, C65, U.S. Army [chaplain], Brooks South, 26

Allen G. Orcutt, US62 C66, U.S. Marines [helicopter pilot], Buck House, 323

Rob Ostenberg, US65 C69, U.S. Army [infantry], Rackham East, 194

William H. "Chip" Ostenberg IV, US64 C73, U.S. Army [Corps of Engineers], Rackham East, 215

Elizabeth Pond, C58, international journalist, Howard House, 166

David Potter, C68, U.S. Navy [Supply Corps], Rackham East, 108

Steve Sandberg, US61 C65, U.S. Navy [helicopter pilot], Buck House, 283

Scott L. Schneberger, C70, U.S. Navy [intelligence], Rackham East, 405

Steven Ostenberg Spaulding, C63, U.S. Army [supply], Rackham East, 271

Peter Stone, C64, U.S. Navy [combat information], Brooks North, 313

Richard E. Upshaw, C66, U.S. Marines [helicoptor pilot], Rackham East, 222

Steve Wells, US62 C66, U.S. Navy [ordinance disposal], Rackham West, 55

Wally Wethe, C68, U.S. Air Force [pilot, DIA], Rackham West, 91 *www.hellgatepress.com*

CPSIA information can be obtained
at www.ICGtesting.com
Printed in the USA
FSHW01n1208100618
49057FS